Witness from the Pulpit

Rabbi Harold I. Saperstein in the 1930s.

Rabbi Harold I. Saperstein in the 1970s.
Carol Studios, Lynbrook, N.Y.

Witness from the Pulpit

Topical Sermons
1933–1980

Harold I. Saperstein

Edited with introductions and notes by
Marc Saperstein

Preface by Emanuel Rackman

Foreword by David Saperstein

LEXINGTON BOOKS
Lanham • Boulder • New York • Oxford

LEXINGTON BOOKS

Published in the United States of America
by Lexington Books
4720 Boston Way, Lanham, Maryland 20706

12 Hid's Copse Road
Cumnor Hill, Oxford OX2 9JJ, England

Copyright © 2000 by Lexington Books
First paperback edition 2001

Cover: Rabbi Harold I. Saperstein in the 1930s; Rabbi Harold I. Saperstein in the 1970s, Carol Studios, Lynbrook, N.Y. Photographs courtesy of the author.

British Library Cataloguing in Publication Information Available

Library of Congress Cataloging-in-Publication Data
The hardback edition of this book was previously cataloged by the Library of Congress as follows:

Saperstein, Harold I.
    Witness from the pulpit : topical sermons, 1933–1980 / Harold I. Saperstein ;
edited with introductions and notes by Marc Saperstein.
        p.   cm.
    Includes bibliographical references and index.
    1. Jewish sermons, American.   I. Saperstein, Marc.   II. Title.

BM740.2.S27 2000
296.4'7—dc21
                                                                    99–048714

ISBN 0-7391-0099-8 (cloth : alk. paper)   ISBN 978-0-7391-0259-6
ISBN 0-7391-0259-1 (pbk. : alk paper)

Printed in the United States of America

♾™ The paper used in this publication meets the minimum requirements of American National Standard for Information Sciences—Permanence of Paper for Printed Library Materials, ANSI/NISO Z39.48–1992.

To Marcia

Love of my life,
Cherished companion,
My most discerning constructive critic

and

To All Those Who Listened

את אחי אנכי מבקש
"I seek my brothers"
(Genesis 37:16)

ואני זקנתי ושבתי ובני הנם אתכם
ואני התהלכתי לפניכם מנעורי עד היום הזה
"I have grown old and gray—
now my sons are with you—
and I have walked before you from my youth until this day"
(I Samuel 12:2)

Contents

Preface

Rabbi Emanuel Rackman

This century has seen a proliferation of Jewish Studies programs in American universities. This accounts for the abundance of scholarly publication in virtually every area of Judaica. In one area alone there is a shortage of titles—the area in which there once was the greatest number: homiletics. Few are the rabbis who now publish sermons, although that genre of Jewish literature, best represented by the Bible itself, received maximum attention from rabbis in the past. Now rabbis prefer to be recognized as scholars rather than as orators. This may explain the decline in the excellence of contemporary preaching, though, needless to say, there are notable exceptions in English, Hebrew, and Yiddish.

The present volume is one such exception. Its author, Rabbi Harold I. Saperstein, preached to one congregation in Lynbrook, Long Island, for almost half a century. What a feat that was! They did not tire of hearing the same voice and cherishing the same style of message—timely, relevant, meaningful to Americans and Jews, action-oriented. The sermons reveal a knowledgeable, learned Jew who brings his command of Jewish literature to bear upon his presentations.

This volume of his sermons is elegantly edited by one of his sons, Marc, a professor of Jewish history at George Washington University in Washington, D.C., who heard many of the sermons as they were delivered. His introductions and notes make us aware of the value of sermons as a contemporary source for the study of Jewish history, revealing the way the rabbi considered the events of his day and communicated his reactions to his congregants. It is a continuation of Marc's distinguished research and publication on the history of Jewish preaching in earlier periods.

I have known the father, Harold, for almost seventy years, and I feel honored to have been invited to write this preface. Though his commitment is to Reform Judaism and mine is to Orthodox Judaism, we have remained close friends, with the profoundest love and respect for each other. The community of Lynbrook, in which we served together for seven years, is a relatively small one, but from there both of us volunteered in 1943 for military service in World War II. When we retired from military service, he returned to Lynbrook for forty additional years.

For half of that period, I served two metropolitan synagogues and for the other half I was involved in Israeli academic life. We did not then see each other often, but our commitment to the same values that made us friends in Lynbrook did not weaken. During that period we each served as presidents of the New York Board of Rabbis. Jewish unity was an ideal that we not only espoused but lived. The two of us, an Orthodox rabbi and a Reform rabbi, had no problems in working together civilly and respectfully for so many causes that were and are cherished in common. We learned this together in our military experience and never forgot it.

The period in which these sermons were delivered included the horrendous Holocaust and the almost miraculous rebirth of the State of Israel; reading them now helps us to relive what was perhaps the most challenging era of Jewish history in millennia. We are indebted to Harold Saperstein for having appreciated the historic character of our generation and having carefully preserved his homiletical output as a legacy to our posterity for generations to come.

Foreword

Rabbi David Saperstein

My work as director of the Religious Action Center of Reform Judaism involves extensive travel and speaking all over the country. There is hardly a synagogue I visit, a conference I address, a television interview I give, that is not followed by at least one person—often more than one—coming up to me with excitement or writing a note saying how influenced they were by my father and particularly how moved and inspired they had been by his sermons, stories, and speeches.

They remember. Some, the specific sermon or story. Others, simply the power of his speaking and the values his sermons conveyed. They remember a rabbi who had the gift of conveying from the pulpit something of his caring, his passion, and his vision in a way that deeply touched and inspired others. This effect was achieved by a combination of natural gifts, carefully cultivated through exposure to the eloquence of his mentor, Rabbi Stephen S. Wise, and other great exemplars of pulpit oratory, and of diligent preparation in advance of delivery. (This although he could better speak extemporaneously than I and many of my colleagues can do no matter how much we prepare.)

During the first half of this century, preaching was the centerpiece of much Christian and Jewish worship. American clergy worked hard to craft the sermon as a powerful and effective medium for communicating core values. In the first decades of this century, many of the great Christian orators were purveyors of what was called the "social gospel," the liberal Christian movement that viewed the Bible as a living message for the great social issues of our time. It arose out of many of the same "age of reason" underpinnings—the rational basis of ethics and morals, the belief in the potential (some would say the inevitable) perfectibility of individuals and society—as did the understanding of the "prophetic tradition" that Reform Judaism held to be the essence of Jewish faith and the foundation for Jewish life in America. Many of these Christian clergy were leading activists for social justice; they believed that their sermons played a vital role as a moral goad not only to their congregants but to the community at large, and that this mode of preaching was a central responsibility of their ministry.

I am aware of no formal study focusing on the Jewish social justice sermon, a type of sermon that played a central role in my father's preaching throughout his entire career, and that clearly had a tremendous impact on me personally and on many other social activists who emerged from our synagogue.

Such social action sermons are likely to provoke controversy, both as to the appropriateness of political subject matter for the pulpit and on the substance of the position espoused. On "Jewish" matters, the rabbi was clearly the expert; on "political" issues, by contrast, congregants felt they were the rabbi's equals. To be effective, the social action sermon required mastery of the facts, statistics and policies involved; rooting the arguments in Biblical or other traditional texts; connecting the positions espoused with those taken by the preacher's denomination or faith group; avoiding a tone of hostility, condescension or denigration; acknowledging the moral commitment of those with whom the preacher disagrees; putting a human face on social problems; and connecting the sermon to the preacher's personal involvement with the issues discussed. The impact of such preaching depends not merely on the power of persuasion but on the trust established between congregants and preacher in and outside of the pulpit.

My father came to Temple Emanu-El of Lynbrook with a well-established commitment to social justice. As a college student when the Depression struck, he spent several days on a Bowery bread line and wrote a powerful paper about the experience, expressing commitment to a socialist restructuring of society. In rabbinical school, influenced by Wise and Wise's colleague and friend, the Rev. John Haynes Holmes, he took the pacifist "Oxford Pledge." It is not surprising that the early social justice sermons delivered in Lynbrook reflect the youthful passion of uncompromising commitments on behalf of fellow Jews in Europe and the disenfranchised of American society.

The sermons I remember having heard in the late 1950s and '60s, on racial justice and civil rights, poverty, the war in Vietnam—many of them included in this book—were less combative in tone, but just as clear and compelling on their values. These sermons worked, arousing little opposition; they would be discussed after services without anger and resentment. More important, they influenced many congregants to establish an effective social action program at the synagogue. As for me personally, there is hardly a speech or sermon that I give without using one of my father's homiletical illustrations. The power of these words, together with the model of my parents' personal lives, have continued to inspire me, and countless other congregants and colleagues as well, to go and do likewise.

Introduction

Marc Saperstein

The following sermons were selected from a repository of some 800 extant type-scripts, written for delivery by my father, Rabbi Harold I. Saperstein, in an active rabbinic career of more than fifty-five years, beginning in 1933. Some words about the criteria for selection are therefore necessary.

I decided, first, to make the cut-off date 1980, the year Saperstein retired as rabbi of Temple Emanu-El of Lynbrook, New York.[1] He had served this one congregation for forty-seven years, during which it grew from some eighty families when he arrived in 1933 to a peak of about 1,000 families. One of the salient characteristics of the material is that it reveals a rabbi speaking to the same congregation over a period of almost two generations. There are a few exceptions. The first sermon, from the spring of 1933, dates from before Saperstein went to Lynbrook. The Rosh Hashanah sermons of 1944 and 1945 were delivered in Europe while he was a chaplain with the American Army. There is an address at a 1970 rally protesting the verdicts in the "Leningrad Trials," given while he was President of the New York Board of Rabbis. There is a sermon to

---

1. After 1980, he returned to speak many times in Lynbrook. He also served in temporary rabbinical positions—twice (for six months each time) in the West London Synagogue of British Jews as a temporary replacement assisting Rabbi Hugo Gryn, once as interim rabbi for a year in Central Synagogue of New York, and finally in a similar role for a year and a half in New York's Rodeph Sholom Congregation. He and his wife Marcia traveled through regions of the Union of American Hebrew Congregations as "circuit riders"—in the southwest, southeast, and Midwest—speaking at each small congregation that they visited. He conducted High Holy Day services in several different locations, including Dallas, Alaska, Costa Rica and South Africa. But the sermons from these years were to a large extent drawn from older material, and I have not considered any of them for use here.

the convention of the Central Conference of American Rabbis in 1957 and a sermon at ordination ceremonies of the Hebrew Union College—Jewish Institute of Religion in 1972. Except for these, all of the sermons in this book were delivered in the Lynbrook Temple.

I will return to the implications of this factor for a preacher later. Here I want to emphasize that remaining in one suburban congregation for forty-seven years did not in this case imply a narrow range of experience. The specific contours of Saperstein's career—as a young rabbi close to Stephen S. Wise near the dynamic center of American Jewish issues; a visitor to Palestine, Poland, and a delegate to the Geneva World Zionist Congress while the clouds of war were gathering in the summer of 1939; a chaplain in the European Theater during the war, entering Dachau with American forces days after its liberation, helping survivors in France, Germany, and Belgium; one of the early rabbis to visit and speak out publicly about Soviet Jewry after visits in 1959 and 1961; a volunteer working on voter registration with Stokely Carmichael in Lowndes County, Alabama during the turbulent summer of 1965; a resident of the Hebrew Union College bordering no-man's land in Jerusalem during the Six-Day War; President of the New York Board of Rabbis at the time of the Leningrad Trials verdict, on the cutting edge of confrontation with the Jewish Defense League; an inveterate, almost compulsive traveler who, with his wife, Marcia, visited Jewish communities in more than eighty countries on six continents—seem to reflect a sustained effort to be "where the action is," and to use the pulpit of his suburban Temple to report on personal encounters with great issues of the day.

Because of this distinctive rabbinic career, and because of my own interests in the academic study of Jewish sermons, I set as my goal to find among Saperstein's many extant typescripts *topical* sermons, which addressed specific issues of the day. Most homiletical collections tend to avoid the topical sermon, for a simple and obvious reason: what may have seemed an urgent, pressing, burning issue at the time of delivery looks very different ten, twenty, forty years later. Frequently it will have diminished into a historical footnote. The precise questions that once loomed so large are all but forgotten with the passage of time. References and allusions to then current matters of discussion seem almost opaque. What was once a front-page headline now seems dated and trivial. "Who will care about this anymore?" one thinks. Furthermore, subsequent years often reveal that prognostications made with confidence by the preacher have turned out to be totally misguided, and positions held with deep conviction but later abandoned may appear somewhat embarrassing. There is thus a natural tendency to prefer for publication the "timeless" sermon, homiletical in nature, textual in orientation, the kind of material that will speak to people as directly today as when first delivered a generation ago.

Especially for other clergy, there are undeniable attractions to the "timeless" sermon that can be delivered, or heard, with undiminished impact twenty years after its original creation. As a historian, however, my interest in past sermons is different. For me, the most fascinating texts are the ones that bring us back to a unique moment in the past and allow us to recover the complex dynamics, the agonizing dilemmas, the deep passions of a point in time that seems ever more elusive. Such are the sermons I have chosen for inclusion in this book, trying to find, on the average, one for every year from 1933 through the 1970s. Cumulatively, they portray the hopes and fears, the triumphs and failures, of a rabbi and a suburban congregation from the Reform movement, representing a significant component of the American Jewish community, over the course of two generations. To say that these were turbulent times seems almost trite. Nazism and the Holocaust; Zionism, the birth of the State of Israel and its subsequent ordeals and triumphs; the withering and revivification of Soviet Jewry; the Civil Rights Movement and the Vietnam War; the assassinations of President Kennedy and the Rev. Martin Luther King—these were not trivial events that could be easily ignored. What were rabbis saying at these times? What were Jews in their congregations hearing?

One example will illustrate. Having taught an undergraduate course on the Holocaust for more than ten years during a period when my academic research focused on medieval and early modern Jewish preaching, I was fairly certain about the value of sermons for determining what was known and thought during the Holocaust era. Memoirs, for all their importance and inspiration, are problematic as historical sources because of the natural tendency to reconstruct the past by projecting backward what was known only at a later time. Contemporary, datable sources are obviously preferable in this respect. Diaries are invaluable, but they are by nature private documents; they reflect the views of the author, but how do we know how well they represent anyone else? Considerable study of late has been focused on newspapers and periodicals of the period. This has demonstrated what information was available, accessible; it does not show what people actually read, heard, internalized and absorbed.

The sermon addressed to a congregation arguably takes us beyond the newspaper, especially since much of the most important information about the murder of European Jews tended to be buried on inside pages. Obviously, not every member in the congregation attends services, not everyone seated in the pews listens or hears; some people tune out or fall asleep even when the best preachers are speaking. Nevertheless, a case can be made that when a rabbi delivers a message during a worship service, especially on the Days of Awe, when Jews tend to be in a more than usually receptive mood, the evidence of actual communication about matters of utmost urgency is especially pertinent.

What was being said about Nazism to an average New York suburban congregation of Reform Jews? Was the danger of the Hitler regime to German Jews recognized? What was being urged about the economic boycott of Nazi Germany? About American participation in the Olympic Games? How much was communicated from the pulpit about the actual murder of Jews during the war itself? What was the mood of rabbis and congregants as news about European Jewry—and Europe itself—became worse and worse, and what homiletical efforts were made to lift that mood? What did rabbis advocate about America's role between the beginning of the war on September 1, 1939, and December 7, 1941? Is it true that American Jewish leaders "remained silent," "did nothing," were guilty of indifference, afraid of confrontational protest? Is it fair to state that "the destruction of the Jews of Europe was all but ignored when it was happening"?[2] I am not aware of any study of such questions based on sermons delivered between 1933 and 1946. The texts published below will provide the foundation for some preliminary answers. For this period, I have focused on High Holy Day sermons (primarily from Rosh Hashanah) because they were delivered to the largest group of listeners, at especially poignant occasions.

Because of this principle of selection, the sermons in this book are not intended to be a representative sample of Saperstein's preaching. Most of them are not textually based. They do not deal with an issue from the Torah reading and move outward from there to a topic of "relevance." They start with an issue of the day, often articulated in the very first sentence. Except for the ones given on Rosh Hashanah mornings, these were Friday night (or holiday night) sermons, delivered in the late (8:30 P.M.) evening service, the main occasion for Sabbath worship in Reform congregations. On Saturday mornings, the service tended to be focused on the bar mitzvah, and Saperstein's message then was always textually based (and usually not written out in full).[3] During this period, it was considered fully appropriate to address an issue of importance—which might include a new book, movie or play of Jewish or general interest, a classical work of general literature, a historical or theological matter, descriptions of experiences in travel to a distant Jewish community—with no necessary grounding in the Torah lesson or other classical Jewish texts. The religious message drawn was thought to be more important than the text from which it was derived.

It will be clear to the reader that these texts are not great works of literature. They were not intended to be. They were written as drafts for an oral delivery. From personal observation and conversation, I can report something about Saperstein's method of preparing the Friday night sermon. The title was announced at least one week in advance (at the end of the previous Friday night service), and usually, in the Temple Bulletin, even before that. During the first days of the week materials would be gathered, books and articles read, notes taken, sometimes a brief outline jotted down. Friday was the day set aside for preparing the sermon, and the actual writing would rarely begin before Friday morning. At that time, Saperstein would sit down at the typewriter and compose a draft of the entire text. The typescripts reveal that sometimes there were false leads—a paragraph begun then crossed out after a sentence or two followed by a new start, a few sentences near the bottom of the page with an arrow for insertion higher up. But for the most part, they were typed out from beginning to end in a couple of hours.

If these drafts had been intended as articles for a weekly newspaper column, the polishing process would have begun at this point. The quickly written typescripts are lucid, well organized, literate, but they do not reveal a particularly

2. Ruth Wisse, in the *New York Times*, August 8, 1998, A17.

3. Furthermore, many of the more "timeless" sermons delivered in the evening services—on Jewish holidays, works of classical Jewish literature, history, and values—reveal more extensive use of traditional and modern Jewish texts. The topical sermons selected for this book thus underrepresent the use of Bible and Midrash in much of his preaching.

elevated writing style, or a natural facility for witty formulations or memorable phrases. They are conversational, even colloquial in places. They contain repetitions of words, awkward formulations, typographical errors, occasional lapses in syntax, all of which would have been changed in retyping. The polishing that would have gone into a second or third written text was applied instead to the oral delivery of the sermon. From the moment the draft was complete, the major effort was devoted to mastering it to the point where it could be delivered freely, with hardly any need for the text.[4] This included the stylistic corrections that frequently result when one reads a written text aloud. There are places in the typescript where one finds changes written in, but most of the improvements would have been expressed in the way the sermon was spoken.

The High Holy Day sermons were different. They were started longer in advance, corrections were made in the typescripts; sometimes they were even retyped. Some of these, particularly from the 1930s and 1940s, reveal a conscious effort to create a rhetorical effect. But that was not the essence of Saperstein's homiletical style. He did not aspire toward the memorable phrase, but toward the compelling idea and the vivid illustration. He valued literary elegance less than clarity and naturalness of expression.[5] The impact he wanted came from the power of the content together with the forcefulness and conviction in the delivery.[6]

---

4. This was not a matter of memorization, but rather of internalization. As a youngster, I remember my father pacing the floor of the basement before Friday night dinner— or walking with him the mile from home to the Temple after it—as he "spoke out" the entire sermon without reference to the draft he carried in his hand. He once said to me that his goal was to know the material so well that if there was a thunderstorm and the lights went out in the sanctuary, he could complete the delivery of the sermon without hesitation. In speaking, he always maintained eye contact with the listeners; the technique he shared with my brother and me was to look at an individual in the audience and imagine he was speaking just to that one person, then pick out another individual for the next thought, and so forth. That way, he said, "Everyone in the congregation will think you are speaking especially to them."

5. In the middle of his career, Saperstein spoke of two contemporary preaching models from Long Island: Rabbis Jacob Rudin, of Great Neck, and Roland Gittelsohn, his neighbor in Rockville Centre until Gittelsohn moved to Boston in 1953. He admired Rudin for his poetic language and eloquence; he admired Gittelsohn for the crystalline clarity of his analysis and his sermon structure. Saperstein clearly thought of his own preaching style as closer to that of Gittlesohn, although alongside clear, convincing exposition, he also aspired to achieve emotional impact through the vivid homiletical illustration or vignette. For a statement of his homiletical approach, see his contribution to "Six Statements on Preaching Techniques," published by the Central Conference of American Rabbis" following presentations at its June 1951 Convention.

6. The sermons were delivered fluently and freely, in a natural, conversational manner that did not preclude building to moments of considerable passion and dramatic effect, in the manner of the great pulpit orators of the first half of the century. At other times, he would grasp the sides of the lectern, lean forward, and lower his voice to make a point, effecting a sense of intimacy with the congregation. Modulation of volume and pace and the natural use of hand gestures provided variety and liveliness. Congregants

It should be emphasized as well that, for the most part, the material here is neither philosophically profound nor deeply original. Saperstein was a voracious reader, and he kept massive files of homiletical materials, which he used to good effect. During the first third of his career, he was very much the disciple of Rabbi Stephen S. Wise. The positions he took on the pressing issues of Jewish concern were molded by Wise's public stance, and some of the formulations and emphases in his preaching may well have been drawn from listening to the masterful oratory of his mentor. Some of the homiletical frameworks (though not the actual content) for sermons were derived from other published works by such great contemporary preachers as Rabbis Abba Hillel Silver and Louis I. Newman and their Protestant colleagues Harry Emerson Fosdick and John Haynes Holmes.

Yet sermons are not where we should look to find the profundity or original-ity expected in a philosopher's treatise. Who, after all, can come up with some-thing profound and original week after week for almost fifty years? These ser-mons are more valuable in representing a significant trend of American Jewish leadership than they would be if they were highly idiosyncratic. The fact that we find material echoing Wise in the 1930s, for example, does not diminish its his-torical importance; on the contrary, it reveals the dissemination of principles and positions beyond the audience that Wise could reach in person. I have therefore identified as many of the sources as I could in order to demonstrate how a preacher worked to prepare his material.

While no single sermon may deserve the description "historic," I would imagine that in their totality, these sermons significantly enhance the historical record of American Jewry. It would be surprising if there are many comparable repositories of typescripts spanning most of five decades, written for delivery in a single congregation. More important, the wide range of significant experiences refracted through these sermons make the aggregate more than a representation of the average Reform rabbi. To some measure, it reflects a rather extraordinary personal involvement—from the perspective of mid-level leadership—in twenti-eth-century Jewish history.

Some Comparisons

For some years I have been working on the sermons of Saul Levi Morteira, rabbi of the Portuguese community in Amsterdam from 1619 until his death in 1660. (His was the synagogue in which the young Baruch de Espinosa grew up and was educated, until his 1656 excommunication.) In addition to a published volume of 50 sermons (*Giv'at Sha'ul*, Amsterdam, 1645), Morteira wrote more

---

actually looked forward to the sermons; at its peak (in the 1960s and 1970s), the atten-dance for Friday night services averaged 300 a week. While the content was undoubtedly important, the reputation Saperstein enjoyed both within his congregation and beyond as an extremely dynamic preacher was justified by his sermon as delivered, not as preserved in the typescripts.

than 1,400 Hebrew manuscript sermon texts, some 550 of which are extant—the largest repository of Jewish sermons by one preacher from any period before the nineteenth century.[7] This present work on the Saperstein collection leads to some illuminating points of comparison.

First as to the similarities. Perhaps most important, both preachers wrote out the texts of their sermons in full before delivery and kept these texts throughout their careers. This is not at all to be taken for granted. In the medieval and early modern periods as in the twentieth century, many preachers did not ascend the pulpit with a completed text in hand. They spoke from brief notes, from an outline, or without anything written at all. However profound, artistic, or inspirational these sermons may have been, their record has been lost except in the relatively rare instance where listeners have later recorded the sermon as they remembered it. Whatever may be said about the relative merits of preaching from a written text, the historical record is certainly enriched by those who employed this technique.[8]

Both collections represent the work of rabbis who served in the same congregation for more than four decades and who delivered a full sermon weekly through much of that period. (After the union of the three Portuguese synagogues in 1639, Morteira preached just three weeks out of every month, while his younger colleague, Menasseh ben Israel, took over on the fourth Sabbath; during his later years in Lynbrook, Saperstein had assistant rabbis who shared homiletical responsibilities). The kind of public speaking required in this context is totally different from that of, let us say, an itinerant *maggid*, or the politician running for office, who constantly addresses different audiences, and who can therefore get by with a few basic "stump" speeches, each with its amusing quips, clever lines, vivid illustrations and moving vignettes, modified for the specific occasion. Nor is the task like that of the professor with tenure, who will face a totally new group of undergraduates every four years, and may need to have a fairly large repertoire of lectures, but can offer the same course every other year or even more frequently.

The primary challenge of a preacher who remains in the same congregation for more than a generation is the audience's expectation of novelty.[9] It is difficult to determine the source of this expectation, why it applied to the preacher but not to, let us say, the cantor—who could sing the same "Kol Nidre" every year while the rabbi would never dream of delivering the same sermon—but there is no questioning its reality. Whether in seventeenth-century Amsterdam or in twentieth-century Lynbrook, Jews looked to the sermon as the one component

---

7. For examples of Morteira's sermons, see my *Jewish Preaching, 1200–1800* (New Haven: Yale University Press, 1989), 270–85, and *"Your Voice Like a Ram's Horn"* (Cincinnati: HUC Press, 1996), 367–444.

8. Most texts of pre-modern Jewish sermons that have come down to us were prepared by their authors some time after delivery; see *Jewish Preaching*, 20–26. Morteira's published volume is thus the exception. Like the present volume, it was not prepared for publication by the preacher himself (but rather by two of Morteira's students).

9. On this expectation, see *Jewish Preaching*, 55 (including n. 31), 400, 428.

of the service that would be new: different each week, like the Scriptural read-ing, but also—unlike the Scriptural reading—different each year. This expecta-tion—similar to that which applies to the syndicated columnist—placed enor-mous pressures on any rabbi's creativity and ingenuity.

Stability in a pulpit has its advantages as well as its challenges. It means that the preacher has an established relationship with a congregation. A visiting *maggid* may arrive with an outstanding reputation, but he needs to sustain and justify it with every appearance. Each time he faces a new audience, he feels the need to bedazzle his listeners once again. If he is preaching rebuke, criticizing the behavior that fails to measure up to the standards of the tradition, there is a different problem, for he faces the natural resistance of those who think, "By what right does this stranger come to attack us?"[10] The rabbi, by contrast, comes to the pulpit each week able to draw upon a reservoir of respect and good will. He has presided at life cycle events for most in the audience or for members of their families. He knows them; they trust him. If one particular sermon is not fully satisfying, there will be many other opportunities.

In addition, this relationship ensures a continuity of discourse. As a genre, a sermon is a discrete entity, complete in itself—like a short story, a poem, a one-act play—and it should be analyzed as such. But for a rabbi who addresses the same congregation week after week and year after year, the individual ser-mon also becomes part of a larger cumulative message. Just as there is an ex-pectation of novelty, so there is an expectation of consistency and continuity. Not the consistency of a philosophical treatise; it is understood that different occasions may require different emphases. But blatant contradictions between one sermon and another or fundamental shifts in position are problematic and need to be explained. The advantage of this situation is that not everything need be covered on any one occasion. The preacher knows that most of the listeners have heard him before, and he can refer back to an earlier communication. He also expects that his audience will return in the future to hear more, and he can promise to address a topic in further detail on another occasion.

This common situation leads to a striking degree of what might be called "self-referentiality" in the sermons of both preachers. Almost every sermon by Morteira after the first few years refers back to earlier ones, which he para-phrases, summarizes, or recapitulates, in order to lay the foundation for the cur-rent discourse. Sometimes he will begin by referring to a sermon he delivered the previous year on the same Torah lesson, or on a different lesson several years in the past. This way of introducing a topic saves time; there is no need for a full discussion of a particular point at present, and the preacher can, after a brief summary, go on to a new aspect assuming that the foundation is in place. Occasionally he will even invite interested listeners to read the text to which he refers if they want full details.

Saperstein does not use this self-referentiality nearly as much as Morteira; when he does, it is usually for rhetorical effect rather than as a pedagogical aid.

---

10. I have discussed some of the dynamics of this problem in *Jewish Preaching*, 49–50, 57–61.

Examples would be the reference to his sermon on lynching—one of his first sermons in Lynbrook—in the introduction to his sermon on the riots against the appearance of Paul Robeson in 1949; his citing of a mid-1930s sermon warning of the dangers of Nazism to all of human civilization in a sermon for Rosh Hashanah morning, 1940; the invoking of a 1933 eulogy for his uncle in his 1949 eulogy for Wise; his reference to sermons on pacifism from the 1930s in the 1975 sermon "How My Mind Has Changed." The rhetorical function of such references in these contexts is clear, and it is enhanced by the awareness that some of those seated in the congregation had actually heard the earlier delivery. But Saperstein's self-references point to the future as well as to the past. Where Morteira frequently says something like, "I do not have to discuss it in detail as I have already done so," Saperstein's point will more often be, "I will not speak of this in detail as I intend to do so in the near future."

There is also considerable reuse in the work of both preachers. To be sure, this contradicts the expectation of novelty, and strict limits were self-imposed by the preachers, but the evidence is present in the texts. Many of Morteira's sermons bear at the end the words—often in discernibly different ink—"I preached it again in the year. . . ." Sometimes additional lines appear: "I preached it a third time in the year . . . " or "I preached it a fourth time." Occasionally additions will be noted: "and I added the following." These repetitions tend to come at seven- to ten-year intervals.[11]

Saperstein rarely repeated the same sermon without change. And obviously, the topical sermons in this book could not be used again. But some sermons could be recycled. Thematic sermons: on the relationship between religion and politics, on Jewish attitudes toward labor. Or homiletical motifs and structures. For example, "The Chains of the Messiah" was a sermon he used on several occasions after its original delivery in 1950—after a minimum of seven years had elapsed, or if he were speaking in a different place. The illustrative material would change each time: what *was* the evidence of the messiah's chains, how could they be broken? On a number of the typescripts there are notations—as with Morteira—"reused in 1958," or "based on sermon from 1938, with changes."[12]

Why do preachers reuse their materials? The creative powers usually begin to wane as one grows older, and the challenge of novelty becomes more daunting. In addition, the more one has already said, the more difficult it becomes to find something new. While younger preachers often depend on ideas from the published works of older colleagues, more established preachers generally feel more comfortable drawing from their own archives. Congregations may come with an expectation of novelty, but rabbis have their own expectation: of forget-

---

11. I have described such notations at the end of his sermons in "The Manuscript/s of Morteira's Sermons," *Studies in Jewish Manuscripts*, ed. Joseph Dan and Klaus Herrmann (Tübingen: Mohr Siebeck, 1999), 171–98, esp. 176–77.

12. For example, a text entitled "Foes of Freedom," intended for the Sabbath during Passover, has appended at the end in a manner strikingly similar to the Morteira manuscripts: "Preached around 1939; repreached April 15, 1949, April 11, 1979."

fulness. They may desperately—often futilely—want their congregants to remember what they say, but they do not want them to remember everything forever.

Moreover, there is turnover in every congregation; after seven to ten years, enough new people will be present to justify bringing an old sermon back to life. Finally, there may be some question about the very assumption that no sermon should ever be repeated. People do not mind hearing a great symphony or seeing a great play more than once; why should we *not* repeat a sermon? Yet the uneasiness with this decision is indicated by the fact that preachers who do reuse their old material generally do not advertise this; rarely do they announce, "this sermon from ten years ago is being repeated by popular demand" or "because it is one of my own favorites."

Unless a preacher has a photographic memory of everything he ever said, both self-referentiality and reuse require a filing system that allows the texts to be accessed for subsequent use. As noted, Morteira's sermons are so filled with cross-references that he must have had an elaborate system of organizing his texts. I cannot deduce from internal evidence whether it was strictly chronological, with each sermon in the order that it was written, so that all the sermons from the same year would be together, or by *parashah*, so that all the sermons on the same Torah lesson would be together. Different volumes of the bound manuscripts were organized according to each of these systems. But either way, there must have been a kind of indexing, no longer extant, that would have enabled the preacher to find his way in the increasingly large corpus of his own writings.

Saperstein's filing system became apparent to me only upon my initial investigation in June 1998. I had always assumed they were filed by year. They turned out to be filed by topic. High Holy Day sermons were grouped together in files so labeled. The other files, arranged alphabetically, were labeled Books and Plays, Germany—Nazis, Israel, Jewish Education, Marriage, Social Problems, Soviet Jewry, War, and, of course, Miscellaneous. Another large set of files contained homiletical material on these same topics: clippings from newspaper and magazine articles, pamphlets, material distributed by various Jewish organizations.

There were several drawers of 4x6-inch cards with quotations organized by subject matter, including many of the poetic passages used in the sermons published here. There were drawers with a 3x5-inch card for each sermon giving the title and a brief outline of its content, and other sets of such cards with ideas for new sermon themes. Upon examining the system, I realized that while the topical organization was less useful for the historian, who might want to reconstruct exactly what was said in any particular year, it is more useful for the active preacher who, addressing a particular topic, will be able quickly to refer to relevant predecessors. (In the 1975 sermon "How My Mind Has Changed," Saperstein actually refers to his file of sermons on pacifism and reads several titles; two of them are published below.)

So much for the oeuvre as a whole. What about the individual text? Both preachers used a title for each sermon. Morteira's were invariably Biblical phrases relevant to the topic of the sermon. The function of these titles is not entirely clear, in that Morteira apparently did not announce the title at delivery, and he did not at first think of publication. Their only use in the manuscripts themselves is as a shorthand way of referring to a sermon already delivered. By contrast, Saperstein's titles had an obvious function in that, as noted above, they were published in advance in the monthly Temple Bulletin, and the title for the following week's sermon would be included in an officer's announcements at the end of each Friday evening service. As can be seen in this volume's table of contents, they might be literary phrases, but were often more prosaic ways of communicating the sermon's contents.

In both cases, there was a striking regularity in the physical preparation of the texts. With the exception of the longer ones for the Sabbath of Repentance, virtually all of Morteira's sermons were written on two sheets of paper, front and back. Most of them end somewhere on the second half of the third side (i.e., the first side of the second sheet), with the fourth side empty except for indications of the circumstances of delivery or redelivery. Saperstein's sermons were typed single-spaced on three sheets of 8½-by-11 inch paper, turned sideways and then cut in half to make six sheets, each one 5½-by-8½ inches. This unusual technique has an obvious advantage: unlike full-sized sheets, the half-sized sheets can easily fit inside a prayer book, or inside a jacket pocket, without being seen, and are quite unobtrusive to handle in the pulpit.

While the text would be fully written, the delivery would ideally be so free and the pages so inconspicuous that no one in the congregation would realize there was a written text. (I imagine that was generally true, as I remember having often been asked, "Does he write his sermons out?"). Quite striking is the standardized length of the texts, regularly ending near the bottom of the sixth side, or with a few lines—usually less than a paragraph—spilling over to a seventh: a regularity that is rather remarkable for first drafts. I remember hearing this as a preaching "rule": six sides of a page, single-spaced in elite type yield about 20 minutes, and that was the desired length.[13]

Neither the Morteira manuscripts nor the Saperstein typescripts appear to be suitable as scripts for public speaking. Saperstein's were, as noted, single-spaced, with minimal margins, occasional corrections squeezed in between the lines. Morteira's texts, written in his own difficult hand, were even more crowded and dense; they also present the problem of having been written on both sides, so that often the ink shows through, making the material extremely challenging to read. Finally, Morteira wrote his texts in Hebrew but he delivered his sermons in Portuguese.[14] Both sets of documents, therefore, reveal what was

---

13. After delivery, the six half-pages were stapled together and put into a file folder. Sometimes the final page became detached from the rest and disappeared, leaving the sermon incomplete, and producing a considerable number of "orphan" pages. I have succeeded in reuniting some of these, but two of the sermons below from the early years are published without their concluding page.

14. I had long been troubled by the feasibility of this linguistic transposition, but I recently found confirmation in a description of Leo Baeck's public speaking in the United States: "Baeck's remarkable sense of duty and propriety dictated that he had to

emphasized above: the importance of the preparation that occurred after the text was written, the work involved in moving to the oral stage of the sermon, which was ultimately independent of the text.

As I have shown elsewhere,[15] there are various techniques of organizing the material in a sermon. In some homiletical styles, the preacher moves from one point to another without ever indicating the overall structure of his message, so that after fifteen minutes, the listener will have no way of knowing from internal cues whether the sermon is nearing its conclusion or still near the beginning. Both Morteira and Saperstein had a far more listener-friendly style. They clearly considered structure to be an important component of their communicative technique. Their sermons can be readily outlined; there is usually an introduction that (among other things) articulates the topic to be addressed, three or more divisions in the body of the text, and a homiletical coda. Both preachers often provided signals to help their listeners keep track of where they are in the sermon, and they recapitulate at the end so that the listeners might more easily remember the main points that had been made. Morteira's structures are often more complex, involving unexpected correlations of disparate component elements, making these sermons models of an important genre of Hebrew literature,[16] but both preachers obviously made the effort to present their material in a manner organized for a pedagogical purpose.

One final point applies to the respective congregations. Especially in the first generation, Morteira's community was composed almost entirely of men and women who had grown up as Christians in Portugal, left that country, and decided to join a Jewish community and came to Amsterdam. Many of them had been educated in the best universities of Portugal and were highly successful in their chosen professions. They knew that they wanted to be Jews—although there is evidence of ambivalence at times—but they had very little systematic Jewish education or thorough knowledge of classical Jewish texts. The preacher's challenge was therefore to present Jewish issues through his sermons in a sophisticated and aesthetically appealing manner, but one that did not presuppose extensive prior knowledge. I view these sermons as an ongoing program of adult education.

A Reform congregation in the New York suburbs was more diverse. Lynbrook, Long Island (settled primarily by émigrés from Brooklyn, who retained its name but reversed the syllables), was primarily a middle to lower-middle-class community, as was its Jewish population. Because Temple Emanu-El was one of the first Reform synagogues in the area (founded in 1920),

---

prepare a new address for each occasion. These were the work of a man in his seventies, writing out his remarks in German, searching the dictionary to be certain of the precise meaning of every English word that he wanted to use, and then pacing up and down in his room until he had his text by heart." Marianne C. Dreyfus, "Remembering My Grandfather, Leo Baeck," *CCAR Journal* 46 (Winter 1999): 52.

15. See the section on "Structural Options" in my *Jewish Preaching, 1200–1800*, 63–79.

16. I have analyzed this structure in some detail in "The Sermon as Art-Form: Structure in Morteira's *Giv'at Sha'ul*," reprinted in *"Your Voice Like a Ram's Horn,"* 107–25.

it drew from a large number of surrounding communities. Its members in the 1930s and 1940s were first- or second-generation Americans of Polish, German, even Dutch-Sephardic backgrounds. Many had grown up in traditional families and—like Saperstein himself—made the break from orthodoxy; a few were second-generation Reform. Lynbrook Jews of a more traditionalist orientation could affiliate with the smaller Beth David Congregation.[17] During the first decades, many were lower-middle class, few had graduate degrees, many had not attended college. The wealthier members were self-made business people, with a sprinkling of professionals. Like Morteira's listeners, they were not, on the whole, steeped in Jewish learning. After the war, with the massive move to the suburbs, the enlarged membership of upwardly mobile commuters to New York firms became increasingly well educated and successful. Yet for most of Saperstein's career, they still looked to the sermon as a primary access to contemporary Jewish issues and traditional Jewish knowledge. For some, especially in the early years, it was a primary access to general culture as well.

The two groups of sermon texts also reveal some significant differences. Morteira's sermons are all fundamentally textual in nature. Each one is structurally linked with a single verse from the Torah lesson, and secondarily with a selected rabbinic dictum, both read at the beginning. Much of the content of the sermons is devoted to exegesis of statements from Bible or rabbinic literature, or grappling with exegetical problems. In a few instances, Morteira addresses issues of the time, but usually in an allusive manner, not directly or explicitly. Many of his sermons could be delivered a century later without anyone knowing (and indeed in some cases they were—by an eighteenth-century Italian rabbi).

The center of gravity in Saperstein's Friday night sermons was quite different. Some of his sermons were explicitly focused on topics from the Bible, or structured by statements from the rabbinic literature. In others, the Torah reading and other classical texts are brought in, if at all, for homiletical effect. It is the topical material that is of the essence, especially in the selections published here.[18] In the seventeenth-century repository, except for a very few occasional sermons responding to events in the life of the congregation, there is nothing really comparable to these topical sermons.

A second fundamental difference relates to the personal voice of the preacher. Unfortunately (from the historian's perspective), only on the rarest of occasions will Morteira use the first person singular. He hardly ever speaks about himself, his experiences, his anxieties, his hopes. This is the kind of mate-

---

17. An early rabbi of this congregation was Emanuel Rackman, Saperstein's colleague in Lynbrook from 1936 to 1943; both of them left Lynbrook for the chaplaincy in 1943. As rabbi of Shaarey Tefilah in Far Rockaway and the Fifth Avenue Synagogue in New York, assistant to the president of Yeshivah University, and president and chancellor of Bar Ilan University, Rackman became one of the most distinguished leaders of modern Orthodoxy.

18. An exception to this generalization is "When Leadership Fails," which is structured by three interpretations in traditional commentators to the failing of Moses at the Wilderness of Zin. Delivered at a convention of the Central Conference of American Rabbis, it was written with colleagues in mind, though it was later used in the congregation.

rial that abounds in Saperstein's sermons. His personal voice is pervasive. Experiences described to the congregation are intended to provide a kind of vicarious encounter with aspects of Jewish life to which they did not otherwise have access. Some readers may view this personal element as overly pronounced; by current standards, they may appear to be too much about the preacher's experiences and memories, not enough about the tradition. That was certainly not the reaction of most congregants upon hearing the sermons delivered.

Another contrast pertains to the use of "external" material—from outside the Jewish tradition—in the sermons. Morteira used remarkably little of this; a reconstruction of his library based on explicit citations in the sermons would suggest an overwhelmingly Hebraic collection: Bible and commentaries, Talmud and Midrashim, medieval halakhic, philosophical, homiletical, ethical, and occasionally kabbalistic literature. Occasionally he will refer to non-Jewish works, such as classical historians (references he may have derived from other Hebrew sources such as Abravanel), and on rare occasions, "one of the works of the [contemporary] Gentiles." It is not that Morteira was reluctant to read Christian literature. His polemical texts written in Spanish and Portuguese, including a recently published monumental treatise on the eternity of the Law of Moses, reveal many specific citations from Christian historians and theologians. Apparently he did not consider this to be appropriate content for his preaching.

As will be quickly seen in the material below, Saperstein's sermons are quite different. In addition to frequent references to material drawn from the *New York Times* and other periodicals, they are filled with citations of general literature, both the classics—Shakespeare, Ibsen, Browning, Longfellow—and the novels, poems and plays of such contemporary writers such as H. G. Wells, Ernest Hemingway, Sinclair Lewis, Carl Sandburg, Maxwell Anderson, Thomas Mann. While Bible, Midrash and medieval commentators are sometimes cited to make a homiletical point, the experiences of Jewish history and the works of modern Hebrew writers (Bialik, Berdichevski, Frishman, Alterman) are invoked just as frequently as the classics of the Jewish tradition. These sermons were not intended as a way of teaching the congregation the unfamiliar, traditional way of grappling with problems of Biblical exegesis; that was done more in his Torah-lesson-oriented Saturday morning preaching, or in his highly attended adult education courses during the week. The sermons used what was familiar in the general culture in order to illustrate or strengthen a point about issues of Jewish or general concern.

Finally, it should not come as much of a surprise that the fundamental problems faced by the respective congregations, as reflected in the sermons, are quite different. In Amsterdam, the predominant external problem was the pressures of Christianity. This was a community of people who had broken with their Christian upbringing. This break often produced the "zeal of the convert," a powerful impulse to defend Judaism and attack its religious adversary. The polemical passages against Roman Catholicism in many of Morteira's sermons suggest he believed that the construction of a new Jewish identity required the tearing down of the old Christian one. In the 1930s, the crucial external problem was, of course, antisemitism, not only in Nazi Germany but in the rest of Europe as well and even in the United States. Many of Saperstein's sermons from the 1930s are devoted to this theme: why is the Jew hated, why are people prejudiced, why do Jews suffer so much?

Internally, the central problem for the Portuguese Jewish community of Amsterdam was the questioning of classical Jewish tradition. In some individuals, the same mind-set that led them to challenge and ultimately break with the authoritative tradition of the Catholic Church opened the door to similar questioning of rabbinic authority. The most extreme and dramatic instance from the first generation was Uriel da Costa, who began by repudiating the belief in the immortality of the soul as alien to the Hebrew Scripture, and went on to reject aspects of rabbinic law. Many of Morteira's sermons defend the rabbinic tradition, particularly in areas that had come under challenge. In the Long Island Reform congregation, the internal problem was not the questioning of rabbinic tradition. The congregants had already made that break. The problem there was radical assimilation, denial of Jewish identity, opting to keep nothing at all.

Editing Decisions

No significant substantive changes have been made in the texts. Some editing was required, as these were quickly typed drafts not intended to be seen by anyone except for the writer. Obvious typographical errors have therefore been corrected. I have also regularized punctuation and format so as to make the text appropriate for reading rather than a cue-sheet for speaking. I have indulged in minor stylistic polishing to smooth out an obvious infelicity where I am convinced that this is consistent with improvements that would actually have been made in the oral delivery. Most of the dates of delivery are taken from the typescripts themselves, or determined from a calendar where the typescript states something like "Rosh Hashanah Morning, 1941." In a few cases they have been reconstructed by internal or external evidence.

I have preserved the original mode of discourse as part of the historical authenticity of the texts, even though they seem quite distant from 1990s standards of "political correctness." The universally accepted style throughout the period of these sermons was what today would be considered insensitively gender-specific language: "men," "mankind," "our brothers in Europe," "the Jew and his responsibility." To talk about "the Negro" in the 1930s through the 1970s was considered natural, not insensitive. The use of "Hitlerites" as a synonym for "Nazis" was common in the 1930s and early 1940s in the speeches of President Roosevelt as well as those of American preachers. "Antisemitism" is written several different ways over the years.

I have not attempted to standardize the transcription of Hebrew words used in the sermons. Readers who know Hebrew will recognize a shift from the East-European Ashkenazic to the Israeli Sephardic pronunciation about the time of the four-month sabbatical stay in Israel between March and June of 1967. Even within each mode, inconsistencies of transcription appear and have been allowed to remain. I have identified in parentheses the source of Biblical verses quoted in the sermons, though the chapter and verse were usually not spoken.

In my brief introductions to each sermon (printed in italics), I have tried to "set the stage" by reviewing some of the significant historical events that provide the background to the message, as well as biographical developments relevant to an understanding of what is said. As a time-bound communication, the topical sermon is often filled with references or allusions to matters that would have been known to virtually everyone in the congregation, but are frequently unintelligible today to all but the historian who specializes in the period.[19] In my annotations, my goal has been to fill in the resonance that the words would have had to listeners when the sermon was delivered.

My primary tool for this task has been the *New York Times Index* for the appropriate year and the microfilms of the actual editions of the *Times* to which Saperstein was often referring. I have also identified other sources for references and quotations. Wherever possible, I have cited books that I know to have been in Saperstein's own library and used by him. In addition, I have included some contemporary bibliography for readers interested in pursuing the various topics further. While these notes may be necessary to understand the original meaning and appreciate the historical significance of the words, I am aware that they may interrupt the flow of the discourse. The reader may therefore wish to read the text once consulting the notes, and then a second time straight through, perhaps aloud, as it would have been spoken.

There are many constituent elements of a sermon. First is the written record of what was said. Second is everything associated with the word "delivery": voice quality, pace, intensity, pitch, emphasis, gesture—all the things that in a musical score would accompany the notes to indicate how they were actually to sound. Third is the preacher: the personality of the speaker, his reputation and prestige, the esteem in which he is held by the congregation, the associations his very presence has in the minds of the listeners. Fourth is the audience and what they bring to the sermon: their level of knowledge and their expectations, their mood, their needs. Fifth is the physical setting: the sanctuary with its symbolism, the lectern, the physical position of the speaker in relationship to those who are listening. And sixth is the unique historical moment in which all of the above are conjoined: what from the outside world imposes its presence into the serenity of the synagogue service and demands to be addressed.

The words of the sermons below have been preserved in the extant typescripts and are now accessible to a reading public. But the other elements are largely missing. The original setting is preserved only in photographs, as the

---

19. This allusiveness is perhaps the greatest challenge in reading topical sermons from any age; see my *Jewish Preaching 1200–1800*, 81–84. For an example within the memory of most readers, one might consult the text of President Reagan's address to the nation following the explosion of the shuttle Challenger on January 28, 1986. It is filled with phrases such as "the events of earlier today," "we've never had a tragedy like this," "sometimes painful things like this happen," "what happened today." The word "explosion" never occurs, and one can imagine future readers wondering exactly what happened. When the words were spoken, there was not need for specifics.

sanctuary was replaced in the late 1950s.[20] There being no videotapes or even tape-recordings of any of these sermons that I know of, the delivery has been lost forever, except in the memory of listeners who heard them, and who may indeed remember the tone of voice as well as the actual words or ideas. The preacher, the audience, and the historical moment are—to some extent—evoked in some of the passages where Saperstein speaks about himself, reports the views or the mood of members of the congregation, and reviews events that have triggered his message. I hope that my introductions and annotations will fill in more of this rich context. But even through an exercise of the imagination, most contemporary readers will never be able to put themselves back in the position or re-create the mood of Jews gathering for worship in the 1930s or early 1940s, when so much of the world around them seemed to be collapsing; or in May 1948 when the State of Israel was established; or even on November 22, 1963, when President Kennedy was assassinated. The written words of the sermons delivered on those occasions are only a pale reflection of the sermons themselves.

Nevertheless, I believe that those words should be preserved. Some of the sentences may seem obviously dated, some a bit bombastic, a few uninspired, prosaic and trite. But far more frequently, reading this material conveys to me a glimmer of the genuine power that the original message carried.[21] The sermon as a form of religious discourse is currently in disrepute within much of the contemporary Jewish community. It is thought to be undemocratic, authoritarian, placing too much upon the shoulders of the preacher and leaving the listeners too passive. These texts convince me that there is still a role for the topical sermon. As the Gettysburg battlefield was not the place or the occasion for Lincoln to conduct a town meeting, so there are times that require a mode of discourse more elevated than the *d'var torah* or "discussion" that is the contemporary vogue. The Friday night of the Kennedy assassination is an example that comes readily to mind. The process of discovering texts I had not known, and re-encountering texts of sermons I remember having heard, has validated for me an intuition of adolescent years in synagogue surrounded by a congregation listening to an admired and beloved preacher—an intuition about the potential power of the sermon to educate, challenge, uplift and inspire.

---

20. Saperstein refers back to the original sanctuary in his 1973 "Days I Remember." In one dramatic instance—the Vietnam War sermon of 1968—the current sanctuary is invoked as the preacher points to the words on the doors to the ark—*emet, din, shalom*—to introduce each of the component parts.

21. Compare a contemporary review of Wise's *As I See It*, written by Harry Salpeter: "I had not read far into this volume when I began hearing again, in undiminished force, the thunders of that moral authority which is Stephen S. Wise. . . . Only in the case of a Fosdick, or a Holmes, or a Wise (among contemporaries) is it possible for the spoken sermon to survive on the printed page, on which within the actual text it may achieve a second life." *Jewish Book Annual* 3 (5705) (Philadelphia: JPS, 1944), 62.

Acknowledgements

This book, which began with the need to clean out boxes and files from the office of a synagogue's Rabbi Emeritus, soon became transformed from an expression of filial responsibility into an adventure of discovery and an exciting intellectual challenge.

I am deeply indebted to my brother, David, for the countless hours of work that he devoted to this project. This would indeed have been a fully collaborative effort had he not been living in Jerusalem during the summer and fall of 1998 when the selection of sermons, their transcription onto computer disk, and the preliminary annotations were done. From that point on, he reviewed every word with me, added material for many of the annotations, and deliberated with me on questions of style. (He graciously accepts responsibility for any errors that may remain in this volume.)

We are all most grateful to my father's brother, Rabbi Sanford Saperstein, for having kept letters written to him from Europe during the Second World War and making them available for quotation.

My daughter Adina read and commented on much of the material in its early stages, and my daughter and son-in-law, Sara and Stephen Frug, were extremely helpful in the proofreading of the finished product.

Most of the research for the introductions and annotations was done at the Gelman Library of The George Washington University, recently enriched by its wonderful I. Edward Kiev Collection of Judaica. Indispensable to my work were the yearly index volumes of the *New York Times* and the microfilm collections of the actual issues. I also used Harvard's Widener Library, and the Libraries of the Hebrew Union College—Jewish Institute of Religion in Cincinnati and New York.

Many colleagues and friends made themselves available for consultation on specific textual and historical problems (not all of which we were able to solve). They include Eugene Borowitz, Eugene Fisher, Allen Kaplan, Gertrude Langsam, Arthur Mattson, Michael Meyer, Philip Miller, Jehuda Reinharz, Howard Sachar, Allan Satin, Julie Spitzer z"l, Michael Stanislawski, Sara Witt and Yosef Yerushalmi.

Rabbi Stuart Geller and the other leaders of Temple Emanu-El of Lynbrook have enthusiastically supported this entire project—among other things a record of the history of that congregation—in many ways.

Based on a table of contents and a rough sample of fifteen annotated sermons, Serena Leigh at Lexington Books ratified my judgment that this was a publishable volume. She has guided the book and its editor through the various stages of production with professional aplomb.

To all those named above, and to Rabbis Hertzberg, Malino and Rackman, whose words are a cherished adornment to this book, I am delegated to express the heartfelt gratitude of the author and preacher of the following sermons.

1

Nazi Nationalism
April 28, 1933

During the months immediately following Hitler's accession to power on January 30, 1933, the Nazi regime launched a dazzling series of initiatives. The mass arrests justified by the "emergency" of the Reichstag fire, the establishment of the first concentration camp at Dachau, the passing of the "Enabling Act" by which the Parliament ceded almost all of its powers to Hitler's government (thereby effectively voting itself out of existence), legislation squeezing non-Aryans out of the civil service, all were part of a well-orchestrated process transforming the republic—without a revolution—into a totalitarian state. Violence against Jews was sporadic. The first coordinated effort was the one-day boycott of all Jewish businesses held on April 1, publicized by widespread propaganda and enforced by brown-shirt storm troopers standing guard.

American Jews were appalled at the developments, but deeply divided on questions of tactics. Would Hitler be able to remain in power? Would the responsibilities of office moderate his antisemitism? Should the opposition to the regime and its policies be expressed by overt criticism and large-scale public protests, or by quiet diplomacy behind the scenes? Was the regime sensitive and vulnerable to the antagonism of world opinion, or would a campaign of hostile criticism play into the hands of the Nazi leaders, who would use it to justify an anti-Jewish response? The militant, confrontational approach was spearheaded by the American Jewish Congress, led by the founding president of the Jewish Institute of Religion, Rabbi Stephen S. Wise. The mass protest rally that filled Madison Square Garden on March 27 revealed Jews deeply concerned, determined to make their voices heard. Yet there was powerful opposition within American Jewry to this kind of approach.

All this was a heady atmosphere for a rabbinical student a few months beyond his 22nd birthday, in his second year at the JIR. Close to Wise, he seems to have become a kind of foot-soldier in the cause at the same time that he was engaged in intensive study of Jewish history and classical Jewish texts. In April, he was assisting Rabbi Morton Berman in putting together the first issue of a new periodical called "American Jewish Congress Courier" in response to the turbulent events (see the sermon "A Prince in Israel," below). Asked to speak at a Friday night service held by a group of Jews who came together to form a new synagogue, he delivered the following sermon. The message begins with the rally and moves onward with full youthful fervor and self-assurance, unswerving in the prediction that the extreme nationalism of the Nazis will never compromise on its antisemitic component, urgent in the warning that this antisemitism could spread beyond Germany, insisting that vocal opposition to the regime must not diminish.

THE MASS MEETING HELD AT MADISON SQUARE GARDEN a month and a day ago to express the protest of American public opinion against the anti-Semitic outrages in Germany is now history.[1] It is a noble thing to raise one's voice in fearless protest when his fellows are suffering from inhuman and well-nigh unbearable persecution. And the mass meeting was not only noble but effective. The universal outcry of protest heard from all corners of the world at that time did much to mitigate the horrors of Nazi excesses and alleviate the condition of our fellow Jews in Germany. Yesterday I had the opportunity of reading several letters received by Dr. [Stephen S.] Wise from prominent German Jews who had fled the country, acknowledging their gratitude for what he was doing on behalf of their countrymen.

One from a prominent Jewish attorney who had escaped to Zurich, Switzerland, after describing the scenes of terror he had witnessed, said, "It was only foreign protests, particularly that of America, which prevented even worse happenings, a greater number of kidnappings and bloody beatings, and possibly one big general pogrom."[2] One pathetic letter, written on March 23, when the agitation for the meeting was starting, and forwarded to Dr. Wise—a letter which

---

1. The rally was held on March 27, 1933, at the initiative of the American Jewish Congress. This provides a date of Friday, April 28, for the sermon. Speakers included, in addition to Rabbi Stephen S. Wise, former New York Governor Alfred E. Smith, Bishops William Manning and Francis McConnell, and Senator Robert F. Wagner. On the rally, see Stephen Wise, *Challenging Years* (New York: G. Putnam's Sons, 1949), 246–47; Melvin Urofsky, *A Voice that Spoke For Justice* (Albany, SUNY Press, 1982), 264–67; Moshe Gottlieb, *American Anti-Nazi Resistance, 1933–1941: An Historical Analysis* (New York: Ktav, 1982), 33–34. For the speech Wise delivered at the rally, see his *As I See It* (New York: Jewish Opinion Publishing Corporation, 1944), 85–89. See also the impact of the event as recorded by the Unitarian Minister John Haynes Holmes in his *A Summons Unto Men*, ed. Carl Voss (New York: Simon and Schuster, 1970), 80–81.

2. Wise later incorporated this quotation into his autobiography, *Challenging Years*, 248.

escaped the censors only because it was mailed outside the country—after telling of the terrible humiliation and suffering they had undergone, continued:

> We are outlaws. The least announcement might break our neck. Therefore please be careful when you write to us. We are apt to suffer for it. P.S., I have just read the papers and find that our situation is known abroad. Thank God.

It is not necessary to belabor the point. Certainly it is clear to every man who sees and weighs the facts clearly that the limitation of the official boycott against the Jews in Germany to one day[3] and whatever easing up there has been in the conduct of the Nazi program have come as direct though unadmitted concessions to the pressure of world opinion.

But merely to protest is not enough. Now that the heat of emotional fervor that permeated all discussion on this subject a month ago has cooled—although, Heaven knows, our vital concern has not abated—it is time that we, to whom the welfare of Jews and Judaism is precious, take inventory. It is time that we analyzed the situation, to determine not only what the facts are but also what they signify. It is time that we realized what the implications of the German situation are for us. It is time that we Jews awoke from our lethargy, that we abandoned our policy of drifting, that we faced squarely the problems of Jewish life today, and that on the basis of that analysis we formulated and acted upon a definite program of Jewish living.

What then is the significance of Hitlerism? Since the first notice of the mass meeting came out more than a month ago, there have been conflicting reports and opinions. It has always been one of the terrible tragedies of all Jewish endeavor that our energy is constantly vitiated by internal strife, our strength dissipated by internecine struggle. At the time of the destruction of Jerusalem by the Romans in 70 C.E., the Jews held the Roman legions at bay, suffering famine and thirst, giving their lives gladly for their land and faith. Yet while the Romans

---

3. Reference is to the first coordinated anti-Jewish act of the new regime, the one-day boycott of all Jewish businesses, held on April 1, 1933. See, most recently, Saul Friedländer, *Nazi Germany and the Jews*, vol. 1 (New York: HarperCollins, 1997), 19–24. The Nazi regime actually used such events as the anti-Nazi rally in New York as a pretext to justify this boycott, though it had been discussed at the highest levels before its official announcement on March 29. See also J. Noakes and G. Pridham, eds., *Nazism: A History in Documents and Eyewitness Accounts, 1919–1945*, 2 vols. (New York: Schocken, 1983), 1: 524: "Originally, the boycott had been intended to be indefinite, but concern about its negative impact on the economy and opposition to it from the Reich President and the Foreign Minister persuaded Hitler to limit it to one day—1 April—in the first instance, with the intention of reviving it if, as he put it, international Jewry did not cease its anti-German activities." Another letter from a Jew in Berlin, dated April 2, published in part by Wise in *Challenging Years*, 247–48, does indeed make the point in the sermon—that the action would have been far worse (i.e., plunder rather than just peaceful boycott of stores, and for more than one day) had it not been for the foreign protests.

were at their very gates, within the walls, instead of uniting for their last stand in a common cause, the Jews were at each other's throats, fighting the enemy without and their fellows within at the same time.[4]

So there are those among the leaders of American Jewish life today who, moved by personal animosity to those who are sponsoring the Jewish protests, willfully blind themselves to the great issues at stake, and not only refuse to participate but even exerted their influence to doom protest activities to failure. As I said, it has been one of the tragedies of Jewish life. But that is another sermon.[5]

There was another type of Jew whose sympathies are not wholeheartedly with the work of Dr. Wise and the American Jewish Congress in their handling of the problem of German Jewry. These were those who, admitting the evils of the situation, yet think that the best policy for Jews is one of silence. There are many people who sincerely believe that the violence of the antisemitic program of the Nazis is only a temporary matter, that it is the natural effluvium of a political party just come to victory, that with the passage of time it will of its own accord be modified. And they point to the apparent surcease of physical violence in the treatment of Jews as proof of their contentions. They therefore feel that the easiest way to end the situation is to ignore it.

In my opinion, however, the facts belie this analysis. For Antisemitism is not just a temporary phenomenon in Nazi policy. It is not merely a body letting off steam for the time being, before starting in on more serious work. Rather, it is a basic element of the Nazi program and the natural fruit of the principles and platform they have been enunciating for thirteen years. The program of the Nazi party was first made public by Hitler on February 25, 1920, and it has since been repeated on every possible occasion. This program contains twenty-five items, of which seven are devoted to the purpose of eliminating the Jew from public life. The official statement on the program expresses the conviction that the program cannot be carried out—and I am quoting—"until the bacillus which is poisoning our blood and our soul has been exterminated. It is against the Jew who has led our people astray, and against the Jewish spirit which has poisoned the German people, that a merciless war must be waged."[6]

---

4. The factionalism and divisiveness of the Jews within Jerusalem during the Roman onslaught is emphasized both by Josephus (e.g., *The Jewish War*, Book 5, beginning of chapter 1) and the rabbinic texts (e.g., B. Gittin 56a). Compare Heinrich Graetz, *History of the Jews*, 6 vols. (Philadelphia: JPS, 1891–1898), 2: 301.

5. On public opposition within the American Jewish leadership community (especially the American Jewish Committee and the B'nai B'rith) to the protest rally, see Urofsky, 264–65 and Moshe Gottlieb, "The First of April Boycott and the American Jewish Community," *American Jewish Historical Quarterly*, 57 (1967–68): 516–56, esp. 522–23. One Reform rabbi from Baltimore charged that if such activities continued, "Dr. Wise will kill the Jews of Germany," a charge that infuriated Wise (and undoubtedly his students). See Urofsky, 268.

6. The twenty-five point Program of the Nazi Party has been frequently republished: see, e.g., Noakes and Pridham, *Nazism*, 1:14–16; Joachim Remak, ed., *The Nazi Years: A*

No, my friends, Antisemitism in Germany is not merely a temporary phenomenon. It is not merely a matter of temporary political expediency. It goes far deeper than this. The Nazi Antisemitism is a necessary part of the political theory of the dominant party in Germany today. Behind the entire Nazi movement lies the spirit of ultra-nationalism. What we are witnessing in Germany today is a recrudescence of that spirit of narrow patriotism and jingo nationalism which has time and time again swept through Europe, bringing in its wake disaster and ruin.

It is one of the paradoxical but fundamental laws of nature and society that good things, when falsely distorted or carried to unnatural extremes, are most conducive of evil. In the individual man, ambition, a trait which in right proportion spurs one on to greater effort and finer achievement, when it becomes so powerful a stimulant that the love of power becomes an end in itself, may not only distort all his finer sensibilities, but may even bring him to folly and crime. So it is that nationalism, which in its finer form has inspired the greatest art and literature, has stirred the noblest emotions in man's heart—this quality of nationalism, distorted and falsified, has been perhaps the most potent influence for evil in the history of the Western world.

It breeds the worst social diseases of our civilization. One of these is invariably war. Another is invariably Antisemitism. For wherever the monster of chauvinism rears its head, there in the shadows lurks the serpent of Antisemitism. As we trace Jewish history, whether it be in Egypt or in Spain or in Russia or in Germany, wherever there has been a rise of extreme national feeling, wherever a people has become intoxicated with a sense of its own prestige and superiority, there the forces of persecution have risen to harass the Jew.[7]

For the presence of the Jew and the spirit of ultra-nationalism are irreconcilable. The Jew, staunch and proven patriot though he may be, must always stand as evidence of an international brotherhood which transcends local and national lines, linking him with fellow Jews throughout the world. Though he may be able to trace his ancestry in a country for generations, though he speak its language, wear its national costume, engage in its national industry, pay the national taxes and fight in the national army, though he himself, not satisfied with 100 per cent patriotism, may insist on proving to the world that he is a 150 per cent patriot, still his very presence belies the theory that material nationhood is all. As a Jew, whether he will it or not, yes, even whether he know it or not, he

---

Documentary History (Prospect Heights, Ill.: Waveland Press, 1990), 28–30. The quotation accompanying the Program appears in the "American Jewish Congress Courier" of April 21, 1933 (the first issue) on p. 5: no specific attribution is given, and I have not been able to find it in any subsequent literature, though it is typical of the rhetoric of Nazi antisemitism in general and of Hitler in particular.

7. This generalization reveals the influence of Salo Baron, who then taught Jewish history at Wise's Jewish Institute of Religion. See his article, "Nationalism and Intolerance," *Menorah Journal* 16 (1929): 405–15 and 17 (1930): 148–58, and *A Social and Religious History of the Jews*, 1st edition, 3 vols. (New York: Columbia University Press, 1937), 2:39–40, 3:107–8, n. 18.

stands for ideals which are universal, which recognize the basic fact that mankind is greater than any one nation that goes to make it up, and that nationhood can justify itself only by the extent of its contribution to the universal good of mankind. It is because he stands for such ideals that the Jew must of necessity be anathema wherever a self-centered nationalism runs rampant.

We can appreciate and sympathize with Germany's desire for a square deal, and with her demand to occupy her rightful place among the company of the nations.[8] But we can neither appreciate nor sympathize with the Germany that maintains the superiority of the Aryan race—whatever that may be: a thing that scientists have not been able to discover; the Germany that seeks to win its way back to the sun by a relentless and systematically cold-blooded extinction of political and national minorities; the Germany that refuses to recognize the right to citizenship of a group which has yielded the finest fruit of German culture, which has lived and worked and suffered in Germany for more than a thousand years.

If it were not for the consistent reports from reliable sources, it would be difficult to realize the extent of combined cruelty and idiocy to which the zeal of the Nazis has brought them. My friends, do not be of those who maintain that because we no longer read of Jews being murdered and beaten, robbed and kidnapped, things are on the road to recovery.[9] Though the Executive Committee in charge of the boycott in Berlin declared that the battle against the Jew will be completed in perfect quiet and with greatest discipline, the last words of the Nazi regulations maintain, "We shall finish with the Jews through the relentless power of our regulations."[10]

Economic strangulation may be worse than physical torture. He who takes away a man's livelihood takes away his life. What greater brutality could there be than to compel Jews to remain in Germany while making it absolutely impossible for them to earn a living?[11] The condemnation of children to ignorance

---

8. A recognition that the conditions imposed by the Treaty of Versailles engendered legitimate grievances within the German population.

9. This may allude to a telegram sent on March 26, 1933, to heads of American Jewish organizations by Secretary of State Cordell Hull, based on a report from the American Embassy in Berlin, stating that "whereas there was for a short time considerable physical mistreatment of Jews this phase may be considered virtually terminated." See *American Jewish Year Book* 35–5694 (1933–34), 30; Robert Abzug, ed., *America Views the Holocaust, 1933–1945* (Boston: Bedford/St. Martin's, 1999), 17.

10. Based on Wise's address to 2,000 delegates from 600 organizations meeting in New York on April 19, as reported in the "American Jewish Congress Courier" of April 21, p. 1. This refers to the manifesto announcing the boycott, published originally in the *Völkischer Beobachter* of March 29, 1933, paragraph 11. See the full text in *The Jews in Nazi Germany*, published by the American Jewish Committee in 1935 (republished New York: Howard Fertig, 1982), 42 (this booklet contains a text of all Nazi anti-Jewish legislation from the first two years of the regime, 123–77). The chairman of the "Executive Committee" in charge of the boycott was the notorious Julius Streicher, editor of *Der Stürmer*.

11. This theme was emphasized in the "Courier" of April 21 on p. 4.

through limitations on the number of children admitted into schools, the barring of the doors of opportunity to talented youth through exclusion from professional schools,[12] the reduction of Jewish merchants and professional men to despair through starvation, through the picketing and boycotting of shops, and the dismissal of Jewish lawyers, doctors, professors and public employees[13]—this is cruelty of the most hateful kind!

But even this is not enough. The Hitlerites are not satisfied with making the participation of Jews in the public life of Germany impossible. Having cleansed themselves of the influence of living Jews, they still fear the pernicious influence of Jewish ideals, which are expressed in literature. And so they are extending their warfare to inanimate books. First came the notice of the attempt to eliminate the Hebrew Old Testament from the German Bible and to substitute for it the ancient Germanic sagas.[14] In other words, due to fear of the subtle influence of Hebraic thought, they aim to substitute their legends of primitive and barbaric society and of a company of gods who fought and schemed and laughed and sinned, for the book that has given the world the moral ideals upon which all the lasting and worthwhile elements of our civilization are based.

And not content with this, a great demonstration has been planned for May 10, at which all books of Jewish authorship are to be publicly burned.[15] Ladies and gentlemen, if that demonstration is carried through on May 10, it will be the final proof of the return of the German leaders to the barbarism of the dark days of the Middle Ages. Such a thing might have been conceivable in 1242, when by order of Louis IX of France, twenty-four wagonloads of Talmudic literature

---

12. Reference is to the "Law Against the Overcrowding of German Schools and Institutions of High Learning," April 25, 1933 (just a few days before the sermon was delivered). See Lucy Dawidowicz, *A Holocaust Reader* (New York: Behrman House, 1976), 42–44.

13. By means of the "Law for the Restoration of the Professional Civil Service," and the "Law Regarding Admission to the Bar," both dated April 7, 1933. See Dawidowicz, *A Holocaust Reader*, 38–40.

14. This effort, which pre-dated the Nazi Party, was resisted even by conservative Christians who made their peace with the regime and its antisemitism. See the 1933 "Advent Sermons" of Cardinal Faulhaber, in which he summarizes the position he is attacking: "Judaism and Christianity, it was maintained, were incompatible; the Jewish Bible must be replaced by a German Bible. . . . Today these single voices have swelled together into a chorus: Away with the Old Testament! A Christianity which still clings to the Old Testament is a Jewish religion, irreconcilable with the spirit of the German people." In defending the position of the Old Testament, he insists that "Antagonism to the Jews of today must not be extended to the books of pre-Christian Judaism." (In this context, Faulhaber did not seem to view Nazi antisemitism as inconsistent with Christian doctrine, which does not, of course, suggest that he would have endorsed the "Final Solution"). Text in George Mosse, *Nazi Culture* (New York: Shocken, 1981), 256, 259.

15. On the famous book-burnings of May 10, 1933, see William Shirer, *The Rise and Fall of the Third Reich* (New York: Simon and Schuster, 1960), 241; Noakes and Pridham, *Nazism*, 1: 401–3; Friedländer, *Nazi Germany and the Jews* 1: 57–58.

were burnt in the public square of Paris.[16] But to think that we are witnessing a repetition of this atrocious act after almost seven centuries!

When, on May 10, those flames arise, they will mean more than the destruction of certain books of Jewish authorship and the finest expression of German culture. These flames will mean the negation of all the progress man has made toward the goal of peace and liberty; they will mean that all the blood that has been spilt, all the lives that have been sacrificed for such fundamental rights as freedom of speech and of religion and of conscience, have been for naught. These flames on May 10 will light up the utmost depth of degradation to which it is possible for a nation to descend. And against it we will protest[17] and continue to protest, not only for our sake but for their own.

For Germany, these excesses mean that they are canceling all the progress they have made in building up a favorable world attitude toward themselves in the last twelve years. The harm they have done to the prospect of establishing a permanent international unity among the nations of the world, and particularly of Europe, is immeasurable. But what does this mean for us Jews? For us it means that Judaism is facing a crisis in its history, a crisis that involves every Jew wherever he may be. This is far more than a German-Jewish problem. It is a universal Jewish problem, for it is the Jew who is being attacked. The hatred engendered by Nazi propaganda goes out against every Jew, as a Jew, whether he lives in Germany or not. As Dr. Wise told us at his birthday luncheon, several days before the great mass meeting,

> Germany is not Eastern Europe. It is not Poland, Roumania, Hungary, Austria. It is GERMANY, land of culture, land of *Freiheit*. If this thing can happen in Germany, without being challenged and rebuked by the civilized world, then it can, and it may, happen tomorrow in any land on earth.[18]

Already we have seen repercussions of the Nazi anti-Jewish propaganda, in far away Japan, in England, Greece, Yugoslavia, and even in our own country, when at the trial of the "Scottsboro boys," the prosecuting attorney denounced

---

16. The burning of all manuscripts of the Talmud discovered in France following the "Disputation of Paris," in which the Talmud was defended by French rabbis against charges of blasphemy, became a symbol of medieval intolerance. See the account in Graetz, *History of the Jews*, vol. 3 (Philadelphia: JPS, 1894), 578–80.

17. The April 19 New York conference (see above, n. 10) unanimously called for a "'Protest March' through the streets of New York on May 10, the day on which books of Jewish authorship are to be publicly burned in Germany" ("Courier," 1).

18. A luncheon was traditionally held on Wise's birthday, March 17, including students from the JIR and other friends and colleagues. In 1933, remarks made by Wise on this occasion were reported in the *New York Times* of March 21. See Moshe Gottlieb, "The First of April Boycott," 523.

what he called the "attempts of Jew money from New York to buy Alabama justice."[19]

Yes, it is our problem. But what are we going to do? Our protests may help the immediate situation in Germany. But when the protests are over, we must have a definite plan of action upon which we can embark to guarantee the perpetuation of Jewish communal life throughout the world. The solution to our problem lies in two directions.

The first part of the solution is that of Palestine. We must keep open at least one nation where, come what may, the doorway of hope and the possibility of living among their own brethren will be open to Jews by right and not by privilege. We must establish one nation where Jewish creative life can be maintained, radiating strength and inspiration to the less vital Judaism of the Diaspora. It is therefore our duty to support the cause of Zionism, which, in the final analysis, is the cause of effective Jewish survival.[20]

But the other side of our solution lies even more closely at home. The survival of Judaism outside of Palestine can be made possible only by the fortification and strengthening of our internal Jewish life. Our best defense against the continuance or reappearance of the conditions that are now prevalent in Germany is by a strengthening of Jewish spirit all over the world. Every Jew must become actively associated with Jewish life and Jewish efforts.

There is a great lesson to Jews in the fact that it is particularly Germany that is the scene for the tragic pages of Jewish history now being written. For it was in Germany that these inner bonds of Jewish association were weaker than in any other nation. It was just in Germany that Jews have abandoned Jewish communal life to the utmost degree in order to participate most completely in German national and communal life. It was the German Jews who denied the peoplehood of Israel and maintained that they were Germans who merely happened incidentally to be of the Mosaic persuasion. It was in Germany where perhaps the greatest percentage of Jewish apostasy and conversion to Christianity took place. And by the paradoxical force of history, it was just those Jews who had weakened and attenuated their Jewishness to the greatest possible ex-

---

19. In the 1931–1933 Scottsboro case, two young white women accused nine black youths of raping them. During his summation, the prosecutor, Wade Wright, pointed at Samuel Leibowitz, a New York Jew who went to Alabama to serve as defense counsel, and said to the jury, "Show them that Alabama justice cannot be bought and sold with Jew money from New York." The quotation appears in the *New York Times* of April 8, 1933, 30, less than three weeks before the sermon. Scholars believe that this dramatic statement had a significant effect on the jury's decision to convict. See Dan T. Carter, *Scottsboro* (Baton Rouge: Louisiana State University Press, 1979), 235–36; Robert Leibowitz, *The Defender: The Life and Career of Samuel S. Leibowitz, 1893–1933* (Englewood Cliffs, N.J.: Prentice-Hall, 1981), 242; James E. Goodman, *Stories of Scottsboro* (New York: Pantheon, 1994), 133.

20. Note the endorsement of both Herzl's political Zionism, emphasizing the need for a sovereign Jewish refuge, and Ahad Ha'am's cultural Zionism, emphasizing a spiritual center that will invigorate Jewish life in the Diaspora.

tent who are now suffering from the effects of the most poisonous antisemitic venom. Even baptism has not helped. For the official definition of a non-Aryan, as stated in the latest anti-Jewish decree, is "Anyone who springs from non-Aryan, especially Jewish, parents and grandparents. It shall suffice if only part of the parentage or grandparentage is Jewish, particularly if such parentage or grandparentage professes or had professed the Jewish faith."[21]

It is a lesson that we may well take to heart. An unorganized and weak Judaism is paving the way for its own destruction. The strengthening of Jewish communal bonds not only insures our own survival as Jews, but is the best means of securing for the Jew the good will and respect of all creeds and nationalities. It is not an easy task to embark upon the venture of organizing a new synagogue in these days of economic stress. It is an enterprise for brave men. But to you who are undertaking such an enterprise[22] go the best wishes and earnest congratulations of myself and others who have [one illegible handwritten word]. For you, my friends, are helping to lay the foundations for a rich and dignified Jewish life in the future.

---

21. This is taken from the "First Decree for Implementation of the Law for the Restoration of the Professional Civil Service, April 11, 1933." See Dawidowicz, *A Holocaust Reader*, 40.

22. I have not been able to determine where this sermon was delivered, what group was addressed, and whether indeed they went on to establish a synagogue. Presumably it was in the greater New York metropolitan area.

2

Are We Civilized?
December 1, 1933

For most Americans today, lynchings seem almost as remote a part of our history as do the Salem Witch Trials. To the extent that we think of them at all, we associate them with the Deep South. It is therefore rather shocking to be reminded by this sermon that three horrifying lynchings occurred in October and November of 1933, two of them in the same week, none of them in the South. The locations were Princess Anne, Maryland, San Jose, California, and St. Joseph, Missouri. In California, the victims of the mob violence were white. Governor James Rolph of California refused to condemn the lynchers. And apparently, public opinion in the rest of the nation was not at all unanimous in condemnation.

    This sermon to the Lynbrook congregation on the Friday night following the California and Missouri lynchings was a fierce polemic, bound up with an appeal to the American self-conception of being a "civilized" people. The explicit comparison was with the witch trials, but the implied comparison seems to be with Nazi Germany. This comes to the surface in the only paragraph of the sermon where—beyond its general social justice sensibility—any specific Jewish content is evident. It invokes an appeal not to Jewish texts or values, but to Jewish self-interest: the Jew always suffers in a society of lawlessness. The examples are the Kishinev pogrom of 1903, remembered vividly by many in the congregation, and the excesses of the early months of the Hitler regime, known by everyone. The message is driven home in the final paragraph: America, which has "raised its voice in protest against the barbarity of Nazi Germany . . . has its own house to clean." The young rabbinical student, like many Christian and Jewish clergy of the day, champions the values of what Reform rabbis

*called "prophetic Judaism" and what Christian colleagues termed "the social
Gospel."*

IN THE YEAR 1692, THE CITIZENS OF SALEM, MASSACHUSETTS, went on a
wild orgy of witch burning. For four months the tempest lasted. Hundreds of
people were accused of having the power of the evil eye, and many were executed by an outraged citizenry. The fanatical witch-hunters considered themselves to be doing the work of God by hanging and burning those they thought
to be the representatives of Satan on earth. But that was almost two and a half
centuries ago.

Today, with our civilization of skyscrapers, automobiles, and airplanes, with
our sophisticated attitude toward life, we look back half in condemnation and
half in pity on those ignorant witch-burners of two and a half centuries ago. We
pride ourselves that since then we have abandoned ignorant superstition and
have developed civilization. And it is true that we have developed a material
civilization beyond the highest reaches of the imagination of previous centuries.
But true civilization is not a matter of automobiles and railroads and skyscrapers. True civilization means primarily one's attitude toward one's fellow man,
and the degree to which primitive passions are controlled for the good of society.

My friends, in light of some of the things that have happened during this past
week in our nation, I say that it is doubtful whether we are really any more civilized than were the Salem witch-burners of 1692. The total number of victims
put to death in those notorious witch huntings was only 20. My friends, thus far
in this year of 1933, in these United States, the richest and perhaps the greatest
nation on earth, there have been more than 20 lynchings. This business of
lynching has come to a climax during the last month, and especially during this
past week.

On October 18, an enraged mob at Princess Anne, Maryland, broke into the
jail, seized a young Negro charged with the rape of an aged white woman,
dragged him through the streets, stripped him of his clothes, and hung him naked from a tree in the sight of cheering throngs. Then they tore down his body
and burnt it. When local and country officials refused to take any steps to appre-
hend the leaders of the lynching mob, the governor sent a group of armed militia
men who seized four of the alleged leaders. This act was followed by an upris-
ing in which a mob of 3,000 went on the rampage, unleashing its fury upon the
representatives of the law in a desperate fight to wrest the prisoners from the
officers.[1]

---

1. See the report in the *New York Times*, October 19, 1933, 1, reprinted in Ralph Ginzburg, *100 Years of Lynchings* (Baltimore: Black Classics Press, 1962, reprinted 1988),
200–2. The murdered prisoner was George Armwood; the *Times* article began, "In the
wildest lynching orgy the state has ever witnessed, a frenzied mob of 2,000 men, women
and children, sneering at guns and teargas, overpowered 50 state troopers, tore from a

This past Monday, a mob in San Jose, California, broke into the jail where the kidnappers and murderers of Brooke Hart were kept, dragged the prisoners across the street, beat them unmercifully, tore their clothing from them, and hanged them. Then, cutting down one of the victims, they saturated his clothes with gasoline and tried to burn the body. The occasion was made almost a public holiday. A crowd of sightseers gathered around and parents held their children high, that they might get a good view of the proceedings.[2]

The other day, a mob of 7,000 in St. Joseph, Missouri, defying gas and guns, smashed the door of the jail, seized a nineteen-year-old Negro youth charged with attacking a white girl, dragged their victim to a tree in the courthouse lawn and hanged him there. While the body swung in the air, members of the mob tried to burn the body with torches of flaming gasoline-soaked rags.[3]

This is the story of the last month. In all the records of human brutality and bestiality, in all the atrocities of the Salem witch burnings, it would be hard to find a picture of greater human degradation. When I read the stories of these bloodthirsty mobs, venting their lust for brutality, my blood turned cold. I said to myself, "How can this be possible in our day? Surely this can only be the work of a crazed and drunken mob of perverted sadists. Surely every normal and sane person will rise up in indignation at such acts of mob violence. Surely there will be a country-wide and universal demand that such practices must cease."

Suddenly, my attention was distracted by the voice of a man opposite me in the subway talking to his friend. His voice was raised so that it could be heard over the din of the train. "I see where the people of California gave these kid-nappers what they deserve. We need more of that sort of stuff in this country. Justice, swift and sure, that's what we need. Those people in California are all right."

The same day I was talking to a man I have known for years, one of the gentlest souls I have ever met, a man whose conscience would hurt him if he killed a fly. What was my surprise, when I started talking about the lynchings, to hear him say, "Those villains got better than they deserved. Hanging was too good for them. If I had anything to do with it, I would have had them killed by slow torture." And then, to my amazement, this gentle soul went off into a prolonged

---

prison cell a Negro prisoner accused of attacking an aged white woman, and lynched him in front of the home of a judge who had tried to placate the mob. Then the mob cut down the body, dragged it through the main thoroughfares for more than half a mile and tossed it on a burning pyre. Fifty State policemen and deputies battled vainly with the crowd in front of the jail, tossing tear bombs in an effort to disperse it."

2. The San Jose lynching was featured in *The New York Times* on Monday, November 17, 1933, 1; the two white prisoners who were killed were T. Thurmond and J. Holmes. For a full account, see Harry Farrell, *Swift Justice: Murder and Vengeance in a California Town* (New York: St. Martin's Press, 1992), 210–37.

3. The lynching in St. Joseph, Missouri was reported graphically in the *New York World-Telegram* on Wednesday, November 29, on page 1, reprinted in Ginzburg, *100 Years of Lynchings*, 205–7, beginning "They didn't hang Lloyd Warner. They burned him alive."

discussion of the horrible means of torture he would have utilized if he had charge of the punishment of the Brooke Hart murderer. Compared to his catalogue, the Spanish Inquisition was only child's play.

Then, to add to my amazement, three New York newspapers came out condoning and praising the attitude taken by Governor Rolph of California, who made no attempt to prevent the lynching and afterward expressed his approval of it. Apparently the condemnation was not as universal as I expected.[4] What is there which has caused so many people to condone these acts of mob violence and unlawfulness?[5]

What reasons can be given in defense of overstepping the bounds of law in this way, in order to wreak vengeance upon lawbreakers? In the South, the argument is often put forth that it is necessary to keep the "nigger" in his place. For these Southerners, lynching is a pleasant expedient reserved usually for colored offenders, in crimes for which, if they involved a white man, lynching would never be considered. Lynching to them is a weapon to be used in racial warfare. However, as far as the great majority of the American people go, I feel I am justified in saying that this is not a satisfactory explanation. Outside of the South, I feel that the American people are in agreement that there must be justice and equal treatment for all before the law. At least we Jews, who have suffered so much from class legislation and from the unjust persecution of minorities, must realize that freedom and justice are meaningless unless there is freedom and justice for everyone regardless of color or of creed.

No, the general condoning of the recent lynchings by people of high character and intelligence does not arise from so base a source as that of race prejudice. After all, the most widely approved lynching was the one in San Jose, California, in which the victims were white men. It is rather the intense horror at the brutality of their crime that has brought so many people to feel that no punishment could be too severe for the criminals. The approval of the recent lynchings represents a countrywide revulsion against the terrible wave of kidnapping and murder which has been sweeping through the country. In the mind of everyone who has a son or a daughter or a little brother or sister, no crime could be crueler than that of kidnapping and murder. Everyone sympathizes with the families of the victims of such tragedies, for it does not take much imagination to place ourselves in their position. It is this sympathy which roused the flame of indignation

---

4. On the reactions to California Governor James Rolph Jr.'s refusal to send National Guard troops and his statement justifying his decision, see Farrell, *Swift Justice*, 271–80. His actual statements are quoted below.

5. The following passage was crossed out in the typescript, and probably not included in the delivery: "'Come, let us reason together,' said the Judge at the Scottsboro case, quoting from the prophet Isaiah, in his charge to the jury. And I say to you, 'Come, let us reason together,' and see what the true significance is of this epidemic of lynching that seems to be sweeping the country." Compare the reference to the Scottsboro case near the end of the previous sermon.

against the criminals and the universal desire that just punishment be meted out to them.

I can understand this. But I cannot justify or condone lynching. I do not attempt to minimize the gravity of the offense of the kidnappers and murderers of Brooke Hart. Nor do I defend the act of a man who attacks an eighty-year-old, helpless woman. But the question is not whether these crimes are defensible or not. The question is whether it is right for the mob to take the law into its own hands. The question is whether in a modern state the people have the right to disregard due process of law regardless of the gravity of the offense. The question is whether or not lynching is the act of a civilized people.

And I say, no! There could be no greater challenge to our claims of being civilized than the pictures that filled the press during the last few days, showing parents gleefully holding children high above their heads to watch a crazed mob beat two men to a pulp, strip them naked, hang them writhing from a tree, and then burn their bodies with gasoline-soaked torches. If it were a case where the law had really failed, if it had seemed as if the devilish criminals were going to escape just punishment, then my attitude might be different. If the legal machinery of justice had really broken down, then there might be some reason for praising this deed, as a renewal of the spirit of the old Vigilance Committees.[6] Then, much as we might lament this necessity, perhaps we would have had to excuse such acts as a necessary warning that the people of our country demand an end of kidnapping and murder and terrorism, and that if necessary they will take it upon their own shoulders to see that justice is meted out.

But here, the instruments of justice had not broken down. Do you suppose that there was even the slightest chance that any jury would have brought in a verdict of not guilty against the Brooke Hart slayers? Conviction and the death penalty at the hands of the law were as certain as the fact that night follows day. No, that lynching was not an act of the enforcement of law, but rather of the destroying of law. It was not the spontaneous indignation of a high-minded citizenry, but the hideous, bestial act of a maudlin drunken gang of potential and actual murderers.

Listen to the testimony of the nineteen-year-old farm boy who had come to town for a spree, and who asserts that he was the leader of the lynching mob. "I saw the crowd around the jail and decided to organize a necktie party. Mostly I went to the speakeasies and rounded up the gang there. That is why so many of the mob were drunk." In other words, it was a gang of speakeasy drunks, led by a farm boy who wanted to have some fun, who have been hailed as the defenders of American institutions and the representatives of American justice. No, it was not the act of a people roused by a love of justice, but of a mob which let its emotions master it. To me, the crime of the lynchers is worse than the crime of the lynch victims. For while the acts of Holmes and Thurmond were the acts of

---

6. These "committees" were formalized vigilante groups found originally in frontier towns of the nineteenth century before the establishment of regular governmental institutions.

mentally diseased and heartless desperados, while the act of the Negro who attacked an eighty-year-old white woman was the act of a sex-crazed and perverted mind, the act of the lynchers was perpetrated by thousands of ordinarily
normal men. And I say again that so long as such acts are approved by masses of
the people, we, the people of America, are telling ourselves flattering lies when
we claim to be civilized.

Not only are these exhibitions of mob violence an indication of the low order
of public morals, and of the disregard of law and order so prevalent in our land.
They will also undoubtedly bring in their wake a long chain of sorry consequences. This danger is increased by the fact that these acts were approved and
justified by the Governor of California. This Governor, bound by oath to execute
the laws of his state, is quoted as saying, "Why should I call out troops to protect
those two fellows? If the people have confidence that the troops will not be
called out, there will be swifter justice and fewer kidnappings." He actually delayed a visit to a Governor's convention in Idaho for fear that someone else
might call out the troops in his absence and prevent the mob from doing its will.
Again, this high-minded Governor says, "If anyone is arrested for the good job
I'll pardon them all. I hope this will serve for a lesson in every state of the Union."[7]

I don't suppose much else could be expected from a governor who refuses to
pardon Mooney and Billings, who have been rotting away in the jails of California for fifteen years although the judge, the jury, the district attorney, the witnesses, and in fact everyone who had anything to do with their original conviction are now willing to testify to their innocence.[8] But if Governor Rolph had
any friends left after his handling of the Mooney-Billings affair, his abominable
conduct in the present case should forfeit him the goodwill of any right-minded
citizen. Governor Rolph is guilty equally with the lynchers. A man who encourages mob lawlessness within the state where he has sworn to uphold the law
does not deserve to hold office.

---

7. See the *New York Times*, November 27, 3, and Farrell, *Swift Justice*, 241.

8. On this now largely forgotten case which was once a *cause célèbre* in California
and much of the rest of the country, see Curt Gentry, *Frame-Up: The Incredible Case of
Tom Mooney and Warren Billings* (New York: Norton, 1967), and Richard Frost, *The
Mooney Case* (Stanford: Stanford University Press, 1968). The case originated in a bomb
that exploded in the midst of a San Francisco patriotic "Preparedness Day" Parade on
July 22, 1916, killing nine people and wounding many others. Thomas Mooney and War-
ren Billings were arrested and each convicted of first degree murder. Though later inves-
tigations revealed gross irregularities and problems with the prosecution's case, the appeals were unsuccessful, and no California governor would pardon the two men. For
Rolph's position, see Gentry, 360–63. In some circles, the case became known as "The
American Dreyfus." Rabbi Stephen S. Wise was a member of the National
Mooney-Billings Committee (Gentry, 318), and after Rolph's statement on the lynchings,
said, "This is the same governor who keeps Mooney in prison for not committing a crime
of violence" (Gentry, 376).

What do you suppose are the results of a spectacle such as that enacted in San Jose, California? It provided a holiday for thousands of people, but let me tell you the cost. First, it left a vile and obscene memory burned into the mind of everyone concerned. What do you suppose is the effect of such an experience on the minds of people, particularly of the children, who stood about cheering while two men were beaten and hung and burned by an impassioned mob? The corrupting influence of such an experience can never be wiped out. From this incident will come innumerable crimes and cruelties in the future. What of the sixteen-year-old boy, crazed with sadistic excitement, who climbed to the top of a nearby shed and shouted, "Come on, fellows. Let's burn 'em"? Many a future crime will owe its origin to the germs of bestiality and lawlessness injected into children's minds by that one depraved experience. It is a high price to pay for an afternoon's holiday.

But even more dangerous than the effects of the act itself is the principle it establishes. Yes, Governor Rolph, in his own words, has taught a lesson to the entire country. The lesson he has taught is that the mob may take the law into its own hands. A more dangerous lesson could not be imagined. He says that "Hereafter, there will be less cause for lynching." But remember that a mob makes its own causes for lynching. In this particular case, perhaps the victims deserved their punishment. But in the next case they may be innocent. Mob psychology is a curious thing. A mob is easy to convince but hard to stop. Whether its actions are right or wrong, just or unjust, the mob is always right in its own eyes. Who is to draw the line, and where is it to be drawn? Who knows where the principle may be asserted next?

Think one moment, my friends, who it is that suffers whenever the mob takes the power and the law into its own hands. Yes, it is the Jew who suffers. For the mob is moved by passion and not by reason. And always the first victim of the mob has been the Jew. The mob that participated in the pogrom in Kishinev in 1903 thought that they were fighting for the right and for God.[9] The Nazi mobs who attacked and tortured Jews in the early months of the Hitler regime thought that they were fighting in the cause of right. Once the right of the mob to take the administration of justice unto itself becomes established, there is danger in store for the Jew.

My friends, the way to eliminate crime is not by passion and violence. If justice is uncertain and slow, then our duty is to speed it up and make certain its administration, not to overthrow it. The measure of a nation's civilization is determined by the extent to which even-handed justice by the state has been substituted for passion and revenge by individuals. America has raised its voice in protest against the barbarity of Nazi Germany. But, my friends, America also has its own house to clean. In view of the events of the past weeks, the United

---

9. Saperstein's source for the Kishinev pogroms was probably Simon Dubnow, *History of the Jews in Russia and Poland*, 3 vols. (Philadelphia: JPS, 1916–1920). 3:66–86; on the religious component, bound up with Passover, Easter, and ritual murder accusations, see 69–75.

States stands condemned before the world. We will reap the fruits of these events in sorrow and in pain. May God grant that never again will our civilization be negated and the name of our country besmirched by such acts of horror and shame.

3

The Call to Battle
September 10, 1934
Rosh Hashanah Morning

Should the Nazi regime be engaged through a network of contacts that might moderate its extremism, or should it be isolated, treated as a pariah, brought to its knees through an economic stranglehold? This question divided Jews and other Americans. Wise and the American Jewish Congress did not originally support the boycott, but they came aboard in August of 1933; the American Jewish Committee and the B'nai B'rith remained opposed. Saperstein's Rosh Hashanah sermon of 1934 contained a powerful endorsement of the boycott policy. How could any self-respecting American Jew continue to purchase German products?

The progression of this sermon would become a pattern replicated frequently over the next eight years. It begins with the negative, reviewing the suffering of Jews in Germany and other European nations (especially Poland), emphasizing the utter bleakness of their lives. Then there is a shift to a message intended to galvanize and inspire. The transition is made here by appeal to a statement of the French General Foch in World War I: when the situation looked bleak, he announced, "I shall attack." Thus the sound of the shofar becomes a "call to battle," not military battle, to be sure, but an organization of unified support for the boycott, a means through which Jews could assert themselves with the self-respect and dignity that would be such important themes in Saperstein's early preaching.

ANOTHER YEAR HAS PASSED INTO HISTORY. A New Year begins. And once more in the ears of Jews all over the world rings the blast of the Shofar. The Shofar in ancient times had a deep religious significance. We read, for instance, that the revelation on Mount Sinai was accompanied by the blast of the Shofar. But the Shofar also served another function in ancient Israel. It was used as a call to battle. It was the signal that warned the people in moments of great national danger. It meant that every Israelite must forsake his own activities, forget petty differences, and join the ranks of his brothers ready to fight against the common enemy.

Today once more the blast of the Shofar must be our clarion call to battle. For as we gather on this Rosh Hashanah to usher in the New Year, the shadow of national danger hovers over us. Once more the enemy has gathered its forces and threatens our destruction. Once more our people must take up arms and fight for their existence. This past year has been one of the most tragic in all Jewish history. A year ago the world stood aghast at the spectacle of the barbaric persecution of German Jews at the hands of the Nazis. Today it is true that the stories of brutal physical torture, which were rife then, are no longer so much in evidence. But this does not mean that the position of the Jew in Germany has been made secure. There has been no letup in the moral and economic and legal persecution.

The Jew in Germany is still a second- or third-class citizen. He is still denied every opportunity of worthwhile activity. Schools are still closed to him, public service is still closed to him, the professions are still closed to him, the boycott of Jewish business continues. Particularly tragic is the lot of German Jewish youth, who face a future dark and without hope, a future where opportunity is an unknown word. Indeed, every class of German Jewry has been affected. The masses live in abject terror, faced by the prospect of starvation and dangers of which they can only surmise. And the latest authentic report shows that as many as 15,000 families of German Jewish professionals, doctors, lawyers, artists, professors and journalists have been reduced to degrading beggardom. Once the leaders of the intellectual and communal life in Germany, the very cream of German Jewry, but now forbidden to practice their chosen professions by the infamous "Aryan paragraph," they find themselves dependent for the barest necessities upon help from Jewish charitable organizations.[1]

Thus in Germany a new type of pogrom is being waged: a pogrom that works by killing not the body but the spirit, a pogrom that degrades and humiliates, destroys self-respect and crushes all hope. A type of pogrom that is far more cruel than the bloody ones of former days—for it works quietly, stealthily, but all the more effectively.

And the events of the past few months bode ill for the future. For with the growing opposition to the Hitler regime and the harassing economic problems that the Reich must face this winter, it will be necessary again to divert the interests of the German masses. When we consider the new powers which Hitler

---

1. The "Aryan paragraph" was a provision of the Civil Service law of April 7, 1933, stating that "civil servants who are not of Aryan descent are to be retired." This was soon applied to other professions as well. See Saul Friedländer, *Nazi Germany and the Jews*, vol. 1 (New York: HarperCollins, 1997), 27–31.

wields[2] and the presence in his cabinet of men like Goering, an inveterate Jew-hater with an arrogant German contempt for world opinion, we do not need the recent speeches at Nuremberg to show us who will be made the scapegoat.[3]

But not only in Germany is Jewish life in a critical position on this Rosh Hashanah. In Austria, caught in the three-cornered struggle for power between Nazis, Reds and Fascists, oppressed by constant fear of the spread of Hitlerism, the Jews are beaten on every side. It would be difficult to distinguish the views of the leaders of the new regime, Chancellor Schuschnigg and Vice Chancellor Starhemberg, with regard to Jews, from those of dyed-in-the-wool Nazis. Both are outspoken in their opinion that Jews should be eliminated from all fields of public and economic activity. Already great progress has been made unofficially in this direction. Jewish children have been segregated into special schools. The other day Chancellor Schuschnigg was reported to be negotiating with the Austrian Nazis to include them in the Fatherland Front which now rules Austria. But there is a saying current in Austria that by the time the Nazis get into power, there will be nothing left for them to do. Whatever turn the unstable politics of Austria may take in the near future, the prospects look equally bad for the Jews.[4]

In Poland, the situation of the Jew is just as tragic. Inspired by a new wave of Nazi anti-Semitic propaganda, there has been a terrible recrudescence of Jew-hatred. When a delegation of Jews came to Col. Slawek, head of the government party, pleading for protection against the attacks of the anti-Semitic Naras, his only answer was, "The Jews are now hated all over the world. Poland is no exception. I am sorry, I can do nothing for you."[5]

Economic ruin and distress is the common lot. A recent visitor described the situation in terms that seem incredible even to Depression-conscious Americans.

---

2. Following the death of President Paul von Hindenburg on August 2, 1934, Hitler combined the offices of Chancellor and President and assumed the title of *Fuehrer* and Reich Chancellor, including Commander in Chief of the Armed Forces, members of which were required to take an oath of allegiance to him personally.

3. Referring to the Nazi Party rally beginning September 4, 1934, the subject of Leni Riefenstahl's propaganda-documentary "Triumph of the Will," William Shirer described the rally as "the most frenzied adulation for a public figure this writer had ever seen" (*The Rise and Fall of the Third Reich*, 230). Against this background, the reference earlier in the paragraph to the "growing opposition to the Hitler regime" seems a bit like wishful thinking if it applies to Germany itself. Yet contemporary writers did speak of "evidence that unrest and opposition to the economic policies of the Hitler government are growing": *American Jewish Year Book* 37, 5696 (Philadelphia: JPS, 1935), 182.

4. On the situation in Austria, see *American Jewish Year Book* 37, 5696, 187–190. Schuschnigg became Chancellor following the assassination of Chancellor Dollfuss on July 25, 1934, heading a "Fascist dictatorship in opposition both to the National Socialists and to the radical parties" (187).

5. "Naras" refers to members of the National Radical Camp (*Obóz Narodowo-Radykalny*), a group formed in April 1934 and composed of unemployed workers who engaged in antisemitic attacks in Warsaw. It was outlawed by the government during the summer of 1934, but it remained active illegally. See Emanuel Melzer, *No Way Out* (Cincinnati: HUC Press, 1997), 6–7; *American Jewish Year Book* 37, 5696, 204–5, 230–32.

A man ordering a pair of shoes would never think of giving the shoemaker money to buy the leather, he said, for the destitute shoemaker would immediately rush off to buy bread for his starving family. Denied all government aid, such as is given to non-Jewish citizens, the average Jew in Poland is fortunate to be able to earn a few cents a day to keep body and soul together. In the large Polish cities like Warsaw, so dire is the situation that as many as 40 percent of the Jewish population applied last year to charity organizations for Passover aid.[6]

These are but indications of the Jewish situation throughout the world today: everywhere gloom and desolation, nowhere a spark of hope; everywhere the menace of Nazism and rising anti-Semitism, nowhere a vision of Jewish strength and solidarity. Surely, if ever, this Rosh Hashanah ushers in a critical year in Jewish history. What are we do to? How are we to answer the call of the Shofar?

I am reminded of the celebrated report of Marshall [Ferdinand] Foch to General [Joseph] Joffre, at the first battle of the Marne. You will recall how Foch was suddenly thrown into the battle in command of the French troops to fill a gap in the line of defense. The Allied army was crumbling before the powerful German offensive. The situation seemed almost hopeless. It was under these circumstances that he sent the thrilling message, which was to take its place among the great military documents of all time. "My center is yielding," he said. "My right is retreating. Impossible to maneuver. Excellent situation. I shall attack."[7]

Dear friends, the Jewish people today are in just such a situation—a situation where danger threatens on every side. There is no time for compromise, no use in self-deception. Our only hope is to gather our strength and to fight for our existence. But as always, it is the tragedy of our people that there are those among us who never learn their lesson, who refuse to see the necessity for action, who put their factional interests above the common good. Blind cowards, they fritter away their strength by stupid internal dissension and dicker with the enemy at a time when every bit of strength is necessary to forestall the doom, which hangs over our heads.

In Germany, for instance, we find the League of National German Jews issuing an appeal before the recent plebiscite asking all Jews in Germany to vote for Hitler.[8] Later we find this same organization protesting against the activities

---

6. On the deteriorating economic conditions of Polish Jews in 1932–34, see Melzer, *No Way Out*, 3–4.

7. Foch was not "Marshall" at the time (September 1914); he was under the command of Joffre. His actual report was apparently far less concise; it concluded, "The situation is therefore excellent; the attack directed against the Ninth Army appears to be a means to assure the retreat of the German right wing." According to his biographer, "This was the phrase magnified by legend into the famous message, "My right is driven in, my centre is giving way, the situation is excellent, I attack" (in the French original: *Mon centre cède, ma droite recule, situation excellente, j'attaque*). See B. J. Liddell Hart, *Foch: The Man of Orléans* (Boston: Little, Brown & Co., 1932), 108.

8. The *Verband nationaldeutscher Juden* was founded in 1920 by Max Naumann, a nationalistic veteran of the World War. It supported German nationalism and was there-

of the World Jewish Conference[9] and its advocacy of the anti-Nazi boycott. "Jews who feel themselves Germans," they said, "oppose every foreign intervention in German affairs." Such Jewish cowards—willing to accept shame and disgrace, willing to cringe before their oppressors, willing to kiss the Nazi boots which kicked the Jewish people in German—deserve the contempt of every human being with a spark of dignity and self-respect. Fortunately, the League of National German Jews represents only a small minority of the Jews in Germany. Yet the distressing fact remains that in no European country has Jewish unity as yet been achieved.

In America too, we have those Jews who counsel silence rather than outspoken truth, and still condemn democratic action of the masses, favoring diplomatic dickering which avails naught. Thus while the World Jewish Conference was being held, the American Jewish Committee felt called upon to deliver a statement to the press denying that the conference represented American Jewish opinion.[10] And in a similar vein, the *American Hebrew* carried in its editorial columns a scathing criticism of the Conference and its leaders.[11] These same groups from the very beginning have refused their support to the boycott of Nazi Germany. Thus we find on every side a lack of vital determination, a lack of unified organization, a lack of purposeful effort for self-preservation.

Jews and friends, on this New Year's Day, let us cry, "Enough of such stupidity, enough of such cowardice, enough of such selfishness!" It is high time for the Jew to straighten out his bent spine and to raise his bowed head. For 2,000 years the Jew has been a homeless wanderer, everywhere considered an alien, everywhere oppressed and persecuted. For 2,000 years he has been the scapegoat of every national tragedy, the victim of every hateful backward force.

---

fore vehemently opposed to the Zionist movement and all links with international Jewish organizations, or even Jewish organizations in other countries. During the Weimar years, it tried to ally itself with right wing German Parties and opposed immigration by *Ostjuden*; after Hitler came to power, it attempted to prove its German loyalties by supporting the new regime. It was eventually disbanded by the Nazis. See *EJ* 16: 106–7; Steven Aschheim, *Brothers and Strangers* (Madison: University of Wisconsin Press, 1982), 220–24; *German-Jewish History in Modern Times*, ed. Michael Meyer, vol. 4 (New York: Columbia University Press, 1998), 90, 271–72.

9. The "World Jewish Conference" met in Geneva in August 1933 to plan for a "World Jewish Congress." A second Conference met in September 1934; the Congress, eventually in August 1935. The idea was for a representative, democratically elected body authorized to make decision on behalf of the Jewish people throughout the world. See references to the Conference below.

10. On the American Jewish Committee's public dissociation from the World Jewish Congress movement, see Naomi Cohen, *Not Free to Desist: The American Jewish Committee, 1906–1966* (Philadelphia: JPS, 1972), 222–25 and bibliography 584, including a pamphlet on "The Proposed World Jewish Congress," which I have not been able to consult.

11. The *American Hebrew*, a New York Jewish weekly founded in 1879, offered a more conservative outlook than Isaac Mayer Wise's *American Israelite*. Taken over in 1906 by a group of leading New York Jews, it was generally anti-Zionist and held positions on Jewish affairs similar to those taken by the American Jewish Committee.

Yes, for 2,000 years and more the Jew has been beaten, crushed, and twisted. How long will the tragic spectacle continue? How long will the Jew continue to bear his shame in groveling cowardly obsequiousness? To turn the other cheek, to kiss the hand that beat one—these are not and never were fundamental Jewish teachings. Rather, to fight for the right, to struggle against tyranny, to combat every wrong and every injustice—this is what prophetic Judaism should and must stand for.

What shall we answer to this new challenge to Jewish dignity and to Jewish existence? At the World Jewish Conference in Geneva, the answer of the Jewish people was given. For one thing, in the words of Dr. Wise, "The boycott of Germany must continue until the Hitler regime cancels every law or practice violating human freedom, political equality, and the ideals of civilization."[12] That must be our answer to Nazi hatred and Nazi persecution. Germany must realize that she shall continue to be isolated economically and otherwise until she comes back into the realm of civilization. The importance of the boycott far transcends narrow Jewish interests. Not only German Jewry, not only world Jewry, but civilization itself is under attack. It is the protest of humanity against Nazidom's return to barbarism.

The boycott of Germany has thus assumed a world-historic importance. It will prove whether or not the righteous indignation of the civilized world has an instrument by which, without resort to bloodshed, it can oppose the trampling of fundamental human rights. The Jew, as always, is in the vanguard of the battle between paganism and civilization. It is a place of honor. Any Jew who, because of personal gain or lack of interest, does not support the boycott while Germany continues to deny civilization's demands, has sacrificed his honor, betrayed his people, and forfeited the respect of humanity. Already the boycott has shown its effectiveness and power. Germany today must yield shortly or face inevitable material ruin. No compromise must be accepted. We must not cease until the battle is won.

But even this is not enough. World Jewry has at last come to realize that the problem of one nation's Jews is the problem of all Jews. We must not let this lesson be wasted. Out of the chaos of contemporary conditions, there must arise some permanent representative organ to defend Jews all over the world from the hatred of their enemies and from the infringements upon their rights. The World Jewish Congress, which will convene next August, will give us such a body, able to champion the cause of the Jewish people before the world.[13]

Through the centuries in which Jews have been in *Golus* [exile], they have never yet been able to join all forces for the common good. Now at last the opportunity is in their hands. Unless they take it, the Jews will merit the contempt of their Christian neighbors. This is no occasion for hesitancy or timidity. We have nothing to do that demands secrecy. We are merely fighting for equal hu-

---

12. Compare Wise. *Challenging Years* (New York: G. Putnam's Sons, 1949). 256–57.

13. On the August 1935 meeting of the World Jewish Congress. see Melvin Urofsky, *A Voice That Spoke for Justice* (Albany: SUNY Press. 1982). 300–2.

man rights for our people. Must we sneak into the back door and beg for them? I, for one, would rather demand them from the housetops.

Most of you will recall the intensely moving scene in the motion picture presentation of "The House of Rothschild," wherein the aged Mayer Anschel Rothschild dies. His five sons are grouped about his deathbed listening to the venerable father's last words of advice. Gasping for breath, he tells them how they are to carry on the banking business that he has worked all his life to build up. "Remember," he says. "Unity is strength. All your lives you must stand by one another. No one brother must be allowed to fail while another brother succeeds. The Rothschilds work always together. That will be your power. And when that power comes, remember the Ghetto. Remember this before all: that neither business nor power nor all the gold in Europe will ever bring you happiness, until. . . ." He pauses a moment. Gathering together his failing strength, he lifts himself out of the restraining hands of his wife, and sitting erect for a moment, his voice rings true and clear, as he continues, "until we, our people, have equality . . . respect . . . dignity. . . . To deal with dignity . . . to live with dignity . . . to walk the world with dignity."[14]

My friends, as we enter a New Year in Jewish life, there is no message more significant than that embodied in those memorable words: that nothing matters, that no success can ever bring true happiness so long as the blessing of self-respect is lacking, so long as Jews fear to hold their heads erect and face the world like men.

At the peal of the Shofar on this New Year's day, every Jew must feel that it is the call of his people who need him. Once more, the battle cry is heard. "Arise, ye sleepers. . . ."[15] Join your brothers to fight for the cause of Israel. No Jew can afford to stand alone. Your strength, your will, your support is needed. Come, gird your loins for the fray, that we may hasten the day when the Jewish people shall truly be able to deal with dignity, to live with dignity, to walk the world with dignity."

---

14. The United Artists movie, based on an unproduced play by George Hembert Westley, and starring George Arliss as both the elderly Mayer and his son Nathan, opened on March 14, 1934. See the review in the *New York Times* of March 15, 1934, which does not even mention the death scene of Mayer, focusing on a very different climactic episode from that emphasized here for homiletical purposes. For Rothschild's will and death-bed charge to his sons, see, most recently, Amos Elon, *Founder* (New York: Penguin Books, 1996), 174.

15. Echoing the famous formulation in Maimonides' "Laws of Repentance" 3,4 on the deeper meaning of the shofar. Maimonides uses the phrase in the context of a spiritual awakening to ultimate values, here it is political.

4

The Great Olympic Idea
November 1, 1935

On Rosh Hashanah 1935, days after the rallies at which the Nuremberg laws were announced, Saperstein delivered a sermon entitled "Civilization at Bay," in which he said, "I do not relish being a preacher of mournful tidings. Would that I could bring you a message of comfort and of hope. . . . I know that you have heard time and again of the tragic plight of the Jew in Germany, in Poland, in Austria and Roumania. And yet you have not heard enough. Until your heart aches with theirs, until through the depth of your sympathy you too feel the pangs of hunger and the deeper pangs of humiliation which they feel, you have not heard enough." Clearly, there was to be no letting up with this message.

In the months following the High Holy Days, the burning issue became American participation in the Berlin Olympic Games scheduled for the summer of 1936. Those who believed in a confrontational policy toward the Hitler regime urged a boycott. The issue began to get ugly with the return in October of General Charles Sherrill, the American member of the International Olympic Committee. After claiming success in his efforts to convince the Germans to allow a Jew to be part of the German Olympic Team, Sherrill warned the American Jewish community that pushing the United States to boycott the games might unleash a wave of antisemitism comparable to that in Germany. That was a challenge that could not be ignored from the pulpit. The rhetorical climax of the sermon is couched as a personal address to Sherrill, arguing forcefully the point that was frequently asserted during these years: that opposition to Hitler's Nazism was much more than a narrowly Jewish issue, and should forge an alliance of all decent people.

Needless to say, the Olympic boycott campaign, fostered by the Non-Sectarian Anti-Nazi League and other organizations, failed to reverse the decision by the AAU to participate in the Berlin Olympics.

ON JANUARY 15, 1894, BARON PIERRE DE COUBERTIN, a Frenchman, sent a circular to all sports organizations, saying,

> Before all things it is necessary that we should preserve in sport those characteristics of nobility and chivalry which have distinguished it in the past so that it may continue to play the same part in the education of the people of today as it played so admirably in the days of ancient Greece.

That was the beginning of the Olympic Games, and thus was created the Great Olympic Idea.[1] Its purpose was to create a closer, friendlier relationship between the nations of the world—through athletic contacts—to bring these nations to understand and know each other better.

In the years since, the athletic contests of the Olympics have been fought with all earnestness. Every nation made the greatest effort of which it was capable to win the crown of victory. But first of all, the rivalry was fair and square, and the contests themselves were a symbol of international respect and good will.

In 1916, the Olympics were to be held in Berlin. But Germany's part in the World War made it necessary to cancel them.

Next year, the Olympics are again scheduled for Berlin. Once more the forces of civilized humanity cry, "We cannot participate." Because again, Germany is at war, not yet with other nations it is true, but still at war—at war with humanity.

In the course of the last few months the problem of whether the U.S. should participate in the Olympics has been given a great deal of publicity. Arguments have been offered pro and con. The radio and newspapers have been the fields of combat between those who favor and those who oppose American participation.

There have been many attempts on the part of certain members of the American Olympic Committee in recent weeks to insure American support by persuading the American people that there will be no discrimination against any group in the coming Olympics. They maintain that Germany will abide by all the rules of the Olympic Games. But no amount of explanation on the part of these so-called leaders of amateur sport can conceal the fact that in Germany the principles of Olympic competition are being violated.

They maintain that there is no discrimination against any capable athlete competing for the German Olympics. Yet the rules of the German Olympic Committee require that every competitor be a member of the official Nazi sports societies. Since membership here is open only to Nazi Aryans, not only Jews but Gentiles—Catholic and Protestant non-Aryans—all those who refuse to become cogs in the Nazi machine—are ineligible.

---

1. For the January 1894 circular of Pierre de Coubertin, see Bill Mallon, *The 1896 Olympic Games* (Jefferson, N.C.: McFarland, 1998), 4 (in a slightly different translation from the original French).

They maintain that Jews have the same opportunities as others to qualify. Yet German Nazis are not even permitted to compete in sport with Jews. On May 29 of this year, the *Schwarze Korps*, the official organ of the Hitler Guard [i.e., the SS], carried an article criticizing the fact that in Berlin a woman's team representing an Aryan sport club had competed with a team of Jewish women. On July 3, the same periodical carried an announcement that the facts had been investigated, and "we are glad to announce that all members who participated in those games have been excluded from German sports organizations." In other words, even Aryans who commit the sin of playing against Jews are disbarred from their organizations and thus made ineligible to compete.

They claim that no Jew will be molested during the games. Yet the Prague press recently carried the report of eye-witnesses to the fact that a Nazi mob had stoned to death Edmund Baumgartner—a twenty-one-year-old Polish Jewish football player, during a match between German and Polish teams in Upper Silesia.[2]

They maintain that Jews have been invited to compete. Brigadier General Charles H. Sherrill, who returned from a visit to Germany last week, and is one of the most ardent defenders of the German Olympics, proclaimed, "My purpose in going to Germany was to get a Jew on the German Olympic team. I succeeded in getting the acceptance of Miss Helena Mayer, a woman fencer, now in California."[3] Yet that same General Sherrill was standing beside Hitler at Nuremberg when he announced his infamous and shameful decree stripping all Jews in Germany of their citizenship.[4] And one of the Olympic rules requires every

---

2. This is based on a two-paragraph notice in the *New York Times* of September 21, 1935, A5:3. The report was apparently never confirmed, and may possibly have originated in Nazi "disinformation." The following account appears in the *American Jewish Year Book* 38 (5697) (Philadelphia: JPS, 1936), 317–18:

> In October [1935], reports began to appear in the European press to the effect that a Jewish youth named Edmund Baumgartner, who had attended a football game in spite of the prohibition of Jews, had been set upon and killed. According to some reports the scene of the alleged outrage had been Ratibor in Upper Silesia; other reports placed it at Breslau. The Nazi News Service issued a strong denial of the story. Investigators expressed the opinion that the report had been invented by the Nazi Propaganda Department, so that if it were used in connection with foreign agitation against the Berlin Olympics, it would be truthfully refuted and cited as an instance of the spreading of foreign "atrocity" propaganda.

3. *New York Times*, October 22, 1935, A1, "I went to Germany for the purpose of getting at least one Jew on the German Olympic team, and I feel that my job is finished." See the account in Richard Mandell, *The Nazi Olympics* (Urbana: University of Illinois Press, 1987), 75, and 76–77 on Helena Mayer.

4. This is not quite precise. According to the *New York Times* of September 14, 1935 (5:2), "General Charles H. Sherrill, American member of the International Olympic Committee, left Nuremberg for Paris today [September 13] after having been the personal guest of Hitler on the train that brought diplomats from Berlin to the convention." The

competitor to be a citizen of the country he represents. Therefore, no Jew under any circumstances is eligible. And incidentally, the invitation [to Mayer] has not yet been received anyway.

But even if all these things were not true; even if our good friend General Sherrill were successful in getting one Jew to compete on the German team; even though for the brief period of the Olympics the German nation halted its persecution of Jews and Protestants and Catholics; even then we could not with honor compete. For the fact would still remain that Germany has trampled the Olympic ideal of tolerance and international brotherhood into the mud.

They have dishonored the appeal of world public opinion. They have denied fair play to their Jews, refused justice to their minorities, defied the ideals of civilization and humanity. We appreciate General Sherrill's working for two years in the attempt to get one Jew on the team. But the fact remains that the Jews of Germany have, after a thousand years of residence, been robbed of their citizenship, their businesses, their properties. Thousands of them have been forced to flee from the country penniless and friendless. No self-respecting Jew, whether from Germany or anywhere else, could go to the Olympics if staged in Berlin.

To me the argument is simple. Germany has denied, opposed and repudiated the Great Olympic Idea. The Nazi regime in Germany is the negation of all those concepts of international friendship, which the Olympics represent. Under these circumstances, the Olympics in Germany will be but a farce, a gigantic act of international hypocrisy. America must not so demean itself as to participate in such hypocrisy.

But a new slant was given to the problem when General Sherrill in his statement warned the Jews of America that their attempt to boycott the Olympics might boomerang.

> In the last two years, attitude has changed. There is a grave danger of an anti-Semitic wave here because of agitation of Jews for German brethren. I would not be surprised if it reached such proportions as it did in Spain in 1492, when the Jews were expelled from there. It is all due to the Jews over-playing their cards. The whole trouble in Germany starts when the Jews, who held a disproportionate number of high positions, over-played their cards.[5]

---

infamous "Nuremberg laws" (technically, the "Reich Citizenship Law" and the "Law for the Protection of German Blood and German Honor") were dated September 15. An editorial in the *Congress Bulletin* 2:1 of November 1, 1935 (the day the sermon was delivered), stated that Sherrill discussed the Olympics with Hitler.

5. Although this appears in the typescript as a direct quotation, it seems rather to be a paraphrase imprecisely remembered. The *New York Times*, October 22, 1935, A1 (continued on 10), quoted Sherrill as saying that "I have a warning for American Jewry. . . . There is a grave danger in the Olympic agitation. . . . It would be overplaying the Jewish hand in America as it was overplayed in Germany before the present suppression and expulsion of Jews was undertaken. The anti-Semitism resulting here might last for years." See Mandell, *The Nazi Olympics*, 75. It does not seem, however, that the breathtaking offensiveness of the quotation as it appeared in the *Times*—blaming German Jewish be-

And the tragic thing is that there are some Jews who listen to this and are convinced. "Perhaps we *are* over-playing our cards," they say. "Perhaps we do call too much attention to ourselves. Maybe it would be better when we are kicked from behind to smile and pretend we didn't feel it. Otherwise our enemies may get all the more angry. Perhaps it would be better when we see our Jewish brothers crushed and beaten to stand by silently and look the other way, lest our turn come next."

Those of you who know my position on Jewish problems know that I have no patience with such Jews. Craven cowards, the fear of persecution is in their bones. Afflicted with a Jewish inferiority complex, they show their inferiority in their every word and action. They are not afraid to play a role of shame and degradation—but they are afraid lest we "over-play our cards" by uttering the truth and standing for justice. What they need is a little backbone. A little courage. A little self-respect.

If we must suffer persecution merely because we stand for what is right and will not be silent in the face of injustice and terrorism and the persecution of our brothers—then let us suffer! If it is our fate to bear the brunt of the attack from the forces of hate at loose in the world, then let us accept our fate! Anti-Semitism is then no longer our problem. It is the problem of those who persecute us. Ours shall be the suffering. But theirs shall be the shame. Our backs may be broken. But our self-respect, our human dignity will remain unshaken.

What shall we answer to our self-styled friend, General Sherrill? (God save us from friends of your caliber!). We shall answer, "You have made a mistake, General Sherrill. You talk of this as though it were entirely a Jewish matter. Yet the fact is that the Jews as yet have had a relatively small part, an all too small part, in the fight against the Nazi Olympics.

"No, General Sherrill, it is not only a Jewish question. It is a *Catholic and Protestant* question as well. You know as well as we do that Protestant pastors and Catholic priests have been plunged into Nazi concentration camps because they defied the attempt to paganize the church. You know that Protestant and Catholic athletic organizations have been ruthlessly crushed. That Protestants and Catholics recognize that it is their problem as well is shown by the fact that hundreds of the leading Christian clergymen of America have signed a statement repudiating your views, and such organizations as the National Council of Methodist Youths addressed an open letter to ministers, priests, and rabbis calling for a ban of the Nazi Olympics.[6]

"No, General Sherrill, it is not a Jewish question. It is an *American* question. Every American citizen is in this fight because they believe in the American

---

havior for Nazi persecution and warning American Jews of a possible similar consequence—is misrepresented or exaggerated by the paraphrase. The *Congress Bulletin* editorial of November 1 (see above, n. 4) describes Sherrill's statement as discourse "taken from Goebbels and Rosenberg."

6. Mandell, *The Nazi Olympics*, 77; *American Jewish Year Book* 38 (5697) (Philadelphia: JPS, 1936), 181–87.

doctrines of liberty, democracy and fair play. And the swastika of Hitler is opposed to everything for which the American flag stands. When you threaten us with an anti-Semitic crusade, you are flinging an insult at every American who cherishes the American tradition. You can't get by claiming, as you did, that the Nazi treatment of Jews is no worse than our treatment of Negroes.[7] After all, Negro lynching in America is not an official program of the government, as is Jew-hatred in Germany.

"No, General Sherrill, it is not a Jewish question. It is a *human* question. We are trying to show that a nation cannot put might over right, cannot violate every principle of civilization and every rule of the Games, and get away with it. Participation in the Olympics would not only bring Germany millions of dollars. It would also enhance the prestige of Hitler's rule within the country and give tacit consent of the outside world to Nazi terrorism. The boycott of the Olympics would be an effective means of expressing the moral indignation of the civilized world at Germany's return to barbarism, and hasten the day when the people of Germany will come back to their senses."

Victory at the Olympics is a great honor. But America can win a greater victory without being there at all. The great stadium will be filled. The flags of all nations but one will be raised. But that one will be more conspicuous by its absence than all the others. Louder than the roar of voices cheering the athletes will be the silence of America—a silence proclaiming to the world, "We cannot join in celebrating good sportsmanship in a land that has made a mockery of fair play." That reproach would be heard around the world. It would ring more resoundingly than all the speeches of statesmen and all the pronouncements of governments.

Other nations would carry off the prizes, in running and jumping and swimming. But to America would go the true Olympic victory—such a victory as has never been won before in Olympic competition: a *moral* victory.

For other nations would be competing and winning in the Olympic Games.

But America would be symbolizing the Great Olympic Idea.

---

7. In the same *New York Times* article (October 22, 1935, A1), Sherrill was quoted as saying, "As to obstacles placed in the way of Jewish athletes . . . in trying to reach Olympic abilities, I would have no more business discussing that in Germany than if the Germans attempted to discuss the Negro situation in the American South."

5

Must There Be War?
November 11, 1936

*This is the first of two pacifist sermons included to show the power of this con-
viction for Saperstein during the 1930s, establishing the basis for the intellectu-
ally and emotionally wrenching decision to abandon this position during the
following years. The arguments in both sermons are drawn largely from the
experience of "The Great War," so devastating that it led many to conclude that
war was the ultimate evil, that nothing—not even Nazism—could possibly justify
becoming involved in another world war. This must have seemed an especially
important message to communicate against the background of the Italian invasion of Ethiopia launched in October 1935 culminating in the conquest of Addis
Ababa the following May, the eruption of civil war in Spain in July, and the
formal establishment of the Rome-Berlin Axis in October.*

*The present sermon, dated November 11, 1936, on a file card that contains
its title and outline, was actually delivered on "Armistice Day." In contrast with
the following sermon, delivered about a year later, which focuses on the Jewish
issues involved in pacifism, this sermon is striking in its lack of specific Jewish
content. The realm of discourse is that of liberal pacifists such as the Unitarian
minister, friend and colleague of Wise, John Haynes Holmes, whose play is cited
below. Only the references to "the streets of Lynbrook," "this pulpit," and boys
"dedicating themselves to the cause of Judaism in their Bar Mitzvah speeches"
situate it in the synagogue. In both sermons, we find arguments from the experience of the recent past applied to the present which appeared to be similar, but
which Saperstein would eventually realize was fundamentally different, so that
the tense balancing of a militant and confrontational anti-Nazism and a princi-
pled opposition to war under any circumstances would ultimately collapse.
Texts of several others of Saperstein's pacifist sermons from this period remain.*

FIFTEEN YEARS AGO, ON NOVEMBER 11, 1921, a solemn funeral procession wended its way from the Capitol Building in Washington to Arlington Cemetery. The lifeless form of the "Unknown Soldier" went to his last resting-place. Shrouded with the flag he died to save, the casket slowly moved down an avenue of bowed heads and grateful hearts. With him, though we knew him not, the entire nation marched in spirit. In many a heart there was pain, and in many an eye a mournful tear.

The "Unknown Soldier" was a symbol of the sacrifice our nation had made. Fathers had given their possessions, mothers their beloved sons, the finest youth of the land had given its lifeblood—in a war proclaimed as "the war to end war." Sir Philip Gibbs, the famous war correspondent, tells us that the idealists in the ranks really believed that by their agony and sacrifice humanity would learn new lessons. As the Unknown Soldier was laid to rest, in the hearts of our people was the conviction that with his burial, the god of war had been vanquished. "It shall not happen again," the whole world said. It was the pledge the living made to the dead.[1]

How are we keeping that pledge? Today, the world stands closer to the brink of another world war than at any time since the Armistice. Once more, machine guns crackle and bombs explode. Once more aeroplanes zoom. Long lines of boys, each one a mother's son, start on the long, long trail.

We resolve that we will stay out. We have learned our lesson. We shall not become embroiled. Ethiopia seems far away.

But, my friends, so did Sarajevo twenty-two years ago. It was the assassination of a Grand Duke that started the ball rolling then. All it needs is one such incident now and the spark may burst into flame that will blaze around the world.

And what will happen to us? Day after day the newspapers will carry screaming headlines. Night after night the radios will pound, pound, pound. Orators will whip mobs into a frenzy with appeals to national glory and patriotism.

The great American humorist, Mark Twain, has described the process in a prophetic warning. I read you his words:

> The loud little handful—as usual—will shout for the war. The pulpit will, warily and cautiously object—at first; the great, big, dull bulk of the nation will rub its sleepy eyes and try to make out why there should be a war. . . .

---

1. The focus on the "Unknown Soldier" as a symbol of sacrificial death to end all war may have been inspired by an "Armistice Sunday" sermon by John Haynes Holmes entitled, "The Unknown Soldier Speaks." As his life ebbed, the soldier reports having said to himself, "It's all right boy. You've done your bit. This war's the last war. They'll never do this sort of thing again. You're dead, or as good as dead; but other men, through all the centuries to come, will live. . . . That's what I died for, or thought I died for. But look at things now!" Holmes, *The Sensible Man's View of Religion* (New York: Harper and Row, 1932), 123 (a book in Saperstein's personal library, as were many others of Holmes's sermons).

Then the handful will shout louder. A few . . . men on the other side will argue . . . against the war with speech and pen, and at first will . . . be applauded; but . . . those others will outshout them, and presently the anti-war audiences will thin out and lose popularity. . . .

And now the whole nation—pulpit and all—will take up the war cry, and shout itself hoarse, and mob any honest man who ventures to open his mouth; and presently such mouths will cease to open.

Next the statesmen will invent cheap lies, putting the blame upon the nation that is attacked, and every man will be glad of those conscience-soothing falsities, and will diligently study them, and refuse to examine any refutations of them; and thus he will by and by convince himself that the war is just, and will thank God for the better sleep he enjoys after this process of grotesque self-deception.[2]

Only a miracle must save us from the course that warning pictures. That miracle must happen.

In the years that have passed, we have come to realize more fully what the actual cost of war was. The direct costs of the World War to all concerned were almost 300 billion dollars. Do you know what that means? It means if you had been paying 400 dollars every minute, night and day, since the year one, you would still not yet have spent that much. The cost of the war amounts to 215 million dollars for every day that it lasted. People talk about the terrible extravagance of the Administration in voting 4 billion for unemployment relief. The war cost the world that much in twenty days. The direct costs of the war to the United States alone were a billion dollars more than have been spent for education during the entire history of this country.[3]

But these are only money costs. What about human costs? Ten million soldiers directly killed. Thirteen million civilians. Twenty million wounded non-combatants. Nine million orphans crying out in vain for the return of their fathers. Five million widows left helpless and alone. Ten million exiles, up-

---

2. The passage is from Twain's posthumously published story, "The Mysterious Stranger." The text, taken from some other publication, was clipped and pasted on a page of the sermon; ellipsis marks represent words that were crossed out in pencil and not actually read.

3. The enormous cost of the "Great War" and the constructive social uses to which that money could be devoted were a standard part of the pacifist repertoire of arguments. Compare, for example, a little book written by Abraham Cronbach, an influential pacifist Professor of Social Studies at the Hebrew Union College: *The Jewish Peace Book for Home and School* (Cincinnati: Union of American Hebrew Congregations, 1932), 56 (giving the figure $337,846,189,657 as the total cost of the war). This does not however seem to have been the direct source for the above passage. See also Clyde Eagleton, *Analysis of the Problem of War* (New York: Ronald Press, Co., 1937), 25–26: "Bitter complaints are raised when, in times of peace, millions of dollars are spent for relief, to save human lives; but the extravagant prices of war, paid to destroy human lives, are regarded as well justified."

rooted from their native soil, men without a country.[4] We read with horror of a single human sacrifice to ancient idols. What shall we say of this modern offering to the pagan god of war?

And we shall not even take into consideration the tragic losses which follow in war's wake: of depression, the breakdown of moral standards, the disregard for life, all the social ills that came as the aftermath of the World War.

No problem in the world is more vital today. You parents who think you can be indifferent to it now, you may be the murderers of your own sons. For it is your sons who will go. I can see them marching down the streets of Lynbrook. Fine, brave-hearted boys, chin up and eyes straight ahead. Boys we know and love, boys whose voices we have heard from this pulpit, dedicating themselves to the cause of Judaism in their Bar Mitzvah speeches.[5] Your hearts will thrill with pride as you see them march.

The years will pass. A weary, shattered, broken world will declare another armistice. The boys will come back. But not all of them. Some who come back will not come back the same as they went. And some will curse God for having permitted them to live and suffer. Perhaps there will be another "Unknown Soldier." Perhaps it will be one of your sons who did not come back. And we will say again, "What fools we've been. It must not happen again."

---

4. Cronbach, 55, provides the figures 9,998,771 soldiers killed, 20,297,551 wounded, five million widows, nine million orphans. These figures apparently were circulated by the National Council for Prevention of War.

5. Fast-forward seven and a half years. In June 1944, Saperstein, now a chaplain in the American Army, wrote a newsletter from "Somewhere in Italy," in which he described soldiers he had met, including the following:

> Another evening the door suddenly opened again. This time a youngster stood there, puffing and panting, his eyes shining with excitement. "I just got here this morning," he gasped, "and somebody told me that the Chaplain was a Rabbi from Lynbrook. I ran all the way up." . . . It hadn't been so long since I had seen him. A little more than five years before he had been in my Bar Mitzvah class. . . .
>
> Now he was here, thousands of miles from home, a soldier, talking about GI problems and about going to the front. We talked together for a long time. Then he rushed back to his tent to write a letter to his mother before retiring for the night. About a week later I was bidding a group of boys God-speed as they left [for the front]. Among them was Arnold [Levy, whose Bar Mitzvah was celebrated in Lynbrook in September 1938]. I could see his eyes shining with eager excitement as I spoke. I remembered the same light in his eyes as he stood before the pulpit of the Temple back home and read his Bar Mitzvah blessings.

But a month later, on July 11, he would be responding in a private letter to news of the death of a boy from the Temple in the Pacific: "I was terribly shocked at the news. . . . Like all those whom I've seen grow up, I never was able to realize that they were reaching maturity. I remember in my pacifist days talking about the next war, and telling how when it came the boys who were being Bar Mitzvah would go out and some of them wouldn't come back. . . ."

What can we do to avoid it? It is not enough for the government to proclaim its neutrality. Governments can change their minds. Wilson was elected in 1916 on the basis of the promise to keep America out of war. It is the people, in the last resort, who fight wars, and it is they who can keep us out of war. But it is not an easy task. We must be ready to struggle and sacrifice for peace in the same way we have been ready to sacrifice for war.

We are pledged to destroy war.[6] It is our pledge to the boys who gave their promising young lives that war might be destroyed forever. We must carry on the torch of peace they flung to us with dying hands. We must advance upon war on every front, religious and political. It is not the counsel of sentimentality; it is the counsel of common sense. General John F. O'Ryan, who knows war as an expert, declares, "War cannot be successfully abolished except through the complete mobilization of all peace powers for peace purposes. Let us wage peace."[7]

But there are some who say, "But sometimes war is inevitable. Sometimes there arises the occasion when we must fight." I answer, "War is never inevitable unless you make it so."

Some say, "War is part of human nature. It is a natural instinct." I answer, "The same thing was said about slavery seventy years ago. If man requires struggle, there is none more glorious than the struggle for peace. He need not go out to kill and be killed."

Others say, "There are causes for which it is honorable to sacrifice one's life." I answer, "Yes, there are such causes: liberty, justice, truth, peace. But war is not one of them. Give your lives for these causes, as I am willing to give mine, but do not use war as a means, for by now we should know that the issue in war is not democracy or world peace or any of those ideals for which men are willing to die. The issues are colonies and foreign investments and the profits of armament manufacturers. Are these worth the sacrifice of your life?"

Others say, "There are evils worse than war." I answer, "There are no evils worse than war. For war carries all other evils in its train. War eliminates no evils but only intensifies them, [as we see in] Nazi Germany."[8]

But they continue, "What can we do when our government declares war? Must we not fight or be accused of cowardice and lack of patriotism?" I answer, "You can refuse to fight, and insist that some means more rational than war be found of settling our disputes. Perhaps you will be accused of cowardice, but you can know that yours is the greater heroism and the truer patriotism.

---

6. This is likely merely rhetorical (as on the first and final pages), but it might also be an allusion to the "Oxford Pledge" that Saperstein had taken as a student. See the 1973 sermon, "Days I Remember."

7. Major General O'Ryan, author of *The Modern Army in Action* (New York: McBride, Nast & Co., 1914) and commander of American forces in World War I, is cited by Cronbach in *The Quest for Peace* (Cincinnati: Sinai Press, 1937), 176, as saying, "I would be a traitor to my country if I did not do everything in my power to abolish war."

8. The words "Nazi Germany" stand alone. If they were intended to belong to the previous sentence, the idea would be that the World War is what produced the evil of Nazi Germany, which therefore serves as an example of the preceding generalization.

Recently the Theatre Guild presented the play, "If This Be Treason," one of the authors of which was the clergyman John Haynes Holmes. The play, which had all too short a run, dealt with the theme of whether it is possible to stop a war once it is on its way.[9] It told of a newly elected President of the United States who found that his predecessor had left him with a war against Japan on his hands. He decided to make peace before the war actually begins. To do so, he seizes upon the device of going personally to Japan to negotiate a peace conference before the war rather than after it.

His arrival creates a sensation. He is placed under military arrest by the Japanese government. But in a climactic scene, when all seems lost, the guards refuse to arrest him, the people rally around the peace leader, the military cabinet is deposed, and peace is established.

The play has been criticized as being too naive. But it embodies one fundamental truth. That is that the people of no nation want war. No people wants its young men killed, its children starved, its country destroyed. If a nation is ready to fight, it is only that they are the dupes of lying propaganda, just as we are, that they feel that they are being attacked and must fight a war of defense. If only the peoples of every nation would declare that "We will not fight," then war would be impossible.

As we celebrate Armistice Day, I would like to see an Armistice Day parade in every town. But it would be a different kind of parade from what we are accustomed to.

First would come the wounded veterans of the World War—maimed and crippled, some on crutches, others being carried. Before them would be a sign, "We Are the Victims." Then would come the mothers of the community; before them a sign, "We Are the Mothers Whose Sons War Kills." Then the children, and before them a sign, "We Are the Ones Whom War Makes Orphans." Then the youth: "We Are the Ones Who Are Asked to Go Out and Kill and Be Killed in Order That Ammunition Workers May Make Profit." And then the workers of the community: "We Are the Ones Who Suffer in the Depressions Which Have Followed and Must Follow Every War." And before them all would be a great banner, on which would be inscribed in letters of gold, "We Are the Legions of Peace, the Makers of a Warless World."

We shall keep our pledge to the "Unknown Soldier" and the millions of martyrs who gave their lives that war might be banished from the earth. We are the Legions of Peace, the Makers of a Warless World.

---

9. The play opened the Theatre Guild season of 1935–1936 and ran for six weeks; according to Holmes, it was "acclaimed by those who agreed with its thesis, and quite generally neglected by the theatergoing public. So in due course it was withdrawn for lack of support." See Holmes, *A Summons Unto Men*, ed. Carl Voss (New York: Simon and Schuster, 1970), 152–180 (115–52 for a selection of other pacifist writings by Holmes). The Theatre Guild, founded in New York in 1919, produced noncommercial plays for a subscription audience and had a significant influence on American theatre.

- 6 -

Can Jews Afford to Be Pacifists?
December, 1937

A little more than a year after the previous sermon, the possibility of a renewed war seemed greater and the position of pacifists more precarious. The apologetic note taken in the first two paragraphs indicates clearly the opposition to the pacifist viewpoint within the congregation. Here the focus is specifically on the Jewish perspective. The title is somewhat ironic in light of the dramatically different situation once the war began, when many were asking the question, "Can Jews afford to be urging the United States to become involved in the European War?"

In common with the earlier sermon, the arguments here are drawn almost entirely from the experience of World War I, in which Jews, caught in the middle, suffered worse than any other group. That experience led to the claim that this must necessarily happen in any war and that therefore, from a strictly Jewish point of view, war is the ultimate evil. In retrospect, it seems to be a fine example of drawing a lesson from the past but applying it without recognizing the fundamentally different situation in the present. Not surprisingly, at this time, the possibility that Germany would undertake and implement a policy of systematic mass murder of all European Jews, a policy that could be ended only by the military defeat of the Nazi state, was inconceivable.

Thus, despite the aggressive and activist anti-Nazi stance in the sermons of 1933–1935, the preacher still concludes that resorting to war will lead to an even greater evil. That this was not an idiosyncratic stance can be seen in a "Peace Day" sermon by Rabbi Philip S. Bernstein in late 1938. Bernstein recognized that "There is only one way by which Fascist aggression can possibly be stopped and that is by opposing it with armed force." But he continues to argue, based on the experience of the prior World War, that the United States must not become involved in another European conflagration and its "evil conquences." "If we wish to save democracy, if we wish to preserve an island of sanity in a mad world, let us avoid such involvement." Sabbath Sermons, 5699-1938 *(Cincinnati: The Tract Commission), 43, 45. The eventual abandonment of this position would be for Saperstein an agonizing process.*

IN DISCUSSING THE THEME I HAVE CHOSEN, "Can Jews Afford to Be Pacifists," I realize I am touching upon a delicate subject. I would emphasize that, as always, I am speaking as your rabbi, not for the congregation but to the congregation. I know before I begin that not all of you believe as I do. I am realistic enough to know that after I finish some of you will still disagree.

I speak on this subject because I feel that as a rabbi, concerned with Jewish values and with Jewish welfare, I must. War is no longer a vague possibility. It is an imminent danger. And as we come closer and closer to it, today as before the last war, pacifism is becoming more and more unpopular. The rise and threat of Fascist powers have made many former pacifists begin to abandon their views. "We believe in peace," they say," but we are convinced that it will be necessary to fight one more war—a war to save democracy."

No one could be more opposed to Fascism than I am. But to me it seems that I've heard words like these before—back in my childhood years at the time of the last war. And it seems to me that our experience in the past war should prove to us that no matter how great an evil may exist, war is not the right instrument with which to operate upon it. I, like others of my colleagues in the Rabbinate and in the Christian ministry, believe that there is no such thing as a good war—for war itself is evil and the source of evil. So we find ourselves compelled to be pacifists—and then we come face to face with the problem: can Jews, and particularly Jewish leaders, *afford* to be pacifists?

In times like this it is not easy to be a pacifist. The drama presented by the Theatre Guild a month ago called "The Ghost of Yankee Doodle" dealt with this theme. The events were supposed to take place eighteen months after the outbreak of the next world war, with the United States still undecided. It showed the difficulty of keeping one's mind clear in a period of war hysteria, the forces that tend to sweep along even those who are sincere lovers of peace. Those who adhere to pacifism open themselves to the charge of being unpatriotic.[1]

And if it is hard to be a pacifist, to be a Jewish pacifist is twice as hard. For we recognize that we are a minority group. In this, as in other respects, the ac-

---

1. Sidney Howard's "The Ghost of Yankee Doodle," starring Ethel Barrymore, opened formally in Boston on November 1, 1937, and at the Guild Theatre in New York on November 22. It was reviewed in the *New York Times* on Sunday, November 21 (Section XI, 2:1), and published by Charles Scribner's Sons (New York and London), in 1938. This provides a date of late December 1937 (or possibly January 1938) for the sermon, which has no date on the typescript.

tions of individuals are taken as the basis for charges against the whole. And there are many Jews who feel most sincerely that in times like these, we must tread lightly. "The position of the Jew is none too good," they say. "We must be careful that we do not make it worse. We must guard our reputation for patriotism jealously. Look what is happening in Germany and Poland and Roumania. Jews are being attacked as surplus population. Let's not bring anything on ourselves here. This is the wrong time to make ourselves conspicuous in unpopular movements. By doing so you may make yourselves responsible for bringing hatred and pogroms and death upon your people. By speaking out so frankly, you are undermining our existence."

It is a grave dilemma. On the one hand is the choice of being untrue to one's convictions. On the other hand is the danger of being the cause of sorrow for the Jewish people. To take the latter is to take upon oneself a grave responsibility. And yet, after careful consideration, I feel that the Jew not only can afford to be a pacifist but that he owes it to himself to be a pacifist.[2]

First of all, and this must not be overlooked, we have a moral obligation to work for peace. We are the people whose watchword through the centuries has been *Shalom*.[3] Our prophets uttered imperishable words on the subject.[4] Our ancient seers set it as the crown of the messianic era. The Rabbis of the Talmud spoke of it as one of the foundations of the earth.[5] War is the repudiation of our basic teaching: the fatherhood of God and the brotherhood of man. If they are to mean anything, that bond of brotherhood must extend to all mankind—even to the Nazis in Germany. We will not answer hatred with hatred, we must not answer slaughter with slaughter. It was no accident that in the famous picture of the four sons in the Passover Haggadah, the evil son is pictured as a soldier.[6]

Exaltation of peace is one of the deep, strong currents of Jewish faith through the ages. We must not turn from it to change our policy with every shifting eddy. Perhaps it means suffering; it may even mean martyrdom. But as Jews, we need not be taught that there are causes for which it is worthy to suffer, worthy even to die. To most people, national honor in war is such a cause; to me war isn't, but peace is. To abandon the ideal of peace for the sake of physical security and self-protection is a betrayal. Safety at the cost of our ideals is unworthy of our Jewish heritage.

---

2. The following words are crossed out in the typescript: "For the service which he renders to the Jewish people when he does everything in his power to oppose war far outweighs the dangers which he chances."

3. Referring probably to the use of the word *shalom*, "peace," as a greeting among Jews. For the mandate to love and pursue peace, see M. Avot 1, 11 and frequently elsewhere. For expressions on the greatness of peace in rabbinic literature, see Leviticus Rabbah 9, 9 and Numbers Rabbah 11, 7 and 21, 1.

4. For example, Isaiah 2:4, Zech. 9:10, statements which associate peace with the messianic age, as in the following sentence.

5. Referring to Simeon ben Gamaliel's statement in M. Avot 1, 18.

6. See examples in Yosef Yerushalmi, *Haggadah and History* (Philadelphia: JPS, 1975, Plates 11 (Prague, 1526), 60 (Amsterdam, 1695), 134 (Berlin, 1923).

In Remarque's novel *The Road Back* there is a scene, which shows the demobilization of the German army. Heel, the typical Prussian officer, stands before Weil, the Jewish soldier. "Now your time begins, Weil," he says.

> "It will be less bloody," answers Weil, quietly.
> "And less heroic," Heel retorts.
> "That's not the only thing in life," says Weil.
> "But the best," Heel replies. "What else is there?"
> Weil pauses a moment. "Things that sound feeble today, Herr Lieutenant—kindliness and love. These also have their heroisms."[7]

Weil represents the eternal Jew, preaching the heroism of peace, of kindliness, and love. But unfortunately, as Germany has proved, war does its work so well, planting seeds of hatred, that the Weils coming afterwards don't have a chance.

But there are more practical reasons why I as a Jew regard the struggle for peace to be worthwhile regardless of its cost. For no matter how terrible that may be, it cannot be half as bad as the reality of war for the Jew. Once the spirit of brutality is unleashed, it does not take long before it finds the Jew as a ready victim. The story of how much the Jew suffered during the last war will never be fully told. In the last war, 10 million Jews were in the warring nations of Europe. Three million of them in Poland, the very center of the conflict. Whole communities were uprooted again and again, forced to carry the sick and the dying with them.

When the Germans took Poland, the Jews were attacked as Russian agents. And when the Russians took it, they were hounded as German spies. No people suffered more than did the Jews during the last war. And so it will ever be. War means certain destruction to the Jew. And the horror of war is intensified by the fact that the Jew, dwelling as he does in every nation, must inevitably find himself fighting against his brother. So it was in the last war. So it must be in any war. Jew fighting against Jew. Brother taking the life of his brother.

Recently I read a story told by the Hungarian correspondent for an American newspaper. During the war he had fought with the Hungarian army on the Italian front. In one battle, his army was driving the enemy in retreat. Climbing into an Italian trench, he saw a soldier seriously, perhaps fatally, injured. Stretching out his arms, he cried, "Bitte, Wasser, bitte, Wasser." Something in the accent and tone of the words caused the Hungarian to look closer. Hungarian and Italian faced each other and recognized each other as Jews. He handed over his canteen, wept silently for a moment, then, leaving him probably to die, went on to continue the work of killing.

---

7. Erich Maria Remarque, *The Road Back* (New York: Grosset & Dunlap, 1931), 48. Heel responds by articulating the romantic cult of the heroic, the antithesis of the pacifistic worldview that Saperstein associates with the Jewish character, Weil: "No . . . They [i.e., kindliness and love] offer only martyrdom. That is quite another thing. Heroism begins where reason leaves off; when life is set at a discount. It has to do with folly, with exaltation, with risk."

According to his story, he has never been able to forget that incident. Sometimes he relives it in his memory. "Perhaps it was my bullet that killed him," he tells himself. "And why? The whole system that set us to murdering each other was the damnedest lie ever invented."

The final reason why anything is preferable to war for the Jew is that the suffering caused by war never stops with the war, particularly insofar as the Jew is concerned. In the aftermath of war there always comes an intensified nationalism, which bodes ill for minority groups, particularly the Jew. And there always comes a cycle of economic distress, which demands a scapegoat, and who makes a better scapegoat than the Jew? At the Paris Conference held after the last war, Paderewski, as the leader of Poland, was negotiating with Wilson and Clemenceau. As his ace card, he threatened, "If these claims are not granted, the Polish people will be so furious they will massacre all the Jews." "And what will happen," asked Wilson, "if we do grant them?" "Ah," said Paderewski, "that will be different. In that case the Polish people will be so delighted that they will massacre all the Jews."[8]

One way or another, when war is over, the troubles for the Jew have just begun. Nazis and Endeks and Cuzists—Germany and Poland and Roumania— our suffering in every one of them is the fruit of the war.[9] As Secretary Hull said in a speech last year, Religion, science, social betterment only go forward in a world without war.[10] War is a mill, whose grist is death: death to youth, death to hope, death to civilization.

We must realize this truth: that whatever evils there may be, war cannot cure them, for it is in large part responsible for them. War cannot wipe out Fascism. No matter who wins, it can only succeed in spreading Fascism. War cannot wipe out anti-Semitism. It can only plant the seeds for more virulent anti-Semitism in

---

8. On Paderewski's opposition to the rights granted Jews in the Polish Minorities Treaty, including his warning that the treaty would create a new Jewish problem rather than solve an old one, see Oscar Janowsky, *The Jews and Minority Rights, 1898–1919* (New York: Columbia University Press, 1933), 356. The vignette itself was apparently apocryphal, or a joke: see Henry D. Spalding, *Encyclopedia of Jewish Humor* (New York: Jonathan David Publishers, 1969), 183, which gives no source.

9. "Endeks" (in Polish, Endecja), were a right-wing nationalist group responsible for many physical attacks against Jews in 1936–1937; see Emanuel Melzer, *No Way Out: The Politics of Polish Jewry, 1935–1939* (Cincinnati: HUC Press, 1997), Index, s.v. "Endecja." "Cuzists" were followers of Professor Alexander Cuza, the head of a Romanian anti-Jewish party which became part of a United Parliamentary Party in December, 1935; anti-Jewish attacks were led by the Cuzists in the following years. See *American Jewish Year Book* 38 (5697) (Philadelphia: JPS, 1936), 291–97 and 39 (5698) (Philadelphia: JPS, 1937), 440–42.

10. This appears to me to be a paraphrase of the view presented in Secretary of State Cordell Hull's Brown University Commencement address, delivered June 15, 1936, entitled "Peace and War" (see the State Department publication of this address, 3–4). It was quoted extensively in the *New York Times* of the following day (A13:1–2). See also *The Memoirs of Cordell Hull*, 2 vols. (New York: Macmillan, 1948), 473–74. It is not clear from the typescript whether the final sentence of the paragraph was intended to be attributed to Hull or was Saperstein's own formulation.

the future. Whatever the cost of peace efforts may be for the Jew, it is as nothing compared to the cost of war. War means the annihilation of our values and of our existence.

Can Jews afford to be pacifists? My friends, if we wish really to serve the Jewish cause, we must seek peace and pursue it:[11] serving it as our mission, holding it aloft as our banner, counting no gain enough if we lose it, no sacrifice too much if we keep it, ever striving, ever seeking, until *Shalom*, peace, shall be the watchword not only of Israel but of all mankind.

---

11. Echoing Ps. 34:15.

Return to Thy People
September 30, 1938
Shabbat Shuvah

In the traditional Ashkenazic communities, Shabbat Shuvah, the Sabbath be-
tween Rosh Hashanah and Yom Kippur, was one of the major preaching occa-
sions of the year for the rabbi of the community. The weekly Sabbath sermons
were ordinarily delivered by other preaching specialists holding the title of
maggid *or* darshan, *while many rabbis, whose primary role was as a legal*
authority and scholar, preached only on this Sabbath and "the Great Sabbath,"
preceding Pesach. For the American Reform rabbi, however, the situation was
different. The major sermons of the period were given on the Days of Awe, eve-
ning and morning; in congregations such as Lynbrook which observed two days
of Rosh Hashanah, this meant full sermons at times of maximum attendance for
the evening of Rosh Hashanah, the first and second morning, Kol Nidre and
Yom Kippur morning, and possibly also at Yizkor (the Memorial Service) on
Yom Kippur afternoon. With all the best material used on these occasions,
Shabbat Shuvah often became a less formal preaching occasion.

No other sermons by Saperstein from the High Holy Days of 1938 appear to
be extant. Based on the sermons from prior years, it seems likely that at least
one of the Rosh Hashanah sermons would have been devoted to events of the
previous twelve months. The present sermon alludes to such events—in Italy,
Austria, and Poland. But it focuses on a theme drawn from the central motif of
the Sabbath Haftarah (beginning with Hosea 14:2), the motif of return (though
return to the Jewish people is substituted for the return to God in the prophetic
text), and less directly, from the Torah reading (whereby Moses' final message
becomes an occasion for reviewing elements of his biography). The experience
of the past year demonstrates that antisemites will not allow Jews to escape
their identity. Rather than producing deeper self-hate and despair (represented

by the suicides of Austrian Jews in the months following the Anschluss), the
healthy response is a return to the potential richness of a full Jewish life.

IN THE PORTION OF THE TORAH to be read tomorrow [*Va-Yelekh*], we hear the farewell address of Moses to the Israelites before he departs from them to seek an unknown grave upon Mount Nebo. What must he have been thinking at that poignant moment when he was about to confer the charge on his successor, Joshua, who was to achieve the goal to which he, Moses, had dedicated his life? Who can doubt that he remembered the days when he had lived amidst the splendor of the Egyptian royal court, when he was accorded all the honors of a prince in Egypt? All this he had given up. Why? To help a lowly slave, oppressed by his taskmaster. But the slave was a fellow Jew.

Then he fled into the wilderness, and there, as a shepherd, he had established his family and found peace. What was it that led him to give up his simple pastoral life and return to Egypt with all its dangers and difficulties? Perhaps it was because even in the wilderness, amidst a strange people, he had not been able to put from his mind his responsibilities a Jew, and it was as though the voice of God spoke to him, saying "I am the God of thy father, of Abraham, Isaac, and Jacob. I have seen the affliction of my people that are in Egypt. Come now, go thence and lead them forth from slavery" (Exod. 3:6,7,10).

Now the end had come. He had sacrificed his years and strength in pursuit of a goal, only to be compelled to relinquish his leadership to another just as the goal was in sight. Who knows what doubts may have crossed his mind at that moment? He suspected that the people would not be true to the law he had given them, but his doubts are dissipated with the one clear light that had always been his guide and strength. It could not have been other than the will of God. With all their failings, they were his brothers and sisters in Israel. They were his people.

The theme of this Sabbath is return. And in this spirit, the message of this Shabbas Shuvah comes to us as a call to duty: "Return, O Israel, return unto thy people. When thy brother is oppressed, how can you close your eyes? When the cry of his suffering rises to the heavens, how can you shut your ears?"[1]

In bringing this message to you, the task of a rabbi today is far easier than that of rabbis of the Western world in previous generations. They spoke to a Jewry that thought it could escape, that believed it was only necessary to renounce its Jewish heritage in order to be welcomed into the outside society with all its attendant benefits.[2]

It was only at the end of the century that with the Dreyfus Affair—when this gallant French captain was pilloried before the world for no other reason than that he was a Jew—Theodor Herzl saw that not one man but the whole Jewish

---

1. In this passage, Saperstein takes several Biblical phrases (Hos. 14:2, Lev. 25:25, Gen. 18:20 and Deut. 15:9) and transforms them into a message for the time.

2. Probably alluding to Heinrich Heine's famous statement that "the baptismal certificate is the ticket of admission to European culture."

people stood on trial. He realized then what now even the blindest might see: that an eternally homeless people must ever remain in the eyes of the nations a despised horde of wandering beggars.[3] It was the same historic episode that brought Edmund Fleg, who had renounced his Judaism in his youth, to realize that there was a bond between Israel's past and his own empty soul, that if he was to find happiness in life he must do so in that group that shares with him a common past and a common future.[4]

But even then the mass of Jewry was not convinced. It took a Hitler to make them realize that there was no escape, that flight from Jewishness was both impossible and cowardly. And we have seen that lesson dramatized during this past year by the fate of the Jews of Italy. They number less than one-half of 1 percent of the Italian population. There has been a Jewish population in Italy for more than 2,000 years. In fact, the Jews are the only element in the Italian population today that can trace their history unbroken back to the days of the ancient Roman Empire, when they were granted citizenship rights. If this does not constitute a right to residence in a country, then the whole world had better pack its bags.[5] If it had seemed rationally impossible for an anti-Jewish reaction in Germany, then it seemed totally inconceivable in Italy. And yet it has happened.[6] Now at last the Jewry of the world has to realize that they must be Jews whether they wish it or not. It is an inescapable destiny. Whether or not it becomes a tragedy depends on you.

---

3. This language is actually closer to Leo Pinsker's *Auto-Emancipation*: "[The Jew] is not a guest, much less a welcome guest. He is more like a beggar; and what beggar is welcome? . . . The stigma attached to this people, which forces it into an unenviable isolation among the nations, cannot be removed by any sort of official emancipation, as long as it is the nature of this people to produce vagrant nomads. . . . How great must be the irritation at the beggar who dares to cast longing glances upon a land not his own" (Arthur Hertzberg, *The Zionist Idea* [New York: Atheneum, 1975] 187–88).

4. Stephen S. Wise wrote the foreword to Fleg's autobiographical *Why I Am A Jew* (New York: Bloch, 1929, translated by Louise Waterman Wise), which he describes as "summing up an epoch in the life of the Westernized, deghettoized Jews who think as humans, philosophize as Westerners, feel as Jews" (ix). For the impact upon Fleg of the Dreyfus Affair, see 22–37.

5. Saperstein apparently took this language from an article by Cecil Roth in *Jewish Frontier*, September 1938 (which must have been read just in the process of preparing the High Holy Day sermons). It was later cited in Abram Sachar, *Sufferance Is the Badge* (New York: Alfred A. Knopf, 1940), 289.

6. This refers to the intensification of anti-Jewish agitation in various periodicals, culminating in the "racial laws," anti-Jewish legislation promulgated over the summer of 1938, most of which would become official in November. For a review of the year before the sermon (September 1937–September 1938), see *American Jewish Year Book* 40 (5699) (Philadelphia: JPS, 1938), 230–34; *Contemporary Jewish Record* 1 (Nov., 1938): 12–13, with texts of the legislation from September 5 and September 7; Susan Zuccotti, *The Italians and the Holocaust* (New York: Basic Books, 1987), 36–37.

Many of you must remember the great dramatic pageant, "The Eternal Road," present in New York two years ago.[7] In that moving spectacle, the most pitiful figure, to my mind, is that of the "Estranged One," who in the hour of trial comes knocking at the door of the synagogue. "What do you seek here?" he is challenged. He answers,

> Long, long ago I had forgotten this community into which I was born. I had forgotten when I was a boy like my son here. For I had become wholly at one with the people of this land. I was wholly contented so, and did not wish to be reminded of you, and of the past—and of the dark. Now we must seek protection in this forgotten house, my son and I. . . . I wanted to spare [him] this heaviest of burdens. Now [he] must bear it all the same.

How much wiser are they who have not thought to escape the burden but have strengthened themselves in order to bear it. How much more noble are they who need not look upon their Judaism as a necessary evil, but welcome it as part of their being—not to be thrown off, and not to be borne with shame, but to be accepted as our most precious possession. How much happier must they be who have brought up their children to know and cherish their faith, to assert their identity with dignity; who in the hour of trial can come to the synagogue not as aliens seeking admittance to a strange refuge, but as those who come to their home. And how much stronger will they fare in this hour of trial.

One of the members of our congregation recently brought to me a striking fact. She pointed out the terrifying number of suicides that were reported in Austria at the time when the Nazis came into power.[8] She contrasted the plight of the Jews of Poland. There were millions of Jews starving, hopeless, their physical plight far worse than that of the Jews of Austria. Yet rarely does one hear of suicide in Poland. Why? Because poor, backward, lacking in Western culture as the Jews of Poland were, they possessed an inner strength, which was lacking in the Jews of Austria.

---

7. The spectacular pageant, written by Franz Werfel, with music by Kurt Weill, directed and produced by Max Reinhardt, opened in New York at the Manhattan Opera House in early January 1937. Despite quite enthusiastic reviews (see the *New York Times*, January 8, 1937, 14, it closed on May 15, and the consortium of backers filed for bankruptcy. For the script, see Franz Werfel, *The Eternal Road: A Drama in Four Parts*, translated by Ludwig Lewisohn (New York: Viking Press, 1936); the quotation is on 6–7 and 9. Saperstein preached a sermon on this pageant the week he saw it, including a reference to the "estranged one" and his son. The *New York Times* of June 28, 1999 (B1,3) reported a new production of this pageant in Chemnitz, Germany, to be presented in the year 2000 in New York, Tel Aviv and Cracow.

8. Following the *Anschluss*, the formal German annexation of Austria on March 13, 1938. This was followed, almost immediately, by legal measures degrading the status of Jews in every realm, accompanied by unofficial acts of humiliation and maltreatment. According to the *American Jewish Year Book*, "At the end of April, the Jewish Telegraphic Agency was informed by a prominent person that he estimated the number of suicides [by Austrian Jews since the *Anschluss*] at 2,000." *AJYB* 40 (5699) (Philadelphia: JPS, 1938), 214, with acts of persecution described 208–13.

An example of that strength is afforded when the Polish Minister of Instruction ordered that "Ghetto Benches" be established in all university classrooms for Jews. Something happened then. The Jewish students entered the classrooms. But they refused to sit in the "Ghetto Benches." They remained standing. That was their answer to the challenge to their human dignity. Their standing was the symbol of their own spiritual integrity and self-respect. [9]

At the Rabbinical Conference in Atlantic City last June, one of my colleagues described an experience on a recent visit to Palestine. He was standing outside the renowned Habima Theater in Tel Aviv. This famous theatrical troupe was presenting the play, "Hard to Be a Jew," by Sholem Aleichem. Two Jewish children were passing by; they read the sign with the Hebrew title, one turned to the other and asked, *Madua kashe lihyot Yehudi*? "Why is it hard to be a Jew?"[10] If Palestine had done nothing else for the Jewish people, all the labor and money and sacrifice that have gone into it would have been justified by that one little sentence. "Why is it hard to be a Jew?" Here was a youngster living in a land where Jews must build a new homeland in the face of every difficulty, in constant danger. But that youngster is of a generation that has never known the psychological rags of *Golus* [Exile], a generation that has breathed the clean air of freedom.

That is the only freedom the Jewish people shall ever achieve. Not the unworthy freedom that comes from the bounty of others, nor the false freedom that comes from trying to disguise one's identity. It is true that ultimate freedom will come to the Jew only when the whole world shall be redeemed. But before that, the Jew must first liberate himself. One of the leading modern Hebrew writers, the late David Frishman, has presented this theme in one of his poems. In it, he describes the Messiah bound. Weighted with irons, his hands and arms shackled, he gazes upon the earth, where he sees Israel tortured. In the anguish of his soul, he cries, "Let me be free." But God answers, "Not until there comes a generation that is worthy of freedom."[11] [May this Sabbath of Return inspire us to re-

---

9. The saga of the enforced segregation of Jewish students at Polish universities began earlier in individual institutions, but escalated in 1937–1938 when rectors of the major universities of Poland acceded to the demands of right-wing students that Jews by confined to "Ghetto Benches." Education Minister Swietowslawski at first resisted, but on September 24, 1937, he granted university officials total autonomy to regulate the seating of Jewish students, and in March he defended the policy of segregated seating as necessary to prevent violence. On October 14–15, 1937, all Jewish students in Poland called a protest strike, and resolved not to occupy the benches but to remain standing in the lecture halls until the regulations were revoked. See *Congress* Bulletin 4:1 (October 29, 1937), 3–4, *American Jewish Year Book* 40 (5699) (Philadelphia: JPS, 1938), 264–68 and, most recently, Emanuel Melzer, *No Way Out* (Cincinnati: HUC Press, 1997), 71–78.

10. See *CCAR Yearbook* 48 (1938): 286.

11. For further citations from this poem and identification of the source, see below, the sermon entitled "Chains of the Messiah." That sermon, dated 1950, is (as will be noted there) based on a sermon published by Louis I. Newman delivered on the "Message of Israel" in March, 1949. The use of the motif here in 1938 indicates that Saperstein had

turn to our people and our God, that we may be part of the generation that is worthy of freedom.][12]

---

come across it before reading the Newman sermon, perhaps in his studies with Shalom Spiegel, professor of Hebrew literature at the Jewish Institute of Religion.

12. It seems as if there is a final page of the sermon that is missing, but that the sermon was quite close to the end in citing the Frishman poem. All that was necessary was an application and a concluding statement. The sentence in brackets is a reconstruction of the way it might have ended, modeled after similar endings in Saperstein's sermons.

- 8 -

Unconquered
September 14, 1939
Rosh Hashanah Morning

On June 5, 1939, Saperstein embarked on a trip lasting close to three months that would bring him to Danzig and the great Jewish communities of Poland, Romania, Palestine, Egypt, and the World Zionist Congress in Geneva. During that summer, the world staggered at the precipice. By the time the trip ended (with a return voyage described at the beginning of the Rosh Hashanah, 1941, sermon), the German invasion of Poland on September 1 had launched another European war.

The outbreak of war did not come as a surprise, but the impact was devastating to a committed pacifist. This would be the first of four successive New Years when every rabbi had to face a congregation under circumstances unimaginably worse than the year before, and summon up something to say. Predictably, Saperstein drew upon his experiences from the previous summer, in the present sermon dramatizing the fate of the Jews by detailed sketches of two individuals he had met, one in Danzig, the other in Alexandria. After prolonged evocation of the pathos, the homiletical underpinnings of the positive message is provided by a passage from the Midrash and the description of the performance of a Yiddish opera seen in Cracow. Each appeals to a moment of danger and potential disarray in the past—the Israelites at the Red Sea, and the crushing of the Bar Cochba revolt—and each concludes with the counsel not to lose hope, but to move forward. Having started by emphasizing the unprecedented character of the present tragedy—the full dimensions of which, of course, still lay in the future—the sermon ends by appealing to encouragement from the models of the past.

THIS PAST SUMMER, I took what might be called a busman's holiday. For three months, I did almost nothing else but study Jewish life and investigate Jewish problems. I visited synagogues and spoke with Jewish people in seven different countries. I met in [the Twenty-First Zionist] Congress [held in Geneva, August 16–26, 1939] with Jews from all over the world. I came into contact with all kinds of Jews—Polish peddlers and Palestinian farmers, pious Jews and atheistic Jews, Oriental Jews and Western assimilated Jews. And so, just as last night, I dealt with the general world situation, so this morning I intend to discuss the Jewish situation in this hour of crisis.[1]

As one who has long been concerned with Jewish history, it seems to me that the present crisis is unique in several respects. For one thing, the tragedy of the Jew has become universal. There was a time when disaster struck the Jew in one country at a time. While Jews were crushed in one land, they were rising in another. While one nation oppressed them, another granted them freedom. Today, the forces at work in one nation spread like wildfire to its neighbors. Our attention in recent years has been riveted on Germany. Only the desperate need for aid of Polish Jewry finally made us realize that their situation is almost as bad. And while America and the nations of Western Europe still stand out as centers of democracy, it would take a rash optimism to ignore the rise of the Father Coughlins and the Moseleys and the Bunds and the innumerable anti-Semitic organizations in recent years.[2]

---

1. One passage from that Rosh Hashanah evening sermon is worth citing as reflection of the anguished outlook of someone beginning to question earlier pacifist assumptions, yet still unable to imagine the nature of the threat to European Jewry and the need for American military involvement to stop the Nazi onslaught:

> When I visited Danzig and Poland this summer, I wrote back and prophesied that war this autumn was inevitable. It was too late then. It is a terrible world indeed in which I, who hate the very word "war," looked upon war as the lesser of two evils—preferable to seeing civilization yield once more to the triumphal march of Nazi barbarism. This war had to come. The time to stop it was twenty years ago, but then men were unwilling to listen. . . .
>
> America owes it to herself and the world to stay out of this war. We can serve the cause of democracy best if we will preserve the principles of freedom and fellowship which today we possess almost alone among the peoples of the earth. The time will come when this war will be over. How it will end, no one knows. Who will be living and who will be dead, no one knows. But when it comes, America must be willing to take the leadership of the world on its path to peace. In the meanwhile, we must preserve the sanity which the world will need after its period of madness; we must preserve the spiritual ideals which the world will need after a period of brutality; we must preserve the breadth of vision which the world will need after a period of nationalistic hatred.

2. For a review of antisemitic expressions in American society during the 1930s, see Leonard Dinnerstein, *Antisemitism in America* (New York: Oxford University Press, 1994), 105–27. Father Charles Coughlin of Detroit was a charismatic figure whose radio addresses became more overtly antisemitic in the late 1930s. General George Van Horn Moseley was also known for consistently antisemitic statements. The German-American

Secondly, the doors of the world have been closed to the Jew. In former times, when Jewish life was crushed in one land, another stood ready to welcome them. So, for instance, after the Jewish massacres that accompanied the Crusades in Germany, Poland invited the Jews to settle in its towns. Perhaps the example closest to us was the great migration at the end of the nineteenth century, which found refugees from the pogroms of Eastern Europe in this haven of America. Today, the Jew knocks at the doors of the world in vain. The few who succeed in finding new homes only touch the surface of the problem. In essence, the world is shut to the Jew.

Sometimes when we discuss the Jewish problem in general terms in this way, we forget that we are dealing with human beings. And so perhaps I can best portray the tragedy of the Jew today through personalities I met this past summer.

The first I met in Danzig.[3] I had been in the same compartment with him on the train from Gdynia, but I had not dared to speak to him. Now as I got off the train, I felt confused. On every side there were Storm Troopers, and I did not know where to turn. Finally, I summoned up courage and turned to my aged traveling companion. "Perhaps you can help me," I said; "I am a tourist from America." "What is it?" he asked. I held my breath a moment. "You're Jewish, aren't you?" I asked. He looked at me strangely for a moment, as if uncertain whether he was being trapped. "Yes," he said, "I am a Jew." In a few moments we had taken care of the necessary details and had started out together on an inspection tour of Danzig, which has burned itself into my mind like a nightmare, the terror of which is softened only by the memory of the character of my newly made friend.

Fifteen years before he had been called to Danzig to assume the managership of a newspaper that had just been taken over by a famous German publishing company, the Ullstein Press. He had loved his work, and adored his wife, and they lived happily together in their own home. Now his wife was dead, his home was lost, his work was taken away; he was destitute and alone.

As we walked through the street we passed a group of young Nazis, who had apparently come on a pilgrimage excursion to Danzig. "They're really not bad-looking fellows," I remarked. "They're murderers," he answered, and something in his voice made me realize he knew whereof he spoke. We stopped for a moment in an old historic tavern for a drink of the famous Danzig *Goldwasser*.[4] Upstairs there was an exhibit of all the books and newspapers in which articles had been written about the tavern. He stopped in front of one, the *Danzi-*

Bund had organized a mass rally in Madison Square Garden in February 1939, with Nazi flags and banners proclaiming "Stop Jewish Domination of Christian America!"

3. Polish: Gdansk: an important port on the Baltic Sea, established as a "free city" in 1919, with a corridor to Poland that separated East Prussia from the rest of Germany. In 1939, Hitler demanded that the Danzig region be annexed to the Reich. This was Saperstein's first stop in Europe.

4. A highly reputed beer brewed in Danzig.

ger Zeitung. "That was my paper," he said, and there was infinite pathos in his voice.

After seeing the sights of Danzig until my head was swimming with swastikas and "Jews Not Wanted" signs,[5] he brought me to his room, a crowded, musty, tiny room in a dilapidated house. There, after a bite to eat, he showed me his treasures: the pictures of happier days—pictures in France, at the seashore, in the mountains of Switzerland. From all of them, the face of a woman looked up at me, stout, good-natured, smiling. "She was my wife," he said, "a *goyah* with a *yiddische neshomoh* [a Gentile woman with a Jewish soul]. She died two years ago of a broken heart, for she loved me with all her life. It's hard to be alone, but sometimes I'm glad she couldn't see all that's happened since."

He showed me more pictures. I saw his face shining forth at me. His voice was sad. "Then I used to smile," he said. "I was always smiling and she was always smiling. How happy we were together." My attention was caught by the cover on his large, overstuffed bed, a remnant of better days. On it was embroidered an inscription: *Zieh fröhlich heraus, komme glücklich nach Haus*, "Go forth in happiness, return home in joy." Once those words had meaning, I thought.

In the evening, he insisted that I go with him on the bus to Olivia, one of the suburbs of Danzig. We went for a walk. From the distance could be heard the sound of cannon. Probably military maneuvers, we thought; or maybe the war has already started. Suddenly he stopped in front of a house. "Here is where we lived for thirteen years," he said, the tears dripping down into his beard. When we parted, I wanted to thank him for all he had done for me. "What can I say to you?" I said. "What is there to say?" he answered simply. *Bruder seinen wir, beide b'nei Yisroayl.*"[6]

As I read the papers, I wonder if my old friend in Danzig is still alive. But after all, he is not unique. He is only one of millions whose lives have been destroyed, who live on in darkness except for the hope that comes from the realization that we, their more fortunate brothers, have not forgotten them. What had he done to deserve such a fate?

My other friend is a young Jew. I was at Alexandria, embarking on a ship, the *Cairo City*, en route to Marseilles. As I walked up the gangplank, I noticed a commotion in another part of the ship. Several of the crew were gathered threateningly around a boy, apparently about 19 years old, who stood backed against the rail. "If you give me over, I'll jump into the water," he said. "What's the matter?" I asked a bystander. "He's a refugee," he answered. "He stowed away on the boat. He's got money, but no papers." On my promise to the captain that I would be responsible for him, the boy was permitted to come to travel to Marseilles. Later, I got his story.

---

5. One of the sights that made the strongest impressions on him was of the great synagogue that had been destroyed by the Nazis the previous month. See "Undying Fires," below, n. 8.

6. "We're brothers, both of us Jews."

He had been a student in Vienna. At the age of 17, he was imprisoned in Dachau. One night, he was taken to the Yugoslavian border and secretly put across, with the warning never to return to Germany. Throughout the night he walked, and in the morning he was arrested by the Yugoslavian police, who brought him to the Italian border, where once again he was put across. After many adventures, he crossed back into Yugoslavia, walking at night and sleeping in fields. Helped with a little money from Jewish organizations he reached Bulgaria, then Turkey.

At Ankara he was imprisoned for three weeks. When he learned of a transport that was leaving with illegal immigrants for Palestine, he was permitted to embark. There were 200 people crowded on a 360-ton boat. They were treated like animals during a voyage of five weeks of indescribable suffering, with hardly any food or water. Finally, he landed in Palestine illegally, swimming to the coast at night. After almost a year in Palestine, he was arrested as an illegal immigrant and imprisoned at Akko. Finally he was brought to the Lebanese border and put across. Here once more he became familiar with the inside of a prison, this time in Beirut. Five times the police gave him the opportunity to escape as a stowaway on departing vessels. Four times he had failed, the fifth time he succeeded. The vessel was the *Cairo City*, and they had just discovered him as I walked up the gangplank.

This boy too is not unique. His fate could be duplicated by thousands who were trapped in the no man's land between Germany and Poland, by others compelled to sail the seas endlessly on refugee ships, seeking some haven that would accept them, by others set adrift on the Danube and not permitted to land on either shore. Many of the children born in no man's land were called *Niemand*, "Nobody," as an indication of the fact that there was no place where they belonged. What have these people done to make them outlaws in the eyes of the world? They had committed no crime. And yet they are men and women without a country. The only right the world will grant them is the right to leap into the sea and end it all.

There was a time when the Wailing Wall was localized in one particular spot in Jerusalem. Today, the Wailing Wall of Israel's tragedy has been extended until it reaches throughout the entire world.

What path shall we follow in this hour of darkness? Charity we have given. But charity is not enough. We must have a positive program. I like to think of the story in the Talmud about the Israelites as they went forth from Egypt. Before them was the Red Sea, behind them the pursuing Egyptian army. The people were terrified. Some yielded to despair. "Let us throw ourselves into the sea and end our sorrows," they said. Another group was ready to return to slavery. "Let us surrender to the Egyptians," they said, "and go back to Egypt." A third group, more courageous, said, "Let us shout and try to confuse the enemy with our noise." Others were in favor of meeting the enemy in battle. But Moses would not hearken to the counsel offered by his people. "O God, help Thy people in their hour of distress." And the voice of the Lord came to Moses. "Why dost thou cry unto Me? Speak to the children of Israel that they shall go forward" (Exod. 14:15). As they marched onward, the water that had seemed an insurmountable obstacle opened before them and became dry land.[7]

In that story of the Rabbis is contained the key of Jewish history. The Jewish people have never yielded to the counsel of despair, they have never permitted tragedy to become the totality of Jewish experience, they have insisted on marching forward despite everything.

Today, there are two fronts on which we can and must advance. The first is Palestine. I say this with full knowledge of all the difficulties in our path. I went to Palestine [this summer] with some apprehension about its future. I return with full confidence that Jewish Palestine will go on. Some other time I shall tell you more about my impressions. Now I shall merely tell you this: that Jewish Palestine is a reality which no force on earth—whether it be British politics or Arab terrorism—can stop or destroy. There are some who say that what we need is not one national home but a number of little national homes scattered all over the world. I know that Palestine cannot absorb all the refugees. No one knows more than I, after what I have seen in Europe this summer, how desperate is the need to find homes in any place and in any way for the millions of Jews whose homes have been turned into hells.

But the building up of places of refuge in the far-flung corners of the earth—in Africa, in Australia, in South America, in Alaska—important as this is, must not be carried out at the cost of Palestine. We must not permit our problem to degenerate into the throwing of bones to dogs; we must not permit ourselves to be dealt with like a band of refugee beggars.[8] We are not dogs or beggars. We are a people of human beings. And Palestine is necessary if the answer to the Jewish problem is to be consonant with our human dignity. There we see united the necessities of the present with the ideal of the future.

The second front on which we must advance is in the strengthening of our own Jewish life. There is no room any more for *parvah* Jews. Either you are *milchig* or you are *fleishig*. Remember this: that enemies can take everything away from us except for two things: our faith and our hope—our faith in the ultimate triumph of right and our hope for a better future. Without these, we are lost. With these we are unconquerable. And these find their expression in the synagogue. Jewish children will need the courage and loyalty which Jewish education alone can bring to them. Are we going to deny it to them? Jews will need

---

7. See Y. Ta'anit 5,2; *Mekhilta Be-Shallah* 3 (ed. Lauterbach, 1:214); Ginzberg, *Legends of the Jews* 7 vols. (Philadelphia: JPS, 1911): 3:15 and 6: 4–5. (The formulation here may have been influenced by a sermon by Morris Feuerlicht for Rosh Hashanah, 1933, called "Watchman, What of the Night?" published in *A Set of Holiday Sermons 5694–1933* [Cincinnati: The Tract Commission], 6–7.) Rhetorically, this midrash takes the place of the quotation from General Foch in the Rosh Hashanah, 1934 sermon. Compare the use of this rabbinic passage (somewhat modified), in the sermon for Rosh Hashanah evening, 1944 and for 1947. Note that Abraham Sachar used this aggadah to structure the concluding chapter of his *Sufferance is the Badge* (published in 1940, see 564–67), and he may also have used it before this publication.

8. Compare the formulation about Herzl in the 1938 sermon, with accompanying note.

the strength and inspiration that emanates from the synagogue. Shall we deny it to ourselves? No. Let us go forward—to a richer, more positive, more purposeful Jewish life. A new century is beginning.[9] New worlds are in the making. We Jews must not fall by the wayside.

My heart bled the other day as I saw the picture of the city of Cracow, the most beautiful and richly historic city in Poland, in flames.[10] I was reminded of the evening several months ago, when I visited the Yiddish theater in Cracow. The performance was Goldfaden's opera, "Bar Cochba."[11] You recall the story of that magnificent struggle for liberation which ended in defeat. I looked around and thought: How timely this drama is; these people are seeing the story of their own lives. When we came to the closing scene, to my amazement I saw that they had changed the text. Instead of ending on a note of tragedy, they had ended on a note of invincible courage.

The original closes with Bar Cochba taking his own life. Their new closing scene showed Rabbi Akiba, who had given his last strength to the revolt. Now he refuses to escape. "I know nothing better than to die," he said. "I am old. My work is finished. But you, my disciples, are young; you must live." "There is nothing to hope for," says Bar Cochba. "You must never lose hope," answers Akiba. "But what shall we do?" they ask. "Flee," says Akiba, "to the north and the south, the east and the west, to the farthest corners of the earth. They will strike you but they cannot destroy you. We shall be as the stars of the heavens. The Jewish people will live!" The curtain came down, and the audience rose to its feet in a tremendous ovation. They had heard a living message. And as they walked, they held their heads a little higher and their step was a little firmer. They saw a new vision of hope.[12]

Israel is shattered. But its spirit must remain firm. While at any one moment other things may prevail, in the final analysis it is the spirit that triumphs in history. The spirit of Israel is eternal. With God's help, it will march on, as it has through the centuries, unconquered.

---

9. Referring to the beginning of the Hebrew year 5700 at Rosh Hashanah.

10. Referring to a picture in the *New York Times*, September 12, 1939, A6, under the title, "Damage Caused by German Air Bombers and Artillery Fire."

11. Abraham Goldfaden (1840–1908) was known as the "Father of the Yiddish Stage." See Sol Liptzin, *The Flowering of Yiddish Literature* (New York: Thomas Yoseloff, 1963), 33–51 on "The Theatre of Goldfaden," esp. 48 on "Bar Cochba." Akiba is not even a character in the original play; the message seems to be that disaster came upon Bar Cochba and his people because he condemned the saintly leader of the Jewish "peace party" to death.

12. Saperstein's journal for the summer trip describes his visit to Cracow on June 27–28, including the Goldfaden opera, in phrases that are fleshed out in the above passage. Then comes his own notation: "(ch[eck] up on original—perhaps this has been changed). Here emphasized fighting & courage—drew tremendous ovation."

9

The World We Make (Introduction)
Sufferance Is the Badge
October 2 and 3, 1940
Rosh Hashanah

The spring and summer of 1940 were terribly demoralizing to the opponents of Nazism. After a period of relative quiet, Germany launched lightning attacks against Denmark and Norway in April, and against the Netherlands and Belgium in May. Only the saving of a large part of the entrapped Anglo-French armies at Dunkirk in the last days of May prevented a total disaster. Soon after, a massive assault overwhelmed the weakened French forces; France surrendered to Hitler on June 21. The conquest of most of Western Europe had taken only six weeks. Only Britain remained as a serious military power in opposition to Germany. After an abortive attempt to negotiate a separate peace, preparations began for the invasion of Britain.

The German air offensive against Britain began in mid-August, and the first bombing of London occurred on September 7—the most devastating air attack on a single city in history to that date. Bombs from an average of 200 bombers were dropped on London for fifty-seven consecutive nights. While the Royal Air Force had achieved some significant victories over the Luftwaffe, the mood among Jews at the beginning of Rosh Hashanah 5701 must have been truly bleak, bordering on panic and despair. The two sermons below do not attempt to conceal this mood. Like the sermons of previous years and the following one, they articulate these feelings, vividly describing the circumstances in London and for Jews in Eastern Europe, attempting to transcend them by identifying sources of strength within the Jewish experience. The appeal to history as evidence of Jewish survival despite the best efforts of the enemies is poignant, and was perhaps a source of reassurance. (Abram Sachar's book, Sufferance Is the*

Badge, *provided not only the title but also a major inspiration for the morning
sermon.) In retrospect the message seems in one sense to be validated, yet in
another sense still incapable of imagining how different the threat to European
Jewry would be from anything in the past.*

Rosh Hashanah Evening

WHILE WE ARE PRAYING HERE, BOMBS ARE FALLING on the city of London,
heroic citadel of human liberty and dignity. Jews in that city, if they can pray at
all, must pray in bomb-proof shelters deep under the surface of the earth. Fate
plays strange tricks. Four years ago, Dr. Wise called me into his office to ask me
if I would like to go to England. There was an opening for a Rabbi in a settlement house in the East End of London. The idea seemed enticing, but I decided
to remain in Lynbrook. The section of London in which I would have served had
I accepted has since been strafed by bombs again and again. I like to think that if
I had gone, I would have had the courage to remain and would even now be
preaching to my people there. But fate was kind and did not put me to the test.
So I am here where men are free, the skies are peaceful, gas masks are curios,
cellars places to hold parties, and a whole nation becomes concerned over the
fate of one little kidnapped child.[1]

Yet I must admit that in the seven years I have served this Temple, never
have I found myself in so difficult a dilemma at the High Holy Days. Frankly,
when I sat down to prepare my sermons, I was at a loss. What can a religious
leader say to his people in times like these, when ideals as well as worlds are
being shattered? Even we, who are supposed to preach certainty to others, find
ourselves stumbling and groping as if we were blind, for something to which we
might cling.[2]

---

1. This is the kind of allusion that everyone in the congregation would have recognized at the time but is totally unintelligible to later readers. On September 21, 1940, less
than two weeks before the sermon was delivered, the *New York Times* carried on its front
page a report of a three-year-old boy, Marc de Tristan, Jr., who was kidnapped in Hills-
borough, California. Front-page coverage continued for the next three days; the report of
the kidnapper's capture and the child's return unharmed appeared on September 23.

2. The following passage, crossed out in pencil in the original typescript, may not
have been actually said. I include it as an important reflection of the preacher's movement from the strong pacifist position held just a few years before. If not said here, it is
probably because of a judgment that it did not fit the flow of the argument:

> For years, as one who remembers the World War as a child and grew up in
> the post-war era, I have been preaching peace. You who have listened to me
> know that hatred of war has been one of the passions of my life. And yet I
> have come to realize that some things are worse than war, and some things
> are more important than peace. And so as I pray for peace, I find myself
> fearing a peace on Hitler's terms, a peace of submission to the forces of bar-
> barism. For I know that they would blot out everything that we, who look

It is no wonder that as never before, people have begun to lose faith. Where can God be, they ask, when the very heavens are crashing down around us? Angelo Patri, the noted educator and psychologist, tells the story of the little refugee boy, whose teacher asked the class to write a composition on the subject, "My House." His brow wrinkled, his lips puckered up, he hunched over his desk and wrote. After some moments he handed in his composition. "My house," he had written, "was a little house. It had pictures on the wall. My father and my mother lived in my house. I left my house and crossed the sea. I do not know where my father and my mother are. They do not know where I am. God, where are you?"[3]

That childish cry rings in the hearts of many of us on this Rosh Hashanah eve after the tragic first twelve months of the fifty-eighth century. Our spirits have not been tried by the necessity of finding refuge from the imminent danger of death in bomb shelters, or the need of sending tender children across war-infested seas. And yet we, too, need refuge. We must find some island within. We desperately require something unshakable, which will keep meaning in life for us even in this dark and distraught hour. That, I believe, is what people today need more than anything else. And so that, in general way, will be the theme of my High Holy Day sermons. Tonight I shall deal with the problem we face as individuals. Tomorrow morning I shall discuss it with reference to the fate of the Jewish people. . . .

Rosh Hashanah Morning

ONE OF THE GREAT HISTORIANS OF THE LAST CENTURY, writing the history of the Jews during the medieval period, was compelled to lay down his pen, for he was so blinded by tears that he could not continue. One feels very much the same in coming to review our history during the past generation. It is a story of heartbreak and sorrow, the sad saga of a people whose cup of suffering has been filled to overflowing. During the past year, the war has intensified the Jewish tragedy. I recall a little more than a year ago, at the World Zionist Congress in

---

upon men as the children of God, hold precious. We cannot live in a world of dreams. In times like these, long-cherished ideals must needs be reinterpreted in relation to reality."

3. Compare the somewhat more expanded version of this story used in a sermon for Yom Kippur evening, 1940, by Rabbi Sidney D. Tedesche: *A Set of Holiday Sermons, 5701–1940* (Cincinnati: The Tract Commission, 1940), 19–20. As that sermon was delivered after Saperstein's, both must have used a common source, perhaps written by Patri himself.

Geneva, after days of vehement debate on the problems of the Jews of Europe and Palestine, the news that war in Europe was but hours away immediately drove all other problems into the background.

We realized that this was the crisis in the disease of which the Jewish people were the victims, that we were destined to pass through a bitter period of pain and suffering, out of which the patient would emerge cured or crushed. I know, my friends, that others besides the Jews are suffering as well, that this is a period of universal calamity. Bombs crashing down from 10,000 feet in the air are no respecters of persons or races or faiths. Yet can we be blamed if, in a time of great disaster, we feel most keenly the hurt of those who are closest to us? We are all members of one human family. But within that family, the Jews are our nearest and dearest.

I shall not go into a catalogue of Jewish sorrows at the dawn of this New Year. God knows: if words are still needed, then words will never avail. If you do not feel the *herzveitik* [heartache] of the Jewish people now, then your heart is too insensitive ever to feel it. In Nova Scotia, during the summer, I visited the park at Grand Pré, scene of Longfellow's immortal story of Evangeline. My thoughts went back to that tale which we all remember from our schooldays, of a people rooted up from the soil over which they had struggled and labored to make for themselves a home, and driven thousands of miles away, parents separated from children, lovers parted, never to meet again. The experience of Evangeline is today so common that our sympathies have become almost immune. Today the fate of the Acadians is the fate of two-thirds of the Jewish people in the world. Other peoples at least can die in their homes and mingle the lifeblood pouring out of their wounds in the soil of the land that they have loved. But the Jews of Europe today, with fewest exceptions, have no homes.

Poland, once the center of traditional Jewish culture, is now a corpse picked clean by the Nazi and Russian vultures. Its three million Jews are homeless. The freedom-loving lands of Holland and Belgium, which once offered a haven for Jews driven from Spain, no longer proved a safe retreat for the Jewish refugees and residents who had escaped there from the Nazi tempest. Those who managed to find refuge in France had only a temporary breathing spell for their pains and for the risk of their lives. For within a few short weeks, the Nazi terror had again caught up with them. That is the fate of the Jews in the world today: to be harried, uprooted, as driven leaves blown by the wind.

And yet, my friends, at the dawning of this New Year, I dare to speak to you of courage. In "The Merchant of Venice," almost against his will, Shakespeare placed in the mouth of Shylock, after having reviewed the many wounds and indignities he had suffered, these ringing words of nobility and fortitude: "Still have I borne it with a patient shrug, for sufferance is the badge of all our tribe."[4] One of the foremost of American Jewish educators, Dr. Abram Sachar, has taken that phrase, "sufferance is the badge," very fittingly as the title of his recently published book on Contemporary Jewish History since the World War. For 2,000 years we have been able to withstand a war against our existence with

---

4. *The Merchant of Venice*, I,iii.

well-nigh superhuman endurance. How? Because deep down within our souls, in our memories, our faith, our hopes, were sources of strength with which our enemies did not reckon. These reservoirs of resistance are still potent; they are still the guarantees of our survival. They enable us in our own day to bear oppression beyond anything which history relates, still with a patient shrug.

What are these hidden sources of strength? First, there are the memories of our past, our living heritage. In time of affliction, the Jew has turned instinctively to his book, and the book has always proved mightier than the sword. For there in the scrolls of our history, when all other hope was lost, we could read the heart-warming tale of a people that remained magnificently and creatively alive under circumstances that, according to the ordinary laws of history, should have rung its death knell. Before our eyes, there would pass a procession of great-hearted and noble-spirited men and women who stood, like Jacob's ladder, their feet on the ground, but their heads lifted up to the stars. In our ears, there rings the heroic story of a people that has contributed richly to the world, even while it has suffered greatly from that world. It is a history comparable in sheer grandeur to that of any people on earth, and in comparison to which the much-vaunted Aryan tradition becomes the immature boasting of a people in its adolescence.

We, the Jews, accompanied Abraham to Mount Moriah, as he built the altar of his stern faith and of the ultimate sacrifice. We stood with Moses on Mount Sinai, heard the crash of the thunder and saw the flash of the lightning, as we witnessed the everlasting covenant between our people and its God. We stood with him again in his lonely vigil on Mount Nebo, as he surveyed the land upon which he was never to set foot, but wherein his people were to carry forth their magnificent destiny. We walked with the prophets and thrilled to their denunciation of oppression and injustice, wept over their infinite compassion for the weak and the wronged. We stood with Jeremiah as he watched the Temple go up in flames, his people carried into exile, and we drank from the well of hope as this man of sorrows prophesied that the Temple would be rebuilt. We sat with our people beside the rivers of Babylon, and tremblingly took the oath of deathless loyalty, "If I forget thee, O Jerusalem, may my right hand forget its cunning" (Ps. 137:5). We watched with choking hearts as Akiba ascended the funeral pyre with a smile on his lips to spend out his last breath in the affirmation of God.[5]

We wandered into exile with our people along weary highways, through many lands, hearkening as Yehudah Halevi sang his love of Zion, watching over the shoulder of Maimonides as he wrote his imperishable words. We drained sorrow's cup to its dregs as medieval Jews embraced death unflinchingly rather than betray their God. We stood on the windswept decks of ships with immigrants fleeing from lands of oppression, and tears of happiness glistened in our eyes as we saw the Statue of Liberty, symbol of new opportunity and freedom. We stood in the communes of the new Palestine and labored under fire, a trowel

---

5. B. Berakhot 61b.

in one hand, a weapon of defense in the other, raising new settlements on our "old-new land" in answer to the murder of our comrades.

All this lives on in us. In wartime, the first objective of an enemy is to smash the lines of communication: telephone systems, railroads, electric plants. This is the best way to throw a people into confusion and to paralyze their strength. The heritage of our history is our line of communication, connecting us with all the centuries that have gone before.[6] We must keep it open, for should it be destroyed, our strongest defense would be no more.

Our second source of strength is the realization of the nobility of the role we can play in the present world crisis. Our faith has always put its emphasis not on might nor on power, but on the spirit of the Lord. Its concern was never with the power of the state but with the dignity of the human being. Dispersed in every land, the underdog of every civilization, in every age of history we have been the bearers of ideals that more powerful and more favored nations saw fit to ignore. Recognizing in us their natural enemies, the forces of darkness have often sought to destroy us. We were always the first and worst victims when barbarism broke through civilization's thin veneer.

Once more, in the contemporary world, history has placed the Jew on the side of righteousness. Let me remind you that in the first Rosh Hashanah sermon I preached in this Temple, in the fall of 1934, I said, "This is not an attack upon the Jew alone, it is an attack upon all the Judaism stands for, all that religion stands for, all that civilization stands for."[7] We Jews stand in the vanguard of the battle for civilization. Ours is a dangerous but a glorious role. Again and again in Christian pulpits I spoke in the same vein, trying, not always with too much success, to make our neighbors realize that the attack on the Jews was only a surface sore, evidencing the cankerous disease working underneath.

Now at last the issue has been clarified. Side by side with us now stand whatever forces of decency there are left in the world. We still cannot see the end of our suffering. But our suffering is not meaningless. Our very existence is the denial of the principles of tyranny. We are still the bearers of an eternal ideal which, though the nations may deny it, the world still needs and will need more than ever when this war is over. As Thomas Mann, undoubtedly one of the greatest creative spirits of our generation, has said, "This old and much tried race with the very wisdom of its blood is called upon to contribute strongly and decisively to that building the outlines of which we can see today only vaguely

---

6. Compare Abram Sachar, *Sufferance Is the Badge* (New York: Alfred A. Knopf, 1940), 578.

7. See "A Call to Battle," from 1934, above: "Not only German Jewry, not only world Jewry, but civilization itself is under attack." The present quotation, however, seems more to reflect a sermon from Rosh Hashanah 1935, which says, "Not merely the Jewish people, but all that Judaism stands for, all that religion in its truest sense teaches, all that civilization represents—all these are threatened. The forces of war, hatred and tyranny, which are sweeping like wildfire over the world, represent their complete negation. Against them on this New Year's Day, civilization stands at bay." Perhaps there is a conflation here of the two.

and indistinctly, to the building of the future of mankind."[8] Yes, my friends, we have a purpose to fulfill through our existence. Therefore we must and shall survive.

Finally, we have a source of strength in our hopes for the future. It may seem strange to talk of the future when our present is so uncertain, but surely we, if any people, are entitled to take the long-term view of history. We Jews are an old people, and with our historic experience we have no right to yield to despondency. Persecution is nothing new to us. Louis Golding recently published a book called *Hitler Through the Ages*.[9] In it, he points out that the basic type of the anti-Semite has always existed. They have had different names in different lands and ages, but their theme has always been the same. They thought that they could destroy the Jew. But most of them are remembered today chiefly because history records the story of their failure.

Perhaps it seems that Hitler's regimented robots are sweeping the world before them. But can you imagine how dark it must have seemed when the Babylonians led the Jewish people into captivity, when Antiochus desecrated the Temple, when the mighty legions of Rome plowed under the city of Jerusalem and sowed it with salt, when the Crusaders practiced for the recovery of the Holy Sepulcher by slaughtering entire communities of Jews, when the Jews of Spain were driven from the land where they had lived in happiness for centuries, when the pogromchiks of Czarist Russia drenched the streets with Jewish blood unchecked?

Then too, people thought that the story of Israel was finished. But in each case, it proved only the end of a chapter. Our enemies have left their bloody trail behind and disappeared into the pages of history, while our children still sing in our religious school their simple song, "Am Yisrael Chai,"—the people of Israel lives, "ad beli dai"—without any end. In the historic cemetery at Newport, Rhode Island, which I visited this summer, the tomb of Judah Touro bears the epitaph, "The last of his name, he inscribed it in the book of philanthropy to be remembered forever."[10] This must refer to the "Touro," for the name "Judah" still continues.[11]

As we usher in this New Year, the skies are overcast and sorrow grips our souls. But the people of Israel need not lose heart. To Hitler and all his hosts, we can say, "You too will pass. But we will go on. For you are but men of the mo-

---

8. I have not been able to trace this precise quotation, but Mann wrote something similar a few months before this sermon was delivered: "We may all be certain that their [the Jews'] strong sense of this world, and of social justice, will play an important part in the upbuilding of a new humanity struggling slowly out of its crises." "Culture Against Barbarism," in *Contemporary Jewish Record* 3 (March–April, 1940), 118.

9. London: Sovereign Books, 1939.

10. Judah Touro's extraordinary will of 1854, bequeathing a total of $387,000 to various Jewish and non-Jewish philanthropic causes, can be found in *Documentary History of the Jews in the United States*, ed. Morris Schappes (New York: Citadel, 1952), 333–41.

11. That is, he was the last to bear the name Touro, but the name Judah, representing the Jewish people, lives on.

ment, and you have pitted yourselves against an enduring people.[12] We can afford to wait, confident that though times are evil, time is on our side. For we have a rendezvous with eternity, and those who build a timeless structure need not be impatient." In the mind of God, "a thousand years are but as yesterday, as a watch in the night" (Ps. 90:4). Unlike other peoples, we Jews have always placed our Golden Age not in the past but in the future. Ours still must be an unshakable optimism, the profound conviction that though it tarry, the Kingdom of God will some day be ushered in upon the earth, when all men shall be brothers, and man, the child of God, shall rise to the full height of his spiritual nobility.

Some months ago, a poem was printed in one of the current magazines, which expresses the faith by which we should enter this New Year:

> I pray you in this hour's confusion, go
> Not back into the old belief
> That all man's life is brutish, harsh and brief,
> And what has been always will be so.
> Earth has seen many a great hope's overthrow
> And many a noble dream go down in grief;
> Yet still persists the parable of the leaf
> That spring unfolds above the endless snow.
> Be not too sure that evil in this hour
> Has strength to make as nothing all our gain,
> And leave us naked to the whirlwind's wrath.
> Through earlier, darker days than these some power
> Deep down in man endured its night of pain,
> Then strode one footstep higher up the path.[13]

---

12. See Sachar, *Sufferance Is the Badge,* 580 (the last sentence of the book).

13. Checks in reference works for the first lines of poems and in periodicals including *New Yorker, Saturday Evening Post, Harper's,* and *Reader's Digest* for the late spring and early summer of 1940 have failed to yield the author of this poem or the place where it was published.

10

Undying Fires
September 22, 1941
Rosh Hashanah Morning

The textual and homiletical framework of this sermon, based on the popular
Hebrew-Yiddish song "Eli, Eli" (not the current song based on the poem by
Hannah Senesh) and its Biblical source in Psalm 22, was apparently drawn
from a sermon by the New York Rabbi Louis I. Newman, delivered on the even-
ing of Rosh Hashanah in 1940, and published in Volume II of his "Sermons and
Addresses," which Saperstein owned. In the typescript, after the quotation of Ps.
22:4-5, "(Newman)" appears. The historical "meat" of the present sermon,
however, is new, drawing at the beginning from the preacher's own experience,
and from the events of the year since the Newman sermon was delivered.

The German invasion of the Soviet Union, launched in June of 1941, brought
a dimension to the war for which the words "titanic struggle" (used below)
seem not a cliché but an apt description. While it was not yet known in the West
that Einsatzgruppen had already begun systematically rounding up Jews in con-
quered territory for mass murder by machine gunning, the devastating implica-
tions of more than a million additional Jewish civilians now coming under Ger-
man control were apparent to all who cared. Even more than the previous year,
there was a mood of confusion, devastation and despair. The sermon articulates
and confronts this mood directly, with the preacher including himself among
those in a state of spiritual disarray. It speaks to the sense of having been aban-
doned to the overwhelming power of the forces of evil, moving on to find sources
of uplift at a bleak hour.

A LITTLE MORE THAN TWO YEARS AGO, I was returning [to the United
States] from Europe. War had just broken out. Night after night, the *Queen
Mary*, pride of the British fleet, was dark. And the darkness reflected the mood

of the passengers. The usual gaiety of an ocean passage was absent. Our hearts were sorely troubled; some among us were obviously stricken with fear. By a strange accident of circumstance, two of the three passengers who shared my cabin with me were Christian ministers. And much of the time of the crossing we spent in our little cabin—secluded, closed in by our four narrow walls, talking. "What can we say to our people?" That was the problem that troubled us. The foundations of the world were being shaken. Did religion have any message for that day?

How much harder it is to know what to say now that two years of bitter struggle have passed. During this period, the war has steadily spread over ever vaster areas. One nation after another has been dragged into its vortex. Today, while we listen to the Shofar here, across the sea, people's ears are alert for the sound of air-raid sirens. While we are gathered in synagogues, at the Russian border, millions of men are engaged in desperate conflict on a battle front spreading over thousands of miles, a titanic struggle which leaves behind only the bodies of the dead and wounded and a scorched earth of utter destruction.

Now our own nation stands on the verge, and the events of any day may hurl us into active participation in this war, from which we have already recognized we cannot consider ourselves as isolated. During these two years, I, like many of my colleagues of all faiths, have had to search my heart, to reconcile conflicting ideals, to revise opinions which could be given up only after soul-rending inner struggle.[1]

But if all religious leaders find difficulty in knowing what to say, it is doubly difficult for a Jew. As always, our people have suffered in a two-fold capacity: as Jews, and as inhabitants of war-ridden countries. Their treatment wherever the Nazis have come—in Germany, Austria, Poland, Czechoslovakia, France, and the invaded portions of Russia—is a story of sheer barbarism for which there is hardly a parallel in all human history.[2] In addition, as in the last war, the great masses of European Jewry are trapped in the no-man's land be-

---

1. As noted in the Rosh Hashanah 1939 sermon, Saperstein's original stance after the outbreak of war was that the United States should remain out of it. In January 1941, in a sermon entitled "They Shall Not Die" about the devastation of Polish Jewry sixteen months after the Nazi invasion, the climactic appeal made to help save lives was for increased financial assistance from American Jews; apparently, he was not yet prepared to call for America to join the Allies in fighting against the Reich. Now, with the increasing likelihood of American entry into the war, and the increasingly bleak threat faced by European Jewry under Nazi domination, the pacifist position seems to have been fully abandoned.

2. At this point, there was still no policy of systematic murder of Jews except in the invaded portions of the Soviet Union. The first secret experimental gassings—of Soviet POWs and Polish Christians—were being conducted at Auschwitz in this very month. While British Intelligence knew of the Einsatzgruppen massacres in the Soviet Union, this information was not yet available to the public. Thus, ironically, the statement about unprecedented barbarism is made when what was truly unprecedented was just beginning.

tween the German and Russian armies, and as the conflict rages, it is over their communities that the great rival war machines sweep back and forth.

The words of what is perhaps the best known of all modern Jewish songs to Jews and Christians alike throb in our hearts: *Aylee, aylee, lomo azavtanee*—

> My God, My God, why hast Thou forsaken me?
> With fire and flame, mankind hath burned us.
> In every way and in every land have we been put to shame.
> Day and night I kneel and pray.
> Thou alone, O God, canst be our helper,
> Hear, O Israel, The Lord our God, the Lord is one.[3]

That is his only recourse: *Shema Yisrael*, faith in God. But we ask ourselves: is that faith warranted, or is it merely a vain delusion? Has God really forsaken us?

Let us go back to the original Psalm from which the title phrase of the song I cited is taken. In words that describe the eternal history of the Jew, and which seem to be written for our own time, the Psalmist of old continues,

> Trouble is near; there is no one to help.
> My strength is dried up like a potsherd.
> A company of evildoers have enclosed me,
> And Thou layest me in the dust of death (Ps. 22: 12, 16-17).

Yet bearing on his body the wounds inflicted by his assailants, he still affirms the sanctity of life and the goodness of God:

> Yet Thou art holy, O Thou that art enthroned upon the praises of Israel.
> In Thee did our fathers trust,
> They trusted and Thou didst deliver them (Ps. 22: 4-5).

Yes, Israel has suffered throughout its history. We are no neophytes in pain. We have been hammered into shape on the anvil of affliction through forty centuries. The significant thing is that we have never succumbed to suffering, we have never seen it as blind and purposeless.[4]

---

3. This plaintive Hebrew-Yiddish folk song was made popular by Cantor Joseph (Yossele) Rosenblatt, perhaps the most famous and popular cantor of the era, who recorded it and sang it frequently in concert. See *Concise Encyclopedia of Jewish Music*, ed. Macy Nulman (New York: McGraw Hill, 1975), 74.

4. The following passage may not have been included in the delivery, as there is an arrow in the margin from "blind and purposeless" to "Why have we suffered":

> Some of you must have seen the play "Journey to Jerusalem," by Maxwell Anderson. The scene was set in Palestine, when the Jewish people groaned under the yoke of Roman tyranny. One of the leaders of Jewish rebellion explains, "Our help must come from within, from our hearts, from those who are ready to die, rather than accept injustice." But his youthful questioner is not satisfied. "What of the visions of the prophets concerning the

Why have we suffered, why must we suffer? Because humanity has not yet extricated itself from the morass of barbarism. Because injustice and hatred and prejudice are not yet dead. Because with all our material progress, humanity is still taking its first faltering steps on the upward path to the kingdom of God on earth. So long as these things are true, we who have chosen to identify ourselves with the Kingdom must be the victims of the forces of darkness. We knew not what our fate would be. But of the righteousness of our cause we have had no doubt.

The Book of Daniel tells of the three Jewish youths, captives in Babylonia, who refused to worship the image set up by Nebuchadnezzar. Enraged, the king commanded that unless they yielded, they be cast into the fiery furnace. The young men answered, "If it be so, our God will deliver us from the burning furnace, O King. But if not,[5] be it known unto thee, O King, that we will not worship thy gods" (Daniel 3:17-18). In those three words, "but if not," is the great grandeur of the Jewish faith. We have never asked for exemption from pain. We have merely sought to serve the right. If God saw fit to redeem us, good, but if not, still we proclaimed His holiness, and gave allegiance to His ideals.

Like Job in the Bible, we have said, "Yea, though He slay me, yet will I trust in Him" (Job 13:15). And somehow, amidst it all, we have endured. The oldest inscription known to history mentioning the people of Israel proclaims that they have been utterly destroyed.[6] Yet Israel still lives on. And out of the scars of centuries of experience, out of a faith that no power on earth can destroy, out of undying hope planted in the hearts of our ancestors, we know still that Israel falls only to rise again, and that the cause of God's kingdom must ultimately triumph.

Once more we turn to the words of the Psalmist. He began, "My God, my God, why hast Thou forsaken me?" And he ends,

> All the ends of the earth shall remember and turn unto the Lord,
> And all the kindreds of the nations shall worship before Thee.
> For the kingdom is the Lord's
> And He is the ruler over the nations (Ps. 22: 28-29).

Kingdom of God?" he asks. He is told, "Their message may not come to pass for a thousand or ten thousand years. It may be," the old patriot continues, "that our race is chosen, our poor race of Israel, to suffer for other races on earth." And so it has been. It is all told in what is perhaps the greatest chapter of spiritual truth ever written, the 53rd chapter of Isaiah, where Israel is depicted as the suffering servant of God.

5. That is, "even if God does not deliver us and we must die."

6. Reference is to the famed "Mer-ne-Ptah Stela," dated ca. 1230 B.C.E., which contains the line, "Israel is laid waste, his seed is not." See James Pritchard, *Ancient Near Eastern Texts Relating to the Old Testament* (Princeton: Princeton University Press, 1955), 378a.

Here we find another indication of hope at the dawn of the New Year: the moral awakening of the nations. When the Nazi regime first came to power, the Jew stood alone. We called out desperately to the world, "Don't you see that we are a symbol of your own future? We are the first victims; we will not be the last. Can't you realize that this is a struggle against civilization, against religion, against humanity?" But there was no one to heed our cry. Aside from a few Christian liberals, the conscience of humanity remained undisturbed, It was as the temporarily stupefied Agrippa, the last king of Judah, during the siege of the Romans, said to his people: "You are the only nation in the world who think it a disgrace to be servants of those to whom all the world hath submitted."[7] In the beginning of the Nazi regime, though all the world found it easy to reconcile itself to the existence of evil and barbarism, the Jew—partly because he was its worst victim, and partly because of his heritage—realized that this was a life and death struggle between two ways of life which could not exist side by side in the same world.[8]

Today the situation has changed. The democratic nations at last realize what is at stake, and they are facing reality with stubborn determination and unparal-

---

7. Josephus, *The Jewish War*, Book II, chapter 16, part of an extensive oration by Agrippa urging moderation (or appeasement). Saperstein's text was *The Works of Flavius Josephus*, trans. and ed. William Whiston, 2 vols. in 1 (Philadelphia: Lippincott & Co., 1874); the quotation is in vol. 2, 269.

8. Saperstein would later illustrate this confrontation by recalling the sight of the ruined synagogue of Danzig from his 1939 visit. Following is the text of an address he gave over U.S. Army radio in January 1944:

> It had been one of the most beautiful synagogues in Europe. Now it was completely demolished. Not one stone left standing upon another except for the entrance arch. Nearby was a sign, which had not yet been removed although its hate-impregnated prophecy of the impending destruction had already been fulfilled: *Komm lieber Mai*, it read, *und mache von Juden uns jetzt frei*—"Come, O month of May, and make us free from Jews." . . . Then I noticed something else. Carved into the stone of that entrance portal was an inscription, a quotation from the prophet Malachi, in Hebrew and in German translation, so that the barbarians who had destroyed that house of God could read it even though its meaning never sank into their hearts. It read, *Halo ov echod lechulonu, halo ayl echod boro'onu*, "Have we not all one Father, hath not one God created us?" (Mal. 2:10). As I looked, I realized that these two signs represented the essence of the conflict that was rapidly coming to a head. They stood for two ways of life that could not survive together in our world. . . .

For a stunning photograph of the Nazi sign in front of the synagogue, see *Danzig 1939: Treasures of a Destroyed Community* (Detroit: Wayne State University Press, 1980), 8. See also photographs of the *Jüdisches Gemeindeblatt* announcing the final worship service in the Great Synagogue on April 14, 1939 (139), and of the dismantling of the synagogue by the Nazis (11).

leled heroism. Despite what American Quislings[9] may say, President Roosevelt spoke the mind of America last week when he took the step which cleared the mist and gave us one clear-cut national purpose: to see that Hitler and his principles are not victorious in the world. "The Nazi danger to our Western world has long ceased to be a mere possibility," he said. "The danger is here now, not only from a military enemy, but from an enemy of all law, all liberty, all morality, all religion."[10]

The same change is evident in nations abroad, which have already been conquered by the Nazi hordes. The Talmud describes the punishment of those who brought strange fire to the altars of God in the words, *serefat neshamah, ve-guf kayam*, "the spirit was consumed, but the body remained."[11] That sentence describes the condition of the world in recent years. When the policy of appeasing evil was accepted in England while it gave lip service to idealism and religion, when France was tragically betrayed in battle by its own leaders and when, a few months ago, the Vichy government capitulated to the principle of collaboration with the Nazis[12]—they thought they were safeguarding their physical existence, but they were undermining their souls. The first was a blot on a great English heritage which goes back to the Magna Carta, the second was unworthy of a nation in whose history was enshrined the principles of "Liberty, Equality, Fraternity."

Since then, England and France, like the other nations of Europe, have paid the price. England has taken a terrific bombardment. Ancient landmarks have been razed to the dust. But through it all, England stood gloriously, thumbs up, in a symbol of defiant courage, evidence of the fact that the spirit of England is not dead. France has been laid prostrate. It has known the agony of national enslavement. Its people must look upon the victorious banners of an enemy. But in recent months, the spirit of unrest has been sweeping through France and other conquered nations. Daring exploits like that of the young men whose story was told in the press a few days ago, who crossed the English Channel in frail canoes to join the Free French forces[13]—all those seething forces of rebellion symbol-

9. Vidkun Quisling, prime minister of Norway during the Nazi occupation, was known for his collaborationist policy, and his name became synonymous with treacherous appeasement, here applied to the Isolationists.

10. This quotation is from Roosevelt's "Fireside Chat on National Defense" of September 11, 1941. See *The Public Papers and Addresses of Franklin D. Roosevelt*, 12 vols., 1941 (vol. 10), 389.

11. B. Sanh. 52a and parallels. Compare the use of this statement in a 1919 sermon by Israel Levinthal, published in *Steering or Drifting—Which?* (New York: Funk & Wagnalls, 1928), 99-110. Saperstein thought of Levinthal as a master preacher.

12. This undoubtedly refers to the new Vichy legislation, the *Statut des juifs*, promulgated in June 1941 and intended to appease the Germans by purging Jews from the professions, commerce and industry. See Michael Marrus and Robert Paxton, *Vichy France and the Jews* (New York: Basic Books, 1981), 98–106.

13. *New York Times*, September 18, 1941 (three days before the sermon was delivered), 1, col. 4: "Five French Lads Cross Channel in Canoes and Land in England to Join de Gaullists."

ized by the V-for-Victory campaign—give evidence to the fact that the real France still lives and will live, that people with a heritage of freedom will not permit themselves to be permanently enslaved, that the essential spirit of humanity is still unconquered. The Talmudic phrase can now be reversed—*serefat guf, veneshamah kayemet*, "the body has been consumed—brutally beaten—but the spirit still survives—is still unconquered.

No, my friends, God has not forsaken us.[14] Twenty-five years or so ago, H. G. Wells wrote a novel called *The Undying Fire*. The world then, like now, was in the midst of a terrible war, a period of travail and agony. In this book, the hero, Job Huss, like Job of old, is put to the test of pain and tragedy in order to see if he will cast out the spirit of God when his hopes are ruined and his skies blackened. Responding to the ancient query, has God forsaken mankind, the hero of this novel says,

> There burns an undying fire in the hearts of men. By that fire I live. By that I know the God of my salvation. His will is truth and service. He urges me to conflict, without consolations, without rewards. He suffers—perhaps to triumph—and we must suffer and find our hope of triumph in Him. He will not let me shut my eyes to sorrow. Though the universe torment and slay me, yet will I trust in him.[15]

My friends, Job has become mankind. That undying fire will never be extinguished. Let it burn on in our hearts as well. Let us face the New Year with faith in God and with hope for the future, confident that God has not forsaken our generation and that, though all seems darkness, in the blackest hour of night, the dawn cannot be far off.

---

14. The following passage was probably not included in the delivery, as it is crossed out. "God has not forsaken us" is then written in pencil before "Twenty-five years or so ago":

> A dear Christian colleague, Reverend Weiss, formerly of Valley Stream [Long Island], whom many of you may remember, now a chaplain in the service of his country, recently sent me as a gift a little book called "Things Which Cannot Be Shaken" by a group of Christian religious leaders. One of them says something that I think we can all take to heart. "Evil can tear up photographs. God holds the negative. When evil has done its worst, men will begin to translate into terms of human fellowship and action the dream which dwells immortal and secure in the heart of God."

15. Compare H. G. Wells, *The Undying Fire* (New York: Macmillan, 1919), 132. The quotation may have been taken from the end of the Newman sermon.

11

The Mount of Sacrifice
September 11, 1942
Rosh Hashanah Evening

The year between the High Holy Days of 1941 and of 1942 continued the spread of the war and intensified the suffering of European Jews. The most decisive change for the Lynbrook congregation was the American engagement, following the Japanese attack at Pearl Harbor, followed a few days later by Germany's declaration of war against the United States. Yet it was clear that the United States was not yet ready to turn the tide, and the war continued badly for the Allies. Despite severe reversals suffered on the Eastern Front during the winter of 1941-1942, the Germans launched major new offensives during the spring and summer, culminating in a dramatic victory by Rommel in North Africa and advances threatening Stalingrad in southern Russia. As William Shirer wrote, "By the end of the summer of 1942, Adolf Hitler seemed to be once more on top of the world."

The news about European Jewry was unremittingly bleak. In June, radio broadcasts and newspapers carried reported announcements from the Polish Government in Exile of mass murder, totaling some 700,000 Polish Jewish victims to date. During the summer, the deportations from the Warsaw Ghetto began, and—in some ways even more distressingly—from France. A mass rally at Madison Square Garden was held on July 21, the day before the eve of Tisha be-Av, in which the atrocities were denounced. But the only realistic response seemed to be a threat of retribution to the perpetrators following the eventual defeat of Germany, and in the meantime, maximum support of the Allied war effort.

In trying to make sense of the disaster and find some basis for reassurance, the Rosh Hashanah sermon turns to the Biblical archetype for Jewish sacrifice, the account of the Binding of Isaac read from the Torah during the holy day observance. It is linked with experiences of martyrdom in earlier Jewish history and in the recent past, and explained by the claim that Jews suffered because they stood for values that the forces of tyranny could not abide. There was no evidence yet that the struggle would be readily won. The source of encouragement, coming at the end, is that it has now become a World War, that nations all over the world are joining in the conflict against German and its allies. This argument is quite a reversal from those used by the pacifist just five years earlier, and who still believed after the war began that the United States should remain outside the arena of battle.

ANOTHER ROSH HASHANAH HAS COME. The sun has set, and we gather in the House of God as we have done very year. We substitute a new Jewish calendar for the old as we have done every year. But something is not the same as it has been every year. My first Rosh Hashanah in this pulpit was the first after the accession of Hitler to power—and so, we have never known a Rosh Hashanah together that was not fraught with tragedy and foreboding. But this year is different. This year, our beloved nation is at war. In this year, everything we cherish is at stake. Something within tells us that when this year is over, its record will stand as one of the great milestones of human history.

We do not need to look at the past for great events. The greatest the world has ever known are taking place right now, and we are actors in them. There is a legend in the Midrash that a second flood would sweep over the earth even as did the flood in the time of Noah, but this would be a flood not of water but of fire.[1] And man is bidden to write on clay tablets, which are not destroyed by fire, but grow harder and more enduring. Ladies and gentlemen, the flood of fire is rising over the world. Every year we inscribe our prayers in the plastic clay of our hearts. This year, they will be burned indelibly by the fire through which we must pass.

Tradition has associated with this Holy Day the Biblical story of the sacrifice of Isaac, which will be read at our services tomorrow morning. This brief and poignant epic is a stirring example of Biblical style, wherein each word carries with it a picture, and in a brief span of twenty sentences we read a story which has become the prototype of the crucial testing which humanity must periodically undergo.

Let me review the familiar tale with you. Abraham had gone forth from his native land and his father's home as a spiritual pioneer. Against the immoral and degraded paganism of his day, he stood as the bearer of a higher vision—the vision of the one true God. Wandering from land to land, he gathered a group of followers about him. Only one thing was lacking, and that was a son—one who

---

1. Genesis Rabbah 49,9, B. Zev. 116a, and parallels. In these versions, however, the possibility of a new "flood of fire" is raised but rejected as inconsistent with God's promise. I am not familiar with a version including clay tablets. Compare the sermon for Rosh Hashanah evening 1942 by Rabbi Abraham Feinberg, published in *A Set of Holiday Sermons, 5703–1942* (Cincinnati: The Tract Commission, 1942), 10.

would inherit his mission and hold aloft the torch he had kindled. Then his prayer was answered; in their old age, Abraham and Sarah were blessed with Isaac, their only son, who grew into a fine and noble youth and walked in the footsteps of his father. Abraham was content. His cup of joy was filled.

Then the tragic summons came to the patriarch: "Abraham, take thou thy son, thine only son, Isaac, whom thou lovest, and offer him as a sacrifice upon the mountain which I shall point out to thee" (Gen. 22:3). We sense him torn between two great loyalties—his attachment to the human being who embodies all that he personally cherishes most on earth, and his duty to fulfill the will of God. But he makes his choice and sets forth on his tragic journey with his son. They proceed to the mount of sacrifice.

Berdichevski, one of the most stimulating of modern Hebrew writers, points out that there are indications that in the ancient sources from which this tale developed, Isaac was actually killed. But the nameless souls who fashioned the Bible into the form we possess transformed tragedy through faith, and fashioned the story's ending to indicate that the sacrifice of Isaac was forestalled.[2] God had demanded much from Abraham; great indeed had been his sacrifices in the service of the Lord. But this ultimate comfort would be his. Now he knew that his cause would not die with him. After him would be the one to carry on the line of spiritual succession and bring the basic truth of religion to generations yet to come.

An old rabbinic saying points out that the lives of the patriarchs are in a sense symbolic of the history of Israel.[3] In this story of Abraham we see the symbol of Israel's tragic role through the generations, with its commingled sacrifice and hopeful grandeur. Again and again, Israel has heard the divine challenge: "Root thyself up from thy native land and go forth to the land which I shall show thee"—and picking up his wanderer's staff, he has set forth. Again and again he has heard the soul-searing words: "Take that which is dearest to thee and offer it upon the mount of sacrifice to prove thy faithfulness to thy God." And each time Israel has not drawn back. Only one thing was granted to him. Grievous though his sacrifice, his faith and cause did not perish, there were ever those who could carry on as his spiritual descendants.

You who have studied the history of our people know the story—the most dramatic and tragic and glorious story in the world, the story of a people that willingly paid the price that it might keep something which was beyond price. Hannah watched each of her sons in turn face the tyrant, encouraged them to

---

2. For the references in *Sinai und Gerizim* and *Me-Otsar ha-Aggadah* by Micha Josef Bin Gorion (Berdichevski), see Shalom Spiegel, *The Last Trial* (Philadelphia: JPS, 1967), 125. Saperstein was undoubtedly led to these passages by Spiegel, his teacher of Hebrew literature at the Jewish Institute of Religion, under whose direction he did a rabbinic thesis on Berdichevski's use of rabbinic aggadah.

3. *Ma'aseh avot siman le-vanim* ("the deeds of the fathers are a sign [or type] for their descendants"): Gen. Rabbah. 40,6 and frequently elsewhere in rabbinic literature. On this principle of interpretation, see Amos Funkenstein, *Perceptions of Jewish History* (Berkeley: University of California Press, 1993), 98–121; Marc Saperstein, *"Your Voice Like a Ram's Horn"* (Cincinnati: HUC Press, 1996), 24–35.

accept death rather than spiritual surrender, and she blessed the name of God.[4] Akiba donned the cloak of martyrdom rather than ceasing to teach the faith, and from the midst of the flames proclaimed the Shema.[5]

One word from the Jew in the Middle Ages might have meant immunity from death.[6] Yet rather might his tongue cleave to the roof of his mouth than that word be uttered. Thus did Heinrich Heine describe them, "Like a ghost keeping watch over a treasure that had been entrusted to it during life, so in its dark and gloomy ghettos sat this murdered nation, this specter people, guarding the Hebrew Bible."[7] A specter people perhaps, yet one that remained ever capable of renewed and vibrant life. They gave up everything, *al kiddush hashem*, for the glory of God's name, and from that act of sanctification took unto themselves something, which was imperishable.

Our own generation has enacted a terrible chapter in this story. The present war did not begin last December for us. It began with the first World War in 1914, continued almost unabated after the Armistice, and reached in 1933 a climax, which has since risen to greater and greater intensity. The world has been stirred by the fate of Lidice, the little town in Czechoslovakia that the Nazis sought to destroy, in retribution for the assassination of the Nazi hangman Heydrich. "Total annihilation" was the phrase they used. But the result was the opposite of what they intended. Lidice in Czechoslovakia was leveled to the ground.[8] But Lidice was not destroyed. It was built into the hearts of millions of

---

4. See II Maccabees, chap. 7 (which does not give a name for the mother), b. Gittin 57b and parallel rabbinic sources, all discussed in Gerson Cohen, *Studies in the Variety of Rabbinic Cultures* (Philadelphia: JPS, 1991), 39–60.

5. B. Berakhot 61b.

6. See Judah Halevi, *Kuzari* IV, 23: "the prominent men amongst us who could escape this degradation by one word spoken easily and thus become free men."

7. *Heines Sämtliche Werke*, ed. Ernst Elster, 7 vols. (Leipzig and Vienna, 1898), 4:197; cf. Israel Tabak, *Judaic Lore in Heine* (Baltimore: Johns Hopkins Press, 1948), 35, 242. The idea of the Jews treasuring and preserving the Bible in the ghetto is common in his writing; see, e.g., Hugo Bieber, *Heinrich Heine: A Biographical Anthology* (Philadelphia: JPS, 1956), 430–31, 435; S. S. Prawer, *Heine's Jewish Comedy* (Oxford: Clarendon Press, 1983), 610, 611, 622. The idea of the "specter people" (*Volk-Gespenst*) is not.

8. On June 10, 1942, in retaliation for the fatal wounding on May 27 of Reinhard Heydrich, head of the Reich Security Main Office and the Gestapo, Germans murdered all 192 adult men in Lidice and 71 women, deporting 198 women and 98 children, and burning the village to the ground. Compare Stephen S. Wise's reaction to this based on contemporary reports, in *As I See It* (New York: Jewish Opinion Publishing Corporation, 1944), 120–21: "Not since November 10, 1938, the date of the burning of the synagogues throughout Germany and Austria, or December 7, 1941, had a gasp of horror gone around the world such as greeted the ghastly news of Lidice. Mankind felt that a deed had been committed to the shame of which men had not before stooped." He goes on to cite Goebbels' threat that if bombings such as that of Cologne continue, Jews will be held responsible, and the Jews of Europe would be "utterly exterminated." Wise then notes, "The world seemed rather less moved by this unspeakable threat than by the more dramatic extirpation of the village of Lidice, even as it too long remained unmoved by myriad

freedom-loving people throughout the world. It was built into the homes of scattered little communities in lands of freedom who took over the very name as symbol that Lidice had not perished.

We Jews, unheralded, have had thousands of Lidices.[9] Community after community has been destroyed; communities I know, where I walked, talked, and worshipped, now have not a single living Jew. The expressed purpose of the Nazis has been the complete elimination of the Jews from Europe. Fortunately, there are limits to the human imagination. For if we really comprehended what the news items reveal of the unending exile and deportation, the pitiless scourges of famine and disease bound up with ghettoization, the ruthless slaughter, we could no longer eat or sleep. We would not be human if we could ever laugh again. And yet the news reports are understatements of the reality.[10]

Why? What is the meaning of this sacrifice we were singled out to make? Abraham has had to climb the mount of sacrifice once more with his beloved son. It is the price of faith, it is the offering that we who have chosen to be the servants of God must bring. It was not blind chance, which selected us as the first and worst victims of the forces of evil in the world. It was because we stood for something, which they could not tolerate. We stood for the freedom of the human soul and the value of the human personality. We stood for the fatherhood of God and the brotherhood of man. Our very existence was their greatest challenge.[11] The yellow badge, which singled out those who must climb to the mount of sacrifice, was an emblem of honor.

In a recent radio broadcast, Joseph C. Hyman, executive chairman of the Joint Distribution Committee, said, "My work has taken me to places like Warsaw, Bialystok, Cracow, Lemberg, Berlin, Paris, to practically every section of the pale of Jewish suffering. Sometimes when I get home and talk it over with my youngest son, he asks, 'Is the whole story of what is happening to our people so sad? Isn't there anything comforting or inspiring?' And I tell him that to me the whole experience is one of tremendous inspiration. I tell him that the Jewish

---

anti-Jewish atrocities of earlier years. Ought not this threat give the united and civilized nations pause?"

9. Compare Wise, *As I See It*, 123 (his speech at the Madison Square Garden rally on July 21, 1942): "There have been a thousand and more Lidices in the life of the Jews of Central and Eastern Europe in the last year."

10. For "news reports" beginning in late June 1942 of mass murder of Polish Jews, based on the detailed report of the Jewish Bund to the Polish Government in Exile in London, see Martin Gilbert, *Auschwitz and the Allies* (London: Michael Joseph, 1981), 39–49), David Wyman, *The Abandonment of the Jews* (New York: Pantheon, 1984), 23–29. For reports on the deportation of Jews from France, see Wyman, 37–38. In September, Wise, who had received at the end of August a copy of the "Riegner cable" reporting a Nazi plan to annihilate all of European Jewry, could write to his friend the Rev. John Haynes Holmes that "I am almost demented over my people's grief."

11. While this idea is not uncommon in these sermons or in the liberal literature of the time, a card in Saperstein's homiletical file suggests a source in John Macmurray's *The Clue to History* (New York: Harper & Brothers, 1939), 226–67.

people I have met in Germany, Russia, Austria, Palestine and our own country are knit together in an invisible bond of such spiritual brotherhood that in all the blood-stained pages of history that bond has not been broken." It was ever, my friends, a brotherhood that learned how to live so as not to be afraid to die, that could say, "The Lord is my light and my salvation; of whom shall I be afraid?" (Ps. 27:1).

But in the last few years, something new has happened. That spiritual brotherhood is no longer confined to Jews. It has expanded until it embraces all the forces of civilization and decency and humanity. Country after country has been overrun by violence and enslaved by a tyrannical conqueror. Country after country has been compelled to take up arms in defense of its existence, its people and its way of life. No longer do Jews march alone to the mount of sacrifice. They are now the battle-scarred veterans in a vast army of those who hate tyranny and love freedom and dream of a better world.

It includes the valiant people of China who, cast down to the earth, spring up again with redoubled determination. It includes the heroic people of Russia who this very night are fighting desperately along the far-flung battle line to hold back the avalanche of the invader. It includes the battered remnants of the free fighting forces of a dozen nations who have refused to recognize defeat, and those millions of others who are patiently and courageously preparing at home for that great day when they will rise once more against their oppressors. It includes the citizens of noble England who stood in the breach for years and showed that free men can take it thumbs up. It includes our own beloved country, spared until recently, whose modern Isaacs have gone forth gladly to show by valor on land and sea and in the air that the spirit which made this country is not [dead].[12]

---

12. The final page of sermon is, unfortunately, missing. It seems near the end at this point, lacking possibly one final homiletical coda.

12

What Have We Jews to Be Thankful For?
November 27, 1942

Between the High Holy Days and Thanksgiving of 1942, the news of the fate of European Jewry had become even bleaker. On November 25, the New York Times *carried a report from the Polish Government in Exile in London of a Himmler order to kill half the remaining Jewish population of Poland by the end of 1942, a first step toward complete liquidation. Information about mass murder already committed included machine-gunning killings by "a special battalion under the command of S.S. men" (the* Einsatzgruppen*) and cramming Jews into freight cars for deportation to Treblinka, Belzec and Sobibor, where survivors from the journey are massacred. A* Times *article on the following day (p. 16) amplified this by reporting the death of one million Polish Jews, the deportation of Jews to Poland from other European nations, and murder by "mass electrocution."*

On November 24, Rabbi Stephen S. Wise held a press conference in Washington, stating that he had learned "through sources confirmed by the State Department that half of the four million Jews in Nazi-occupied Europe had been slain." This was the first occasion on which he was authorized to disclose publicly the now famous Riegner cable dispatched from Switzerland the previous August, communicating information about a German plan to liquidate all the Jews in Europe in one massive, coordinated blow. American authorities had requested that Wise not publicize this until confirmation could be received, and Wise acceded. The dismal news was carried in a subsidiary notice in the Times *on November 25.*

On the other hand, the Allied war effort showed some early signs of reversing the Nazi onslaught. Anglo-American troops first landed in Morocco and Algeria in early November. A front page Times *article on November 12, under the sub-headline "Casablanca Yields," stated, "By a bold and well-planned stroke the war has reached a turning point where, for the first time, Reichs-*

*fuehrer Hitler is forced into defensive action that stretches his forces in a way
that he had neither planned nor timed." More important, the Russians launched
a counter-offensive at Stalingrad beginning November 19. The New York Times
coverage from November 24 until the day of the sermon was filled with indications of a potential German disaster in the making.*

*These developments served as the background for the post-Thanksgiving day
message, which serves as important evidence for the ambivalent mood at this
critical juncture: the anguish of alarming new revelations of Nazi atrocities, and
the exhilaration produced by the first encouraging reports of Allied advances. It
contains a clear statement of the recognition—in conflict with the pacifist sermons of the 1930s—that the only way to stop the mass murder of European Jews
is by the quickest and most decisive possible military defeat of the Nazi state and
its war machine.*

"WHAT HAVE WE JEWS TO BE THANKFUL FOR?" is my theme for tonight. If it
had been "American Jews," the answer would be easier. Our reasons for thank-
fulness are obvious. We can be thankful that we live here, that we have freedom
and security and a remarkable degree of material plenty, things which are scarce
and doubly precious in the world today. In other words, we can be thankful that
our parents or grandparents had the foresight or luck to migrate to this country,
that they did not miss the boat, as some of their brothers and sisters and cousins
did.

But my subject is not "*American* Jews," but "*Jews.*" And certainly it would
seem as though just at this time there would be very little to say on that subject.
During the last few days, the papers have given the general public information
about what has been happening to the Jews of Nazi-occupied Europe. To me,
this information was no shock. As one who is continually in touch with Jewish
life, reading reports of various Jewish organizations, the horrible things stated in
the papers were long familiar. How many times have I spoken to various groups
and said that if I should tell all that I have learned about what is happening to
our Jewish brethren across the seas, it would be a story so horrible that you
could not believe it. And if we did believe it, we could only thank God that
sometimes we are able to forget, because otherwise no Jew knowing these things
could eat or sleep or laugh again. I have said that outside of the casualties on the
Russian front, the suffering of the Jews of Europe exceeds that of all other people combined. They suffered not only as conquered nations, but doubly, because
they were Jews, victims of the diabolical plan of extermination by the Nazis.

Further I did not speak. But the news reports of the last few days have carried the story of what I might have told you: of Jews used as guinea pigs for
testing poison gasses, of Jews as victims of mass electrocutions, of countless
new and ingeniously contrived methods of killing people, buried by the thousands in mass graves.[1] And even their dead bodies did not remain inviolate; they

---

1. Mass electrocution, which turned out to be inaccurate as a technique of mass murder, appeared in the report of the Polish Government in Exile from November 24, de-

were being used, believe it or not, to supply some of the lubricating oil which the Nazi war machine so badly needs.[2] All history has not known anything so fiendish. As we read these reports, we can well ask, "What have we Jews to be thankful for?"

First, then, let me say that in this situation of unprecedented tragedy, we can be thankful for the faith of the Jews of Eastern Europe who are suffering and dying. Do not misunderstand: I do not say that suffering and death are good. But when suffering and death are inevitable, it is easier and nobler to die with faith than without it. The Jews of Nazi-occupied lands are victims of a monster of evil that has spread its sway over a great part of Europe. No appeals to mercy or human conscience will save them, no international diplomacy will save them, only one thing will save them, and that is the defeat and destruction of the monster itself.[3] Until that defeat is engineered, Jews will die—by the hundreds of thousands and the millions—until those left in those countries that were once the richest springs of Jewish culture and learning are decimated and reduced to a remnant of those who once lived.

What a terrible tragedy it would be if they died, when die they must, with a sense of futility and meaninglessness—like rats cornered in a trap. But if you knew these East European Jews, if you had seen them, you would have confidence that they at least know how to die. They may be dressed in outlandish garments, with long beards and *payis* [sidelocks], they may not all be overly clean, their bodies may be bent and broken from privation and suffering, but they have in their eyes and their hearts a dignity and strength that might inspire us all. They know that though they die, the cause of human freedom and of God's kingdom does not die with them. They know that there are things more precious than life, and foremost among these is the purity of one's immortal soul and the steadfastness of one's conscience. When they die, they die with the Shema on their lips, for they know that ultimately wickedness must perish, and truth must triumph, and those who die *al kiddush Hashem* are eternally blessed.

That is the spirit of martyrdom we Jews have learned through centuries of history. In the time of the Maccabees, Hannah saw her seven sons choose death

---

scribed in detail in the *New York Times*, November 26, 1942, 16, as having occurred in Belzec. On this report, based on the eye-witness account of Jan Karski, see Martin Gilbert, *Auschwitz and the Allies* (London: Mitchell Joseph, Rainbird, 1981), 93–95.

2. Wise was paraphrased in the *Times* article of November 26, 16, as saying the State Department documents included affidavits about "such atrocities as turning Jewish bodies into fats and soap and lubricants." For a fascinating account of this report reaching Wise, who disclosed it to Sumner Welles, who checked with sources in the Vatican, from which it leaked back to Himmler, who in turn sought to verify from the Reich Security Main Office that this was *not* true, see Richard Breitman, *The Architect of Genocide: Himmler and the Final Solution* (New York: Alfred A. Knopf, 1991), 6 and 251–52, n. 5.

3. This echoes the position taken by Wise in a mass rally at Madison Square Garden on July 21, 1942, in which he said that "the salvation of our people and all peoples who would be free can only come under God through a victory speedy and complete of the United Nations [referring to the Allies]"—*As I See It* (New York: Jewish Opinion Publishing Corporation, 1944), 123.

rather than betray their faith and retain an ignoble and cowardly life.[4] Only last Wednesday, in a class on literature that I am reading with our High School group, we studied the story of the massacres of 1648 at the hands of the Cossack leader Chmielnitzki. Fifteen hundred Jews were gathered in the city of Tulchin, and there they were massacred. But to the amazement of their captors, they showed no fear but joy, as they sang with their last breath the Hallel, the prayer of praise.[5] The Jews in Poland today are the descendants of those Jews in Tulchin. We can thank God that the glory of martyrdom has not departed.

Secondly, we can thank God for the strength that is America. At the same time as Jews were dying in Tulchin, Pilgrims were celebrating Thanksgivings on these shores. Here an ancient dream was fulfilled. It is not merely that Jews as well as others were able to find refuge in this land. It is that America stands as a symbol to the oppressed and suffering of the world—to the Jews as well as others—that freedom and justice do exist. The light of the Statue of Liberty is not only a light of welcome to the outcast and poor, the tempest-tossed and needy who came here to live. It is also a light promising to all humanity that some day darkness will be dispelled from the entire world.[6]

When you approach the historic bridge at Concord near Boston, inscribed on the figure of the Minuteman is the verse from the poem, "Here once the embattled farmers stood, And fired the shot heard round the world."[7] It told the world that America would henceforth be free, but it also promised the world that all humanity would some day be free. The news reports tell us that when American troops marched into North African cities, the civilian populations met them not with sullenness and bitterness—as the peoples of Norway and Holland met their conquerors—but with rejoicing and happiness, for they knew that behind the American flag came their liberators.

And today the strength of this great country is girded for victory against the enemies of civilization, who are at the same time the worst enemies of the Jews, and its pledge is behind our assurance that when the war is over, justice will be done for all, even for our oppressed Jewish brethren. The greatest symbol of this is the fact that the President has seen fit to appoint an American Jew to a position that after the war will be the most important in the world: in charge of the

---

4. See II Maccabees, chapter 7 (which does not give a name for the mother); B. Gittin 57b and parallel rabbinic sources. This model was invoked in the Rosh Hashanah evening service a few months earlier.

5. On the martyrdom of Jews in Tulchin in 1648, see Heinrich Graetz, *History of the Jews*, 5 vols. (Philadelphia: JPS, 1891–95), 5: 9–10. The text being studied would appear to have been Sholem Asch's *Kiddush Ha-Shem*, first published in English by the Jewish Publication Society in 1926 and reprinted in 1936. For the description of the martyrdom of Jews singing the Hallel, see chapter 14, 204–10 (the number killed is given there as 1400). In chapter 11, Asch emphasizes the military prowess of the Jews defending Tulchin and holding off the Cossack besiegers until they were betrayed by their Polish allies; this motif apparently did not seem appropriate in the present context.

6. Note that "the American dream" would become an important theme in sermons of subsequent years, but rarely in as overtly a messianic sense as here.

7. From Ralph Waldo Emerson's "Concord Hymn."

feeding and the relief and the reconstruction of the war-torn world.[8] A Jew will go to Europe to bring help not only to stricken Jews, but to the stricken victims in all lands, yes even to the stricken Germans themselves, that they may learn what America means to the world. And again, we can thank God for America.

A third thing we can be thankful for as Jews is the promise that is Palestine. It looks now that the danger that that country would be overrun, which loomed so large, is now a thing of the past.[9] Now we can evaluate its positive features. There the Jews are half a million strong. Though a people with a history of 4,000 years, Palestinian Jewry is not an old people but a young people: fertile, growing, with promise of rich harvests in the future. It may well be that when the war is over, the Jewry of Europe, as I am convinced, will have been so badly crushed that it will no longer play a significant part in Jewish history. But in the meantime, Palestine will have arisen to stand side by side with the great Jewish community of America, the two pillars of an indestructible people.

Even now they are doing their share and more in the fight for freedom. When the war is over, those who will have escaped the wave of destruction that is sweeping over Europe will need a land where they can find healing and home. It is too much to ask them to be strangers once more. Only in Palestine will they be at home. Palestine Jewry will await them with open arms. It is for us to see that the doors are not closed.

We thank God for the prayers in the hearts of the Jewish people that would not let Zion die though absent for 2,000 years; for the prophetic vision of a man like Herzl, who wore his life away to an untimely death at age forty-four in the attempt to transform a dream into reality; for the labor and sacrifice of those pioneers who in little more than a generation have carried on in the spirit of Herzl, laying foundations in the land with strength and making the land fertile

---

8. This type of allusion appears to be to a recently publicized item recognized by most in the audience, and indeed it was. The *New York Times* of November 21 (six days before the sermon) carried on page 1 a story that began, "Governor [Herbert] Lehman of New York will soon be named to direct the feeding, clothing and rehabilitation of countries which are friendly to or occupied by the United Nations. . . . He would be responsible, it was said, not only for feeding, clothing and sheltering the starving millions of Europe, Asia and Africa but also would have charge of the efforts to get these countries back on their feet industrially and agriculturally at the end of the war." The following day reported the formal appointment of Lehman as Director of Foreign Relief and Rehabilitation. On December 8, Roosevelt held a meeting with a small group of Jewish leaders, arranged by Wise. Reports of that meeting indicate that the president expressed satisfaction in appointing a Jew to this post, in that after the war, "Junkers" would have to go to Lehman on their knees to ask for bread. See Richard Breitman and Alan Kraut, *American Refugee Policy and European Jewry, 1933–1945* (Bloomington: Indiana University Press, 1987), 243.

9. The threat of German military conquest of Palestine was acute in the summer of 1940, the spring of 1941, and for the last time in the fall of 1942. Rommel's retreat from El Alamein in early November meant that Egypt and Palestine were no longer in danger. For the responses in the Yishuv to the German threat, see Tom Segev, *The Seventh Million* (New York: Hill and and Wang, 1993), 68–72. For Wise's reaction to this danger in July 1942, see *As I See It*, 124–25.

with their sweat and their blood; for those in all lands who have remained loyal to the cause of Zion and have made Palestine truly the land of hope for the Jewish people.

Finally, we can thank God for the dawn of victory, which already can be seen over the horizon. We whose lives and destinies are bound in this struggle have known dark days and nights of anguish. We have seen the forces of Fascism ride roughshod over nations. We have seen our own beloved country caught unprepared, yielding to the might of the enemy when confronted with overwhelming numbers and superior preparedness. We have waited and asked ourselves, "When will the tide turn?"

Now it seems that the tide has indeed turned. On every front, the Axis powers are meeting with reverses. On every front, the Allied powers are garnering new strength, and ever greater will to victory. The Nazi monster is being hemmed in with a ring of steel that will close in tighter and tighter until the monster is utterly crushed, never to rise again. Victory will be ours. And in this achievement the world is learning a lesson: it is learning that all humanity must henceforth stand together, that in condoning the attack on the Jew, the world condemned itself to the ordeal of suffering through which it must now pass. In that world on which the sun of victory and peace will eventually rise, we trust that men will at last realize that each must be his brother's keeper and that all men are truly brothers.

If so, then even as for Jacob of old, the suffering and struggle, the wounds and scars we bear will have been transformed into blessing, and though we may still limp, the sun will rise upon us, and we will again render thanks unto God.[10]

---

10. A reference to the Torah lesson for the week, *Va-Yishlah*, which includes the story of Jacob's wrestling, receiving of the blessing, and walking away at dawn with a limp.

13

Farewell
June 20, 1943

I have not been able to find any sermon text in which Saperstein announced and explained his decision to take a leave of absence from the congregation and volunteer to serve in the American Army as a chaplain. The initial impetus for this decision was provided by a letter from Wise to Saperstein dated December 10, 1941—three days after Pearl Harbor and the day before the German declaration of war on the United States. It said, in part: "In confidence I beg to send you herewith a copy of a telegram, which has just come to me from the President of the Jewish Welfare Board, summoning me and other heads of rabbinical schools and organizations to a meeting . . . with a view to securing additional qualified men for chaplaincy service on a full-time basis. Would you be willing to take a leave of absence from your congregation for the duration of the emergency in order to serve as a Chaplain in the U.S. Army? . . . I realize that this might entail a great sacrifice on your part, but nothing short of the greatest sacrifice on the part of all of us will carry us through to victory."

The present text shows the eventual results of that letter. It is not formally a sermon, but rather a response following tributes paid at a Sunday evening gathering celebrating ten years of rabbinical service to the congregation and providing a sendoff for the leave of absence. A testimonial document signed by all members of the congregation and special guests is in Temple Emanu-El. Wise was invited, but could not attend. His letter dated June 16, 1943, reads, "I cannot tell you how much I appreciate your note and how I wish it were possible for me to join you at the farewell party which you are giving in honor of Rabbi Saperstein. He is one of my very dear and honored young friends. Sunday, June 20, is so crowded with engagements that I cannot manage it." Representing the faculty of the Jewish Institute of Religion was Professor Shalom Spiegel, mentioned below. The Program for the occasion reveals a mixture of classical music, greetings, addresses, and presentations.

The personal character and distinctive genre of the text make it different from most of the others. There is no reference to the earlier pacifist position, though the assertion that "there is not a family that has not some loved one in the service" is painfully ironic in juxtaposition with the language of the 1936 pacifist sermon: "For it is your sons who will go. I can see them marching down the streets of Lynbrook." Neither is there any romanticized enthusiasm for the prospects of Army life. I have included it because of its human interest as a reflection of a young rabbi's role in a small congregation during a difficult and tragic period.

THE ONE FAILING THAT WE RABBIS ARE OFTEN CHARGED WITH is a lack of practicality. But I am now very proud of the practicality of one decision I made recently. I didn't order my army hat until after this evening's affair.

This has been a wonderful testimonial, but not really to any merit on my part. It is rather a testimonial to your generosity expressed in word and deed. There still echo in my ears your more than kind words, which I shall try desperately to remember to bolster my morale while I am learning how to take orders in the Army. . . . I need not tell you how much I cherish your tributes. They are particularly meaningful to me coming as they do from my co-workers and friends, my beloved teachers, and you who represent so well the larger American community within which our Temple functions.

With all the allowances for the exaggeration that is an accepted part of these occasions, I should like to feel that they indicate something of what I have been trying to do with greater or lesser success. I came here, ten years ago, younger than most of the members of our Young Folks League. I have spent with you the most important decade thus far in my life. I think perhaps that I am in as good a position as anyone to evaluate it. I haven't become the great Jewish leader of Dr. Wise's stature that my mother envisioned then (although I have a secret suspicion that she wouldn't admit it even now). But I have tried, in the tragic period of history with which destiny decreed my service should coincide, to hold before my people an ideal of Jewish dignity and unity, and to awaken my fellow Americans to something of the grandeur of our American heritage.

I haven't become the scholar that you, Dr. Spiegel, who influenced me more than any other teacher in my many years of study, might have hoped for.[1] Yet I have known something of the creative joy of sharing with young and old in the adventure of learning, and of trying to transmit to them something of the vision I was privileged to receive from my teachers.

I certainly haven't become the miracle rabbi *à la* Peretz Chesterfield of our musical comedy which some of our congregation must secretly have hoped for.[2]

---

1. Shalom Spiegel, who taught Hebrew literature at the JIR before moving to the Jewish Theological Seminary of America, was Saperstein's advisor for a rabbinic thesis on the treatment of Jewish legends by Berdichevski.

2. The Sisterhood and Men's Club of the Temple regularly put on plays from this period through the 1960s. This play was identifiable solely through the fortuitous survival

But I can say that with the limited gifts that God has given me, I have tried to serve the Temple without stint of time or strength.

That's all I have done. Mine hasn't been a big job. Lynbrook is not a big town. But it's our town, and in it babies are born and people die, children grow up and go away to college and get married, and boys put on uniforms and go away to fight for their country; people feel secret hopes and fears, the challenge of American patriotism and the sorrows of stricken Israel. All this I have shared with you, and in the process, although I may not have taught you much of life, there is much of life that I have learned myself.

You have talked as though this wonderful thing you've done for me tonight were a reward for what I have done. I feel as though I am accepting it under false pretenses, for I have already received my reward while all this was going on. It's hard to describe it. It was the pride in the eyes of my parents when I was ordained. It was the smile on the lips of my wife when you so graciously welcomed her to our community. It was the wordless grip of a friend's hand after I had conducted a funeral service for one whom he had loved. It was the light that brightened the eye of some member of the congregation as the message of my sermon spoke to some inner need. Above all, it was the joy of doing the work I would rather do than anything else in the world.

I have heard your tributes; now let me pay mine. First, to those of you who planned for and brought about this wonderful evening, which I shall never forget. Second, to those of you with whom I have had the privilege of working side by side, and to whose labors the progress of the Temple is due. Third, to the memory of my beloved grandfather and uncle, who have blazed the trail of Jewish service before me.[3] Fourth, to my family, who have lived with me through the greater part of this decade, and whose love and confidence have given me strength when I most needed it. Above all to my wife who, as my severest critic, has put me on my mettle, and who, as my partner in life, has made real to me the words I had been speaking at wedding ceremonies for many years before my own.

We part now. I leave you, not because I want to leave Lynbrook, but because I feel that at this moment I can be of greater service where I am going. There is

---

of the "playbill," including the cast of characters, among Saperstein's miscellaneous papers. Performed at Temple Emanu-El on June 21, 1941, it bears the title "So let 'em foreclose: a Musical Farce," but no author is given. It was actually written by the distinguished Boston attorney Lewis Weinstein, with the full title "So let 'em foreclose! Or, Temple Olov Hasholom ["peace be upon it"], Inc.; a merry, modern, musical mirrorscope of American Jewish community life" (Boston: Walter H. Baker Co., 1934).

3. His grandfather, Rabbi Hyman Max (Chaim Mordecai) Lasker (1864–1932), received ordination in 1886 from Rabbi Isaac Elchanan Spector in Kovno, came to the United States in 1889, and served orthodox congregations in Portland, Maine, in Buffalo, N.Y., and—for thirty-eight years—in Troy, N.Y. His son, Adolph, Saperstein's uncle (1898–1933), was a social worker before entering the Jewish Institute of Religion, from which he was ordained in the fifth class, of 1930. He served in the Lynbrook congregation from 1929 until his death, at age 35, in December 1933. Saperstein had begun to substitute during the period of Lasker's illness, and continued after his death.

not a family that has not some loved one in the service. Think of me as being with the boy whom you love wherever he may be, trying to bring to him, in his bitter task, an understanding of why he has been called upon to sacrifice. Think of me as providing to him a bond with eternal values. I may not be with him, but some other rabbi will be, and I will be with the boys that others love.

You back home must continue to give to your rabbi the loyalty and support you have given to me, for he will be here in my place.[4] The Temple will continue to need you, and you will continue to need it. My prayers shall be with you, as I know your will be with me.

Let us fervently hope that before long, we shall meet again to begin a new decade together. Just as the last was inaugurated with the accession of Hitler to power, so the new shall be inaugurated with the triumph of democracy. Just as the last has been one of worldwide tragedy and destruction, so the new shall be one of worldwide hope and rebuilding. Only one thing shall remain unchanged. That is that we shall carry on together in the love of God and the fellowship of Israel, in loyalty to America and in service to our fellow men.

As for tonight, all I can say, from the depths of my heart, is, "Thank you."

---

4. Zev Bloom and Morrison D. Bial served as Rabbis of Temple Emanu-El while Saperstein was on leave with the U.S. Army.

14

The Call of the Shofar
September 17, 1944
Rosh Hashanah Evening,
Grenoble, France

Saperstein went through the chaplaincy-training program, held at Harvard Divinity School, during July and the first half of August 1943. Upon finishing the course, he was assigned to Fort Banks in the Boston harbor defenses; he conducted High Holy Day services at Camp Myles Standish, a staging area for troops being sent overseas. Texts of these sermons do not seem to be extant, but the following description in a letter of October 3, 1943, is of interest:

> *All my army sermons thus far have been simple and direct. Since I spoke to small groups I adopted the personal, conversational style, and found it to be very effective. With the larger crowd I found for Rosh Hashanah, I reverted to the oratorical style I used to use in the Temple on such occasions. The sermons I gave were similar to those I had given in the Temple—fairly long, well developed, illustrated, using fine phrases, etc. Ordinarily I would have considered them pretty good; somehow, however, they didn't click as well as I would have wished. For the last two sermons I used the simple technique again. I found that it was much more successful.*

And in a letter of October 19, "Never in my life have I conducted services where the response was so genuine."

Service at Fort Banks continued until March, when he was transferred overseas, landing first in Algeria for Pesach, then, by April, in Italy (see the references to Tunis and the Anzio campaigns in the February 1946 sermon, and to Rome in the March 1964 sermon). Despite heavy fighting in Italy, the war was clearly going well for the American forces. By August 11, he was writing from "Somewhere in France." In that letter, he describes Jews who

fled to the countryside, where they lived in hiding. They are now just begin-
ning to emerge and the tragic story of the living and the dead will soon be
ready to be told. There is not a family some member of which has not disap-
peared or been killed Thus far, not a word has been heard from a single one
of those who were deported to forced labor battalions or concentration
camps. . . . By and large, the Jews of France are a people who have suffered
and become embittered and disillusioned. It will take a long time for their
scars to heal, if they ever do. . . . Many of the atrocities mentioned above
were committed not by Germans but by French Vichy police.

The High Holy Days of 1944 were observed in a spirit different from any
since 1932. German forces were reeling in retreat, large areas of occupied
Europe had been liberated by Allied Armies, the end of the war seemed to be
within the foreseeable future. The services were intended for American army
personnel, but—as described in a letter from the time—there was an earlier
service for French Jewish civilians, and many of them stayed on for the Army
service. The combination of the first public worship after liberation and praying
together with American Jews made it a deeply moving experience for the
French, and also for the rabbi who led the worship, as he would recollect in his
1973 sermon, "Days I Remember."

Saperstein had used before the three components of the Rosh Hashanah
Musaf service to structure a Rosh Hashanah sermon. Here he used them in an
order different from the liturgical one, starting with Zichronot in order to begin
with the theme of memory and grief, and move on to a more upbeat message
from there.

THE SUN HAS SET. ANOTHER YEAR HAS ENDED and a new one begins. We
are gathered in synagogue as we have done every year. Tomorrow we will listen
to the soul-stirring sound of the Shofar as we have done every year. But somehow, in the light of the memories and hopes that flood our hearts this Rosh Hashanah, the message of the Shofar this year will be more significant and more
real than ever before.

In the Musaf service tomorrow, there are three sections where the Shofar is
blown, and the prayers accompanying each of them represent three distinct
themes. One section is called *Zichronot*. It is a summons to each human being to
stand before God to render account of the past and to seek guidance for the future. Never did we feel the need for God so much before, because whether we
are Jewish soldiers in the American Army or Jewish civilians in France, the experiences through which we are living are the most profound and moving of our
lives. We in uniform are far from our loved ones, and many have known—or
will soon know—what it is to pass *be-gei tsalmoves*, "through the valley of the
shadow of death" (Ps. 23:4)—an apt way of describing war. You, the Jews of
France, have come through the *Emek Habacha*, the "vale of weeping." In
America, we had known of the trial and suffering you were undergoing, but they

still seem distant. Only now are we beginning to appreciate, when they are no longer words on a printed page, but tales from the lips of our brother Jews.

And as we try to throw off the tragedy of the past, the question throbs in our hearts: How shall we go on, how face the future? The Midrash tells us that when the Israelites had escaped from Egypt, they found themselves at the Red Sea, behind them the pursuing hosts of the Egyptians. Their plight seemed hopeless. Some counseled, "Let us return to slavery in Egypt. We shall never be free." Others cried, "Our burden is too great to bear. Let us cast ourselves into the waves to die." Still others said, "Let us pray to the Almighty, there is nothing we can do." As the sound of their weeping rose to God, He spoke to Moses, and said, "Why do you cry unto me? *Daber el b'nai Yisrael va-yiso'u*, ["Speak to the children of Israel that they may go forward" (Exod. 14:15)].[1]

That is our answer. Not backward must we look but forward, where there are new and greater tasks to be performed. Heavy though the burden of our hearts may be, we must face life with dignity and courage, with heads held high—determined that the lives we live in the period of freedom and peace that lie before us will be worthy of the sacrifice that has gone to make these blessings possible.

Another section is called *Shofarot*. This is a challenge to the Jew to be true to his heritage. In the past few years, the Jewish people have had their cup of suffering filled to overflowing. Our people has been the victims of the most inhuman and barbaric program in history—a program designed simply and openly to exterminate the Jewish people, to solve the "Jewish problem" by destroying every Jew. The program almost succeeded. The soil of Europe will long remain saturated with the blood of the Jewish people, its very air will long echo with the cries of those who have perished. As the forces of the enemy are being driven back, the story of the tragedy of Jews in lands they had conquered are being are being revealed. The number of those who have died *Al kiddush Hashem* ["for the sanctification of God's name"] can hardly be counted.

I said "almost succeeded," but not quite. Out of our experience comes a new realization of an ancient truth: that Israel is one and eternal. This very service is evidence of that truth. Here we are Jews, whose native languages differ, whose national backgrounds differ, but who feel the bonds of a common heritage and common destiny. When we say *Shema Yisroayl* ["Hear, O Israel"], we affirm not only one God, but also *Yisroayl echod* ["Israel is one"]. Let me assure you, my Jewish brothers of France: though our lot in America has been more fortunate than yours, your pain has been our pain, your suffering has been our suffering, your tragedy has been our tragedy.

And we shall go on as a people. Our experience corroborates the testimony of history: Israel has ever lived to stand at the graves of those who sought to destroy it. A few months ago, I stood before the Arch of Titus in Rome, in the company of a group of Palestinian [Jewish] soldiers. This arch had been erected

---

1. See Y. Ta'anit 5,2; *Mekhilta Be-Shallah* 3 (ed. Lauterbach, 1:214), Ginzberg, *Legends of the Jews* 7 vols. (Philadelphia: JPS, 1911): 3:15 and 6:4–5. Compare the use of this rabbinic aggadah in the Rosh Hashanah, 1939 sermon, "Unconquered" (and the note ad loc.) and in the 1947 sermon, "Thieves in the Night."

to celebrate the destruction of the Jewish nation, whose leaders had been compelled to walk under it in chains. For almost 2,000 years, no Jew had walked under that arch, the symbol of our national tragedy. And now I, a Rabbi of a free land, and those Chalutzim, who were rebuilding the ancient land of their people, stood there as evidence of the fact that our enemies can burn our synagogues, they can lay waste our nation, they can kill and enslave our people—but so long as the will to live persists in the heart of a single Jew, *Am Yisroayl Chai*, the People of Israel lives![2] And some day, this tragic story of our day will be but a page in one chapter of one volume of the story of a people that would not die. And at the conclusion of that story will still be written not "The End," but "To Be Continued."

The third section [of the shofar service] is called *Malchuyot*. It challenges us with the reminder that the ultimate ruler of the universe is God, that there is a moral order in this universe which cannot be violated. The very stars in their courses fight with us.[3] A year ago, the pattern was not so clear. We prayed for victory and hoped for peace—but that prayer and hope were not based upon realistic observation but on the yearnings of our heart. Today, only the blind cannot see the handwriting on the wall. The struggle is not yet over. But a ring of steel has been forged around the enemy that will relentlessly tighten until he is crushed.[4]

Those who plant seeds of hatred and death shall reap a harvest of hatred and death. Those who have sought to build a tower of Babel and storm God in his heavens are seeing that very tower come crashing down upon them bringing destruction. Evil and tyranny may triumph for a day, or a year. In the long-term view of history, righteousness must ever triumph. The furies of slavery may trample everything before them. But freedom will rise, from the grave if necessary, to throw off the yoke.

And so we turn to the New Year. The darkness has not yet passed, but the first light of dawn is beginning to shine over the horizon. From the darkness comes the query, *Shomer, mah mi-layil?* "Watchman, what of the night?" (Isa. 21:11). And the answer rings back, clear and strong: *oso boker*, "the morning cometh" (Isa. 21:12). Human beings—our stricken people—the freedom-loving world—take new courage and rise to face the new day. For while the shadows still linger, we are confident that some day we shall be able to say, in the words of the poet, "Out of the shadows of night, the world rolls into light, it is daybreak everywhere."[5]

---

2. Saperstein's later account of this event was published in Louis Barish, ed., *Rabbis in Uniform* (New York: Jonathan David, 1962), 173-74.

3. Echoing Judges 5:20.

4. Note the use of this metaphor, somewhat prematurely, at the end of the post-Thanksgiving Day sermon of 1942, above.

5. The poet is Henry Wadsworth Longfellow, in "The Bells of San Blas." The typescript reads "Out of the *darkness* of night," perhaps quoted incorrectly by memory.

15

The Voice of Joy and Gladness
September 8, 1945
Rosh Hashanah Morning
Namur, Belgium[1]

Saperstein conducted services for Pesach 1945 in France, but soon after he was moved into Germany. A letter dated May 15, 1945, describes the experience: "One drove through the completely devastated cities of a country that had brought ruin and desolation to so much of Europe. One passed countless trucks of prisoners moving back, crowded with soldiers who had set out to conquer the world. The mills of historic justice grind slowly but surely." After being stationed for a few weeks in Worms, he was in Munich on the day of the German surrender, and the following day he entered Dachau. The same May 15, 1945, letter states, "No description in words could exaggerate or even compare with the sheer horror and gruesomeness of the reality. The heart of everyone who sees it fills with terrible anger at the hideous efficiency and unbelievable inhumanity of the Nazi beast."

After meeting with survivors in June, he was transferred to Namur, Belgium. There he discovered Vicar Joseph André, a local priest who had hidden and fed some 200 Jews during the Nazi occupation in his own home and in the houses of

---

1. The actual text of this sermon from 1945 is missing. There is, however, a sermon with this title labeled, "preached Rosh Hashanah Morning, Sept. 26, 1946, at Lynbrook." At the end of the sermon, the following words are typed: "(This sermon, with slight modifications, was also preached in Belgium (Namur) at Catholic school where we held HHD services in 1945 and repeated at Thionville [in NE France]." All that remains from the 1945 High Holy Days is the first two pages, slightly torn, from the sermon for the evening of Rosh Hashanah. I have used the introduction from that text and the body of the text preached in 1946 as the best record of what was said on the first Rosh Hashanah after the war.

other Belgian Catholics—a story similar to the now much better known activi-
ties of Pastor André Trocmé and the Huguenot community in Le Chambon-
sur-Lignon, France. Saperstein's report to the National Jewish Welfare Board
about the Vicar André was widely covered by the media, including a December
28, 1945, article in the New York Times. *(See his later account in Louis Barish,*
ed., Rabbis in Uniform *[New York: Jonathan David, 1962], 94–97; a picture of*
Saperstein with the priest and a group of the sheltered Jewish children can be
seen in the account of Father André published in Mordecai Paldiel, The Path of
the Righteous: Gentile Rescuers During the Holocaust *[New York: Ktav, 1993],*
68–71.)

A rather poignant counterpoint to the ebullient spirit that characterized the
first Days of Awe following the defeat of the Nazis is the following private con-
fession in an October 7 letter from Saperstein to his younger brother Sanford,
who had also become a rabbi and was serving in Athens, Georgia:

> *I'm a little worried about my own preaching when I get home. Although one*
> *might think that the opportunity of getting away from civilian routine*
> *preaching for a couple of years, plus the enriched experiences of war, would*
> *give an abundant supply of preaching material, I find the opposite to be*
> *true. In all the time I've been in the army, I haven't thought up or worked*
> *out a single new sermon. In fact, I've never even written down a word. All I*
> *have been doing is rehashing old sermons, trying to give them a little con-*
> *temporary slant, and to flavor them with an occasional new morsel. For one*
> *of my High Holy Day sermons, I tried to think up something new. After*
> *coming home from my evening service, I walked the streets until 12:30 and*
> *couldn't even get an idea. I slept fitfully until 6:30 and as the morning hours*
> *wore on, still found myself inspirationally paralyzed. With less than an hour*
> *to go for the service, I yielded and fell back on an old sermon outline that I*
> *had preached in civilian days—and preached it better then, too. I almost*
> *bawled with frustration and a sense of incompetence. It probably sounds*
> *amazing—but I'm actually scared at the idea of the plunge back to the ci-*
> *vilian rabbinate. People are going to expect such an awful lot. Instead of*
> *feeling overflowing with stuff, I feel squeezed out and dried up. The total of*
> *my war experiences will probably give a touch of interest to two or three*
> *sermons, and then I'm homiletically bankrupt.*

While the material about the laughter mentioned by Sarah upon the announce-
ment that she would bear a son may well come from an earlier sermon, many
would judge that the following texts reveal something quite different from the
homiletical bankruptcy and paralysis of the creative spirit that Saperstein
feared.

TO ME AS TO MANY OF YOU, THIS ROSH HASHANAH has been long and ea-
gerly awaited. The first Rosh Hashanah that I preached before the civilian congregation to which I hope soon to return was in 1933—the first after Hitler had
come to power in Germany. From then until now, the New Year brought no
happiness; only the hope and faith to which we clung in desperation mitigated

the tragedy of reality. As I look back, the period of my ministry has been a period of war—a war that has been aptly termed the war for survival.[2] If that description is true for humanity, it is doubly true from the Jew. For while to other men, it meant chiefly spiritual survival, for the Jew it meant actual physical survival. Other people could somehow have lived on even in the face of a Nazi victory. For the Jew, it meant extinction. For other peoples this war of survival lasted about six years. For the Jew it has lasted more than twelve.

During that period each year, from the bottom of our hearts rose the prayer for life: *Kosvenu besefer hachayim* ["Inscribe us in the Book of Life"]. During the first half of it, we the Jews of America,[3] were living in relative security, as part of the strongest, freest Jewish community in the world. But our hearts were with our brothers across the sea, over whom there hovered the dark cloud of oppression, tyranny, danger and death. The world may have been indifferent, but we knew that they were our brothers, that our fate was bound up with theirs, and we prayed for them. During the last half of that period, since the American nation entered into the war—and we put on the uniform to go out to fight against our enemy—our prayer for life became even more meaningful. To the soldier, the words of the *Unesaneh Tokef*[4] strike home: *Mi yichyeh umi yamus*, "who will live and who will die, *mi vekitzo umi lo vekitzo*, ["who at the end of a full life span, and who prematurely"]—these words are not just poetry.

But this year is different. We have seen the fulfillment of our prayers. The enemy of civilization, decency and humanity has been battered down into the shambles of destruction, the forces of democracy have triumphed, "the reign of evil has perished from the earth."[5] Our hearts are filled with gratitude as we gather on this Rosh Hashanah. Truly we can make a *shehechiyonu*.[6]

Something of the spirit of faith and hope which permeates the High Holy Days is reflected in the Biblical passages that tradition has assigned to be read. On Rosh Hashanah we read the story of Isaac; on the first day we learn the circumstances of his birth. You all recall the familiar details of the Biblical tale. Sarah, despite her fervent prayer, had been barren. Then, when she and her husband no longer dared to hope, the messengers of God appeared to Abraham and prophesied that Sarah would bear him a son. And this son would be his spiritual heir, through whom his seed and his mission would be carried on. They foretold that his descendants would some day be a great people, like the stars of the sky and the sands of the sea for multitude, and through them all the children of the earth would be blessed.

---

2. In the introduction to the September 26, 1946, sermon, these words are followed by "to use Roosevelt's phrase."

3. The sermon was delivered to Jewish soldiers in the American Army.

4. A central prayer of the High Holy Day liturgy. Beginning with the words, "Let us affirm the awesome power of this day," it expresses the belief that the destiny of every human being was determined during this season.

5. Another echo of the High Holy Day liturgy, transposing a future tense into the present time, as if the hope expressed in the prayer has now been fulfilled.

6. The blessing praising God for having "kept us alive, sustained us, and permitted us to reach this time."

The prophecy seemed fantastic. Sarah could not bring herself to hope that it would be fulfilled, for she was already an old woman, more than eighty years of age, and Abraham was ten years older. But as the holy day reading opens, we find the words, "And the Lord did unto Sarah as He had said. And Sarah conceived, and bore Abraham a son in his old age. And Sarah said, *tzechok oso li elohim, kol hashomea yitzhak li*, 'The Lord has caused laughter concerning me; all that hear of it will laugh at me'" (Gen. 21:6).

Now what did the laughter of which she spoke connote? From the context, it would seem that it might indicate the laughter of ridicule. It is as though it meant, Everyone knows how much I longed for a child, how much it would have meant to me and to Abraham to know that there was something to carry on the faith. But the joy of bearing a child was denied to me in my youth. And know when people hear that in our old age a son has been born to us, they will say, "What a joke! They're too old and worn by suffering to rear a child. They'll be dead long before he's old enough to carry on the cause. Life has played a strange, ironic trick on Abraham and Sarah: their prayer has been fulfilled, but too late to do any good."

That would seem to be the meaning of the laughter of which Sarah spoke at the birth of Isaac. But the Jewish tradition was not content to interpret it that way. Rashi, the great medieval commentator, quoting the Midrash, explains it not as the laughter of ridicule but as the laughter of joy. For the Midrash tells us that with Sarah, many other barren women conceived, and many sick people were healed, and many prayers were answered—so that there was joyous laughter through all the world.[7] By that interpretation they expressed their confidence that the Jewish people would never lose its power of creative survival. And that faith is symbolically justified in the incidents of the following passage, which we shall read tomorrow morning, in which we see Isaac climbing the mountain with his father, and through his readiness to sacrifice for his faith evidencing his worthiness to carry on the torch of truth which his father had kindled.

Now we can see the analogy between the Biblical narrative and our own day. Israel, crushed beneath the yoke of the murdering tyrant and oppressor, had long been praying for redemption. Year after year, until it looked as though the hope were vain, as though the goal of the enemy would be brought to completion and the Jewish people and faith would disappear from the earth. Then the prayers of Israel were finally answered; after all its sorrow the day of victory has come. But has the victory come too late? Can the enemies of the Jewish people still mock at him—and from behind their prison walls or from their unhallowed graves, say, "It is true that we have failed in our drive for world conquest. But in one thing at least we succeeded: in our attack upon the Jew. Victory has come too late for them. They are weak and broken and smashed. The moral sense has disappeared from the world. They will never be able to bring it back."

---

7. Genesis Rabbah 53:8; compare Rashi on Gen. 21:6.

There is no denying the extent to which such gloating by our enemies might be justified. A people of sixteen million has had six million murdered. And the crisis is not yet over. For on the one hand, the anti-Semitic propaganda sown by the Nazi regime throughout its history, coupled with the inevitable postwar reaction, has produced an extremely grave anti-Semitic problem throughout most of the world.[8] And on the other, the lofty ideals proclaimed as our goal while men were pouring out their blood on the battlefield now seem to be forgotten, while nations play the game of power politics in which the Jewish people figures only as a ball to be kicked around.

In the face of these facts, it might seem that the mocking laughter of our enemies would be warranted. But the spirit of the Jew has a power of resilience, which cannot be stifled. No, sad though our hearts may be at the realization of the tragedy that envelops us, we refuse to admit defeat. Once again, we have survived the downfall of our enemies. You, Hitler, the latest exemplar of the classical anti-Semite from the time of Haman, thought you could prevail. You did not realize that yours was but the power of the moment, while we are a people of eternity. And we shall survive the tribulations of the night of moral darkness through which the world is now passing. We shall go on to be a blessing to the earth. Through our redemption, others who suffer shall be redeemed; through our healing, others who are sick shall be healed; through our freedom, others who are enslaved shall be freed.

On what basis shall we build this faith? How shall we give evidence to our conviction that, like Isaac of old, we—the fortunate survivors of a people of martyrs—shall be equal to our task, shall be worthy of carrying on our age-old heritage? We can do so in two ways. First, through a renewed sense of Jewish brotherhood and mutual responsibility. We must realize that as God is one, so all Israel is one, however we may be scattered. We must care for each other, for—though it hurts me to the depths of my being to say this—the truth must be uttered: no one else cares. When six million Jews were murdered in the most horrible deaths imaginable, to the average person it was just a number to be read as he glanced at the news columns of the paper before turning to the things that concerned him: the sports page, or the financial page, or the "Blondie" comic strip.

When the atrocity pictures of concentration camps came out, people were shocked as they realized it wasn't propaganda after all. But the shock soon wore off, and they began to complain that you shouldn't show such pictures. They make people feel uncomfortable to look at them. And now that peace has come, the same lack of moral consideration has manifested itself a hundred times. When people read of Jews who escaped the outstretched hand of the angel of

---

8. This sentence seems to me more likely to have been said in September 1946, when the sermon was repeated and somewhat revised, than in September 1945. For discussions of antisemitic agitation during 1945–1946, see *American Jewish Year Book* 48 (5707) (Philadelphia: JPS, 1946), 172–87 (United States), 285–86 (South Africa), 317–19 (Austria), 335–38 (Poland), 362–64 (Hungary). Most dramatic was the blood libel pogrom in Kielce, Poland, on July 4, 1946, killing forty-two Jews.

death during years in concentration camps, dying in order to find their way to Palestine, they become bored and annoyed. "That's all you see in the papers: Jews," they say. "What do they want? Aren't they ever satisfied?"

Do you remember that bitter article by Ben Hecht a couple of years ago called "Remember Us"—in which he described how after the war the representatives of the world's nations would gather round the table. All would be there. Only the Jews would have no delegates—except for the ghosts of those who were murdered in gas chambers and by poison injections and forced to dig their own graves. From their ghostly mouths comes the plea, "Remember us!" But there is no one to hearken.[9]

Did I say no one? There will be some who will remember. The rest of the world may forget; whether it accidentally forgets or purposely forgets doesn't matter. We Jews shall not forget. We shall remember you! The people in other countries who died had something to live and die for; you were caught like rats in a trap. But we will see that you too have not died in vain. In your name and memory we will strengthen the hands of those of your afflicted brothers who

---

9. Hecht's "Remember Us" was originally part three of the memorial pageant *We Will Never Die* performed at Madison Square Garden on March 9 and 10, 1943 (and elsewhere throughout the country), to dramatize the desperate plight of European Jews. After citing several incidents of brutal mass murder, it continues,

> When the German delegates sit at the peace table with their monocles restored to their pale eyes, no sons or survivors or representatives of these myriad dead will be inside the hall to speak for them. And by that time, it will be seen that the Jews are Jews only when they stand up for the hour of extermination. Once dead, it will be seen that they are left without a government to speak for their avenging and that there is no banner to fly in their tomorrow. Only this that I write—and all the narratives like it that will be written— will be their voice that may drift in through the opened window of the judgement hall.

"Remember Us!" was printed in *American Mercury* of February 1943, and an excerpt was published in the *Reader's Digest*. See William MacAdams, *Ben Hecht: The Man Behind the Legend* (New York: Charles Scribner's Sons, 1990), 229–30, and Robert Abzug, *America Views the Holocaust, 1933–1945* (Boston: Bedford/St. Martin's 1999), 146–49. The description in the sermon may also conflate an advertisement written by Hecht for the Emergency Committee and placed in the *New York Times* on November 5, 1943 (A14), entitled "My Uncle Abraham Reports." It begins:

> I have an Uncle who is a Ghost. . . .
> He was elected last April by the Two Million Jews who have been murdered by the Germans to be their World Delegate.
> Wherever there are Conferences on how to make the World a Better Place, maybe, my Uncle Abraham appears and sits on the window sill and takes notes. . . .

See David Wyman, *The Abandonment of the Jews* (New York: Pantheon Books, 1984), 154–55.

remain. In your name and in your memory we will work for the future of the Jewish people and the Jewish homeland. In your name and in your memory we will strive toward that goal of a world of brothers in which no man shall ever oppress his neighbor again. Your memorial will be the degree to which we succeed in these endeavors. But whether we succeed completely or not, we shall not weary nor rest from our labors. For we cannot forget. And remembering, we shall act.

Secondly, if we are to justify our faith in Jewish survival we must preserve our sense of consecration to a purpose. No matter how tragic his fate may have been, the Jew always felt an innate spiritual superiority over those who persecuted him, for he knew that persecution is a sign of weakness. Only in recent generations have we had the tragic spectacle of Jews in any numbers afflicted with a sense of Jewish inferiority, who instead of keeping their own ledgers as any normal people does, began to take themselves at the value assigned to them in the ledgers of their enemies. Hitler tried to do what countless anti-Semites had previously tried to do and failed. He tried to make the designation "Jew" a mark of dishonor and shame. That was the intended significance of the yellow Jew bade. Instead, their suffering served to arouse many people to a deeper sense of Jewish dignity and consecration.

It would have been much to expect this sense of consecration to survive in every case. But the miracle did happen in many cases. I have seen it among Jews in concentration camps who, like Jonah of old, say, "Ich bin a Yid,"[10] and by the way they say it show that they still carry their Jewishness as a designation of honor. I have seen it in the American Army in men who have won the respect of their fellow Americans by respecting themselves as Jews.[11] I have seen it in civilian life, in Jews who have taken a new grip on their Jewishness and have determined that Jewish service and education and philanthropy are to take priority over all other things in their lives. I have seen it most of all in the Jews of Palestine—in the young Palestinian Jews whom I met on many fronts during the war, and who permitted themselves no rest, day or night, in their efforts to rescue their Jewish brothers. And I see it now in the resistance forces of Palestine who are fighting and dying not for themselves but that they may welcome their stricken brothers home.

It is this Jewish responsibility, consecration and faith which are the harbingers of our future and which promise that our lot is not hopeless. Hitler once said, "The Jewish people shall never laugh again."[12] He did his best to carry that

---

10. Yiddish, "I am a Jew," echoing Jonah 1:9.

11. The following sentence was apparently added for the 1946 delivery in Lynbrook.

12. I am not aware of this precise quotation. It may be an allusion to the now famous passage from Hitler's Reichstag address of January 30, 1939: "During my struggle for power, the Jews primarily received with laughter my prophecies that I would someday assume the leadership of the state and thereby of the entire Volk and then, among many other things, achieve a solution of the Jewish problem. I suppose that meanwhile the then resounding laughter of Jewry in German is now choking in their throats." In the recently published translation of his diary, Victor Klemperer, in an entry dated July 20, 1933, wrote, "A sound film recording of Hitler, a few sentences in front of a big meeting—

threat through. Not long after VE Day, I performed a marriage ceremony [here] in Belgium for two refugees who were shortly afterward to leave for Palestine. The words of the last of the seven traditional benedictions took on new meaning to me: "Praised be Thou, O Lord, who has created rejoicing and song, love and brotherhood, peace and fellowship. Soon may there be heard in the cities of Judah and in the streets of Jerusalem, the voice of joy and gladness, the voice of the bridegroom and the voice of the bride."

I thought to myself, despite our sorrows, Hitler has not succeeded. Hope and faith have not perished from the Jewish people. Israel *shall* laugh again. And his laugh shall be not a laugh of bitterness or mockery, but the laugh of a strong and healthy people, that walks the high road of history following a gleam of truth. And as envisioned by the sages of old, through Israel, a greater measure of joy and happiness shall come to the earth. Mankind has wept enough tears. God grant that the time may come soon when the words of old shall be fulfilled, when "He will wipe the tears from all faces, and He will remove from all the earth the rebuke of His people, for the Lord hath spoken it" (Isa. 25:8).

---

clenched fists, twisted face, wild bawling—'on January 30 [1933] they were still laughing at me, they won't be laughing anymore.'" This indicates that the motif of laughter in the January 30, 1939, speech had been used almost six years before. See Klemperer, *I Will Bear Witness: A Diary of the Nazi Years, 1933–1941* (New York: Random House), 26.

16

A Jewish Veteran Returns
February 8, 1946

After some eight months of work with survivors following the end of the war, Saperstein returned from Europe to the United States in December and was re-united with his family in New York, including his first viewing of his then fif-teen-month-old son (the present editor).   Just as there was a farewell event on a Sunday night, in June of 1943, so there was a welcome home event on Sunday, January 27, and the text of his remarks remains. Among other things he spoke of his feelings about his native country: "When, the day the fighting in Europe ended, I stood at Dachau and looked at a pile of what had once been human beings—each one of whom had loved and hoped and dreamed—I suddenly thought, 'There, but for the grace of God, am I.' And the day I came into Boston Harbor and stood out in the freezing cold on deck looking down at a boat that had come out to meet us, on which was emblazoned in great letters, 'Welcome Home,' I thought of the Pilgrims who centuries ago had landed in that vicinity, because they had wanted to be able to stand before God as free men. And I found myself saying, America must be true to itself, and you must be true to America."

I have not been able to find the text of a sermon dated February 1, the first Friday night after the return, although the sermon below, delivered the follow-ing Friday night, refers to what "I explained last week." This one reports on the condition not of European Jews but of Jewish soldiers in the American Armed Forces, characteristically drawing largely on personal experiences for the more general message.

ALTHOUGH MY SERMON IS ENTITLED "A JEWISH VETERAN RETURNS," our service tonight is not a formal occasion in honor of our returned service men— except insofar as every time we gather to worship in freedom, our service is in part a tribute to those who won in war the right for us to do so. What I hope to do is to touch upon some of the effects of army experiences upon the attitudes of the youth of our people toward religion and the Jewish problem. More than half a million Jewish youth during the war bore the uniform of our Army—more than 10 percent of our Jewish population: men, women, and children. This group is bound in a very profound way to affect the future of Jewish life. It is therefore exceedingly important that we realize what we have to work with and what we have to hope for. I shall give some of my own impressions, and after our service we will have a general discussion when some of the men present will have the opportunity to make their contribution.

For part of the time during the war there was some talk about a great religious revival. Some people got the impression perhaps that our young men had turned en masse to religion and religious services. "There are no atheists in fox-holes" became a popular byword, and the hope was fostered that when the war was over we would find these ex-GIs flocking to the synagogue, clamoring to attend services. Actually, that rosy picture represents an over-idealized and somewhat distorted picture of the facts.

What then can we say has been the effect of army life in general upon the attitude of our Jewish young men to religion? Let me be very sober and factual—not rhapsodical—about this. I'm not going to make any glowing claims. To me the chief progress we made lies in two factors. One, a great number of Jewish men who had never known any kind of Judaism except an old-worldly traditional type, which had no real meaning or message for them came into contact for the first time in their lives with a new modern approach to religion—to a Judaism that had vitality and power for our day and our lives.

Under ordinary circumstances, most of these men would have considered it a sacrilege to enter a Reform Temple. While our Army type of service preserved many traditional forms that are not present in our Reform ritual, still—as conducted by the great majority of Army chaplains—it carried out our basic principle of making the service intelligible and meaningful for American youth. In the preaching and educational programs, many men got a new insight into the richness and greatness of our religious heritage. I could count the men by the hundreds who have told me that they had never before realized how much our religion has to offer.

[The second factor relates to prayer.] It is true that attendance [at services] in the army was better than it would have been for the same young people in civilian life. But it must also be admitted that except in exceptional cases, there were usually more men who did not come to services than who did. It is true also that there are very few atheists in foxholes. But the fact that when things get very rough—when the world is crashing and rocking around you, and that terrible unearthly fear creeps into every part of your body—you cry, "God save me" may not really represent a sense of religion. It may be merely a form of fear-hysteria. And when the danger has passed and that same soldier returns for a brief period of rest, he does not always run immediately to find a religious service to express thanks. It is just as likely that he'll go seeking a much more questionable type of inspiration in an environment where the religious spirit is most conspicuously absent.

But this "foxhole" type of experience has fostered one positive result: the acceptance of prayer and religion as a legitimate recourse in time of crisis. Under normal circumstances, there is a tendency on the part of young people—take typical college students, for instance—to have the attitude that there is something a little unmanly about the youth who prays. Not so in the Army. Every man who has been in combat in war recognizes that there are times in life when you yourself don't have the strength to carry through, when you need the support of some power greater than yourself, when no matter how smart you are, you just don't have all the answers. And that's the mood of prayer. They have found that it helps you to pull through, and they accept it not as a sign of weakness but as a normal expression in time of crisis.

I recall, for instance, in Italy—we were stationed about twenty miles south of Casino, and we were sending men to the bloody Casino and Anzio campaigns. Three chaplains—Catholic, Protestant, and myself—gathered for a few minutes with the men before they climbed onto the trucks. It was announced that the chaplains were there and the men could fall out to meet with them. Rarely indeed did it happen that a man would hesitate to spend those few moments in prayer.

Sometimes there are moments that burn themselves into your heart. I remember once there was a group of about a dozen Jewish men on a shipment. I had conducted a little service and as usual at the end I said, "And now, let each of us pray in his own words, in the silence of his heart." Apparently the words "in silence" hadn't registered with one of the men—a mature fellow about thirty—for with tears streaming down his face he started to speak in a choked voice, "O God, bring me back safe to my mother and my father." We were all deeply moved, for there was something fitting about it—he was putting into words the prayer that all of us were praying in our hearts.

So much for religion. Let me now turn to the GI's attitude toward Jewishness. Here again it is possible sometimes to paint an overly optimistic picture. By and large, just as the American soldier in general is a civilian in uniform, so the American Jewish soldier is a Jewish civilian in uniform, and so the attitudes you find in the Army duplicate the patterns that are found in general in the outside world. For instance, in the Army we found the extremes. There was the pugnacious Jew who is ready to fight at the drop of a hat and interprets everything that happens to him as a slur upon his faith and an example of prejudice.

And there was the other extreme—the Jewish escapists and assimilationists. Just as in civilian life they are more common in the upper financial levels, so in the Army this type is usually found among the officers. I refer here to the type of Jew who refused to participate in any Jewish activity that might single him out from the non-Jews, who kowtowed to obtain the favor of the non-Jews, and refused to identify himself with the Jewish group in any positive manner, whether it meant attending services or helping Jewish civilians.

But again I think that there are two aspects in which the Army can be said to have had a helpful influence. By and large, I think it has given to Jewish youth a greater sense of Jewish dignity. They learned that unless you stand up for yourself, nobody is going to stand up for you. They have the satisfaction of knowing that they made their contribution as well as anybody—and that they don't need to make any apology for themselves. That, when they enjoy freedom and equality, it's theirs by right and not as a special favor granted. They have learned, as I explained last week—by intimate living with non-Jews in a way that normal life never makes possible—that the non-Jew understands and admires the Jew who is a Jew, but he distrusts the Jew who isn't anything.

They have learned basic democracy tempered in the crucible of fire: that America is made up of people of all kinds—of all faiths and national origins—and that they have the right to be what they are. They have seen in their chaplains—who, incidentally, were the only men in the Army to wear their Jewishness on their breast—that they are recognized, not in the same numbers perhaps, but in the same category as people of other faiths.

Serving in the Army has had another influence on those in particular who saw service in foreign lands where they had the opportunity of coming into contact with Jewish civilians. It made them realize the bonds that join all Jews in all lands: in a common heritage, in a common faith—though it may be expressed in modified forms and different languages—and to a great extent in a common destiny, and hopes, and problems. It was an amazing thing to see how this realization would come home. Wherever Jewish soldiers went—I've seen it in the countries of North Africa, in Italy, France, Germany, Belgium—always the same: they sought out the native Jews.

I remember in Tunis, where I had to make a stopover: I was seeing the town with a plane companion by the name of Bill Mark. We passed a photographer's shop, and the photographer saw my insignia and came running after us. He was so excited when he found out I was a Rabbi, he begged for the honor of taking our picture, and refused to take any money. A little later we went into an officer's mess. The waitress spotted my insignia and informed me that she too was Jewish and proceeded to give us service such as nobody else in the place was getting. As we were walking back, Bill said to me, jokingly, "It looks to me as though it's an advantage to be a Jew."

The point in this experience—and I've seen it duplicated hundreds of times by others—is that I had something in common with these foreigners that others do not have. I had a great deal in common with Bill Mark too. We're both Americans, about the same age—went to the same kind of college, like much the same kind of music, read much the same kind of books, live in the same kind of community, love the same flag. But I had something else that Bill didn't have: I shared something with this man and girl in Tunisia that he didn't enter into. When a Jew with a true Jewish heart meets another Jew anyplace in the world—it may be in the *mellah* or Jewish quarter of a North African city, and the Jew may be dressed in native robes—it may be on the boulevards of Paris and the Jew may be dressed like people at home—it may be in a concentration camp in Germany and the Jew may be dressed in cast-off rags—but when we look into each other's eyes we know that in some deep, unexplainable manner we belong together.

For the better part of 4,000 years we walked the same road together, said our prayers together, and helped each other along. For a few hundred years our paths have diverged—we've separated and in some cases almost lost contact with each other. But now as we look into each other's eyes and grasp each other's hands, you feel as though long forgotten memories are struggling to consciousness. You realize that in a very unique sense not only is God one and humanity one, but Israel too is one.

I shall not take time to point out some of the things I as a chaplain learned from my experiences: new attitudes toward the relative importance of different aspects of my work as a Rabbi in Israel. That will come out in due time. Tonight I confine myself to those experiences which are shared by all Jewish GIs. The Haftorah which we read[1] told us that workers were sent to mine and hew the stones that would be necessary in the building of the Temple. And then it continues, "And when the house was built it was made of whole stones, as they had been prepared at the quarry, so that neither hammer nor ax nor any tool of iron was heard in the house while it was in building" (I Kings 6:7). The reason for this was that iron was considered the symbol of war and its weapons.[2] Although it was necessary to provide the materials for the building, the building that was itself to be dedicated to peace used those materials, but dissociated itself from the reminders of war.

So it is with the things of which I have been speaking: this realization of the relevance of Judaism for modern life, this sense of its value as a source of help in meeting the crises of life, this deeper sense of Jewish dignity, this consciousness of Jewish unity and mutual responsibilities. In and of themselves, they represent no miracles and they are no answer to our problems. But they are the raw material out of which the Temple of a better world and a stronger Judaism can be built. They came from the grimness of war. But in the hands of loving builders and architects of the future, they can be separated from the forces that gave them origin and used to build a Temple of peace—which shall bring light and joy and goodness to humanity.

---

1. Accompanying the Torah lesson *Terumah*.

2. See Mishnah Middot 3,4: "They dig up whole stones, on which iron has not been lifted up. . . . For iron is created to shorten man's days, and the altar is created to lengthen man's days; it is not fitting for that which shortens man's days to be waved over that which lengthens man's days."

- 17 -

Passover—For Our Day
April 19, 1946

Saperstein had been preoccupied with the fate of the survivors of the Nazi genocidal campaign from the time the war ended. In a later, retrospective sermon (April 1, 1955), he described a meeting he had in Frankfurt not long after VE Day with Lt. General Lucius B. Clay, then in charge of Civilian Affairs in Germany.

> *General Clay is a man of character. Later on, as Commanding General of the Occupied Territory, he showed deep and sympathetic understanding of Jewish problems. But at that time I must say he was still completely devoid of the slightest understanding of Jewish needs. I asked him why, with the Joint Distribution Committee poised on the rim of Germany ready to come in and help the survivors, military permission was still being withheld. "If we were to let Jewish relief groups in now," he answered, "we would also have to let in Protestant and Catholic relief teams"—as though there had been nothing unique about the treatment of the Jews by the Nazis. I asked him why Jews in Germany were being subjected to the non-fraternization laws which applied to the Nazis, though Jews were all victims and none supporters of the Nazis. "We cannot make any distinction between elements of the population," he said. I asked him why Jews were not organized together in their own camps so that they could work out their destiny together. He answered, "We consider only national origins; the Jewish Poles are to be considered as Poles and treated accordingly," not realizing that whereas non-Jewish Poles would be returning to their homeland, Jews from Poland would be returning to a land of persecutors and bitter memories.*

Eventually, he concludes, understanding came.

Yet one year after the end of the war, DP camps in Europe were still filled with Jews who had no place to go. The holiday of Pesach, with its theme of liberation from the oppressor, seemed a cruel mockery to those Jews in 1946. The

Pesach week sermon moved from a description of the previous year's holiday during the last weeks of the war to the need for a new liberation. Particularly powerful is the motif of the "fifth son," who cannot ask because "he is here no more, but his voice rings out louder than all the others." There is a strong insistence that the overwhelming majority of survivors still in Europe wanted nothing other than the opportunity to go to one place where they could consider themselves to belong: Palestine. This motif, already present in many of the war-year sermons, would become a central motif of his preaching in the dramatic period leading to the establishment of the State.

AS WE GATHER TOGETHER ON THIS SABBATH, for many the spirit of the Seder service still rests upon us. I imagine that if you were to ask the average Jew which ceremony of the entire calendar of Jewish observances meant most to him, it would be the Seder. That is true whether the Seder be held at home, in a Temple community hall such as ours was, or for a group of soldiers. I realized that last year.

Let me tell you something about last year's Seder. It will give you an idea of one aspect of a chaplain's work. Passover came at the end of March. Two weeks before Passover, we received word to be ready to move into Germany at 24-hour's notice. I went to my commanding officer and explained to him the extent of preparations necessary for Passover and asked whether he could give me any confidential information as to whether we would be likely to remain at the site we were then in. He was sympathetic but explained that he simply did not know himself exactly when we would have to move. And so I went ahead with my preparations, not knowing whether at the last moment it might not all prove to be in vain.

I had two Seders to arrange—at a distance of about 125 miles apart. One was in a town, the other in a military barracks. In both of them, I had to start from scratch—one for about 300 men, the other for about 200. You start off and make arrangements for a place—in this case one was to be held in a Red Cross Service Club, the other in an army mess hall. Only we couldn't get into either to start preparing until 6:30, and the Seder was scheduled for 7:30. Then you face the problem: where shall we begin?

You haven't anything. You need plates. Of course, the men could use their mess kits, but at that time these men had eaten from their mess kits since they had come overseas. I was determined that this occasion was going to be different: they were going to have plates. I heard that more than a hundred miles away there was a place where a German crockery supply depot had been taken over. So the day before Passover we drove that 115 miles in my jeep and a trailer, and we came back crawling over the shell-torn roads. We got our plates.

The food and its preparation were easier. The Army is very cooperative. We asked them long enough in advance; they could not promise anything until the last minute, but finally they came through with chicken—not canned, but the real thing. One of my boys was an army cook, so we're all set. But what about the special things we need? Wine had come through from the Jewish Welfare

Board, but not enough. Fresh eggs were something you dreamed about. But there were farmers around, who had wine and eggs. Money wasn't any good, but cigarettes and laundry soap did the trick. Dozen by dozen, we got them.

Horseradish was something you simply did not see, and I wouldn't have known how to say it in French anyway. So down to the marketplace I went and tasted every vegetable they had until I found one that tasted bitter enough to do the trick. I still don't know what it was. But whatever work went into such a Seder was more than compensated for when the men got together—some just back from the battle lines—and joined in singing the familiar songs. I couldn't help thinking what a wonderful holiday it was.

What is the reason for this hold that Passover has over Jewish hearts? I think it is twofold. First of all, Passover is one of the few observances where the richness and beauty is still maintained. Traditional Jewish life was filled with meaningful observance. The Sabbath and holidays, even the daily routine, were replete with observance that helped a person to get beyond himself, that added a new dimension to life. Modernism came to Jewish life at a cost of many of these observances. It was impossible for most people to be a part of the modern world and still maintain all of the old customs. The meaning was lost, and since the kernel was no longer there, the shell was thrown away. Jewish ceremonial life became progressively weaker, and many Jews abandoned it completely.

Yet the average human being feels the need for meaningful symbols. It is true that life can be lived without them, but the reaction to Passover shows how strongly felt is the need they still fill. One of the great tasks of modern Judaism is to renew that sanctification of life that comes through ritual and ceremony. I do not mean that we must become more Orthodox; it may mean in some cases the creation of new ceremonies or the modification of old ones. Our Reform Commission on Ceremonies has been working on creating a number of new ceremonies, which are traditional in spirit and modern in form. The observance of the Sabbath and holidays must come back into Jewish homes—in a revised form, perhaps, but in the same spirit as in days of old.[1]

Secondly, Passover has its grip on Jewish hearts because its message seems to have been written for our own day. Last year when we observed it, we were fighting against the modern Pharaoh, and victory was almost within our grasp. This year is our first Passover in a world of peace and freedom. I say a world of peace and freedom—I mean, rather, the potentialities of peace and freedom. Out of the history of recent years, there are certain basic lessons that must be learned. When the Jews came out of Egypt, their national life was still not secure until they had come to the Promised Land. So we have learned that liberation alone is not enough. Those who were liberated must be able to move on to the Promised Land, shaking the dust of Egypt from their feet.

---

1. This call was in keeping with a central principle of Reform Judaism from its early stages. "What was needed, therefore, was to sift old customs and to create new ones that would give poetic expression to the universal truths which Reform had chosen to stress" (Michael Meyer, *Response to Modernity* [New York: Oxford University Press, 1988], 275, on Kaufmann Kohler).

In Geneva, there is now convening a Commission of Englishmen and Americans, on whose decision the fate of hundreds of thousands of Jews depends. These are Jews who survived concentration camps with their gas chambers. They want one thing now: to go to Palestine. A recent poll by UNRAA in displaced persons camps in the American Zone showed that this was the goal of 95 percent of them. When I returned from overseas, I was asked to submit a statement to the Anglo-American Commission.[2] In that statement, I said that I was convinced, after talking with thousands of American Displaced Persons that they wanted to go to Palestine above all else, and that most of them are impelled by the simple realization that Palestine alone offers an answer to their homelessness.

They have been pushed around over the face of Europe, surviving by miracles. They do not want to come to a new country as beggars and strangers. In Palestine alone, they will be coming to their own; they will, at last, belong. It alone seems to offer not only healing for their physical wounds, but also salve for their wounded spirits. There the sense of belonging and of living for a purpose will give them the therapeutic treatment they so sorely need after their soul-searing experiences.

When I was in Poland [in the summer of 1939], I visited a cousin of mine in Warsaw. He was the same age as I, and he was as good a person as I. Only his father had stayed behind when mine came to America. Later, his father with all the rest of his family had moved to Palestine; he remained behind. Then, before the war, he too wanted to go to Palestine to join the others. But he could not get an immigration permit. The war came. The Nazis came. My cousin died in a gas chamber—because Great Britain had said, "It is illegal for Jews to go to Palestine."

I spoke last week about the fifth cup—the cup of Elijah. Tonight let me speak about the fifth son. You recall that the Passover Haggadah tells us that the story of Passover must be told to all the children of Israel. The sages of old said there were four kinds of sons and enumerated them: the wise, the wicked who seeks to separate himself from his people, the ignorant who does not know his heritage, the one who does not know how to ask. But there is a fifth type: the son who cannot ask because *he is no more*—but his voice rings out louder than all the others. It is the voice of the thousands of American Jewish boys who gave their lives in a war for freedom—freedom not only for everybody else but for Jews as well. It is the voice of six million Jews who were murdered. And it asks, *"What is the meaning of this service?"* (Exod. 12:26).

---

2. The Anglo-American Commission was established, at the instigation of British Foreign Secretary Ernest Bevin with the consent of President Truman, to investigate the problem of refugees and Palestine. Commissioners visited DP camps in February 1946 and took polls to determine the wishes of the survivors. In one such poll, more than 21,000 out of 22,000 questioned chose Palestine; this would appear to be the one cited in the sermon. See Abraham Sachar, *Redemption of the Unwanted* (New York: St. Martin's/Marek, 1983), 201–5.

Although we may be able to cover up with words our answer to the first four sons, the question of the fifth son allows no confusion; it demands a clear-cut answer. It demands that we in our turn demand, "Let my people go." It demands that those who survived until now shall continue to survive. I hope that the Commission sitting on the shores of Lake Geneva hears those words.[3] Let them know that the Israelites have been tempered by the fires of slavery. They will no longer consent to being merely a problem. They will make themselves a force. Let them know that regardless of their decision, the Jewish people of Europe will move on to the Promised Land, that no force on earth can hold them back except death itself—and death holds no terrors to those who have gone through what they have gone through.

We began our Passover Seder with the words, "This is the bread of affliction which our ancestors ate . . . . Let all who are in need come and share with us." May the message of this Passover inspire us to generosity and a sense of Jewish brotherhood. This year, many of our Jewish brothers are still strangers in alien lands. Next year, may all the homeless be at home in the land of Israel. This year, although the tyrant has been overthrown, many of them are still not entirely free. Next year, may all of them celebrate as free men.

---

3. The Commission's report was completed and signed on April 19, the day the sermon was delivered, recommending the quick admission of 100,000 refugees into Palestine, but this information apparently came out too late to be incorporated into the sermon.

18

The Resistance Movement in Palestine
October 25, 1946

Beginning in the summer of 1946, exasperation with British policy molded by Foreign Secretary Ernest Bevin led to a radicalization of Palestinian Jewish responses. The Haganah concentrated primarily on "illegal immigration," but two splinter groups—the Irgun or "Etzel," and "Lehi" (also known as the "Stern Gang")—turned to sabotage and attacks on British targets, including personnel. The most dramatic example of this was the Irgun attack on the King David Hotel in Jerusalem on July 22, 1946, resulting in the death of more than 90, severe punitive reprisals by the British against the entire Yishuv, and a fierce condemnation of the Irgun by David Ben-Gurion. September and October brought a new round of political negotiations, as publicity about Jewish DPs intercepted by the British and interned on Cyprus created powerful feelings of sympathy in the United States.

The rhetorical introduction to the sermon, probably not original, appeals to the patriotic self-image of Americans by identifying the resistance movement in Palestine with the "Minutemen" of the American Revolution, both standing up in defiance of the British oppressors. The reference to the Torah recording the divine promise of the land of Israel to Abraham at the end is an appeal to the Jewish self-image. Between these two framing elements, most of the material is expository, clarifying for the listeners the historical background (presented from a clear Zionist perspective), the players and the issues. The sermon dissociates the preacher from the tactics of the militant splinter groups, but argues that their behavior should not be taken to invalidate the larger cause, or the principle of standing up and fighting, if necessary, for Jewish rights, in the "spirit of the Maccabees . . . , the spirit of Bar Cochba."

LET ME PRETEND FOR A MOMENT that I am a foreign correspondent writing a report from one of Britain's hot spots. "Flare-up of Terrorism: British security troops in search for hidden munitions caches were subjected to a terrorist ambush and attack last night. The terrorist bands were fully armed. All indications are that the attack was organized and that responsible native officials were implicated. The Colonial Office, denouncing the attackers as gangsters, announced its determination to seize the ringleaders and to stamp out all further resistance. Troops have imposed stringent security measures and are conducting careful searches for implicated parties."

That sounds fairly familiar, doesn't it? It's almost typical of the reports that have been coming out of Palestine regularly during the past year. But the strange thing is that I wasn't trying to write a dispatch from Palestine in 1946. I was trying to write a report from Boston, Massachusetts in the year 1775.

You see, there are two ways of looking at things. Those Yankee farmers who fought from behind every fence and hedge on the road to Lexington and Concord were undoubtedly denounced by the British as terrorists. To us, they were the patriots of our country, fighting against tyranny, when they fired the shot heard 'round the world. Anyone reading and swallowing the British reports would have received a completely distorted view of the events leading up to the American Revolution. What we call the Boston Massacre, where soldiers shot down unarmed civilians in the streets of Boston, the British undoubtedly explained as soldiers bravely defending themselves when attacked in trying to break up an organized anti-British demonstration. What we proudly acclaim as the Boston Tea Party protesting the policy of taxation without representation, the British undoubtedly explained as gangster violence resulting in wanton destruction of British property.

This brings us to the first fundamental principle I must emphasize in discussing the resistance movement in Palestine. Let us not be duped by British-inspired reports, which use such question-begging terms as terrorists, illegal immigration, gangsters, etc. Let us remember that those Jews involved—regardless of the degree to which we approve of their methods—are sincere patriots, fighting not for profit but for principle, not for themselves but for their people, not carrying on illegal activities but fighting against what they feel to be the illegal program of a tyrannical regime, a program which if allowed to prevail means death to large portions of the remains of an already decimated people.

In order to make my own position clear, let me say now that I am convinced—and I think I know most of the facts—that weighed on the scales of either justice or mercy, the right is on the side of the Jewish resistance. And although I do not agree with the tactics of every group involved, I acclaim them now as heroes whose names deserve the same place of honor in Jewish history as do those of the Minutemen in American history.

Let me try now to clarify for you just what these resistance groups are. Newspaper reports carry references to such names as Haganah, Irgun, Sternists—and the average person finds it quite confusing. Are all of them different names for the same group? If not, what are the differences, how important are they, and whom do they represent? To answer this question, we must go back to the beginning of Jewish self-defense in Palestine.

At the beginning of modern Palestinian settlement, long before the Balfour Declaration and England's entry into the picture, the Jews recognized the need to protect themselves against wandering bands of Arab marauders, who would suddenly fall upon a Jewish settlement, rob and pillage it, then disappear into the desert. It was an old Bedouin custom, thousands of years old, and Arab villages as well suffered from them. Its motivation was not nationalistic.

In response to this need, the Jewish settlers organized the *Shomrim*, the "Watchmen." This was a group of young men, mounted on horseback, with a romantic courage and love of adventure and a deep pride in their organization. Some of them had previously been leaders of the self-defense groups that had sprung up in Eastern Europe in response to the bloody pogroms there. In Palestine, they wrote some thrilling chapters of Jewish heroism and did their job well.[1]

After the Balfour Declaration, the situation changed. It soon became apparent that Great Britain was more concerned with its own imperial interests than with the purpose for which it had been given the Mandate to Palestine: that of promoting the establishment of a Jewish homeland there. While there had been no Arab nationalist opposition at the time when the San Remo Peace Treaty gave official support by the nations of the world to the program of the Jewish homeland,[2] the rapid progress of Jewish settlement soon awakened Arab feudal leaders to the realization that their position, based as it was upon the ignorance and exploitation of the Arab peasants, was being undermined. Taking advantage of the ignorance they were seeking to perpetuate, they began to stir up mass Arab opposition.

This was tough going, because the Arab masses had every reason to be satisfied with their Jewish neighbors, whose presence had hurt them in no way and benefited them in many. But their leaders used every trick of lying propaganda and appeal to religious fanaticism, and the result was Arab rioting. The British, whose job it was to promote law and order and who could easily have quelled any disturbance, seemed not too much interested in doing so. Instead, it often seemed that they were encouraging Arab opposition to Zionism and then making concessions to the Arabs, which resulted in whittling down the Jewish homeland—the establishment of which, I repeat, was the sole purpose of Great Britain being there in the first place.[3]

---

1. On the Shomrim, first organized in 1907, see Howard Sachar, *A History of Israel from the Rise of Zionism to Our Time*, 2nd ed. (New York: Knopf, 1996), 80–82.

2. In the San Remo Conference of spring 1920, the Balfour Declaration was incorporated into the peace treaty with Turkey, establishing the basis for the British Mandate for Palestine.

3. See also Pierre Van Paassen, *The Forgotten Ally* (New York: Dial Press, 1943), 121: Opposition to Jewish settlement in Palestine "did not spring up as a spontaneous reaction in Arab nationalist circles. . . . It originated and was carefully nurtured in the milieus of the newly arrived British civil and military administrators." Saperstein owned this book and read it carefully; note the explicit reference to it below.

The situation became clarified in the riots of 1929. At that time it became quite evident that England, if not guilty of stimulating the riots, was clearly guilty of not having done what it could to stop them. They seemed to have a strange faculty for collecting all arms from a Jewish colony shortly before it was attacked, and coming to quell the attacks after the damage was done. Jewish lives were lost that the British could have and should have saved.[4] The Jews now saw that they could not depend upon the British for protection and would have to take care of themselves.

The 1936-1939 riots saw this program of self-defense under way. The self-defense organization had to be secret, since the British preferred to have the Jews helpless when the Arabs came to attack. But the organization was thorough and effective. It included every able-bodied Jew in Palestine. They were given intensive training and subjected to an unofficial but thorough discipline. I saw evidence of it when I was in Palestine during that period [in the summer of 1939]. In the middle of an evening, a friend would excuse himself and leave a party. No one asked any questions. Every strategic spot in Palestine was under 24-hour volunteer guard. Supplies of munitions were kept secretly cached.

There was one strange thing about this program of military organization. It was used exclusively for defense. The policy of *Havlagah*, self-restraint, represents one of the most amazing stories in history. For Jewish action was taken only in self-defense—not for retaliation, and not for terrorism. When a colony was attacked, they fought to defend themselves. They did not go out as they could have done to attack neighboring Arab villages. This defense organization was the basis of the *Haganah*.[5]

As time went on, a small group of hot-blooded young men became impatient with the program of self-restraint. They were Revisionists, and their philosophy was a militant one. "We have followed moral standards," they said, "and we get pushed around. The Arabs have been terrorists and the British are quick to make concessions. We'll show them that we can be terrorists too." So a small group of extremists broke away from the *Haganah* and formed the *Irgun Zva'i Leumi*. Their policy was to meet violence with violence, bloodshed with bloodshed. One could understand their impatience. But so careful were the masses of Jews

---

4. The 1929 riots in Jerusalem, Hebron and elsewhere, followed an eight-month simmering dispute over prayer at the Western Wall. Sachar gives casualty figures as 133 Jews dead and 399 wounded, with 87 Arabs killed and 91 wounded (174). According to Sachar, British forces in the immediate vicinity were simply inadequate to restore control. Many Jews did, however, perceive the British behavior as blatantly partisan, as in the following Revisionist perspective: "The Arabs, using their variety of weapons, were not interfered with. Where Jews retaliated to an Arab attack, usually driving off the attackers, the British police arrived on the scene to search the Jews for arms. When found, they were confiscated and their owners arrested." Shmuel Katz, *Lone Wolf: A Biography of Vladimir (Ze'ev) Jabotinsky*, 2 vols. (New York: Barricade Books, 1996), 1126. See also the condemnation of British failure to anticipate the violence despite ample warning by Maurice Samuel, *What Happened in Palestine: The Events of August, 1929, Their Background and Their Significance* (Boston: Stratford, 1929), 86–87.

5. See the similar description by Sachar, 213–16.

to keep their case unsullied that this group was repudiated by all responsible organizations in Jewish life.

When I was in Palestine during this period, there had been some attacks upon Jews, leading to several deaths, and this group had retaliated by tossing a bomb into an Arab theater, also causing several deaths. The entire Jewish community of Palestine rose up in protest. Every newspaper had an editorial denouncing the act. Mass meetings were held. "This is not the way Jews act," they proclaimed. "'Thou shalt not murder' is still a basic Jewish law."[6] Nothing like it for moral strength has ever been known in human history.

When the war came, these defense organizations were ready, and they served the Allied cause well. Thirty thousand of them served in Palestinian units of the British Army, and later in the Jewish Brigade. They made a substantial contribution toward preventing the breakthrough of Rommel's forces at El Alamein, which was really the turning point of the war. The British used volunteers from the Haganah and the Irgun for some of their most dangerous missions. Something of this remarkable story is told by Pierre Van Paassen in *The Forgotten Ally*, a truly amazing book.[7]

And then, finally, the nightmare of war was over. The full toll of Jewish losses at the hands of the Nazis was now apparent. Courageously, the Jews of Palestine set themselves the task of saving as many of their surviving brothers as possible. But they found that their battle was still not over. The British—who still were in Palestine only on one legal basis, namely, to assist in the building up of a Jewish homeland—said, "They cannot come in. If they do come, we will consider it illegal. And we will stop them—kill them if necessary—and send them to concentration camps. One thing we refuse to do: to let them come into Palestine, to save their lives."

A few generations ago, the Jews might have taken that, bowed their heads, and said, "It is God's will." Even today, some Jewish communities might still take it. But, thank God, not the Jews of Palestine. The defense organizations, whose function had previously been to protect Jews from Arab attacks, now went into action to bring Jews into Palestine. "If the British call it illegal," they said, "we consider that only an expression of *their own violation* of moral and international law."

What is the strength of these groups? First, there is the Haganah, the official Jewish military force. It has the backing of the entire Palestinian Jewish community, men women and children. It would say that it has about 60,000 to

---

6. The Monday, July 3, 1939, issue of the *Palestine Post* reported a warning by the Chief Rabbis of the Jewish community that "No Jew must entertain even the thought of unjust reprisal and the shedding of innocent blood. Whatever the circumstances, Jews must not commit acts contrary to the spiritual laws of Israel . . . [including] the word of the Almighty, 'Thou Shalt Not Kill.'" That very day, however, another bomb exploded in an Arab café in Haifa, killing one and injuring forty-two.

7. *The Forgotten Ally* (see above, n. 3), 198–208 on Jewish task force activities against Rommel; a summary of activities is on 224–27. The figure 30,000 is on 229. Pierre Van Paassen, a well-known journalist, was a fervent Christian Zionist; see above, n. 3. The Hebrew version of his book was banned by the Mandatory Government in 1946.

80,000 trained soldiers, with as many more in a partially trained reserve. It has a striking force known as the *Palmach*, which numbers 12,000 to 14,000; that is the standing Army of Jewish Palestine serving on a full-time basis. The Haganah does not commit acts of terrorism. It is ready to fight only when such fighting is necessary to carry out its program of bringing in Jews, of saving lives. They say, "We're not looking for trouble. Let the British stay out of our way and everything will be all right. But if they try to stop us, we will show them that Jews fight too."

The Irgun still maintains the principle that the Haganah is too moderate. They maintain that this is actually war, and that we must forget gentlemanly rules of fighting. "Make yourself such a problem to the British, make life for them so dangerous," they say," that you will force them to accede to your wishes." The Irgun numbers about 3,500 to 4,000 men. Finally, there is a small group known as the "Stern Gang," a group numbering perhaps only 200 or so, which believes that even the Irgun does not go far enough.[8] They are zealots, every one of whom has sworn an oath to be ready to give his life without a second thought if it should be necessary for the cause. No assignment is too dangerous for them. Acts performed by the Irgun and the "Stern Gang" are still repudiated by the majority of Jews in Palestine and by all official organizations. We too may not agree with their tactics, but let us not fail to give due credit to their unselfishness, their heroism, and the ultimate justice of their cause.

What about the future? The next weeks and months will be historic ones for Palestine. This weekend, the Zionist Organization of America is gathered at Atlantic City in National Conference. In another month, the World Zionist Organization will assemble at Basle, Switzerland.[9] At these conferences, the position of the Jews of America and of the world will be expressed. There is no doubt what the position of the Jews of Palestine will be. They will not allow themselves to be frightened, they will not allow themselves to be discouraged. The British may intercept ten refugee ships. One will come through, and its passengers will be saved.

The struggle will go on. And in it, we can take pride. The spirit of the Maccabees lives again, the spirit of Bar Cochba. Jews are standing up now, not as beggars pleading for handouts, but as a people of human beings ready to fight for their lives and their honor. I remember a leader of the Jewish Brigade whom I met at a conference in Paris on Armistice Day, 1945. "What will your men do when they return?" I asked. "We will show the world," he said," that Jews are no longer merely a problem. We are now a force that must be reckoned with." Back in 1939, when I was present as a delegate at the World Zionist Congress, one of the speakers was Tom Williams, a Christian member of the British Par-

---

8. On this, see, recently, Joseph Heller, *The Stern Gang: Ideology, Politics and Terror, 1940–1949* (London: Frank Cass, 1995).

9. The 22nd World Zionist Congress, the last before the establishment of the State, convened in Basle on December 9, 1946. See Walter Laqueur, *A History of Zionism* (New York: Holt, Rinehart and Winston), 574–76.

liament. "Hitlers and British governments come and go," he said, "but the Zionist cause can never be stopped."

In next week's *sedrah*, we will read of God's promise to Abraham that the land of Palestine would belong to him and his descendants until eternity.[10] We are confident that that divine promise will eventually be fulfilled. Though we regret the necessity of fighting to make it so, we are determined that the Promised Land will be ours, and through the combination of land and people, in the future as in the past, the nations of the world will be blessed.

10. See Gen. 12:7, 13:14–15, 15:18–20, all in the *sedrah Lekh Lekha*.

19

Thieves in the Night
January 31, 1947

The following sermon continues the treatment of themes from the previous one—
the unconscionable betrayal by the British, the pathos of the refugee in desper-
ate need of a home, the frustration leading some Jews to opt for a radical, mili-
tant, even terrorist form of Zionism. This time it is done through a book: Arthur
Koestler's Thieves in the Night.

In a sermon delivered on December 17, 1976, on The Thirteenth Tribe, *Sa-*
perstein described its author as follows: "Arthur Koestler is one of the most
interesting literary personalities of our time. He was born in Hungary, educated
in Austria and Germany, and currently lives in England. As a young man he
served in then Palestine as a foreign correspondent for three years. Later he
became a communist and spent some time in the USSR, but left the party disillu-
sioned during the Stalinist purges of the 1930s. He covered the Spanish Civil
War as a correspondent, was captured and spent some time in Franco's jails
under a death sentence. During World War II he volunteered for the French
Army and after its collapse fought for the British. His books include novels on
political problems, essays, and autobiography. They reflect his changing loyal-
ties, his ideals and disillusions, his dedication to the principle of individual free-
dom." Clearly, the preacher was attracted by both the narrative and the
pro-Zionist sympathies of Thieves in the Night, *which Koestler had dedicated to*
the memory of Jabotinsky, and he thought that it would be an effective way of
dramatizing the excitement and heartache of Jewish Palestine to his congrega-
tion. He later would express much more serious reservations about Koestler's
negative attitude toward Judaism and Jewishness.

More so than in the previous sermon, a certain ambivalence about the Jew-
ish extremist groups (Irgun and Lehi) seems to be in evidence, perhaps the result
of a conflict between the legacy of the early commitment to pacifism and the
commitment to Jewish self-respect and self-assertion. Thus the condemnation of

terrorism is juxtaposed with a much longer and rather forceful explanation of the circumstances which produce it. Such ambivalence can also be seen in a passage written (and then crossed out) in the typescript for the sermon on Rosh Hashanah Morning, 1947:

> *I do not agree with the extremist groups in Palestine, although I am deeply convinced of the necessity of resistance as conceived by the Haganah, the official resistance forces of the Yishuv. Yet I could not help being thrilled by the bearing of those misguided but magnificently heroic boys who, charged with terrorism, sat through their own trials with the lives being weighed in the balance, ignoring everything that was being said while they read—the Bible. And when the sentence of death was imposed, they rose not to plead for mercy but to sing the Hatikvah.*

And later in the same sermon,

> *Six million Jews are murdered—many of whom might have been saved—the world is coldly silent. Two British soldiers are killed by patriotic Jewish fanatics whose patience has passed the breaking point, and public opinion is shocked, while in England, which prided itself on being the fatherland of freedom and democracy, there are mob scenes against the Jews in retaliation.*

What distance had been traveled from the sympathetic identification with the British standing up against the German bombers seven years before, in the Rosh Hashanah sermon of 1940!

AS WITH ALL SERMONS BASED UPON BOOKS, tonight's sermon is not intended to be a book review. But when I read *Thieves in the Night,* I decided that here was a book to be brought to the attention of the congregation, whose theme deserved discussion from the pulpit. Although perhaps not the ideal novel on Palestine, it is in my opinion the best that has yet been written.

Its author, Arthur Koestler, is one of the outstanding novelists and thinkers of our day. He himself has been a part of a world in turmoil, living in Russia, Spain, and Palestine, and out of these experiences have come his novels, which grapple with the fundamental social problems of our times. In *Thieves in the Night,* Koestler tried to be objective, to present all sides of the problem fairly. But he would probably be the last to claim that he was impartial with regard to this matter where the destinies of human beings are at stake. More so than perhaps any other place in the world, Palestine has a quality of inducing intense feeling. There is little of the middle-of-the-road spirit in the Bible; it is a book of deep passion, great hopes, lofty vision. And so today: it seems that everyone touched by Palestine becomes aflame. I've often said that the best expenditure for Zionist organizations would be to send writers there. Again and again, Christians and Jews visiting there with neutral opinions about this issue have been caught up by the ideal. It is not insignificant that of those who really know the subject well, there are very few unsympathetic to the Jewish cause.

The book moves in three concentric circles. In the innermost, it tells the stories of individuals. Joseph, son of an English aristocratic mother and a Jewish father, who coming against the ugly fact of anti-Semitism is deeply wounded and driven to find his destiny by returning to the Jewish people and joining a cooperative colony in Palestine. And Dina, the girl he loves, who carries bitter memories of unforgettable experiences in concentration camps, with haunting effects that make normal emotional life for her impossible; the tragedy of her life is crowned with an equally tragic death. And a host of other vivid characters as well.

The second, larger circle in which these characters play their part is the story of Ezra's Tower, a typical new colony of Palestine, erected on Jewish-owned land, but against the opposition of both the Arabs and the British. The story of the new colonies would provide material for an epic of modern Jewish history, as full of courage and hope as those of the early settlers on this continent, and with much more justice behind them. Hundreds of such colonies have been established in recent years. A small group of people who have joined together and prepared themselves for months or years finally are given the signal to go ahead. Everything is prepared carefully in advance. Specially trained workers come to join them for the first twenty-four hours, which are the most crucial. In the pitch darkness of night they start out, by morning the foundations of the new colony are already in place: a watchtower has been constructed, an electric generator installed, a protective wall set up. By nightfall of the first day, they are ready to live, work and defend themselves. A new colony exists on Jewish soil.[1]

When I was in Palestine in 1939, I was invited to participate in one of these expeditions. I was given careful directions as to where to come. I promised flippantly, "I'll be there. Nothing but an Arab bullet will stop me." Perhaps I talked too loud. For the morning of the day that had been set, the Arab bullet came and caused a slight change in my plans.[2] But anyone who reads Koestler's story will

---

1. Compare the very similar contemporary description published in Henry Near, *The Kibbutz Movement: A History*, 2 vols. (Oxford: Oxford University Press, 1992, 1997), 1:317–18. For background and context, see Sachar, *A History of Israel* (New York: Knopf, 1996), 216.

2. Most of the listeners would have understood this reference to the preacher's having been lightly wounded in an Arab attack during the 1939 visit. Members of the congregation learned of this by reading a brief article in the *New York Times* of August 3, 1939 under the headline "American Wounded in a Palestine Bus," which began, "Harold Saperstein, an American tourist, suffered a slight gunshot wound today when a bus in which he was a passenger was ambushed outside Haifa." The *Palestine Post* article of the same date (p. 2) states that the attack occurred in Haifa, in a bus travelling to Mishmar Ha-Emek. In a talk given at Cornell in early 1940, Saperstein said that in his speaking to various audiences in recent months, "Invariably, I am introduced as the Rabbi who was shot in Palestine. When, after what I usually consider a stimulating and provocative address, the floor is opened to questions, the first one, without exception is, 'Where were

feel as though he lives through the experience. Then the excitement of the first twenty-four hours is over, and the story settles down to the depiction of the routine of day by day life in the colony, the problems of social adjustment and personality conflict and different people's thinking.

I liked the fact that Koestler didn't try to romanticize. He did not make every *chalutz* as handsome as a motion picture star; he did not make life just one brave round of working with a will and singing songs of joyous hope. Life is much harsher and sterner than that. People in the colonies are human beings, with the virtues and weaknesses that, well, we have. But all in all, they are people we can be proud of, whose lives are bound up with a great ideal, and the pattern of whose existence reveals that the social vision of the prophets and the heroism of the Maccabees are still living forces in Israel.

The third circle is that of international events and the large problem of the rights of the Jews to Palestine. The story takes place between 1937 and 1939, against the background of the rising shadow of Hitler in Europe, with waves of immigrants, mostly so-called "illegal immigrants," coming into the land, and with the British putting into effect the policy of the then newly issued "White Paper," which repudiated the entire reason for the British to be there.[3] The larger problems of Zionism are revealed through the personalities and views of typical individuals. Among the Jews we see the chalutz, the pioneer, to whom Palestine and his right to it and his need for it is a matter not of theory but of life. We see the compromising university professor. We see the [Jewish] terrorist who has reached the conclusion that only steel and bullets are heard in a world where nice-sounding words have become so cheap.

Among the Arabs we see the clever, young, modern, educated politician, combining personal ambition with a theory of renascent Arab nationalism in Palestine, of which the mass of Arabs know and feel nothing. Best portrayed of all is the elderly Arab village chieftain, who represents the preference for the old way of life that is being upset by the new Jewish settlers. His words are a classic articulation of that view:

> We want to live our own way and we want no foreign teacher and no foreign money and no foreign habits and no smiles of condescension and no pat on the shoulder and no arrogance and no shameless women with wriggling buttocks in our holy places.[4]

you shot?' And for some reason, audiences are always disappointed when I answer, 'I was shot between the Emek and Haifa.'"

3. The "White Paper," issued by the British on May 17, 1939, infuriated the Jewish community of Palestine and Zionists throughout the world by imposing a quota of 10,000 Jewish immigrants to Palestine for each of the next five years, plus 25,000 refugees, after which there would be no future Jewish immigration without the consent of the Arabs. It also prohibited sale of land to Jews.

4. Arthur Koestler, *Thieves in the Night: Chronicle of an Experiment* (London: Macmillan & Co., 1946), 214–15. While this quotation seems appropriate for the village Mukhtar, in the book it is actually spoken by the "editor of a moderate Arab weekly."

It doesn't matter that the American non-Jewish reporter reminds him that the Jews "haven't robbed you of an inch of your land, but they have robbed you of your malaria and trachoma and your septic child-beds and your poverty."[5]

Finally, we have the picture of the typical English colonial officials—attracted by the glamour and exotic character of the Arab, enjoying the feeling of the master race that Arab obsequiousness inspires, disliking the keen, intelligent Jews, who are more than a match for them mentally and who see through their pretenses—and of the Englishmen who are basically decent people and find it hard to reconcile their own feelings with official policy, but who have a job to be done.

In all these respects, the book is a strong argument for the Jewish cause, and one that all may read with profit. I would, however, take issue with the conclusion of the book. For it ends with its central figure, Joseph, joining the terrorist group, convinced that every other method must inevitably fail. As the author puts it, "One can reach a point of humiliation where violence is the only outlet."[6] One gets tired of being reasonable, of waiting while nations play politics. As Joseph says, "I was the reasonable fly running in zigzags over the window-pane because there was light on the other side, and I had my legs torn out and my wings burnt off with matches. I am through with your reasonableness."[7]

I don't believe in terrorism. I feel distress—mingled, I must admit, with a measure of admiration—when I read about acts of [Jewish] terrorism in Palestine. But I think it's the wrong way, and that it is doing our cause more harm than good. At the same time, I think it is time for the British to realize that the responsibility for the terrorism lies not upon the Jews but upon themselves.

How would you feel if you were a Jew in Palestine, who had left all his family behind, hoping some day to bring them to join you. When you are ready, restrictions placed by the British prevent you from bringing them. Then the war comes, and a black curtain cuts you off from all contact. When it is lifted, you learn that almost all of them—to use the phrase the DPs would use to describe the fate of their loved ones—all of them "went up in smoke," met their death in the gas chambers of the Nazis. Of the entire family—father, mother, brothers and sisters—only one survived: a younger brother or sister, who had gone through five years of living hell, but who at least was still alive and looking forward to being reunited with you. You can't wait.

But the "powers that be" say, "No, we cannot rush. We've got to look into this matter. We have to send an investigating committee, to see whether your brother really wants to go to Palestine. And if the investigating committee reports that he does, we'll send another one to make sure they didn't get it wrong. And then we'll call a conference of everybody concerned and see whether we can do it. In fact we'll call a couple of conferences." The months go by, and they stretch into years after the war is over, and your brother or sister is still in a DP

---

5. Koestler, 214.
6. Koestler, 227.
7. Koestler, 156.

camp. Let us understand that this kind of experience is what makes the psychology of the terrorist.

My friends, let the British quit their moral posturing and their political hypocrisy and their condemnations of terrorism. When you owe a man a debt, a debt that spells life or death for him and his loved ones, and you can easily afford to pay it, and for selfish reasons you refuse, and, after begging and pleading and appealing to mercy and to justice, he is still refused, he may very well finally decide to try violence. That is very bad, but don't put on any of your moral airs. Pay your debts first.

We can understand what leads to terrorism, though we do not condone it. I think the tendency in certain Jewish circles to approve it is a dangerous one. But I do believe in resistance. I do believe that we must go on with our work.

In commenting on the passage from this week's *sedrah* [*Be-Shallah*], the rabbis tell us that when Israel came to the Red Sea and saw the hosts of the Egyptians pursuing them, there were four groups among them. One group, broken by misfortune, was ready to return to Egypt and continue their lives as slaves. A second group said, "Let us pray to God and leave it in His hands. We ourselves are powerless." A third group, driven to hysteria, said, "Let us fling ourselves upon the spears of the Egyptians," even though they knew that the struggle was hopeless. A fourth group, responding to the command of God [see Exod. 14:15], said, "Let us move forward even though it be into the sea. A way will open if we do not yield to despair."[8]

We find these four groups today. One says, "We will never succeed. Let's give up our hopes and reconcile ourselves that we made a mistake by starting out." Another group says, "There is nothing we can do. Let's just wait and hope that God will not forsake us." A third group says, "Let us fight. Terrorism is the only answer." But the approach that prevailed in ancient days is still the only true answer: "Let us go forward." Let us carry on our work—bring newcomers into Palestine, build new colonies, work on the political front, resist when anyone tries to stop us, but above all, keep advancing. It is not an easy answer. Before us lies the sea. But perhaps in our day too, the path through the sea will again be opened for us, and we will march forward to the Promised Land.

---

8. Compare the use of this rabbinic aggadah in the Rosh Hashanah, 1939, sermon, "Unconquered," and the Rosh Hashanah evening sermon from 1944.

20

Israel and Us
May 21, 1948

In a sermon dated May 6, 1950, Saperstein spoke about his whereabouts on the day when Israel's independence was actually proclaimed, May 14, 1948: "I was listening to the radio, driving up to preach at Cornell University, and how sorry I felt that I could not be with my own congregation on that historic night." The Sisterhood Installation mentioned in the first sentence might have taken place on the previous Friday evening, May 7, or some time during the week following May 14. But May 21 was the first occasion for a regular sermon at Temple Emanu-El after the declaration of the State. The emotions of that moment were expressed at the outset: what a privilege it was for a Jew to be living at this time that so many generations of ancestors had prayed to see. Themes we have encountered in the previous two sermons are reprised—particularly the bonds of Jewish unity, and the disgust with the behavior of the British. But the sermon is primarily an attempt to communicate both the significance of the event against the broad canvas of Jewish history and the specific challenges that face the newborn State at the present moment.

SPEAKING TO THE SISTERHOOD AT ITS INSTALLATION, I noted that eighty generations of our ancestors hoped and prayed for the events of this month, and would have considered themselves blessed to be alive now. It sounds glib; only in personal terms can we realize what that statement means. I know, for instance, that my grandfather, the elder Rabbi Lasker,[1] in the time of Theodor

---

1. Hyman Max (Chaim Mordecai) Lasker, who received ordination from Rabbi Isaac Elchanan Spector in Kovno and served as Rabbi in Troy, New York; his son, Adolph Lasker, a graduate of the Jewish Institute of Religion, was Saperstein's uncle and predecessor in the Lynbrook congregation until his death in 1933.

Herzl, was among the first of the Orthodox rabbis to give their support to the Zionist cause. Before that I have no personal knowledge. But this I do know, for I know the waters from which they drank. For generations before, in Jewish communities of Eastern Europe, my ancestors prayed, *Vesechezena enenu,* "Let our eyes behold Thy return in mercy unto Zion," three times each day.[2] Like other ancestors living in the ghettos of medieval Europe, hounded and afflicted, they gathered each year at Passover in homes that however humble were radiant with spiritual beauty and ended their seders with the words, *Leshono Habo Berushalayim,* "Next year in Jerusalem." And further back still, in that band of Jews who went forth into exile in Babylonia 2,500 years ago, there was one in whose veins flowed blood that at this distant date I have inherited, who sang in sorrow with his fellow Jews, "If I forget thee, O Jerusalem" (Ps. 137:5).

Even without this event, this generation would have been an historic one for the Jewish people. But it would have been historic in negative terms: the greatest tragedy our people has ever experienced. This will not cancel out that tragedy. But it will balance it. Our generation will be remembered as the first generation in 2,000 years privileged to see a Jewish flag flying proudly over our own land on our ancient soil.

Rabbi Irving Miller, speaking to our UJA dinner, said that each day he prays that he may be worthy of living at this hour.[3] I think that all of us should ask: What does this hour demand of us? For it is patently not enough to look upon events merely as spectators. Just as our past is bound up with that of other Jews, so our destiny is bound up with theirs. What then must be our relationship, as Israel in America, to the people of the land of Israel?

First, we must recognize that our brothers are at war. War is a terrible thing, and of all the peoples on earth, there are few that have such a deep horror of war as the Jewish people. Early deprived of power, we have often been among the victims of war, seldom among its wagers. But much as we have hated war, there have been times when we have taken up arms without hesitation or fear because the cause for which we were fighting was so important. This is one of those times.

We intended no harm to the Arab. Our hand was outstretched in friendship. This was not accepted. Some day the Arab peoples will realize that they have been the victims of their own leaders. It is to the eternal shame of the nations of the world that after 2,000 years and six million dead in the past decade, we still must fight for our own. And I say this with deliberation, that seldom in the history of mankind has there been a nation that has fallen so low in terms of moral principles as has the British Empire, which failed not only in administering the Mandate, but also in administering humanity. But what must be must be. At

---

2. This sentence is part of the core liturgy (*Shemoneh Esreh*) of the daily morning, afternoon and evening services.

3. Miller was at the time rabbi of the Orthodox Congregation Sons of Israel in nearby Woodmere, Long Island. He was chairman of the National Administrative Council of the Zionist Organization of America in 1948, and would become president of the American Jewish Congress in 1949 and of the ZOA in 1952.

least we can thank God that our people in Israel are able to fight with courage and honor and skill.

Let us not be too easily discouraged. There will be reverses, as there must always be in warfare. We stand alone in Palestine: 600,000 people against the armies of nations numbering 40 million, a ratio in populations of almost one hundred to one. We must also remember that we have been a legal army only since the 14th of May. Before then, every bit of fighting equipment was contraband. It was illegal to own even a rifle, let alone large equipment; to be caught was punishable by life imprisonment. Our enemies have had complete freedom, plus the active assistance of England, in building up their war potential. Third, the advantage in military strategy invariably lies with the force taking the initiative. They can strike where and when they wish; we must be prepared to meet them on every front.

But we have sources of power that will weigh in the balance before the end. First, we have a new generation of Jews: strong, brave, stalwart and skilled. I remember years ago when I was in college [at Cornell], living at the Cosmopolitan Club, a debate between an Arab and a Palestinian [Jew]. The Arab pointed out that in case of fighting, the Arabs of Palestine outnumbered the Jews seven to one. The young Palestinian calmly answered, without *braggadocio*, "That makes it even, for one Jew can outfight seven Arabs.

Second, we have a cause and a faith. David, coming up against Goliath, said, "You come against me with a sword and a spear, but I come against you in the name of the Lord of Hosts, the God of Israel" (I Sam. 17:45). Judah the Maccabee, speaking to the Israelites before their battle, though hopelessly outnumbered, said, "It is one with God [i.e., it is all the same, it makes no difference] to redeem by many or by few" (I Maccabees 3:18). We today are fighting in the name of God and six million martyrs. They are on our side, an unbeatable combination. Finally, the Jews of the world sacrificed for war against the Nazis. We must be ready to sacrifice again in war for Israel. We are the home front; we must not let them down.

Let us turn now to economic relationships. There are some who say, "Israel can never be a normal state; it can endure only by the largesse of Jews in the rest of the world. It will always be a recipient of charity on an international scale." This shows a lack of appreciation of the facts. Just as the Israelis could have had peace in a moment by relinquishing their freedom, so they could have economic stability by closing their doors to their brothers, by saying "We're here, let them take care of themselves." The money we have been sending to Palestine has not been to take care of permanent indigents. It was sent to help the Jews in Palestine perform a responsibility as much ours as theirs: receiving and caring for newcomers.

Remember that in the last fifteen years, the Jewish population of Palestine has more than tripled. How could we ever have expected the Jews of Palestine to take upon themselves twice their number and absorb them without assistance? This would be like America taking in 300 million newcomers in fifteen years. During the next fifteen years, we will again triple our population in Palestine. There will be large international loans and other ways of financing programs.

But in large part, it will have to continue to depend on the support of the Jews of America, who must not stop giving so long as God does not stop giving to us. One satisfaction we can have in giving is the knowledge that we are no longer pouring into a bottomless pit. We are building so that future generations in Palestine will need help no longer, but will live in peace and plenty on their own soil.

There is also the religious relationship. There has been a great deal of talk about the normalization of Jewish life, the claim that when Jews have the land of Israel, we will have the same sense of loyalty to it that Americans descended from Englishmen have to England, or Americans descended from Greeks have to Greece. That is not true. Our relationship to Israel is different in character. Those other national loyalties weaken and diminish until after several generations they exist only vaguely. We will not owe any political allegiance to Israel any more than these other peoples owe to the land of their origins. But while their spiritual attachment may disappear, ours, we hope, will continue, unweakened, from generation to generation.

The reason is in the strange combination of religion and nationality, the junction of the faith of Israel and the land of Israel, which makes the Jews unique. Our faith is different from that of our neighbors in part in that it is bound up with land. And Israel is a land different from others in that it is bound up with faith. Read our Prayer Book, read the Bible. Tomorrow, for instance, our Bar Mitzvah boy will read the prophecy from Ezekiel, who lived in the time of exile, in which God promised that He would rebuild the waste places and restore His people to their land.[4] We are seeing the fulfillment of prophecies made thousands of years ago. How can it fail to have an effect upon us? Visiting Israel for Jews will be more than a visit to the land of our ancestors. It will be a sacred pilgrimage to the center of our inspiration. Jewish life in Israel will be more than another Jewish community. This will be the only community that can be completely Jewish: in language, in culture, in daily life. I need not here discuss the religious tendencies in Palestine. It is enough to say that back in the land of its origins, Judaism will draw new strength and will be an inspiration to Jews throughout the world.

Finally, the human relationship to Israel. The establishment of the Jewish State is of vital concern not only to Jews, but to all mankind. It does not matter that in numbers we will be tiny. Sooner or later, we will have a voice in the assembly of nations of the world; more than that, we will have the prestige which only the Holy Land possesses. Remember, it was only a little nation when we produced the religious ideals that have kindled light for all mankind. The very miracle of our homeless people, fighting against desperate odds and winning out

---

4. This description would appear to apply to Amos 9:11–15, the Haftarah for *Kedoshim*, which ordinarily would have been read the previous Sabbath. The Haftarah for Emor, the lesson scheduled for May 21, 1948, begins with Ezekiel 44:15 and focuses on the role of the Levitical priests in the rebuilt Temple.

against power politics and selfish interests[5] will itself—when our age is seen in perspective—be one of the great shining lights of our generation. Oppressed groups until the end of time will take courage from it, even as the story of the Exodus from Egypt in ancient times has been a beacon light of inspiration to all peoples seeking freedom. It will bring men renewed faith in the moral law of mankind, in the ultimate triumph of the right. But more than that, out of the magic combination of land and people may come a transcendent good. Here there is a laboratory, a microcosm of all the problems that trouble humanity— human relationships, revitalizing faith, racial tensions, economic justice, nationalism and peace. We must not expect too much too soon. Berdichevski noted that, like Jacob, we must first have a stone on which to lay our heads. But like Jacob, we will dream,[6] and that dream may well kindle once again a light to guide man in the darkness.

It was in 1895 that Theodor Herzl wrote *The Jewish State*. He was called a madman then. He said in response, "If you wish to be right in fifty years, you must be ready to be called mad now."[7] Fifty years have passed, and his dream has come true. His name can be numbered among the prophets. As we read his words, it is as though they throb with the sound of the angels' wings he said he heard as he was writing them:

> The idea [of the Jewish State] must make its way into the most distant, miserable holes where our people dwell. They will awaken from gloomy brooding, for into their lives will come a new significance. Every man need think only of himself, and the movement will assume vast proportions.
>
> And what glory awaits those who fight unselfishly for the cause!
>
> Therefore I believe that a wondrous generation of Jews will spring into existence. The Maccabees will rise again.
>
> Let me repeat once more my opening words: The Jews who wish it will have their State.

---

5. The typescript of the sermon contains at this point the parenthetical remark, "(phrases from Jew[ish] Ed[ucator?] Vol. 19 #2p2)."

6. Based on Genesis 23:11–12. Saperstein repeated this comment by Berdichevski in his Rosh Hashanah 1950 sermon and (with a different application) in his November 14, 1975, sermon below. Shalom Spiegel, the advisor for Saperstein's rabbinic thesis on Berdichevski, cited this as "the profoundest word that has been said in Zionism: 'Give us first a stone whereon to lay our head—and then we shall dream.'" See *Hebrew Reborn* (Cleveland: World Publishing Company, 1962), 356.

7. Compare the following entry in Herzl's diary (February 17, 1896) following the appearance of *The Jewish State*: "Not a word yet in the local press. Nevertheless the pamphlet begins to be spoken of. Acquaintances ask me: 'Did you write that pamphlet people are talking about? Is it a joke or something meant to be serious?' I answer: 'Deadly serious. Naturally, whoever undertakes a thing of this kind must expect to have the street boys running after him.'" *The Diaries of Theodor Herzl*, ed. Marvin Lowenthal (New York: Grosset & Dunlap, 1956), 98. The "fifty years" figure appears in the famous entry following the Basle Conference, September 3, 1897: "At Basle I founded the Jewish State. If I said this out loud today I would be greeted by universal laughter. In five years perhaps, and certainly in fifty years, everyone will perceive it" (*Diaries*, 224).

We shall live at last as free men on our own soil and die peacefully in our own homes.

The world will be freed by our liberty, enriched by our wealth, magnified by our greatness.

And whatever we attempt there to accomplish for our own welfare, will react powerfully and beneficently for the good.[8]

8. Herzl, *The Jewish State*; see Arthur Hertzberg, *The Zionist Idea* (New York: Atheneusm, 1959), 225–26.

21

A Prince in Israel
April 22, 1949

Stephen S. Wise died of stomach cancer on April 19, 1949, at the age of seventy-five. On Friday, April 22, 3,000 people filled Carnegie Hall, with more than 10,000 standing outside, for the funeral service.

Jewish and general newspapers were filled with tributes and eulogies by dozens of the major leaders of American Jewish life, as well as of the liberal Christian community. With the silencing of his powerful voice, many felt that an era had come to an end, that—despite the attacks against his public positions by other Jews both from the left and from the right—he had spoken for American Jewry in a way no one could replace, and that the interests of world Jewry would henceforth be represented most effectively by the leadership of the new State of Israel.

Both explicit references in the sermons of the 1930s and our editorial annotations pointing to unspoken parallels indicate the impact of Wise on Saperstein during his student years and the early years of his rabbinate. The tribute below, disclaiming the role of a "formal eulogy," turns to the personal voice in order to present a picture of the human side of Wise beneath the public persona. The impact of this celebrated leader is dramatized by describing not only the experience of hearing Wise speak for the first time—at Cornell University—but also the time that Wise had taken to talk to an undergraduate, who was then weighing the rabbinate against a career in the law, and who discovered in this encounter a model and an ideal.

The end of the sermon is characteristic of Saperstein's homiletical technique: the reference to an earlier talk, given more than fourteen years previously upon the premature death of his uncle, his predecessor in the Lynbrook Temple, the use of a literary source not from a classical Jewish text (the short vignette by the South African writer Olive Schreiner), and the climax intended to stir the emotions and produce an uplifting, cathartic effect.

MY ADDRESS TONIGHT IS NOT INTENDED TO BE A FORMAL EULOGY of Dr. Wise, or to summarize his contributions to Jewish life. For that you need merely to have read the newspapers when his death was announced, or read the current Jewish magazines, or better still, wait until his true stature is realized in the perspective of time. Tonight, as one who was proud to number himself among his disciples, and was privileged to have been inspired by his influence and to have borne his friendship, I would like to speak informally of Dr. Wise, the man.

The Bible knows no greater distinction than that of being "a man." "The man Moses" (Num. 12:3). Elijah is a "man of God" (2 Kings 1:9,13). "The man Mordecai" (Esth. 9:4). In these expressions, manhood implies more than mere male identity. It is rather the fulfillment of the words of creation, "Let us form man in our image" (Gen. 1:26). That is what we mean when we speak of Dr. Wise, the man.

My first contact with him was back in the spring of 1931, when Dr. Wise came to the campus of Cornell University to speak at the Sunday morning services of Sage Chapel. There, each week, the greatest Christian preachers of the country were invited. But on those occasions when Dr. Wise came, the largest crowds the chapel had ever drawn always turned out. Previously, Dr. Wise had merely been a name to me. Then, as I entered into my last year at college, there came to me a realization of something which had been there all the time but to which I had been blind—the realization that the greatest fulfillment life could bring to me would be if I could devote it to Jewish religious leadership.[1]

At this point, the name Dr. Wise took on new meaning. For he represented the kind of leadership I felt I should like to take as my model. When I learned that the Jewish Institute of Religion was a truly liberal seminary, in that it accepted students of all approaches to Judaism and permitted them the freedom to interpret and practice Judaism as they desired, it seemed to me that that was the school I wanted. Then came the question, would they admit me? Unlike schools for other professions, here there was fortunately no problem of anti-Semitism. The problem was the reverse. All the other applicants had been preparing for this from their earliest childhood. My own preparation was at the time woefully incomplete.

---

1. It is rather extraordinary how many men who went on to distinguished careers in the rabbinate or other areas of Jewish life describe in similar terms the impact of first hearing Wise speak or first meeting with him when they were students. Two examples will have to stand for many. For example, Jacob Philip Rudin (rabbi of Temple Beth-El of Great Neck, Long Island), "Founder's Day Address," HUC-JIR, New York, March 12, 1954, 3–4, describing Wise's visit to Harvard in 1923, when Rudin was a junior: "I heard a man speak as I had never heard a man speak before. . . . I knew then and there that I would go to the Jewish Institute of Religion if Dr. Wise would have me." Robert P. Jacobs (founding rabbi of the Hillel Foundation at Washington University in St. Louis), *By Reason of Strength* (The St. Louis Rabbinical Association, 1998), 22: "In the fall of 1928 my father took me to the 1,000-seat Loew's Theatre in downtown Syracuse, NY, to hear Rabbi Stephen S. Wise speak. . . . That one speech changed my life. I would become a rabbi and go to his school for my studies. I did."

I had written to Dr. Wise and he had arranged an interview following his sermon. I shall always remember the sense of pride I had that morning in Sage Chapel as I looked around and saw the faces of thousands of university faculty and students, practically all non-Jewish, listening with rapt attention and profound respect to this Rabbi. I came up to him afterward with a great deal of trepidation. And then I found out something about Dr. Wise. When one was near him, you had a sense of his greatness. There was something majestic about him—when, for example, you found yourself in a room with him, no matter how large it was, the room seemed crowded—but at the same time he was a very simple man, a man without pretense or artificiality. For an hour we walked back and forth across the campus in the rain while we talked about the problems of Judaism. I found myself soon pouring out my heart to him as though he were an old friend.

That night he spoke at a meeting that our newly formed Hillel Foundation had arranged. The President of the University was there, as was everyone else on campus who amounted to anything. Dr. Wise spoke on Zionism. I had been a Zionist sympathizer from my childhood.[2] But that night for the first time, I heard Zionism with that fervor and understanding of which only Dr. Wise was capable. It moved me more deeply than I can say. I think that in all the hundreds of Zionist speeches I've made myself since that night, I have been subconsciously trying to catch the echo of Dr. Wise.[3]

Apparently my interview was successful, for I was accepted, and the next four years of my life were tied up with the Jewish Institute of Religion and Dr. Wise. As you know, he was its President. In addition, he had his hand in every important cause in Jewish and civil life. Yet somehow he found time to be not merely a President in name and in an official sense, but also to be a friend.

Our day began with chapel. Many of the students found it hard to get to school on time for the service. But each morning, Dr. Wise was there, his head bent in prayer, as he stoked up the spiritual energy for the enormous work that he did—enough to keep six ordinary men busy, work which allowed no more than five hours of sleep a night for the greater part of his life.

Once each week the entire school gathered for the homiletics class. One of the students would preach; Dr. Wise would listen carefully and then, from the wealth of his experience and his great pulpit power, he would criticize it. You might think he was asleep while you were speaking, but after you were finished he could invariably repeat the sermon almost word for word. No commendation has ever been awaited with greater anxiety or received with greater satisfaction than Dr. Wise's, "That was a good sermon."

And once each week we would gather in his study and he would let us peek behind the scenes of Jewish life. He was in constant communication with Jewish leaders all over the world. The great of many nations and of all faiths kept him informed and asked for his counsel and help. He would discuss with us the

---

2. Compare the opening paragraph of the previous sermon.

3. For a discussion of Wise's Zionist preaching, see Robert Friedenberg, *"Hear O Israel"* (Tuscaloosa: University of Alabama Press, 1989), 97–101.

problems that were most pressing at the moment. Sometimes, if he was uncertain, he would ask for our opinion, and he was not above taking notes on what we, his students, might think and utilizing our ideas in his public utterances. He would hand out cigars—not the good ones, which he kept for special guests, but those that he wouldn't dare give to anyone but his students—and every few moments, Mrs. Wise, busy in the child adoption office down the hall,[4] would open the door and stick her head in to make sure that nobody had dared light up one of the cigars, which his doctors had prohibited.

To complete the picture of his humanity, I recall how each Purim the students would present our Purim play. We would caricature the members of the faculty. Nor would we hesitate to lay it on thick when it came to poking loving fun at our leader, for on Purim everything goes. And invariably, the voice that rang out above all others in laughter at himself was that of Rabbi Wise.

From time to time we would have the opportunity to hear him speak from the pulpit or from the platform. He was the greatest orator of the generation in America. Some have said that he would have made a great actor, because of his deep, rich, expressive voice. But they are wrong. Dr. Wise could not act. When he had to read something that was not his own, he read it very poorly. It was only when he was expressing something that he felt very deeply, when the great fire of his spirit smoldered and burst into flame, that his voice became infused with passion. His whole body became transformed; he rose to oratorical heights and lifted his audiences to levels that he alone could do. He was a dramatic speaker, but dramatic quality was not something that he achieved artificially. It was something that flowed out of the fervor and sincerity of his message.

It was my fate to be a student at the Institute during those early years when Hitler first came to power. Of all the great political thinkers, of all the great Jewish leaders, it was Dr. Wise alone who recognized the true menace that Hitler represented to the Jewish people and to the world. (The first three issues of the American Jewish Congress publication—now the "Congress Weekly," were put out by Rabbi Morton Berman, now in Chicago, and myself in that first hectic month in the spring of 1933.)[5] Others attacked him bitterly; they accused him of seeking notoriety because he called great public meetings of protest. I shall never forget that first great mass meeting in Madison Square Garden [on March 27, 1933] when, for the first time, the voice of civilization cried out through the

---

4. Louise Waterman Wise, who was instrumental in establishing the Child Adoption Committee of the Free Synagogue in 1917, the first agency devoted to the fostering of adoption for orphaned Jewish children. The Free Synagogue (later named the Stephen S. Wise Free Synagogue) was adjacent to the Jewish Institute of Religion on West 68th Street in Manhattan.

5. In 1933, Berman, ordained by the Jewish Institute of Religion in 1926, was serving as assistant to Rabbi Wise at the Free Synagogue in Manhattan. The first issue of the new "American Jewish Congress Courier," of which he was editor, was dated April 21, 1933; Saperstein used material prepared for this first issue in his April 28, 1933, sermon printed above. (This periodical was renamed the "Congress Bulletin" in the issue of January 11, 1935, and the "Congress Weekly" in January 1941.)

lips of Stephen S. Wise against the Nazi menace.[6] Hitler himself recognized the significance of this Jewish leader, for he grouped Wise with Mayor La Guardia and Franklin D. Roosevelt as his greatest enemies in America.[7]

But it was not until the war years, when Dr. Wise was already an old man, that I felt the true greatness of his stature. As a matter of course, I mailed him one of the letters I sent out [from Europe] to my congregation. Numerous as were his tasks and responsibilities, I received a long reply by return mail. Throughout the war, this correspondence continued. I almost hesitated to write to him, for I knew how greatly he was burdened, but never did he fail to answer. In his own inimitable style, every letter had not only his signature in his writing, but also some addition or correction in his own hand, to show that it had received his personal attention—no matter how perfectly typed the letter had been. At the time when Marcia and I were married, he left an important Zionist meeting to conduct the service. And he was not too busy to write three personal messages of good wishes when our first child was born.[8]

---

6. See the beginning of the April 28, 1933, sermon, above. Saperstein described the impact of this rally in a sermon given the day after Thanksgiving 1933:

> Shall I tell you of one of the profoundest experiences of my life? It was on March 27 of this year. I was at Madison Square Garden at the great protest meeting sponsored by the American Jewish Congress. . . . There around me was a sea of faces, more than 20,000 of them, my fellow Jews. As I thought of those 20,000, and more than twice that many more milling around the streets outside, and hundreds of thousands more listening to the radio at home, all our hearts beating in unison, petty differences of parties and beliefs forgotten, all united in a common interest and a common sympathy for other Jews more than 3,000 miles away, my heart filled with emotion. I felt as if I would have liked to embrace each one of them and say, "Shalom, my brother." And when I looked at the rostrum and heard Bishop McConnell and Bishop Manning and Alfred E. Smith raising their voices, that the world might hear, against a great wrong perpetrated upon our oft-wronged people, a thought came to my head, and it intoxicated me like wine: the thought that I was standing on holy ground, witness to a great event in Jewish history.

7. I have not been able to find the source for such a statement by Hitler. Wise was, however, frequently vilified by Nazi propaganda. For example, the *Congress Bulletin* issue of April 3, 1936 (2:23) contained an article on p. 8 headlined "Dr. Wise Gets Under Hitler's Skin; So *Stuermer* Erupts." This summarizes and quotes from an article by one Fritz Brand in the February 14, 1936, issue of *Der Stuermer,* reacting to Wise's efforts urging New York department stores to boycott Christmas season toys produced in Nazi Germany. To quote *Der Stuermer* as reported by the *Congress Bulletin,* "Suddenly the love of Chief Rabbi Wise for the contemptible non-Jews awoke. With devilish maneuvering, practiced only by Jews, he warned benevolent Catholics of the peril menacing their churches in Germany. Success was assured. He succeeded in bringing about the participation of prominent Catholics in the Jewish boycott."

8. The three separate letters, addressed to father, mother, and newborn infant, are in the possession of the editor.

As I traveled around, both immediately before and during the war, and met with Jews of all kinds—pious Polish Chassidim and German Jews under Hitler's yoke, Jews in Orthodox Yeshivas before the war and in concentration camps right after the war, pioneer Jews in Palestine colonies and refugee Jews seeking a home—to all of them the name Stephen Wise (or "Shteffan Vise," as they pronounced it) was a magic password. They all knew it, and the mere mention of the name brought a look of pride and strength into their eyes. For to all of them, he was the symbol of the courageous Jewish people, of the unconquerable Jewish spirit.

Those who attended the conference of the World Jewish Congress at Montreux, Switzerland, last summer, at which Dr. Wise presided as its President, speak of the touching tribute paid by the representatives who gathered there, many of them survivors of the tragedy of European Jewry, who saw in Dr. Wise the symbol of the unity of the Jewish people.

It seems indeed an act of providence that he was spared to see the establishment of the State of Israel. For that was one of the great hopes and sublime causes of his life. (He often told me how he, a Reform rabbi, had worked together with my beloved grandfather, [Hyman Lasker of Troy, New York] an Orthodox rabbi.) Back in 1897, shortly after Wise had founded the American Zionist Federation, parent of the ZOA, in a time when Zionism was a very questionable movement, Theodor Herzl, at a World Zionist Congress, said to him, "Stephen, I may not live to see it, but before fifty years have passed you will see the Jewish State reborn."[9] Herzl's prophecy has come true.

When I first came to this congregation, following the death of my uncle [Rabbi Adolph Lasker, an early graduate of the Jewish Institute of Religion], also a disciple of Dr. Wise, I paid tribute to my uncle with this story by Olive Schreiner, which applies even more aptly to the man whom both of us called *morenu verabenu*, "our master and our teacher." It is called, "The Artist's Secret." Once there was an artist whose works were distinguished by a strange shade of red—pulsing, vibrant, and lifelike. Other artists tried to imitate it, but none succeeded. The artist went on painting with all the fervor of his spirit, and all his paintings had that strange, lifelike character and that haunting red tone. He himself grew paler and weaker until at last he died. When the other artists came to pay their tribute, they looked curiously about the room, wondering if they could find the artist's secret, the mystery of the strange red color that no one could imitate. They did not find it. They could not see that underneath his burial clothes, above his heart, was a tiny wound, only now closed in death. The artist had been painting with his life's blood.[10]

---

9. Wise reported this statement (dated to 1904) in his autobiography as follows: "I shall not live to see the Jewish State, but you, Wise, are a young man. You will live to see the Jewish State" (*Challenging Years* [New York: Putnam's, 1949], 37. On the "fifty years" figure, see Herzl's diary entry noted in the previous sermon, n. 4. Wise attended the Second Zionist Congress in 1898 as a representative of American Zionists.

10. "The Artist's Secret" was published by Schreiner in *Dreams*, 1890. See *An Olive Schreiner Reader*, ed. Carol Barash (London: Pandora, 1987), 149. The final explanatory

Dr. Wise has rendered incomparable service to the cause of the Jewish people and democracy. There will be no one to replace him. The pictures he painted on the canvas of Jewish and American life were unique, for he painted with his life's blood. In a sense, all Jews are his disciples and his debtors. May we prove worthy of him as we march on, holding aloft the banner he handed on to us, serving the great causes he advanced so far but left unfinished.

---

sentence of the paragraph is not in the one-page vignette, which ends, "And it came to pass that after a while the artist was forgotten—but the work lived." This was not a point to be emphasized at the present occasion, while the general point of the story, vividly exemplifying renunciation and sacrifice of self in creating something enduring for others, was indeed appropriate.

22

Outside the Law
September 9, 1949

In many ways, Paul Robeson represented for the American black the kind of figure whom Saperstein admired so much in Wise as a representative of the American Jew: widely respected for his talents in the general community, dignified and proud of his identity, an uncompromising champion of the underdog and the oppressed, a tireless spokesman on behalf of the principles to which he was passionately devoted. When Robeson's communist sympathies began to arouse increasingly confrontational opposition against the background of the growing "Red Scare," a homiletical challenge was created.

Despite his socialist leanings in the 1930s, Saperstein had contempt for Soviet-style communism as stifling human freedom and Jewish self-expression. Yet the sermon evoked by the Peekskill riots against Robeson's concerts was not an attempt to define a moderate middle ground. It was in the polemical tradition of the early '30s. Just as his 1933 sermon on lynchings begins with the model of the Salem Witch Trials as a precedent intending to inspire universal revulsion among the listeners, so he begins here with a reference to the 1933 lynchings—and his own sermon on the subject—as an introduction. Here no lives had been lost, to be sure, but the dangers of the mob psychology were just as horrifying. Particularly powerful, of course, is the analogy with Nazi Germany: the events in Peekskill help us understand how "ordinary human beings" could allow atrocities to happen.

The ending is also characteristic: a parable by Arnold Toynbee (whose negative description of Judaism as a "fossil religion" would later be the subject of severe criticism by Saperstein), taken from a popular magazine, providing a vivid, concrete argument that America is strong enough to tolerate even radically divergent political positions, and that indeed such toleration may even strengthen the foundations of American democracy.

IN THE FALL OF 1933, THERE WAS A SERIES OF LYNCHINGS in the South, which for a few days stirred the attention of the press and the people throughout the United States. I had just come to this congregation and had preached only a few sermons. That week, I felt called upon to direct my message to the problem of lynching. The title of that sermon was "Are We Civilized?" My theme was that one of the measures of the civilization of a country is the degree to which justice and due process of law have been substituted for barbarism and passion and vengeance in the determination of, and punishment for, crime. I pointed out that it was not a question of condoning or condemning the acts of the lynch victims. It was a question of whether or not in a civilized country the mob should be free to take the law into its own hands. I concluded that so long as lynchings could occur in a country and be condoned by great numbers of its citizens, there were serious questions about the state of civilization and the security of the citizenry of that country.

Most of us living here in the North, where racial problems are not so acute as they are in the South, can see the subject of lynching objectively and can recognize its evils and dangers. But with something closer to us, we sometimes develop a blind spot. And so today, in my first formal sermon of this seventeenth year of service, I feel called upon to address a similar theme, for it is my conviction that the events of the last few weeks in Peekskill are to be classed in the same category as lynching. The difference is one of degree, but not of kind.

I do not think it is necessary to review the actual events. The newspapers during the last few weeks have contained abundant reports. The essence of the situation lies in these facts:

1. Twice, arrangements were made for concerts to be given by the great Negro singer, Paul Robeson.

2. These concerts were sponsored by organizations that are understood to be Communist Front organizations, and Robeson himself is a strong champion of communism and the Soviet Union.

3. Groups of citizens and veterans of the Peekskill community decided to demonstrate, as evidence of their objection to the singer and the organization sponsoring him.

4. The demonstration resulted, in the first instance, in the forcible prevention of the holding of the concert. In the second instance, the concert was held, but at its termination there was an outbreak of rioting and mob action against those attending the concert. A number of people were injured.[1]

---

1. The events in Peekskill, New York, between August 27 and September 4, 1949, were covered extensively in the *New York Times* and other newspapers and journals. For later accounts from somewhat different perspectives, see Howard Fast, *Peekskill, U.S.A.* (New York: Civil Rights Congress, 1951); Marie Seton, *Paul Robeson* (London: D. Dobson, 1958), 206–17; Edwin Hoyt, *Paul Robeson: The American Othello* (Cleveland: World Publishing Co., 1967), 183–91; Stuart Svonkin, *Jews Against Prejudice* (New York: Columbia University Press, 1997, 135–48.

Let me make certain things clear at the beginning. First, I do not agree with the political views held by Robeson and the organization that sponsored his concert. I believe in democracy. I fought in a war against an enemy that stood for enslavement and dictatorship and the denial of human freedom and dignity. I am convinced that, to a degree, the Soviet Union stands for the same evils of dictatorship, enslavement, and the denial of human freedom and dignity that we abhorred in Nazism and Fascism.

Secondly, I recognize the right of a group of citizens to express their opposition to the public activities of individuals and groups whom they regard as challenging the things they hold precious, by every legitimate means. In other words, in the Peekskill situation, the veterans' and citizens' groups have every right to peaceful picketing and demonstration that will evidence their views. That is the democratic way in action.

But I must condemn what actually happened in Peekskill as evil, representing more of a threat to our ideals and way of life than the activities against which they were protesting.

What are the evils of the Peekskill incident? First, let us think of its effect upon the minds of those participating, particularly the children. The significant thing about the reports of eyewitnesses is that the mob action was carried on in a holiday spirit. Even little children, who could not have the slightest idea of the political implications, were made to look upon the attack on human beings as something to be commended. Witnesses describe the hate-distorted faces and the shocking language of some, and the gay picnic mood of others. Girls not yet in their teens were among those throwing rocks at cars. "I got one, Momma," one thirteen-year-old girl shouted excitedly. Another group of girls giggled as the driver of a bus whom they had hit staggered out bleeding and fell to the ground.

No one can predict what a harvest of criminality was sown in those hours, when bloody violence was encouraged and commended. The impressions of those hours, when the veneer of humanity was lifted and bestiality let loose, will not easily be erased. The scars they left in the minds of children are ugly, sordid and enduring. We wondered when we read of the acts of the Germans under Nazi rule—how was it possible for people who seemed like ordinary human beings to stand by and do nothing, let alone participate, when inhuman atrocities were being performed? The psychology of the people of Peekskill was no different from that of Berlin. It should make us realize that if things like those that happened there can happen while the authorities stand by and virtually encourage it, it could happen here.[2]

That brings me to my second point. More dangerous than the effects of the events themselves is the principle they establish. "Wake up, America!" was the motto of Peekskill. The people there were trying to teach the rest of the country a lesson. That lesson is basically this: that the mob may take the law into its own

2. An echo of Sinclair Lewis's title, *It Can't Happen Here*; Saperstein preached a sermon on this book and its theme in 1935. Other supporters of Robeson branded the anti-Robeson rioters "murderous imitators of Adolf Hitler;" see Stuart Svonkin, *Jews Against Prejudice* (New York: Columbia University Press, 1997), 140.

hands when it feels hatred and senses danger. A more dangerous lesson can hardly be imagined. Remember that mob psychology is a peculiar thing. A mob is easy to convince and hard to stop. The mob, moved by passion not by reason, is always right in its own eyes. Who is to draw the line, and where is it to be drawn?

And who is it that inevitably suffers once the principle is accepted that the mob may take power and the law into its own hands? When passions are aroused, the Jew is vulnerable. The mob that participated in the Kishinev pogrom thought they were fighting for the right, and for God. The Nazi mobs that attacked and murdered Jews in the early days of the Nazi regime—and sent them to gas chambers in its later years—thought they were fighting for the right, and for the security of the fatherland.[3] My friends, the Peekskill story spells danger for the Jew, and even more, danger for America.[4]

How then shall we meet the challenge of communism if we are agreed that communism is a challenge to American ideals? Certainly, my friends, it will not be done by breaking the heads of communists. It will only strengthen their convictions and lend credence to their charges that security and liberty in America are but a mirage. Giving vent to violence against communists will not prove to anyone that communists are wrong; it will win them sympathy and support from sources that would never otherwise have been influenced. The Peekskill enemies of communism probably did more to further the cause of communism in a few hours than all the efforts of the communist propagandists who were there have done in years. You cannot prove the superiority of Americanism over communism by throwing stones at communist sympathizers. When we try to employ the techniques of terrorism, and the denial of rights, against communists, then we have already fallen to their level.

There is a better method that we can use. We can prove our superiority and the bankruptcy of communism by making our democracy more perfect. We must show our own people and the world that here in America, freedom is a living thing. Communism should challenge us, not to fight it, but to negate it by being true to ourselves.

---

3. This and the previous paragraph use language from the November 1933 sermon; see note 9 to that sermon on the Kishinev pogrom.

4. There was actually an overt antisemitic component to the riots. Bumper stickers were distributed saying, "Communism is Treason. Behind Communism Stands the Jew! Therefore: For My Country—Against the Jews!" and Jewish residents of Peekskill were threatened by mail and telephone. Griffin Fariello, *Red Scare* (New York: W. W. Norton, 1995), 75 (with oral histories of the riots, 75–80). Jewish agencies such as the American Jewish Committee and the Anti-Defamation League did not publicly acknowledge the antisemitism of the rioters and repudiated rhetoric linking the rioters with fascism, because of their reluctance to suggest that Jews and communists had a common enemy and were therefore allied. Saperstein's approach is that of the American Jewish Congress, clearly anti-communist, but outspokenly emphasizing the dangers to the Jew of the assault on civil liberties. See Svonkin, *Jews Against Prejudice*, 140–45.

Arnold Toynbee, the distinguished British historian, developed this idea in a recent article entitled "Turning the Tables on Russia."[5] In it, he told the story of the herring fishermen. It seems that with the food shortages in Britain, there is a terrific market for herring. But herring has one failing: if it is not strictly fresh, it loses its flavor. As they had to go further and further out to get their herring, it became increasingly difficult to bring the fish back and get them to the table of the British people before they had reached an unappetizing state. So many of the herring fishermen got what seemed like a brilliant idea. They installed great tanks on their boats, filled them with water, and thus kept the herring alive until they were to be sold.

But strangely, it did not work as well as it seemed in theory it should have. The herring seemed to sense that they were in captivity; they became listless and sluggish, and the flavor wasn't right. Only one enterprising young fishing captain seemed to be able to get herring to market that had the proper taste. In a very short time, he had made a fortune for himself. Finally, he divulged his secret. "I just put a few catfish in the tank with the herring," he said. "They kept the herring active and healthy. True, in the course of the trip, they ate a few of the herring, but the increased value of the thousands they didn't eat made it worthwhile."

Toynbee pointed out that the communists are the catfish of American society. They may win over a few adherents. But their very presence can serve as a healthy and stimulating influence, if we will accept it as a challenge.

The great task that lies before the youth of our generation is to strengthen the bulwarks of our democracy. Ten years ago last week, the great war began. It has been a bloody decade. Our age has seen enough of bloodshed. The next age must be one of peace and democracy. In the Bible reading [for this week], it says, "When you shall cross the Jordan unto the land which the Lord thy God giveth thee, thou shalt set up great stones and write upon them the words of the law" (Deut. 27:2–3). We have crossed the Jordan. Let us not imitate the pagan practices of those who contend against us. Let us follow the law: the law of our land, and above all, the law of God and humanity.

---

5. Arnold Toynbee, "How to Turn the Tables on Russia," *Woman's Home Companion,* 76 (August 1949), 30–31, 92–93.

23

The Chains of the Messiah
September 12, 1950
Rosh Hashanah Morning

Saperstein had concluded a sermon for Shabbat Shuvah 1938 with a reference to David Frishman's poem describing the Messiah in chains, yearning for freedom to redeem his suffering people, restrained by God's response that he must wait until a generation that is "worthy of freedom." In March 1949 Rabbi Louis I. Newman of New York, gave a sermon on the radio program "Message of Israel," entitled "The Messiah in Chains," using the Frishman poem, based on the motifs in this and another of Frishman's messianic poems. This was published in Volume VI of his "Sermons and Addresses" in 1950. Saperstein wrote in his copy over this sermon, "HHD theme," and used it as the organizing framework for the following text. Apparently the Newman sermon reminded him of the motif he had already used and suggested reusing it not just as a dramatic conclusion but as a structuring principle for a Rosh Hashanah sermon.

While the homiletical framework is largely drawn from Newman, the use of this material is somewhat different. The three homiletical passages at the end, using the quotation from Rabbi Herzog, the bell in Geneva, and the "Eternal Light" program, are not in the Newman sermon. More important, the evocation of the contemporary situation as apparently fulfilling the prerequisites for redemption—unprecedented suffering juxtaposed with the external trappings of unprecedented success—is new, as is the application. Its resonance and its moral message, including the reference to Soviet expansionism and the United Nations, require a review of international events during the months preceding delivery. On June 25, 1950, North Korean troops crossed the thirty-eighth parallel and entered South Korean territory. The United Nations Security Council, after calling for a withdrawal of North Korean troops, provided military support for South Korea under a unified command. Through the summer months, the North Koreans continued their advance, reaching their maximum penetration on

September 5. The sermon was delivered, one week later, at a time of deep concern about the military implications of communist expansion.

Saperstein would use this title and motif—the chains of the Messiah—in several subsequent High Holy Day sermons, each time retaining the framework but substituting more contemporary applications.

DAVID FRISHMAN WAS ONE OF THE PIONEER POETS of the Hebrew renaissance. Several of his best poems are built around the figure of the Messiah as it is portrayed in Jewish lore, a symbol of human striving for a better world. In one, he begins with a vision like that of Isaiah, in which we see the Messiah bound to the throne of God with chains of gold. The poet speaks to him: "I have recognized you by your signs," he says," by the burning fire that flames in the eye of every poet, seer, redeemer and prophet, by the lines of pity in the furrows of your cheeks, and most of all by the linked chains that bind your arms." He describes the struggle in the soul of the Messiah, who hears the cry of man's suffering and anguish and strains to rush to their help, but in vain. The Messiah moans, "O God, why hast thou given me this sentient heart, to feel the pains and burdens of the oppressed? Why hast thou endowed me with the strength to redeem, and yet hast bound my hands with chains? Why, O God, didst thou make me to be a redeemer, but to redeem Thou does not permit me?" And as we hear the clanging of the chains, the voice of God rings out,

> When a new generation shall arise,
> A generation that will desire and prepare its soul to be redeemed,
> Then shalt thou also rise to thy role and redeem.[1]

The suffering was present, but the will to be redeemed was not sufficiently strong.

In another poem, Frishman describes the preparation for the coming of the Messiah. First, there is the iron shoe for his horse, then the girdle of silk that he will wear, third the flag that will proclaim his presence. All three are completed and shine in the fullness of their beauty. But one thing remains unfinished: his soul. As the poet says,

> There is not yet enough of the sublime,
> Not enough of light and glory,
> Not even of the sigh pure and true.
> Ah woe, they are not yet to be found.
> Therefore, alas! until this day,
> The soul of the Messiah is not yet complete.[2]

1. David Frishman, "Mashiah," in *Sippurim ve-Shirim* (New York: Hotsa'at Keren Yisrael Matz, 1938), 163–67. It was translated in Leo Schwarz, *A Golden Treasury of Jewish Literature* (New York, 1937), 600–3, but that translation was not used here; Saperstein appears to have translated the material directly from the Hebrew.
2. Frishman, "Bi-shvil ha-Mashiah," in *Sippurim ve-Shirim*, 168–72.

Liberal Judaism no longer speaks of the Messiah in such personal terms. But in these poetic visions and expressions of folklore, we find profound truth for the plight of our own time. Mankind is in desperate need of redemption. After terrible suffering, everything appears to be in readiness. But the redemption is perennially postponed. Something is lacking. The Messiah is still in chains. Mankind is not yet ready for redemption.

If we are honest with ourselves, as we should be on this holy festival, we will see the application of this symbol in Jewish life. Surely the two external requirements for redemption have been fulfilled. On the one hand, our generation has heard the lamentations of our people in their agony. We have endured the most fiendish and catastrophic attack upon our existence of all the sorrow-laden centuries of our history. Our losses have been beyond comprehension, our suffering beyond realization.

On the other, external signs seem to point to a brilliant new day. We have seen the emergence of American Jewry as the largest, strongest, wealthiest and freest Jewish community in all Jewish history, where Jews have risen to highest eminence in every field of endeavor, and where our response to the needs of our brothers in faith marks an epochal achievement of world philanthropy. And Israel: like the Phoenix, from the ashes of Jewish tragedy the new State has risen. A tale of heroism and achievement has been written that future generations will retell with awe. The dream is no longer a dream. All the external trappings are there: the flags, the uniforms, the buildings. Surely it would seem that the time of the Messiah's coming is at hand. But alas, the soul of the Messiah is still incomplete.

The Messiah waits until the Jewish people shall be worthy of him in every respect. They must have knowledge of their heritage. They must have faith that is strong. They must have devotion to their ideals. They must have dedication to humanity. They must have a spirit that yearns for redemption.

These are the goals to which we aspire. Unfortunately, they are not yet completely realized. In Israel, we have a haven for the Jewish body. It is not yet a shrine for the Jewish spirit. The signs and portents are there, but we must still labor for their fulfillment. It is not enough that Israel should be just another country. Surely the object of the age-old aspirations of our people was more than that. There is already too much narrow nationalism in the world. The great promise of Israel is that it may blaze for all the world to see the path of a new type of nationalism in which, in the spirit of the Jewish faith, particularism and universalism will be blended, its people citizens of Israel and citizens of the world at the same time. Of course, we must not expect too much too soon. Like Jacob in the Bible, first Israel must have the stone on which to lay its head before it can dream of heaven.[3] But for that very reason, let us not deceive ourselves that our task regarding Zion is finished. The chains of the Messiah are not yet riven.

---

3. Genesis 28:11–12. Compare the 1948 sermon, above, where the comment is attributed to Berdichevski.

If this is true of Israel, how much more so is it true of American Jewry. With all our opportunities and potential, we have fallen so short of what we might have been. We have given much; we could have given so much more. And when we have given, we have so often given of our means and not of our might, of our savings but not of our souls. The time has come for a great revival of Jewish spiritual values in America. The Stretiner Tzadik, a famous Chassidic leader, once said, "Every Jew has within himself an element of the Messiah which he is required to purify and nurture. Messiah will come when the Jewish people has brought him to perfection of growth and purity within themselves."[4] And so, my friends, every time a Jew worships God in sincerity, every time a Jew becomes more attuned to the spiritual treasures of our heritage, every time a Jew makes loving sacrifice for our cause, another link is severed in the chains that bind the Messiah.

But the Messiah was expected to bring redemption not only for the people of Israel but for all mankind. Surely it would seem that just like the Jewish people, the entire world is in need and ready. How great is the pain with which it has been wracked. Twice in one generation we have known the ravages of total war. Millions of people, innocent and guilty alike, have gone to their graves before their time. How many bodies have been maimed, how many homes destroyed, how many lives shattered. And the external means for this redemption also seem to be at hand. We have an international organization with all the machinery for settling conflicts and disputes between nations. We have unleashed vast new sources of power through which the material resources are available for making the world a paradise.

But the paradise is not here. The Messiah still tarries. He is still bound in chains. And so, instead of welcoming the New Year in peace and security, mankind fearfully faces the possibility of another total war. Many of our countrymen this very day are suffering the hardships and dangers of combat, still fighting and dying.[5] The burden of sorrow has again fallen on many families in the land. A spirit of anxiety broods over many a household, especially where youth may be called to the colors.

There is no doubt as to what our answer had to be to Russia's program of expansion by treachery and force. Unless checked, Soviet Russia represented a fundamental challenge to the peace, security and freedom of the world. The forces of evil had to be stopped. It may well be that the action of the United Nations on this issue may mark its historic transformation from a debating society

---

4. See Newman, *Hasidic Anthology* (New York: Charles Scribner's Sons, 1934), 248. Newman used this passage in his radio sermon, but in a universalized form: "Every Jew—every man—has within himself . . . . Messiah will come when Israel—mankind— has brought him to perfection . . . ." Saperstein used the original text from the *Anthology*, not the version in the sermon, retaining it as a message to the Jewish people. The shift to the universalistic dimension comes in the following paragraph, but is not associated with the Hasidic rebbe.

5. American forces had fallen back between mid-July and early September. The landing at Inchon on September 15, shortly after the sermon was delivered, would mark the beginning of a major counteroffensive.

to the true custodian of the peace and security of the world.[6] If any nation attempts aggression against its neighbors, it must be resisted with all the power that the free nations of the earth can muster.[7] And I say that though I, like many of our congregation, am a member of the Reserve Forces of the American Army, for whom the progress of the war has direct personal implications.

But when we act in the name of the right, we must be sure that our hands are clean. Within our own country, we have sometimes been too prone to overlook the cancerous stories of intolerance and bigotry, of injustice and persecution, which we condemn so readily in our enemies. In our international relations we have been too ready to overlook moral convictions on the basis of expediency. Too ready to do business with totalitarian Spain. Too ready to free Nazi war criminals with blood still on their hands.[8] Too ready to support reactionary regimes throughout the world.

Our moral position is not always as clear as it should be. And that happens to be the crux of the problem. I once heard Rabbi [Isaac] Herzog, Chief Rabbi of Israel, interpret the first sentence of the fourth book of the Bible: *Vayedaber Adonoy el Moshe bemidbar Sinai b'ohel moed*, "And God spoke to Moses in the desert of Sinai in the sanctuary" (Num. 1:1). Rabbi Herzog pointed to a special significance in the order of those words. First comes *bemidbar*; we are now in the desert, he said, in the wilderness of evil and confusion. We are seeking the *ohel moed*, the sanctuary. But before we reach it, we must have Sinai, we must have the moral law.

Before the world can have peace, before true redemption can come, we must have a change in the spirits of men. Insincerity and duplicity must be driven out of the chancelleries of the nations. Brotherhood and love must be instilled through the churches and synagogues, the schools and the homes, the playing fields and the marketplaces of the world. When I visited in Geneva, just before the war, I saw a bell on exhibit in the Town Hall. Molded from the metal of swords and cannons, it had been used to summon the first sessions of the League of Nations. The sound of the bell had been clear. But the spirit behind it had not been unsullied. And the League of Nations [teaches us that without] the spirit of humanity [the United Nations],[9] however magnificently its new buildings may

---

6. Security Council resolutions condemning the North Korean invasion, asking members to provide military assistance to South Korea and establishing a unified command headed by the United States, were taken in the absence of the Soviet Union, which had been boycotting the Council since the previous January.

7. The contrast between this Cold War position and the pacifist stance of the 1930s sermons is, of course, quite dramatic.

8. Referring, apparently, to the recruitment of German rocket and atomic scientists (and other Nazi collaborators), who were brought to the United States beginning in 1948 in order to prevent the Soviet Union from employing them. See John Loftus, *The Belarus Secret* (New York: Alfred A. Knopf, 1988), esp. 82–85. It is not clear to me how much publicity attended this policy at the time.

9. These two phrases are reconstructed, based on context, as the top part of the final page of the text, containing the second part of the first two lines, has been torn off and is missing.

raise their heads over the East River, will have been built on shaky foundations. We will fight one war after another and find ourselves no better off than before.

Some time ago, I heard a drama presented on the "Eternal Light" program called "The Congregation of the Dead."[10] It told of the death of Rabbi Nachman of Bratslav. When his time had come, he summoned two of his disciples and asked them to bring him to a secluded valley far away. The valley was covered with bones. He explains to them that once the valley had been filled with houses, and the houses filled with people. Then came war, and the people perished, and there was no one to lay them to rest. Through the years, their souls had been wandering, waiting for someone to guide them. Now, as he leaves this mortal sphere, Rabbi Nachman has come to them in order to lead them to the throne of the Eternal. He tells the first of his disciples, "My son, you are a rebel, say a rebel's prayer for them. Go back among men and say that we must revolt against injustice or else we lose our humanity." To the second he says, "My son, you are a dreamer. Speak then a dreamer's prayer, the dream of a better world, a world where all men shall be secure." With these words, Rabbi Nachman closed his eyes and breathed his last and went forth to lead his congregation of the dead into God's presence.

My friends, those who have died—of our people under the tyrant's lash, of humanity fighting against aggression—those who have died *al kiddush Hashem* [for the sanctification of God's name]—await our prayers. We must carry on their fight. We must fulfill their dream. We must say the prayer of the rebels and the dreamers. That is the task to which we must dedicate ourselves on this Rosh Hashanah. That is the means by which the chains of the Messiah will be shattered, and redemption made real for Israel and all humanity.

---

10. This radio play was broadcast on October 10, 1948. Saperstein collected transcripts of the "Eternal Light" broadcasts, and frequently referred to them in his sermons. The play was based on a story by Paul Tabori, published in *Liberal Judaism*, August–September, 1947), 16–21; Saperstein's paraphrase seems to have been based on this original version.

- 24 -

Birth of a Nation
November 2, 1951

As the Sabbath before "Armistice Day" (November 11) had become an occasion for sermons devoted to the theme of war and peace in the 1930s, the Sabbath near "Balfour Day" (November 2) evoked discussions of Zionism and the new State of Israel. The following sermon is not inspired by a dramatic event in the news. It uses the occasion on the calendar, and the appearance of a sympathetic and interesting new book, to assess the challenges and achievements of the State of Israel during the first three and a half years of its existence. It brings us back to a time when—with the immediate security problems of its birth period overcome—the excitement of the historic transformation in Jewish life was still palpable.

THIRTY-FOUR YEARS AGO TODAY, ON NOVEMBER 2, 1917, the Balfour Declaration was issued. In it, the British Government, in the midst of war, pledged its support to the Jewish people in the establishment of a Jewish national homeland in Palestine. There is a report that Lloyd George, then Prime Minister of Great Britain, said to a group of Jewish leaders, "We have given you your start. Now it is up to you."[1] That was not really the beginning of the restoration of Zion. Jews had always lived in Palestine, and the modern colonization had been going on already for almost four decades. And it was not so simple after the

---

1. Compare the following statement, attributed to Lloyd George in Milton Steinberg, *A Partisan Guide to the Jewish Problem* (New York: Bobbs-Merrill, 1945), 256 (a book Saperstein owned): "It was contemplated that when the time arrived for according representative institutions to Palestine, if the Jews had meanwhile responded to the opportunity afforded them by the idea of a National Home and had become a definite majority of the inhabitants, then Palestine would become a Jewish Commonwealth."

Declaration was issued; a great many things had to happen before the political process thus begun reached its end in the establishment of the State of Israel. But the Balfour Declaration, for the first time, placed the problem of the Jewish homeland on the world's political agenda, and it was therefore a historic day.

For the occasion of its anniversary, I have chosen to discuss the recent book by James G. McDonald, *My Mission in Israel.*[2] For James G. McDonald saw at first hand the birth of a nation in the land of Israel, having himself played a significant part in the process. McDonald is a Middle Western American of Scotch and German ancestry. For many years he was Chairman of the Foreign Policy Association. He is by nature a teacher and student. But the events of our day brought him out of the ivory tower of scholarship and plunged him into the midst of international political affairs.

In 1933 he was appointed High Commissioner for Refugees for the League of Nations. In this capacity, he had occasion to confer with Adolf Hitler, who said to him, "The world will some day thank me for teaching them how to deal with the Jews" [252]. He came away convinced that this attack was the forerunner of an attack not on Jews alone but on all religion, and all humanity. His interest in the problems of refugees continued through World War II. Then in 1946, President Truman appointed him as a member of the Anglo-American Commission on Palestine.[3] In this position he proved one of the staunch friends of the Jewish cause. In 1948, a few weeks after the Jewish State had been proclaimed, he received a phone call from Washington asking him to be the first Special Representative of the United States to the government of Israel. When the following year our country gave *de jure* recognition to the government of Israel, his position was changed to that of first Ambassador to Israel. The book begins with the phone call, telling the story of his stewardship over a period of two years.

Mr. McDonald was not the traditional diplomat. In his own phrase, he did not wear the old school tie of the State Department. He had little patience with red tape and was concerned with people and issues. Perhaps for this reason, he was resented by some of the State Department's career diplomats. But he was the personal choice of President Truman.

His attitude is expressed throughout the book. As he states in the Preface, he did not seek objectivity in the sense of cold disinterestedness [xiv]. Of course, he was at all times the representative of the American government, and when it was necessary to talk sternly to the Israeli authorities he did so. But through it all, a great personality and a deep human spirit is revealed, and from his humanity and understanding he emerged a major friend of Israel during the early, crucial years of its life.

There are many things that stand out in the book. For example, a series of interesting personal encounters:

---

2. New York: Simon and Schuster, 1951. Page references to this book are incorporated into the sermon text in square brackets.

3. Compare the reference to this Commission in the sermon for Passover 1946, above.

— His interview with the Pope [Pius XII], who was particularly interested in McDonald's status: whether he was merely a personal representative of the President to President Weizmann (as Myron Taylor then was to the Pope) or an official representative of the U.S. Government, such as the President now intends to send [34].

— His interview with Ernest Bevin, of whom he says, "I had to tell myself that this was not Hitler seated across from me but His Majesty's Principal Secretary of State for Foreign Affairs" [25].

— His luncheon with Count Bernadotte, shortly before the Count's assassination, in which McDonald warned, "I have fears for your safety" [67].

— His contact with [Pavel] Yershov, the Soviet Minister, when they were both quartered in the same hotel, where each listened to the other's conversations on the public phone [38].

— The concert of the Israel Symphony with Leonard Bernstein conducting and [President] Dr. Weizmann in attendance; when the alarm came of an Arab air raid, Weizmann remained where he was and the entire audience sat in their seats listening to the magnificent music punctuated by the sound of anti-aircraft guns [95].

— His description of an informal visit to [Prime Minister David] Ben-Gurion's home while Mrs. Ben-Gurion cooked the dinner herself—a typical touch [245]. (I can remember after meeting her casually twelve years ago, she, already one of the two or three most prominent women in the land, took it on herself to phone me personally and make sure I was all right after the newspaper report of a slight injury I sustained in an Arab ambush.)[4]

All of these things impressed me, but thinking back to the contents of the book, three general impressions remain most vivid.

The first is the tremendous effect of the people and the State of Israel upon the observer. There are, of course, many who visit Israel with a deep-rooted prejudice in its favor and refuse to recognize anything but that which is praiseworthy. On the other hand, there are those who come into contact with Israel with preconceived antagonistic prejudices, whose minds and eyes are closed to everything positive and who note only that which can be criticized. There are others who are antagonistic to Israel by virtue of their background and associations and interests—British Foreign Office officials, Christian missionaries, etc. But time and again the visitor to Israel who comes with open mind, ready to learn and then to judge, whether Jew or non-Jew, comes away an ardent enthusiast. It is almost amusing to read McDonald's remark that he, recognized as a champion of Israel, sometimes had to tone down the reports of his associates because of the fervent enthusiasm for the Israeli cause.

What is there about Israel that makes so deep an impression? First of all, there is the sense of *historic* achievement, the fulfillment of an historic goal after two millennia of hopes and prayers. It is a cause that stirs the sense of romance in the heart of anyone who has a sense of world history. To observe the birth of the Jewish State carried with it the sense of privilege of being the one generation out of a hundred [to live at this time].

---

4. See the allusion to this injury and the explanation (including reference to the *Palestine Post* newspaper article) in "Thieves in the Night," note 2, above.

But even more, I think there is a something *refreshing* about Israel. In a world that is blasé and corrupt, where moral values are degraded and ethical ideals are scoffed at, where ideals are used for what they can get you—it is up-lifting to see Israel, where a great ideal is taken seriously, where people are ready to sacrifice for it, where in the forms of social organization, in the ingath-ering of the exiles, unselfishness is the motivating force. Not that there are no political squabbles and personal weaknesses. But somehow, by and large, a visit to Israel makes one feel that the human spirit can still rise to noble heights. I hope the time will come when every Jew and many of the non-Jews of the world will have made at least one pilgrimage to the "old-new land," for the contact not only with the shrine of past religious teachings, but with a dynamic center of living idealism.[5]

Secondly, the book reveals the tremendous achievement of the infant state in so brief a period—a miracle far greater than the crossing of the Red Sea in an-cient times. There are the military miracles, mentioned only incidentally in the book, by which, surrounded by enemy nations, outnumbered forty to one, the little State defended and enlarged its borders. There is the miracle of migration, the taking in of immigrants that doubled its population over a period of two and a half years—an achievement for which there is no parallel in all of human his-tory. The most amazing thing is that this was not a selective migration, that many of those who came were the socially useless: the crippled, the aged, the incurably ill. There is the miracle of internal democracy: the handling of prob-lems arising from a bewildering diversity of political positions, the transforming of the terrorist Irgun into a political party, the surmounting of recurrent political crises initiated by the extreme religious groups. Any of these problems might well have capsized the newly launched ship of state.

No less than any of these was the miracle of diplomacy. During this period there were three basic challenges with which the infant State had to grapple. One was the attempt to diminish its already tiny territory by cutting off the southern Negev. The second was the attempt to take Jerusalem from the new State and set it up under an international regime. The third was the attempt to force Israel to take back Arab refugees who had fled the land.[6] The first would have meant surrendering territory that they had defended with their life's blood. The second would have meant yielding the historic and inspirational center of the Jewish faith. The third would have meant taking back a powerful potential fifth column before peace had been definitely established. As Ben-Gurion said, "We can be crushed, but we will not commit suicide."[7]

---

5. In the summer of 1955, the Sapersteins led the first youth tour to Israel sponsored by the Reform Movement's National Federation of Temple Youth. They subsequently led many tours for teenagers during the 1960s and for congregants during the 1970s.

6. These were the substance of Count Folke Bernadotte's proposals made on June 27, 1948 (except that Jerusalem was to be given to Jordan). See Howard Sachar, *A History of Israel* (New York: Alfred A. Knopf, 1996), 337.

7. For the context of this statement, see Sachar, 439–40.

So they made no compromise. Against them were arrayed the diplomatic forces of the great nations of the world. Great Britain, almost always on the other side of the fence; the United States, all too often starting out by following the lead of Great Britain; Russia, moving from side to side according to its own advantage. But on each major issue, the Israeli government eventually won.[8] The tribute McDonald pays to the Israeli leaders—when he calls Ben-Gurion "one of the few great statesmen of our day" [241], and his associates an extraordinary group, any one of which is equal and some of whom are far superior to those in many of the great countries [272]—is apparently not an exaggeration.

Finally, the book left me with a feeling of optimism for the future. Israel will always be a tiny nation. But McDonald points out that this does not mean that its size must dictate its importance. For, he reminds us, Israel has something unique in its Jewish heritage. Israel must not try to be just like every other nation. It must be true to its Jewishness. It must make itself the fearless advocate of international justice. It must take a forthright stand on every issue. It must be in this sense a spiritual pioneer among the nations. It must follow a creative and moral path, whose direction is pointed by the Jewish past, in order to bring something new into the world.

McDonald ends with these words:

> The future of Israel as a land of refuge is, thanks to the courage of its inhabitants and the devotion of Jews throughout the world, substantially assured. The future of Israel as a spiritual force is not without danger, but it is pregnant with splendid hope. After two and a half rewarding years, I close this account of my mission confident that Israel will triumphantly vindicate the faith of its builders [297].

There are those who will say that this is unrealistic. But the whole story of the birth of this nation is the story of the triumph of ideals over the realists. The following story is attributed to [Revisionist Zionist leader Vladimir] Jabotinsky. When accused of impracticability, he answered, "One day, London was so deeply enveloped in fog that all street movement was stopped. A man emerged from a hotel crying for someone to show him the way to a hospital, where his wife was critically ill. His hand was grasped by a stranger whom he could not see, who led him quickly, despite the fog, to the hospital. When he reached it, he asked his guide, 'How could you lead me through this terrible fog?' 'It was not difficult,' answered his guide. 'You see, I am blind.'" Sometimes, indeed, the idealists see more truly than the realists.[9]

---

8. For a review of the Armistice Negotiations beginning in 1949 pertaining to the Negev, Jerusalem, and the status of the refugees, see Sachar, 347–53, and 339–45 on Israeli military victories determining the status of the Negev.

9. I have not been able to find a source for this vignette.

25

"I Lift My Lamp"
October 31, 1952

During the 1930s, Saperstein devoted a number of sermons to the topic of immigration. Then it was a matter of refugees, and the strong prejudices that prevailed in many circles against German-speaking Jews who were purportedly taking jobs away from American citizens. This issue was addressed by an appeal to the American self-image as a haven for the oppressed, and by a careful presentation of facts to rebut the claims that taking in "foreigners" was undermining American life.

Now in 1952, the issue of immigration quotas again came to the forefront in the political arena. While unemployment was not nearly so pressing as in the 1930s, the nativist, xenophobic sentiments were heightened by the communist scare. In this context, Saperstein once again set forth a consistent argument on behalf of a liberal immigration policy. This was couched not primarily in Jewish terms—as the establishment of the State of Israel had now provided a home for all Jews who needed one. His opposition to the McCarran-Walter Act was based on his commitment to freer access for foreigners of very different backgrounds. This position was again evidence of a rabbi who took the "American dream" with utmost seriousness.

ON THE BASE OF THE STATUE OF LIBERTY on Bedloe's Island in New York Harbor is inscribed the famous poem by Emma Lazarus:

> Not like the brazen giant of Greek fame,
> With conquering limbs astride from land to land,
> Here at our sea-washed, sunset gates shall stand
> A mighty woman with a torch, whose flame
> Is the imprisoned lightning, and her name
> Mother of Exiles. From her beacon-hand
> Glows world-wide welcome; her mild eyes command

The air-bridged harbor that twin cities frame.
"Keep, ancient land, your storied pomp!" cried she,
With silent lips. "Give me your tired, your poor,
Your huddled masses yearning to breathe free,
The wretched refuse of your teeming shore,
Send these, the homeless, tempest-tost to me.
I lift my lamp beside the golden door!"

Better, perhaps, than anything else that has ever been written, that poem expresses the spirit of our country. America has been the land of hope and opportunity. It summoned not the fortunate and those in high places, but the unfortunate, those who sought freedom, who were escaping persecution, who wished to build a new life. From all over the world they came: people of every race and every faith and every nationality. We can imagine what American meant to them. I recall arriving in New York harbor from abroad in [early September] 1939, when war had just begun, and the emotions that filled my heart as I looked upon the Statue of Liberty. And we can imagine what feelings filled the hearts of our parents or grandparents when they first caught sight of the uplifted torch. But we must not be unmindful either of what these people meant to America. For it was these people—immigrants all—who poured their lives, their labor, their genius into the crucible and made America what it is today.

We can see something of this relationship as it applies to the Jewish community if we summarize the history of Jewish migration. It began with those who came in 1654, whose story will be depicted in pictures following our service tonight. They were the forerunners of the first wave of Jewish migration, a wave of Spanish and Portuguese Jews who had escaped the Inquisition and ultimately found refuge here. The second wave came in the middle of the nineteenth century and consisted chiefly of German Jews, escaping the forces of political reaction sweeping over Europe at that time. The third wave came at the turn of the century, from about 1881 to 1914. It consisted of Jews from Eastern Europe—in many cases our grandparents and parents—escaping the tyranny and persecution of the Czarist regime. Each wave successively found here the opportunity they sought, and each made its adjustment and made its contributions to American life.

After the First World War, however, for the first time there was a basic change in our American immigration policy. It was a period of isolationist fervor, anti-foreign hysteria, the emergence of the Ku Klux Klan. Under the influence of these forces, plus the fear that a great influx of laborers might cause unemployment, restrictive immigration laws were passed in 1921 and intensified in 1924.[1] The principles of those laws have been in effect ever since. They basically accomplished two things. First, they put an overall limit of about 150,000 newcomers a year to be admitted. Second, they imposed quotas based on na-

---

1. The Quota Act of 1921 limited annual immigration to three percent of the country's nationals in the 1910 census. The National Origins Act of 1924 defined the quota as a ration of each country's nationals in the United States to the American population, as shown in the census of 1920.

tional origins, which permitted a proportionately large number of immigrants from Northern and Western Europe—England and Germany, for example—and a relatively small number from Southern and Eastern Europe—Italy, Poland and Russia.

We can see the reasons for the overall limitation. But why the distinction between people of different nationalities? If we study the arguments presented at the time, it appears to be simply a matter of the theory of Nordic superiority. It was accepted at that time that Anglo-Saxons were of better stock and that Italians and Jews were eugenically a poorer risk, more difficult to assimilate, of inferior stock. The immigration act made that concept into law.

When the Second World War ended, it was clear that a new immigration law would be required. For several years, the Displaced Persons Act permitted some of the emergency needs in the aftermath of the war to be met, by mortgaging the quotas of countries with large numbers of refugees.[2] But this was only temporary. For five years, the struggle continued to develop an immigration act that would meet the new needs of a new day. The result has been the McCarran-Walter Immigration Act.[3] I venture to say that since the beginning of our history, there have been few acts of legislation so contrary to American principles, so antagonistic to the fundamental spirit of American life, as this.

The new law started out claiming to correct certain unfair elements of the old law. Under the previous law, for example, there was no allotment at all for Japanese immigration and for other nationalities in the Pacific area. The McCarran Act improves on this situation to the extent of allowing about 185 Japanese immigrants as a yearly quota, and about 100 each of other Pacific nationalities. But even here the racial doctrine is maintained, so that if a Chinese marries an Englishwoman, for example, and lives in England, their child would have to come into America under the Chinese quota regardless of the fact that he was born in England. Aside from Oriental nations, the same quota restrictions based on national origins are maintained.

Recently, I was discussing this with one of our members, who responded, "What's wrong with it? It's a codification of what we've had all along, isn't it?" True. But the fact is that we've learned a great deal since 1924, when the National Origins Act was passed. We've learned, for example, that scientifically there is no such thing as a pure race, and that even if we recognize that different nations have different racial tendencies, these differences cannot be correlated in any with differences in intelligence or in moral standards. People of all nations and all national origins run the gamut from bad to good, from morons to gen-

---

2. The Displaced Persons Act of June 25, 1948, permitted 205,000 DPs to enter the United States. This number was increased by amendment to 415,000 two years later.

3. On the McCarran-Walter Act (technically, the Immigration and Nationality Act of June 27, 1952), see Marion Bennnett, *American Immigration Policies* (Washington D.C.: Public Affairs Press, 1963), 212–39; Vernon M. Briggs, Jr., *Immigration Policy and the American Labor Force* (Baltimore: Johns Hopkins University Press, 1984), 58–60; William S.Bernard in David Jacobson, ed., *The Immigration Reader* (Walden, Mass.: Blackwell, 1998), 69–70. The law was passed by Congress over the veto of President Truman.

iuses. The so-called "riff-raff" from Italy and Poland that came to this country at the turn of the century turned into some of the finest citizens America has ever known. Their children include some of the most distinguished political leaders in exclusive Nassau County, and most of the members of the finest congregations, including our own.

The whole problem of "Nordic superiority" is no longer an academic one for us. We have seen tens of millions of people come to untimely ends as victims at that pagan, unscientific altar of cruelty. Certainly we must be concerned at a quota system allowing Germany the second largest allotment of immigrants—smaller only than that of Great Britain—implying that Germany, which has twice brought war to the world in our generation, which has experienced a complete generation of anti-democratic indoctrination and ten years of the viciousness of Nazi rule, is still closer to our traditions and political system than, say, the people of Greece, whose quota is about 1 percent that of Germany.

Our fundamental opposition, then, is that the McCarran Immigration Act, instead of being a true reevaluation of our immigration policy, is merely a cosmetic legislation that, like cosmetic surgery, covers up but solves no problems. It represents an outworn and un-American theory. It does not welcome but rather expresses hostility to the immigrant. It is motivated by prejudice. I say this as a Jew, but even more so as an American. For tragically, this legislation does not primarily affect the Jews. The six million martyrs can no longer migrate to this country. The three million Jews behind the Iron Curtain no longer have freedom of movement. The remaining islands of Jewish community life that must be transplanted are chiefly directed toward the State of Israel. This legislation makes for conflict between the ideals and the realities of America.

There are also other aspects of the bill to which I am opposed, in which the bill goes far beyond any previous immigration legislation. First is its position on deportation as a penalty. For example, it would permit the expulsion of an alien who became a public charge—perhaps through no fault of his own—even though at the time of entry there was no sign of economic difficulty. Or of a person institutionalized in a mental hospital within five years after admission to the country, even though he was perfectly sane upon his entry. It is my conviction that an immigrant should be punished only for a crime that others in the country are punished for, and then only in the same way. The Bible says that the same law must be applied to the stranger as to the homeborn (Num. 9:14). The American spirit demands equal standing under our laws for all within our borders. Deportation is a punishment not only for the individual concerned, but also for innocent members of his family.

And the law further discriminates between the naturalized citizen and the native-born citizen. For example, a naturalized citizen can lose his citizenship if he remains abroad for more than five years. Or his citizenship may be retracted if he joins a subversive organization within five years after it is granted. Now I do not believe in coddling those who are disloyal to America. But there are two dangerous aspects of this distinction. First, once a person has been naturalized, there should be no difference in his treatment from that of other citizens. We do not have classes of citizens; we are all Americans regardless of whether we happen to have been born here—by an accident which reflects no credit to ourselves—or become Americans by choice. Second, "subversive" is a very indefinite and fluid term. The provisions of this bill that place authority in the hands of executives without opportunity even for judicial review or appeal represent a dangerous move toward totalitarianism. Again, our basic principle is a moral one. Immigrants must be treated as human beings.

We have heard a good deal about the McCarran-Walter Bill in recent weeks. This is not a matter to be decided by the elections. It was passed by members of both parties, and both presidential candidates claim to see its imperfections.[4] But there is a great danger that we may get all excited about issues during the election campaigns and then when they are over, sink back into lethargy and allow the successful candidate to forget the things he said when he was seeking our votes. Whoever is our next President, it will be our task as citizens to continue the battle: to require those who govern us to repeal this act so that America may be true to its ideals, so that the lamp of the Statue of Liberty may again shine forth as a symbol of hope and humanity for all the world to see.

---

4. The presidential election, in which Eisenhower defeated Adlai Stevenson, was held just four days after the sermon was delivered.

26

The Fruits of Sacrifice
September 10, 1953
Rosh Hashanah Morning

Two events lay in the background of this Rosh Hashanah sermon for 1953. The first, of a personal nature, was a trip to Europe and Israel provided by the congregation as a gift upon Saperstein's completion of twenty years as their rabbi. It was the first time he had been in Israel since the visit in the summer of 1939, the first of many trips he would take with Marcia, his wife. Many sermons had been devoted to Israel in the late 1940s and early 1950s, but these were based largely on reading. The renewed encounter produced a vividness derived from personal experience at a time when tourism to Israel by American Jews was still relatively unusual.

The second event was the growing influence of the House Un-American Activities Committee and the figure of Senator Joseph McCarthy on American life. Many rabbis raised this issue in their High Holy Day sermons of 1953. Saperstein's homiletical file contains a "New Year Message" by Rabbi Herschel Levine printed in the "Jewish Press" with the following warning: "Today the Communist Party is outlawed; tomorrow it will be the Socialist Party, then the small labor and liberal parties; then Jehovah's Witnesses and other unpopular faiths; then labor unions, cultural groups, service clubs, Masonic orders, until through a blind type of anti-totalitarianism, we shall have achieved totalitarianism." Just a few days after Rosh Hashanah, the dangers of McCarthyism were dramatized to many by the mention of Stephen S. Wise, Judah Magnes and John Haynes Holmes as collaborators with the Communists by one Benjamin Gitlow in testimony to the HUAC. Had this come the week before, it certainly would have been incorporated into the above sermon. Saperstein devoted a separate sermon to the defense of Wise on October 9.

THIS MORNING WE READ THE STORY OF THE *AKEDAS YITZCHAK* ["The Binding of Isaac"] from the Torah. This ancient tale of spiritual testing made a profound impression on the Jewish heart. Its importance is indicated by its inclusion into the liturgy of this holy day. It was a perennial reminder to the Jew that sacrifice was an essential ingredient of his faith.

The ancient sages further developed this thought. As always, they did so not explicitly but through the medium of allegory. The sacrificial ram that took the place of Isaac, they said, was not an ordinary ram. It was brought into being by God at the time of the creation of the universe itself. In later days, they went on, the bones of that ram were used to build the foundations of the *Beis Hamikdash*, the Holy Temple in Jerusalem. The left horn was fashioned into the shofar to proclaim the giving of the law on Mt. Sinai. And the right horn awaits the time it will be used as the shofar with which Elijah on Mt. Moriah will proclaim the coming of the Messiah.[1]

These three aspects of our Jewish heritage are thus all associated with sacrifice. The *Beis Hamikdash* represents the national element in Jewish life. It was the sanctuary of the entire people. Its destruction was considered the end of national Jewish existence. And the prayers for its rebuilding offered by Jews through all the centuries of the exile were, in essence, prayers for the restoration of the Jewish nation. The ram as the symbol of sacrifice can with justice be associated with Jewish national life in our day as in ages past.

We have all heard so many UJA speeches, we have read so many magazine articles, we have seen so many motion pictures, that the story of the rebuilding of the land of Israel and the establishment of the Jewish State has become an oft-repeated and familiar tale. Yet one cannot fully comprehend the scope of these achievements until he has walked over the length and breadth of the land, talked with its people, looked at the dust of its earth and raised his eyes to the stars. It is difficult for us who live in lands blessed by nature's abundance, rich in natural resources, to realize the sheer human sacrifice that has gone into the reclaiming of the land of Israel. It is impossible to exaggerate the degree to which the land had been laid waste through centuries of neglect—its soil eroded, its mountains rocky and bare, its deserts barren and waste. One wonders, how can they ever reclaim it? It takes an effort to realize that the portions of the land now blossoming like a garden were once also rocky crags, shifting desert sands, malarial swamps. The miracle that made them fruitful was the miracle of superhuman sacrifice.

During a *hamsin*, a heat wave of burning desert air which greeted us for our first week in Israel—in relation to which the heat wave with which America greeted us on our return seemed like a welcome relief—Marcia and I traveled to Sodom, site of ancient Sodom and Gomorra, on the shores of the Dead Sea. Hour after hour, under the scorching sun, we traveled along the new highway,

---

1. See Louis Ginzberg, *The Legends of the Jews*, 7 vols. (Philadelphia: JPS, 1911), 1:283.

stretching through desert wastelands that looked like a vision of the inferno. That narrow band of paved highway had conquered the desert, for it made it possible to bring up the rich chemical deposits of the Dead Sea. Just before the final drop down to Dead Sea level, 1,300 feet below ordinary sea level—the lowest spot on the face of the earth—there was a simple monument. On it was an inscription dedicated to the memory of those who labored to build this road but did not live to see its completion. It reminded one that the road took a toll not only in dollars and labor, but also in sacrifices of human life.

No one speaks of the tremendous loss in human life sustained by the infant nation of Israel in its war for independence. It would not be military prudent to publicize the figures. But there is hardly a family—from that of the new President, who lost one of his two sons, to the humblest in the land—which escaped sacrifice. All over the land today, along virtually every road, in every town, are monuments to those who died that Israel might live. We had the great privilege of interviews with Dr. [Izhak] Ben-Zvi, President of Israel, and Rachel Yanait [Ben-Zvi], his distinguished wife. She spoke to me about her son, whom I had met at her home when he was a young boy years before [during the visit of 1939]. I mentioned the sacred responsibility all of us should feel for the new State in view of the youth who lost their lives that it might endure. She paused for a moment, then said simply, "You are right—all the more so because they did not *lose* their lives, they *gave* them."

The State of Israel, my friends, is built on the foundation of sacrifice. And even so, only through sacrifice can our *faith*—[symbolized by the ram's horn on Mt. Sinai]—be preserved. Tradition tells us that before the Torah was given to the children of Israel it was offered to various other people of the earth. But they were unwilling to accept its moral commitments: to relinquish robbery and bloodshed, war and violence. Only the Jews stood ready to make the sacrifice the Law demanded.[2] And so we became in a sense the suffering servant of the Lord. That famous chapter in Isaiah [53], which Christianity applies to the figure of the Christ, is more accurately interpreted as a description of the role of Israel. The Jew was "despised and forsaken of men, a man of pains and acquainted with grief" (Isa. 53:3).

Chaim Nahman Bialik, in one of the greatest of his poems, *Megillat Ha-esh* ("The Scroll of Fire), describes the destruction of the Temple by the Romans. In silent sorrow, God views the ruin of His house. But amidst the still smoking rubble, a tiny wisp of the Holy Flame still burns on the devastated altar. The angel who guards the tears of the world snatches the tiny flame of holiness and carries it away to a distant island. There the Morning Star, representing man's eternal hope for the future, guards the flame. And when the cup of man's tears is filled, salvation will come.[3] Thus there is divine purpose in Israel's suffering.

---

2. See sources in Ginzberg, *Legends of the Jews*, 3:81 and 6:30–31.

3. See Chaim Nahman Bialik, *Complete Poetic Works*, ed. Israel Efros (New York: Histadruth Ivrith of America, 1948), 158–62. There is a card in Saperstein's homiletical file with the beginning of a printed interpretation of the poem by Ben Aronin; the source where this appeared is not noted.

Judaism has never been a device for making life easy. It has been a challenge to make life worthwhile. The saga of the Jew has been a long tale of sacrifice. Yet the Jew never pitied himself, for he saw his faith as part of the divine plan of the universe. Whenever an enemy sought to destroy it, he rose in heroic rebellion. When everything else was lost, he clung to it as his most precious possession. Often one word repudiating his heritage would have brought surcease from his suffering and opened before him the locked gates of freedom—but he refused to speak that word. In our generation, we have reached the very abyss of suffering—yet our faith still endures.

The Sabbath after Tisha b'Av is called "Shabbat Nachamu," the Sabbath of Consolation. After the day of mourning and lamentation comes this blessed Sabbath when the Haftorah begins, *Nachamu, nachamu ami*, "Comfort ye, comfort ye My people" (Isa. 40:1). This year I observed that Sabbath morning on Mt. Zion at the traditional grave of King David, in a synagogue dedicated to all the Yeshivot destroyed throughout the lands of Europe. Later that week, I returned to see the tragic museum set up there on Mt. Zion in tribute to the memory of the six million who perished at the hands of the Nazis.

In that museum were bloodstained scrolls and knapsacks and boot soles, soap made from the fat of human bodies and lampshades made from human skin. It revealed the depths of degradation and inhumanity of which human beings can be capable, and it illuminated the greatness of Jewish tragedy in our generation. But on that day, a special ceremony was being performed. To Israel had been brought a number of Torah scrolls rescued from European synagogues. They were being distributed to communities and colonies in the land. After appropriate prayers, they came forward: men with hands callused by labor and faces darkened by the sun, representing settlements all over the land. Each received and carried away a Torah to be cherished—an *etz chayim*, a tree of life—as a memorial to those who had died *al kiddush Hashem* [for the sanctification of God's name].

Finally, tradition tells us that the advent of the Messiah also will be announced with the horn that symbolizes sacrifice. How true it is that every step forward toward the goal of a better world demands its price. There are no bargains in human progress. For every step forward in the march of mankind, there is a tale of sacrifice. Some years ago, I preached a sermon based on Carl Sandburg's novel, *Remembrance Rock*. In that novel, a Justice of the Supreme Court makes a radio address to the people of the United States during a crucial phase of the war. He speaks to them of the glory of their heritage. "It has cost to build this nation," he says. "Living men in struggle and risk, in self-denial and pain, paid that cost. Has it been worth it? I think it has. You can bury the bones of men and later dig them up," he continues, "to find they have moldered into a thin white ash that crumbles in your fingers. But their ideas won. Their visions came through. They live in the sense that their dream is on the faces of living men and women today. They ought not to be forgotten."

Yes, the price of freedom has always been great. One of the most painful aspects of the contemporary American scene is that we have been frightened into forgetting how great was that price and how precious, therefore, the value it has created. No American name is better known in Europe today than that of McCarthy. No aspect of American life was more frequently questioned than that of McCarthyism. Liberal Europeans could not understand how a nation as strong and free as ours could be terrorized by one man. "Can it be true," they said, "that in America people are so afraid of being labeled Communists that they must guard their words on every political subject?" I tried to balance their views. Yet I felt a sense of shame.[4]

I do not exaggerate when I say that McCarthyism has done more to destroy the prestige of America abroad than anything that has happened since the war. Sometimes we ourselves do not realize the extent to which our responses are controlled by fear of McCarthy. Recently I read of a social [science] experiment carried out on one of the prominent American campuses. A statement of belief was drawn up consisting entirely of selections from the Declaration of Independence and the Constitution. It was presented to hundreds of students without explanation of its source. They were asked to sign it as a statement of principles. Only a meager handful were willing to take the chance of signing it. I think it would be difficult these days to get people to sign the Ten Commandments for fear McCarthy might declare them to be un-American. Peace and freedom and brotherhood cannot be born without pain, [and neither can they be preserved without pain]. The courage to sacrifice is needed today, as in every crucial period when human values are being weighed in the balance.

In the traditional liturgy for the High Holy Day season there is a medieval poem called *Ki Hinei Kachomer*. Translated, it says, "As the potter shapes the clay and proves it, so are we proved in fire by Thee."[5] Let us pray as this New Year begins that even as the generations that have gone before us, from out of the fire of sacrifice we may emerge stronger in our devotion to the land of Israel, deeper in our loyalty to the faith of our fathers, nobler in our allegiance to the ideals of our nation and the cause of humanity.

---

4. This passage apparently referred to conversations on a trip to Europe during the summer of 1953, the first time Saperstein had been back in Europe since his service in the chaplaincy during and just after the war.

5. See Max Arzt, *Justice and Mercy: Commentary on the Liturgy of the New Year and the Day of Atonement* (New York Holt, Reinhart and Winston, 1963), 212–13.

27

Promise and Fulfillment
September 28, 1954
Rosh Hashanah Morning

The sermons of the 1940s and 1950s evince a strong sense of patriotic identifi-
cation with the United States. The "American dream" was a concept taken with
utmost seriousness, a touchstone with which to measure specific failings of
American society and policy, an analogue to the ideals of prophetic Judaism.
The 300th anniversary of the first Jewish settlement in New Amsterdam was a
natural occasion to take the measure of both the larger society and the Ameri-
can Jewish community against the ideals of each. For American society, the
gravest concern was the challenge to liberty in the "Red Scare" represented by
McCarthyism. In the Jewish context, it was no longer just the problem of as-
similationists seeking to escape their Jewish identity, but the superficial knowl-
edge and minimalist behavior of those who had joined the synagogues. There is
also the warning that Israel must not become a surrogate for an authentic
"center of Jewish spiritual life" at home.

ON MY WAY TO THE RABBINICAL CONFERENCE in New Hampshire at the
beginning of the summer, I stopped to see the famous Orozco murals in the
Baker Library of Williams College.[1] This remarkable work, typical of the powerful style, tremendous vitality and social consciousness of the contemporary
Mexican artist, is intended to be an epic of American civilization. It consists of a

---

1. Saperstein had seen the murals of Orozco and Rivera during a visit to Mexico in
the summer of 1938; he spoke frequently about the power of the social consciousness
expressed in these Mexican murals.

series of panels divided into two balanced halves. The first deals with ancient American civilization before the European conquest; the second half depicts American civilization after the coming of the white race.

Both halves reveal a common pattern. They begin with the problem: man with his imperfections and weaknesses, his superstitions, his lust for power, his inhumanity toward his fellow man. Then the vision, the dream of men living in cooperation and understanding, the promise of a brave new world. Then comes reality, with its mingling of constructive and destructive forces, and the old evils reappear in new guise: war, greed, inhumanity. The cycle is completed, and we end with another vision of hope, a promise that is still to be fulfilled.

I shall not pass judgment on the artistic merits of this work or on the specific application of its symbolism. It seems to me, however, that here we have depicted a basic theme of history and life. The ultimate source of tragedy and heartbreak is the separation of promise from fulfillment, the gap between dream and reality. Yet the vision continues to guide us onward.

This Rosh Hashanah marks the beginning of a milestone year: our 300th anniversary as an American Jewish community. Now Rosh Hashanah is the traditional season of evaluation, of taking stock. And just as we evaluate ourselves in our individual lives, so I think we might well take this opportunity of evaluating America and American Jews. For that evaluation I can think of no better measuring rod than the one implied in Orozco's murals: promise and fulfillment. What was the vision? How far have we fulfilled it? What remains to be done?

America has always been more than an ordinary country,[2] more than a geographical area and a political entity, more than its physical reality as manifest in the amber waves of grain, the purple mountain majesties, the alabaster cities. It has been a way of life, an ideal. America is the struggle for freedom at Valley Forge; it is the ordeal at Gettysburg to ensure that freedom might be enjoyed by all men. America is the Bill of Rights, Lincoln's Second Inaugural Address, Roosevelt's "Four Freedoms." America is people: people of all races and faiths, holding their heads straight in dignity, clasping hands in brotherhood.

Maxwell Anderson expressed it in his play *Valley Forge*, when he has George Washington say,

> The spirit of earth
> . . . stands over this, my country
> in this dark year . . . like a pillar of fire
> to show us an uncouth clan, unread, harsh-spoken,
> but followers of a dream, a dream that men
> shall bear no burdens save of their own choosing,
> shall walk upright, masterless, doff a hat to none,
> and choose their gods! It's destined to win, this dream,
> weak though we are. Even if we should fail,

---

2. In the draft of this sermon at this point there is a parenthetical notation: "(adapted from Silver's sermon, 1950)." The reference is to Abba Hillel Silver, "Make Mine Eyes to See" (Yom Kippur, 1950), in *A Set of Holiday Sermons 5711—1950–51*, published by the Commission on Information about Judaism of the UAHC and the CCAR, 30–31.

It's destined to win!³

That has been the promise. And in truth, America has made majestic progress toward its fulfillment. With all imperfections, here man has a greater measure of freedom than in any other land in the world. The spirit of democracy
thrives better here than in any other place under the sun. America has been to the
world a beacon of hope and, again and again, the champion of right. The onward
march continues. For example, the recent Supreme Court decision for
non-segregation in public education was a mighty stride forward for the vision.⁴

But we must not be complacent. Even in the process of fulfillment, the seeds
of old evils take roots. There are those in our midst who have lost faith in
America and would destroy our institutions. We still have our rabble-rousers,
bigots, demagogues and witch-hunters, who prey upon the fears of people to
sow discord and reap their own advantage.

Perhaps the greatest task that lies before us is to keep our democracy vital,
courageous and strong. I despise the communist movement. I know that its adherents are our enemies who would, if they could, destroy our liberties and our
way of life. I know that in Soviet Russia and its satellites, Jewish life is doomed,
and the ax of destruction hangs precariously over the heads of Jews. I believe
that when communists resort to espionage and conspiracy they should be prose-
cuted to the full extent of the law.

But when we begin to tamper with freedom of speech and thought we are
only mimicking the communists. When it becomes a crime to advocate unpopular ideas, then let us beware. For who knows where the process will end. Bishop
Sheil, distinguished member of the Roman Catholic hierarchy, recently berated
the junior Senator from Wisconsin with these words: "An America which has
lost faith in the integrity of the government, the army, the schools, the churches,
most of all an America whose citizens have lost faith in one another, such an
America would not need to bother about being anti-communist; it would have
nothing else to lose."⁵

The great danger in some of those who raise the communist hue and cry is
that they pretend to speak in the name of democracy. I recently read an analysis

---

3. Maxwell Anderson, *Valley Forge* (Washington, Anderson House, 1934), 164. Saperstein's homiletical file indicates that the passage was found in Robert Luccock's collection of sermons, *The Lost Gospel* (New York: Harper & Brothers, 1948), 31–32.

4. This was the unanimous "Brown v. Board of Education of Topeka, Kansas" decision of 1954, reversing the "separate but equal" doctrine of "Plessy v. Ferguson" and
holding that de jure segregation is unconstitutional, violating the equal protection clause
of the 14th amendment.

5. Bishop Bernard J. Sheil of Chicago was the founder and director-general of the
Catholic Youth Organization, whose denunciation of McCarthy (identified as "the junior
Senator from Wisconsin") in a speech made on April 9, 1954, two weeks before the televised Army-McCarthy hearings began, gained national attention. The quotation appears
in the *New York Times* article of April 10, 8. Saperstein may have been reminded of this
by the *Times* article of September 3 reporting that Bishop Sheil was resigning from his
position. A card with the quotation on it was in his homiletical file.

of the art of bullfighting. To kill the bull, the matador must drive the sword straight between the bull's shoulder blades. It is possible to do so only because at the last moment the matador turns the bull's head by showing it a piece of red cloth, the *muleta*. The bull instinctively plunges at the cloth, and that is what makes it possible for the matador to march out in triumph while the dead bull is dragged out by four horses.[6] When people wave a red flag under our noses, let us not act the bull. Let us be sure we look closely at the man behind the rag before we plunge. Otherwise ours may be the fate of the bull.

As we go forward, let us not lose the vision or hope. Before he died, Thomas Edison said something that echoes the words of Moses when he laid his charge upon Joshua: "Be courageous. I have lived a long time. I have seen history repeat itself again and again. . . . Always America has come out stronger and more prosperous. Be as brave as your father before you. Have faith. Go forward."[7] Those words might well be made the litany of our faith.

Let us similarly place 300 years of Jewish life on the scales. America represented something new and unprecedented in Jewish history. In previous countries of our Diaspora, it had always been a matter of choosing: spiritual freedom with practical restrictions, or practical freedom with spiritual enslavement. In other words, if they wanted to be Jews they had to be ready to give up some measure of their freedom, if they wanted to be free men they had to be ready to give up some measure of their Jewishness. The promise of America was that here Jews might achieve freedom and prosperity on the one hand, and maintain their full spiritual life at the same time.

How well has this promise been fulfilled? We cannot say that there is no discrimination in America. But we can safely say that here the struggle against bigotry and intolerance has been continuously fought and won, from the time of Asser Levy fighting for the privilege of standing guard side by side with his neighbors in defense of New Amsterdam.[8] Our confidence in America is perhaps best symbolized by the sealed tunnel in the historic synagogue of Newport [Rhode Island], now a national monument. When that synagogue was first built, a trapdoor was constructed under the ark leading to a secret underground exit. It was a carryover, perhaps, of Marrano traditions and memories of ancient days, when the synagogue was often the last place of refuge for the Jewish community

---

6. The basis for this passage applying bull-fighting to Red-baiting was a clipped column (without indication of source) in the homiletical file. The last name of the author at the bottom is torn; what is clear is "Henri Marc. .". The "analysis of the art of bullfighting" may have been Tom Lea's novel, *The Brave Bulls*, the paperback edition of which (New York: Pocket Books, 1951), was in Saperstein's home library.

7. This was Edison's last public message, sent to a lighting convention in Atlantic City less than two months before his death. See Ronald Clark, *Edison* (New York: G. Putnam's Sons, 1977), 241.

8. On Asser Levy in New Amsterdam, see Morris Schappes, *Documentary History of the Jews in the United States* (New York: Citadel Press, 1952), 6–8.

in time of danger. When the Declaration of Independence was proclaimed, the tunnel was sealed. It remains so to this day.[9]

Material prosperity too we have achieved in measure. It is not true that all Jews are wealthy, as many of us can testify. But by and large we have reached a level of material well being which places us in a unique position in the Jewish world. In the world Jewish crisis of our day, we alone were prepared to give practical relief. The record of philanthropy established by our generation of American Jews is one that would merit an honorable page in Jewish history, though it were our only accomplishment.

But what about spiritual achievements? True, America has produced a new and great force in Jewish life, in the Reform movement. True we have several great institutions of Jewish learning and thousands of magnificent synagogues and Temples throughout the land. But there are those who question whether American Jewish life has any creative future. They point not only to the escapists, trying to hide their Jewish identity; not only to the apologists, stricken with a sense of Jewish inferiority; not only to the assimilationists, trying to merge with the majority. They point to people like you, members of a congregation and ostensibly positive Jews, and they say that even among such as you there is widespread ignorance of our Jewish heritage and indifference to Jewish values. Dr. Mordecai Kaplan, one of American Jewry's most provocative thinkers, stands among them.[10] In a recent public discussion he commented that most of us are Jewishly like "Ol' man river: tired of livin' but scared of dyin'."

We cannot evade our historic responsibility. The twenty-three who 300 years ago set foot on the docks of New Amsterdam have now grown to the greatest Jewish community numerically in the history of our people, six million strong. It is only a decade since six million of our people died as martyrs. With them was destroyed the rich traditions and institutions of a strong centuries old Jewish life. The American Jewish community must now take over the unfulfilled spiritual tasks of the six million who have perished.

At the end of the book of Genesis, we read of Jacob's blessing to each of the twelve tribes. In describing the fate of the tribe of Issachar, the phrase is used, *vayet shichmo lisbol*, "he bowed his shoulder to the burden" (Gen. 49:15). One

---

9. This passage reflects part of the mythos of the American Jewish experience. There was indeed a trapdoor in the floor of the reading platform of the Newport synagogue, with a ladder that leads to the foundations. But there is no evidence of any link with "Marrano traditions," or that it was sealed when the Declaration of Independence was proclaimed. Saperstein's homiletical file attributes this interpretation of the "sealed tunnel" to a broadcast of "The Eternal Light," script no. 239. A modern treatment notes that "secret stairs, rooms under cellars, and secret chambers were common in early American houses": Rachel Wischnitzer, *Synagogue Architecture in the United States* (Philadelphia: JPS, 1955), 18–19.

10. Kaplan, the founder of the Reconstructionist Movement and a critic of the Jewish "establishment" in America, had a significant influence over many Reform and Conservative rabbis of the time. The quotation appears on cards in the homiletical file, including an article reporting Kaplan's address to the Zionist Cultural Institute of Winnipeg in the spring of 1952 on "Can American Jewish Life Be Creative?"

rabbi in the Midrash comments, *lisbol ol shel eretz Yisroel*, "to bear the burden of the land of Israel." Another disagreed. "No," he said," "it is *lisbol ol shel Torah*, to bear the burden of Torah. This is what is meant," he continues, "by the passage in Chronicles which says, 'the children of Issachar are men who know what the time requires to be done'" (I Chron. 12:32).[11]

To extend help to our brothers in Israel: By all means. To buy bonds and give to the United Jewish Appeal and exert our democratic influence that our government may not be a party to the destruction of the new state: By all means. But one responsibility is ours above all others. "To bear the burden of Torah": to make of America a center of Jewish spiritual life. When the Torah was given, God said, according to the Midrash, "If you do not accept this Torah, there shall be your grave."[12] The word used is *shom*, "there," not *po*, "here." In other words, wherever you will be, if Jewish faith and education are neglected, there Jewish life will perish. As we go forward then as American Jews, let us be like the children of Issachar, "men who know that the time requires to be done."

We stand at the threshold of our second 300 years. As Jews and Americans we go forward armed with the potent weapon of the visions from the past. We have gone far toward the fulfillment of their promise. But there is still far to go. May we move forward, that Jewish life in this land of freedom may know a new Golden Age, and that the American spirit may kindle a new light of hope for humanity. Then shall we, our country and our faith, truly merit Gods blessing, for we shall have helped bring blessing to the world.

---

11. Genesis Rabbah 98:12.
12. B. Shabbat 88a.

28

How Leadership Fails
June 27, 1957
CCAR Conference Sermon
Miami Beach, Florida

In several earlier sermons, Saperstein referred to annual conventions of the Central Conference of American Rabbis (see the end of the sermon for 1938 and the beginning of the sermon from 1954). The program of these conventions included a "conference sermon" as part of the Shabbat morning service; Saperstein was invited to deliver this sermon in June 1957.

The difference between this sermon, addressed to colleagues, and those addressed to congregants is readily discernible, and Saperstein's homiletical files reveal extensive preparation, especially with the Biblical commentaries. After an introduction drawing from Hasidic materials to bring life to the topos of unworthiness, the central topic is derived from an exegetical problem of the Torah parashah, Hukkat, containing the dramatic account of Moses at the Wilderness of Zin (Num. 20:2-12). The sermon identifies three different exegetical traditions about the sin of Moses, each one rooted in a specific formulation of the Biblical text. These three traditions are all accepted here and used to provide three kinds of pitfall for contemporary leadership.

This is primarily a homiletical style of preaching. The topical nature of the sermon is exemplified most concretely in the reference to the "Crusade for Christ" of the Reverend Billy Graham, which opened in New York on May 15, was drawing huge numbers, and appeared to be inspiring a major religious revival. Some response seemed necessary, if only to reassure the listeners that their own work was not, by comparison, a failure.

A SERMON HAS BEEN DEFINED as something a preacher will go across the country to deliver but will not go across the street to hear. The character of this congregation, comprised largely of preachers, makes this a sobering and challenging experience. The story is told that when the Gerer Rebbe was selected as leader of the Kotzker Chassidim he said, "I know that I am not more learned nor pious than others. The only reason I have accepted this appointment is that worthy men have requested me to do so. During the days of the Temple," he continued, "a cattle breeder in the land of Israel was required to drive his newborn cattle into an enclosure in single file. As they entered they were all of equal station, but when over each tenth one the owner pronounced 'consecrated to the Lord,' it was set aside for a special holy function."[1] I am apparently the tenth cow at the Conference. And lest this still sound presumptuous may I repeat the words of the *darshan* [preacher] who began each *derosho* [sermon] with the announcement, "I do not preach to you: I preach to myself and allow you to listen."[2]

This week's sedra contains one of the most poignant episodes of the entire Torah. Almost forty years of wandering had passed. In the wilderness of Zin there was no water for the congregation. As they had done so often before, the children of Israel complained to Moses, "Wherefore have ye made us to come up out of Egypt to bring us unto this evil place to die here" (Num. 20:4). God directed Moses, "Assemble the congregation and speak unto the rock in their presence and thou shalt bring forth water from the rock" (Num. 20:8). Moses gathered the people and bitterly rebuked them. Then he smote the rock with the rod, and water came forth. And the Lord said unto Moses and Aaron, יען לא האמנתם בי להקדישני לעיני בני ישראל לכן לא תביאו את הקהל הזה אל הארץ אשר נתתי להם, "Because ye believed not in me to sanctify me in the eyes of the children of Israel, therefore ye shall not bring this assembly unto the land which I have given them" (Num. 20:12).

We can imagine the anguish with which Moses must have searched his heart and conduct. "What have I done to merit this denial? Where did I fall short? How did I fail?" The Bible text never specifically states the nature of the sin of Moses. The Rabbis and traditional commentators, however, had no hesitation in spelling out the pattern of his failure. They are not content with the explanation that he erred in striking rather than speaking to the rock. As they were prone to do, and as we do not hesitate doing, they read into the Bible verses, not necessarily their intrinsic meaning, but a message they could be made to convey. They do not agree in their conclusions on this passage. In fact they do not refrain

---

1. Louis I. Newman, *The Hasidic Anthology* (New York: Charles Scribner's Sons, 1934), 218.

2. Compare Azariah Figo, cited in Israel Bettan, *Studies in Jewish Preaching* (Cincinnati: HUC Press, 1939), 235; Marc Saperstein, *Jewish Preaching 1200–1800* (New Haven: Yale University Press, 1989), 60–61. In Saperstein's homiletical file, there is a card on which is typed "Chayim Brisker—Introduced each sermon—Talk to myself—invite others to listen," but no source is given for this.

from directly refuting each other. But as we read their interpretations and commentaries, we see the pattern emerging. It forms what we might call a critique of leadership. They took the opportunity to present a primer of pitfalls of which a leader must beware. Their discussion may not help us to understand the fate of Moses. It does help us better to comprehend the function of the rabbi.

Some of the commentators derive the failure of Moses from the sentence which says that after hearing the complaint of the Israelites, ויבא משה ואהרן מפני הקהל אל פתח אהל מועד ויפלו על פניהם, "Moses and Aaron went from the presence of the assembly unto the door of the tent of meeting and fell upon their faces" (Num. 20:6). The Tanchuma, followed by several of the medieval commentators, interprets this as *flight* in fear of the threatening faces directed toward them. "They ran away," it is stated, "as an officer of the kingdom in time of revolt flees to the palace of the king." Another Midrash associates their action with the fact that Moses and Aaron were in mourning for the death of their sister, Miriam. And God rebuked them: "Leaders of the people, go out at once. My children perish of thirst and ye have nothing better to do than to mourn the death of an old woman."[3]

The pitfall for leadership thus indicated might be termed flight from reality. The leader misses the mark when, out of fear or out of a confusion of values, he turns his back to the challenge of life. We must not make of faith an escape from the necessity of action, of the sanctuary a refuge from the demands of society. I shall not speak at length of those in our day who succumb to the force of expediency. It is in poor taste for those who do not stand on the combat line of the integration problem, for example, to pass judgment upon the conduct of colleagues who do.[4] Let us each search his own conscience; for within all our congregations and communities, there are questions of standards and values. No rabbi escapes the confrontation of some issue in which he must determine whether he will be guided by principle or the pressure of public opinion. Officially the Reform movement, laymen and rabbis alike, has taken a firm and advanced position on many social problems.[5] The real test is not what we say gathered in convention, but what we do when we stand alone, like Moses, before

---

3. Saperstein found these two interpretations in Bialik and Ravnitzky's *Sefer Ha-Aggadah*. See *The Book of Legends*, transl. William G. Braude (New York: Schocken, 1992), 750, no. 267.

4. This had been debated at the 44th Biennial Assembly of the Union of American Hebrew Congregations held in Toronto in late April of 1957. In the issue of the *CCAR Journal* dated June 1957, Abraham Klausner discussed that Assembly and wrote, "Instead of self-righteously chastising our Southern brethren and colleagues for their failure to implement the mandate of our tradition as emphasized by the Supreme Court of the land, perhaps we should give thought to the nature of their problem and reason with them as to the manner in which we could work towards total desegregation, North and South. It is not for us to impose martyrdom upon others" (61). I cannot determine whether or not this issue was available for Saperstein before this sermon was delivered.

5. This refers to resolutions passed by the UAHC at its Biennial Assemblies of the lay leadership of Reform Judaism, and by the Central Conference of American Rabbis at its annual conferences.

the menacing faces of those who disagree with us.

The flight from reality sometimes has other origins. It may be an outgrowth of theology rather than expediency, evolving not out of fear but out of despair. There is a tendency current in theological circles to separate faith from circumstance, to seek to save the world by forsaking it. Sometimes this may give an erroneous impression of practicality. Billy Graham, drawing almost 20,000 people night after night to Madison Square Garden, would seem to be waging a very real and successful campaign against evil. The numerical results may well make some of us envious. But where does it all lead? I shall not question the sincerity of spirit of Billy Graham and his followers. Nor shall I question, as so many have done, the propriety of the techniques of his organization. I do question the efficacy of his solutions.

There is need for a great religious crusade against the imperfections of the world. Whether on Eighth Avenue in New York, or on Main Street in Montgomery, Alabama, or along Pennsylvania Avenue in Washington, D.C., there are evils to be fought. The question is whether the sawdust trail is the true road to salvation. According to our faith, not those who take issue with sin, and not those who denounce themselves as sinners, and not those who call upon the Lord, whether in a rousing hymn or in a "still, small voice," but those who labor as partners of God in shaping the world are the architects of redemption.[6] The goal cannot be achieved once and for all, even in a moment of genuine exaltation. It is a continuous and relentless battle. The imperfections of New York City, or of any other city, will not be resolved by the charged emotions of religious revivalism. They may ultimately be resolved by the rational application of ethical idealism, painfully and courageously grappling with life. The late Stephen S. Wise also spearheaded a fight against entrenched evil in New York. It is his way, rather than that of Billy Graham, which we must follow.

Among our own colleagues there are those ready to concede not only the imperfection of the world, but its imperfectibility. To them, religious commitment is a sort of honorable discharge from the bankrupt business of society. They consider themselves on sound theological ground, not when they confront life, but when they fall on their faces before the glory of the Lord. Our Sedra reminds us that the sanctuary must not be converted into a harbor of safety where men find refuge in their flight from fear or their leap of faith. "My hair and beard have grown white and I have not yet atoned!" lamented Rabbi Hayyim of Zans. "O, my friend," replied Rabbi Eliezer [of Dzikov], "you are thinking only of yourself. How about forgetting yourself and thinking of the world."[7] The challenge admittedly is eternal and universal; but the place to begin

---

6. This sentence, together with the last three sentences of the previous paragraph, were quoted by the *New York Times* as part of its coverage of the CCAR convention (June 28, 1957, A26:6).

7. Martin Buber, *Tales of the Hasidim*, 2 vols. (New York: Schocken, 1947–48), 2:214.

in answering it is, in Buber's phrase, "Here where one stands!"[8]

Another group of commentators explains the sin of Moses in terms of the anger and impatience demonstrated toward the people. *Hamorim*—"rebels," he called them (Num. 20:10), and by his irritable condemnation he indicated his lack of faith. For he repudiated them, though God himself had not done so. Rashi, in this context, cites the midrashic passage in which, when Moses was searching for the rock, he angrily rejected the use of the one selected by the people.[9] It was then that he called them *hamorim* and the Midrash gives several derivations for the word. One comes from a Greek root, meaning fools. Another is connected with the word meaning teachers, as though he were saying, "You who presume to teach your teachers." A third links it with the word meaning archers implying "you who shoot upon your leaders with your arrows."[10] They conclude that temper and contempt were unworthy of his position as a leader.

The flaw of leadership indicated here is that of alienation from the people. It is expressed in readiness to repudiate them, a reluctance to recognize their function, the tendency to discount their importance. It is not easy for the spiritual leader to work with people who lack understanding, who have the effrontery to try to teach their rabbis when they should be learning from them, who do not hesitate to shoot barbed arrows of criticism, sometimes with deadly effect. There is room for righteous anger in Judaism, and circumstances which demand such anger. But the anger of the rabbi must be constructive, and never the expression of personal pique. He must be prepared, without loss of dignity, to absorb hostility and frustration. Among his primary requisites are patience and tolerance for the limitations of the people whom he must both lead and serve.

A recent anthropological study of East European Jewry was called *Life Is With People*.[11] And we might well say of the rabbi's work that it too is with people. For in the final analysis it is people who are the measure of our achievement. If we do not have impact upon their thinking and lives and aspirations, our labors are but vanity. Unlike the scholar or the artist, the rabbi cannot work in isolation. In modern times particularly, he is the mediator who interprets and transmits the Jewish heritage to the Jewish people. I am not measuring effectiveness in terms of numbers, but that criterion must not be too lightly disregarded. Professor Salo Baron, in concluding a recent study of "The Modern Age in Jewish History," strikes an implied note of hope about the future of American Jewry. Its spiritual health, he maintains, will be determined by whether or not a distinguished leadership can be developed. "If in the next generation," he says, "American Jewry turns from quantity to quality; if, for example, it can produce one hundred truly first-rate scholars and the same number of writers and artists,

---

8. A recurring motif in Buber's writings, e.g., *Hasidism and Modern Man* (New York: Harper Torchbooks, 1966), 172–73.

9. Rashi on Numbers 20:10, based on *Tanhuma, Hukkat* 9.

10. See *Numbers Rabbah* 19,9 on the verse. Rashi states that the word is from a Greek root.

11. Mark Zborowski and Elizabeth Herzog, *Life Is With People* (New York: Schocken, 1952).

of rabbis, of communal executives and of lay-leaders—then one could look forward to new heights of achievement."[12]

Halevai ["would that"] his requirement be fulfilled. But even though it would be, the optimism of his conclusion cannot be taken for granted. It is true that the great epochs of Jewish achievement have been marked by the emergence of uniquely gifted and creative individuals. But great ages have also had communities receptive to their leaders. Without them the latter remain but voices in the wilderness. Five hundred truly first-rate leaders might well make the next generation an historic one. But what of the generation which will follow that? I would feel more confident if the next generation could produce half a million truly devoted and loyal Jews. From them the requisite leadership would emerge. The saving remnant may be, as the prophet indicated, one out of ten. Certainly it must be more than one out of ten thousand.

At rabbinical conferences we are prone to think of the ideal rabbi in terms of scholarship. We all know how important but difficult it is to find time for the study of Torah, and we sympathize with ourselves on this account. I hope I will not be misunderstood in stating that sometimes this involves a mistaken emphasis. The rabbi must, of course, be versed in the literature and traditions of our faith. Without that he cannot be considered a rabbi. And he must continuously enlarge and deepen his understanding. Without that he is not worthy of his title. But we must not confuse qualification with function. Whatever the historic role of the rabbi was, the duty of the modern rabbi is not to study but to teach. For him study must be only the prelude to transmission. The measure of his success should be not what he has imbibed but what he has imparted. In this respect the German *lehren* comes closer to a description of his function than the Yiddish *lernen*. In medieval Christianity the clergy often had a monopoly on literacy. It will be an evil day for Judaism, however, when the rabbi becomes the vicarious custodian of Jewish learning for the community. Rabbi Ishmael did not negate the value of *Torah lishma* [study for its own sake] when he reminded us in the *Pirke Avot* (4,5) of the special merit of learning in order to teach, and the even greater merit of learning in order to practice.

I repeat—we must guide and teach, not chastise and denounce. It is easy to speak disparagingly of the low standards of American Jewish life. It is not hard to prick the bubbles in the veneer of suburban Judaism, to make scintillating and devastating criticisms of the superficiality of the contemporary religious resurgence. If these be warranted, let us not judge except as we judge ourselves. In reality the level of American Jewish life is far higher than it was a generation ago. There is room for criticism. But there is also room for commendation. Let us not alienate ourselves from our people. If they lack the living waters of knowledge and of faith, let us not condemn them. Let us help to meet their needs.

Again we return to our Bible passage. A third approach of commentators is

---

12. Baron, "The Modern Age," in *Great Ages and Ideas of the Jewish People*, ed. Leo Schwarz (New York: Random House, 1956), 483–84.

deduced from the phrase, הַמִן הַסֶּלַע הַזֶּה נוֹצִיא לָכֶם מַיִם, "Are we to bring you forth water out of this rock?" (Num. 20:10). The Ramban [Rabbi Moses ben Nahman] indicates that the shortcoming of Moses lay in his use of the word נוֹצִיא—"are *we* to bring forth"—giving the impression that he and Aaron and not God were to perform the miracle. The danger for the rabbi implied here is loss of perspective. It is revealed when he comes to consider himself the source of authority rather than its instrument, the end of Jewish life rather than its servant.

The modern rabbi is uniquely susceptible to such distortion. We often complain among ourselves that the prestige of the rabbi is waning. In reality, his status has rarely been at a higher level. The trend is not towards too little *kovod* [honor] for the rabbi, but towards so much *kovod* that it sometimes leads to an unhealthy manifestation of hero-worship. For we are tempted to take this adulation seriously, and this is a deadly danger. With the donning of our rabbinical robes, we must never assume in our own eyes the aura of perfection and infallibility that the admiration of many congregations implies. We must not evaluate our work as it affects us, but measure ourselves in relationship to our work. It is not we who give meaning to Judaism and the synagogue. It is Judaism and the synagogue that should give meaning to our lives.

There is an old legend concerning the return of the captured Ark of the Covenant by the Philistines. It was, you will recall, placed in a cart drawn by two cows. As it approached Beth Shemesh the reapers there, seeing the ark, rejoiced and bowed down before it. And the cows said each to the other, "See how the people give us reverence. Surely we must be divine." But when they came to the field of Joshua, the Beth Shemite, the Levites took down the ark and the people offered up the cows as a burnt offering unto the Lord. Poor creatures, they had not realized it was not to them that men paid homage, but to the precious treasure they bore.[13] In similar vein, the Chassidic Moses of Kobryn reminds us, "A leader must not think that God chose him because he is a great man. Does a peg on the wall on which the king hangs his crown boast that its beauty attracted the king's attention?"[14] Colleagues, *De nobis fabula narratur.*[15]

---

13. This passage was a puzzle, as the story is not found in rabbinic aggadah, which presents a positive view of the cows. In Saperstein's homiletical file, I found a clipped printed paragraph (no identification of the source) containing the story (introduced by "There is a parable . . . ") and the application to the "vain synagogue functionary." On it is a hand-written note, "cited by Simon Singer in Where the Clergy Fail." The "Rev. Simeon Singer" (1848–1906) was Minister of the New West End Synagogue. His *Lectures and Addresses*, ed. by Israel Abrahams (London: Routledge, 1908), contains the address, "Where the Clergy Fail," delivered in 1904 as Honorary President of Jews' College Union Society, and this address indeed contains the story (205–6), which Singer attributes to "the Russo-Jewish fabulist, Gordon." See, for the original source, *Kitvei Yehudah Leib Gordon: Shirah* (Tel Aviv: Dvir, 1956), 189; on 353, Gordon indicates that the story was his own invention (*yelid ra'ayonai*). There is no indication that Saperstein actually used anything else from the Singer address in this sermon.

14. Buber, *Tales of the Hasidim*, 2:167.

15. "It is about us that the story is told."

These then are some of the ways in which leadership fails: in flight from reality through fear and confusion; in alienation from people through contempt and impatience; in loss of perspective through arrogance and forgetfulness of purpose. The force of the message is intensified because it is expressed through the medium of Moses, the pattern of whose life as portrayed in the Bible was essentially the contradiction of these failings. Again and again we have seen Moses courageously confronting the imperfections of the world, unselfishly identifying himself with his people, retaining his basic humility and sense of consecration. Yet even Moses failed. And in his failing we are warned. But at the same time we are comforted. מתחיל בגנות ומסיים בשבח.[16] For though Moses did not see his task carried to completion, there is no indication that his labors were in vain. Though he had failed, in Jewish tradition he is still Moshe Rabbenu, regarded by the sages and the Rambam [Rabbi Moses ben Maimon, Maimonides] as preeminent among the prophets. Moses did not attain perfection. It is not expected of us. We are human, as our people are human, as even Moses was human. The glory of our work lies in the fact that though we are finite, the cause itself is infinite. So long as we strive in sincerity, even with our failures we may succeed.

Let us seek to avoid the pitfalls on our path. But whatever our limitations the important thing is that as servants of God we strive courageously, unselfishly and humbly to bring the waters of life to our people.[17]

---

16. "We begin with blame and conclude with praise," B. Pes. 116a and elsewhere.

17. The text of this sermon is taken from *The Central Conference of American Rabbis Yearbook*, 67 (1957): 139–44; hence the quotations in the original Hebrew letters.

29

Message from the Movies
December 19, 1958

On October 12, 1958, an explosion rocked the large Reform Temple of Atlanta, Georgia, causing major destruction. This was the most dramatic of a series of attacks against Jewish institutions in the South that year, including the bombings of Beth El Temple in Miami, Florida, and the Jewish Center of Nashville, Tennessee, on March 16, the bombing of the Jacksonville, Florida, Jewish Center on April 28 and the attempted bombing of Beth El Temple in Birmingham, Alabama, on the same day, an effort foiled by a wet fuse. Anonymous phone calls linked these bombings with Jewish involvement in the movement for integration and civil rights.

Saperstein spoke about the Atlanta incident on October 17, arguing a theme we have encountered in sermons from the 1930s and 1940s on Nazism, lynching and anti-communist riots: that "once the spirit of disrespect for law and the separation of group against group and man against man is accepted, though it be at first directed against the Negro, it is not long before the application is expanded and . . . directed against the Jew, even as once it is directed against the Jew, it will inevitably be directed against other groups, until the spirit of democracy is destroyed." The juxtaposition of the two motion pictures discussed in this sermon given two months later was a compelling way of illustrating the connection between prejudice against Negroes and against Jews. Here the emphasis, however, was not on the destructive power of hatred but rather on prejudice transcended when people thrown by circumstance into a common situation come to know each other not as stereotypes but as human beings.

The brief discussion of church-state issues at the end was prompted by the Christmas season, which invariably raised issues of conflict among Jews re-

garding such matters as activities in the public schools and Nativity scenes on public property. Whether or not the actual examples given would have seemed compelling to listeners without a fuller exposition, the underlying message, emphasized at the end, is that the rights and interests of a minority group cannot be abridged without damaging the community as a whole.

MY SERMON TONIGHT IS BASED UPON TWO MOVIES. Now it is a rare experience for me to go to even one movie. I see only special ones, of particular interest. But on this occasion, there were two movies I wanted to see. I had only one free evening. I went with my family to the earlier one, then coming out, we realized that we could make the other one in a neighboring community. In spirit, in subject matter, in treatment and background, the two pictures are as different as they could be. But after seeing them both, I realized that insofar as they expressed a message, their theme was the same. It was the same picture, in different form.

"The Defiant Ones" is a powerful, gripping drama with a theme of important social significance.[1] It is the story of two prisoners in a Southern chain gang. The truck on which they and other prisoners are being transported gets involved in an accident. In the confusion, the two men get a chance to attempt an escape. But their escape is complicated by the fact that they are chained together. It is further complicated by the fact that one [played by Tony Curtis] is a white man who hates Negroes, and the other [played by Sidney Poitier] is a Negro. In a sense, they become temporarily married; the chain is their wedding ring.

They have not gone far before their animosity breaks out. The white man wants to go south, the Negro wishes to head north. Soon they realize that they are bound together and that they must go together. But this realization does not eliminate their animosity, which seethes inside the white prisoner and evokes a bitter reaction from the Negro. As they continue they manage to get along together and begin to understand each other better. But they are still white man and Negro.

Then they get a chance to cut the chain. They are now separated. The white prisoner has a chance to escape by himself with the aid of a white woman, who sends the Negro off on a trail across the swamp. When he realizes that the Negro is going to his death, he suddenly turns his back on his chance of escape and runs to warn his chain mate. Again they are together. Just in time, they reach the bridge where they had hoped to hop a train that would bring them to freedom and safety. They run for it; the Negro makes it and holds out his hand for the other. The train is moving faster. He grasps the wrist of his partner and tries to pull him up, but he doesn't have the strength. If he lets go, he's got it made. Instead, he clings desperately until he can no longer hold on, and he himself tum-

---

1. The message seems much less radical, more commonplace today than at the time of its release, when the goals of integration and racial equality were still quite controversial. See on this *Magell's Survey of Cinema: English Language Films*, Second Series (Englewood Cliffs: Salem Press, 1981), vol. 2, 604, 608.

bles from the train. And so they are caught. They are going back to prison. But now in a sense that they are no longer bound by an iron chain. Each had given his chance of freedom for the other, and they are now bound by a chain of humanity.

The second picture, "Me and the Colonel," is an adaptation of a play presented during the war years under the title "Jacobowsky and the Colonel."[2] The story is built around a Jew [played by Danny Kaye] named Jacobowsky. After flight from one place to another, he now finds himself a refugee in Paris when the Nazis take over, and once again he must flee. His own experience and the experience of his people over the ages have given Jacobowsky two things. First is an outlook on life. No matter how bad things are, he will not allow himself to despair. "There are always two possibilities," he says again and again; "one is always worse than the other. So you can always hope that the one that is not so bad will develop." The other quality is resourcefulness. His mind is quick and alert, fertile with techniques; he is inured to danger, always able to take advantage of circumstances, never completely nonplussed.

Seeking to escape at the same time is a colonel of the Polish Army who has been entrusted with important papers that he must transmit to London. Fate throws them together. The colonel has an immense disdain and contempt for Jews. He is of aristocratic stock, a soldier. He still lives in the aura of medieval chivalry. As Jacobowsky says, the colonel has one of the best minds of the twelfth century. He does not want to become involved with Jacobowsky, but he can't help himself: their fate is bound together. For there is no means of transportation out of Paris, except that Jacobowsky has managed to get himself an automobile and some gasoline. And so they set out together.

While dealing with a potentially tragic situation, the story is presented as a comedy. Franz Werfel, the author of the original play, used the light and ironic touch. We see the Polish colonel, who thinks of drinking and romance and war as the most important things in life, and the Jewish refugee—sensitive, intelligent, alert, endowed with ancestral wisdom. The colonel has a love of life, Jacobowsky has a love of living. The colonel despises his travel-mate even when he must depend on him for his own survival. Near the end, when they are separated and Jacobowsky is in danger, the colonel rejoins him. The story concludes as they make their rendezvous with the submarine that will carry them to freedom, and they become aware of a new bond. In the course of surviving danger, they have touched the basic humanity that links them.

These are the two movies. And like the two dreams of Pharaoh we read about last week, the two stories are one (see Gen. 41:25). Their theme is exemplified in the chain that binds Negro and white, in the antique automobile that represents the hope of escape for Jew and Pole. It is simply this: that we are bound together, all of us, that we rise together and fall together, that all who

---

2. "Jacobowsky and the Colonel," written in German by Franz Werfel was adapted for the American stage by S. N. Behrman. Produced by the Theatre Guild and directed by Elia Kazan, it opened in March 1944.

seek freedom must seek it together, that the destiny of one cannot be separated from that of the others.

The Rabbis of the Talmud recognized this and expressed it in a parable. A group of men was crossing a stream in a boat when one of them started boring a hole in the bottom. The others protested, "What are you doing?! You'll kill us all!" "Why are you concerned?" the man replied. "I'm making the hole under my own seat." "But can't you see?" they answered. "We're all in the same boat."[3]

We can see the application of this message in many ways. I first came to this pulpit just after the beginning of the Nazi regime in Germany. I was then still a rabbinical student under the tutelage of my great mentor, Rabbi Stephen S. Wise. Already his great voice was lifted up to alert not only the Jewish people but also the entire world to the menace of Nazism. Under his influence we, his students, also sought to bring this awareness to our communities. I remember the first Thanksgiving service at which I preached. There were then three Protestant churches participating. I stressed the point that Nazism represented a threat not only to Jews and Judaism, but to all religions, to all free people, to all civilization.

I can still remember the reception. The response was one of attentively listening to an obviously young preacher, with a kind of tolerant attitude, as though in my zeal and inexperience and concern for Jewish welfare I was exaggerating. Yet it was not too many years later that the real nature of the menace of Nazism became apparent to all, when our nation went to war because of it. Today, each Memorial Day, we pay tribute outside this Temple to those who died because of the truth of what we had said.[4] If the truth had been comprehended in time, the great sacrifice might have been avoided.

Yesterday, reading my copy of the "National Jewish Post," I came across the report of a statement by a prominent Orthodox rabbi serving the congregation in Memphis, Tennessee. He made the point that he thought it was wrong for Jews to take the lead in the anti-segregation movement. He did not go to the extreme of saying that protests against segregation were alien to religion. But he felt that Jews should concern themselves with strictly Jewish problems, and that there were other agencies to be concerned with problems of Negro civil rights. I'm sure that a great many readers will agree with him, particularly those in the South who are concerned about what anti-segregation activities may do to the position of the Jewish minority there. But how shortsighted their view is. Being in the spotlight of an unpopular position may be uncomfortable and even dangerous. On the other hand, in the long run, it is more dangerous to pretend that this problem does not concern us.

---

3. A paraphrase of a parable from Leviticus Rabbah 4,6.

4. "Outside this Temple" refers to the memorial monument of the village of Lynbrook in a square just across the street from the Temple property.

Psychological studies in recent years have demonstrated that the prejudiced personality rarely isolates his prejudice against one group alone.[5] The person who is prejudiced against Negroes is usually also prejudiced against Jews and other minorities. Of course there are such things as regional social patterns. Prejudice against Negroes may be the pattern in sections of the south, accepted even by people otherwise non-prejudiced. But these are not the dangerous people. These people are reasonable; they do not resort to violence and dynamite.[6] The ones who are dangerous do not need to wait for Jewish participation on behalf of the Negro to hate Jews. Note that the same hate sheets that have been attacking Jews for decades in the South are now linking the Jews with the Negro problem. Safety for Jews in the South is directly associated not with joining an anti-Negro bandwagon, but with the recognition of the dignity and rights of all human beings.

Now to deal with a problem that is particularly current at this season of the year: the problem of church and state with particular reference to holiday observance in the public schools. Here we find the Jews virtually isolated in our insistence upon the wall of separation. Only such splinter groups of the non-Jewish religious world as Ethical Culture and the Unitarians are aligned with us. Other groups insist that our schools are anti-religious, that we must bring more religion into the schools if we are to meet the menace of communism. They cannot understand the position of the Jew, and we are accused of being against religious education, among other things. Superficially it sounds convincing, and it is hard to make the non-Jewish world recognize that this affects them as well as us.

Right now, the main emphasis is upon Christmas, and there we are alone. Once the principle is established that religion has a legitimate right in the schools, however, suppose the Catholics then insist that there be public financing of parochial schools. If we say that this is discriminatory, favoring one group, the answer will be, "There is nothing to prevent any religious group from building parochial schools. This is a way of strengthening religion." And when the Protestants insist that this is against the principle of the separation of church and state, the answer comes back, "But we have established that that principle should not be applied to religion in the public schools."

Or take another issue. Suppose the Protestants decide there should be brief religious services in the public schools at holiday time, not merely festival celebrations. This is only an expansion of the argument that we need more religious training. Jews object. But this time the Catholics object as well. It is against their principles to have their children attend worship services other than their own. The Protestant argument is that this will strengthen religion. The Catholics re-

---

5. From the beginning of his rabbinate in the 1930s, Saperstein had frequently discussed from the pulpit the nature of prejudice, using reports of current psychological and sociological studies.

6. All listeners would have recognized this as an allusion to the bombings of Southern synagogues, culminating in the bombing of the Temple in Atlanta that had occurred two months earlier. See introduction.

ply, that it has no place in the public schools. But the Protestants answer that "It has already been established that a religious observance can be held in the schools."

In other words, the interests of all groups, not just Jews, ultimately indicate the desirability of complete separation.

It comes down to this. All mankind are bound together. We are like the limbs of a single body. You cannot hurt one without doing harm to the entire organism. In the Bible reading for this Sabbath, the spirit of family unity that connected Joseph with his brothers proved stronger than any resentment he may have nurtured (see Gen. 45:1-15). John Donne expressed it long ago when he said, "No man is an island, entire of itself; every man is a piece of the continent, a part of the main. Therefore never send to know for whom the bell tolls; it tolls for thee."[7]

---

7. John Donne, *Devotions upon Emergent Occasions*, Meditation XVII. Compare the end of the sermon on "The Deputy" from 1964.

30

Jewish Life Behind the Iron Curtain
September 11, 1959

Beginning in 1953, with a trip to Israel and Europe, the Sapersteins began a series of summer travels that would bring them to Jewish communities on six continents. Over the years, congregants learned to expect that the sermon delivered on the first Friday night following Labor Day would probably be a report on experiences during the summer involving Jewish communities outside the United States. Material from these trips also entered the High Holy Day sermons, although these were less factual and more homiletical in nature.

Following the death of Stalin, the overt persecution of the "Doctors' Plot" type had ceased in the Soviet Union. But word was getting back of a systematic repression of Jewish culture and religious identity in the Soviet Union and many of the other "Iron Curtain" countries. The highly negative reports of a few rabbis who visited in the second half of the decade led the Soviet authorities to refuse to grant visas to those who answered "rabbi" to the question about profession on the visa application, and indeed, Saperstein's original application for a visa was rejected. But in Europe, they applied for and received visas to Czechoslovakia; in the Soviet Embassy of Prague they received visas to the USSR, and in Moscow, visas to Poland.

The sermon below was a summary report delivered against the tense background of Nikita Khrushchev's arrival for a state visit to the United States (see below, n. 5). It contains an extremely pessimistic, almost fatalistic, evaluation. From the plethora of facts, what stands out for the listeners are the capsule characterizations of Jewish life in the three countries which signal the conclusion of each section—Czechoslovakia: "a set of museum pieces," Poland: "a great unmarked grave," Soviet Russia: "an iron paroches [ark curtain] preventing access to the Torah." The bleak conclusion about the likely need to say kaddish *[the mourner's prayer] for another three million Jews less than one generation after the six million would be repeated on numerous occasions in the following decade, until the revival of Jewish identity following the Six-Day War suggested an alternative scenario. Compare the 1970 address on the occasion of the Leningrad Trials.*

THE BIBLE TELLS US THAT WHEN JOSEPH WAS SENT BY HIS FATHER to seek out his brothers and report on their welfare, he met a stranger who found him wandering and asked, "Whom do you seek?" Joseph answer, *Et ahai anochi m'vakesh*, "I seek my brothers" (Gen. 37:15–16). That phrase could be the theme or text of our travels this summer. It sounds like a roster of the countries of Europe: Spain, England, Ireland, Scotland, Germany, Austria, Czechoslovakia, Denmark, Sweden, Finland, Poland, and Russia. In each of them we sought out our brothers—to visit their sanctuaries, to report on their welfare. Tonight I am particularly concerned with the countries behind the Iron Curtain.

I have a rather unique passport. Here is a canceled Russian visa, a canceled Polish visa; here is a valid Czechoslovakian visa, obtained by a fluke in London, here a valid Russian visa obtained in Czechoslovakia, here a Polish visa obtained in Moscow. It is interesting to note that this summer, out of literally dozens who applied, only three rabbis obtained visas for the Iron Curtain countries, and I was the only one who started out listing myself as a rabbi. As you know, when I started out, I thought I would be denied the opportunity. The tale of how I got the visas—of my pilgrimage in and out of Russian consulates all over Europe—is itself a revealing story.

All in all it was a strange, exciting, and tragic trip. Strange, because we never knew from day to day how things would gel, and each new development required revising our plans. Exciting, because we were conscious of blazing new trails in travel—establishing contact with Jews who had been cut asunder from Jewish contacts for more than forty years. Tragic, because it is my sad duty to report that, while others may evaluate the situation differently, on the basis of what I have seen, we must say *kaddish* for Jewish life in Central and Eastern Europe—this great area once the center of Jewish spiritual, cultural creativity. I say it is my conviction that Jewish life there is dead—not only because of external pressure, but more tragic because after survival through centuries of persecution, the Jews of these countries by and large have lost the will to live as Jews. I was, as you know, in concentration camps of Germany, days after liberation.[1] What I saw now was more tragic than what I saw then. For then I saw the crushed bodies of our people, this time I saw their crushed spirit.

There are two pictures that the observer will get of Jewish life in countries behind the Iron Curtain. Both of them, though contradictory, have elements of truth. When you speak to "official" representatives of the Jewish communities, they will speak to you in positive terms, tell you that everything is fine. In doing so, they obviously speak out of fear. We must not hold it against them. This is no game they are playing; they are only too well aware of the consequences of

---

1. See the letter cited in the introduction to the 1945 sermon, "The Voice of Joy and Gladness."

what they might say. Jewish spokesmen in the South who are wary of speaking out on the integration problem must be similarly understood: their livelihood is at stake.[2] Jewish leaders in Russia know that their *lives* are at stake. They are all too aware of the tendency of American leaders to quote their negative statements to the press—and all too aware of the consequences for themselves. We must therefore take their statements for what they are. The other picture is derived from personal observation, from conversations with ordinary Jews. It is possible to have such conversations. There is still fear on the part of many people of speaking to strangers, but the political climate is different than it was under Stalin, and the fear is disappearing. Particularly in the precincts of the synagogue, Jews are eager to unburden their hearts.

Let me take Czechoslovakia first. Before the war there were 350,000 Jews; now the estimates are 20,000 to 30,000—5,000 in Prague. In once colorful, now rather drab Prague, we find two functioning synagogues. One of them is the famous Alt-Neu Shul—since the destruction of the historic synagogue in Worms, the oldest synagogue in Europe. It is called the "Old-New Synagogue" because it was first built in the twelfth century, and rebuilt anew in the thirteenth century. There are four other synagogues now converted into Jewish museums. We had a long, interesting discussion with Dr. Rudolf Iltis, Secretary of the Jewish community. He pointed out to me that there is freedom of worship. Jewish education is permitted—they have a library, a kosher kitchen and a mikveh, all under supervision of the Gemeinde—the Jewish community organization—and financed by the government. They publish a yearbook, a copy of which I have here; they print a religious calendar without interference; they need no help. Much of what he said was true, but must be seen in perspective.

I spoke with another representative, with whom I became a close friend in the days I spent in Prague, but whose name I am not free to mention. He pointed out that attendance at services is exceedingly limited. Religious supplies must be imported from Israel by various means. No professing Jew occupies an important government position. No Jewish organizations of any kind are permitted. Children may be given religious instruction, but only on written request of both parents—and many parents are reluctant to make such a request. There are about 500 Jewish children in Prague, virtually none above the age of 14. About 300 are between the ages of 8 and 13; of these only fifty are receiving any education.

Prague has a wonderful Jewish museum, one of the finest in the world. Before the war there were nine small museums. The Nazis combined them all with the intention of making an anti-Semitic museum. Three Jews—qualified and dedicated—were selected for the job of setting it up. They knew that when their task was completed, they would be put to death. They did their job so well, that despite the intention of the Nazis, they laid the foundation for a constructive, impressive museum. Since the war, about 150 synagogues once vibrant with life throughout Czechoslovakia have been closed, their ritual objects gathered together. At the end of the war, the museum had 1,300 catalogued items; today it has 30,000—2,000 ark curtains, 8,000 Torah mantles alone.

---

2. Compare "When Leadership Fails," above, n. 4.

I spent an evening in the home of the rabbi. It is located inside the cemetery, on property that had belonged to the Jewish community. This seemed symbolic. We attended Tisha b'Av services in the Alt-Neu synagogue. In accordance with tradition, we turned over the reading desks, sat upon the overturned desks on the floor, and chanted the Book of Lamentations, lamenting the loss of the ancient glories of Jerusalem. This too seemed symbolic. Perhaps I can summarize by saying that the living spirit of Czechoslovakian Jewry has been transformed into *a set of museum pieces.*

We turn to Poland, the "Old Country" for so many of our parents or grandparents. It meant a great deal to me because I had visited here before the war in 1939. I had gone to the towns where my parents had been born, and made pilgrimages to the chief centers of Jewish culture and life. On the train from Brest-Litovsk to Warsaw, we passed once again through the town of Mezrich where my mother was born. Our visas would not permit us to get off, but it would not have mattered—there is no Jewish life there any more.

Once there were three million Jews in Poland. They were poor; they knew the dangers of anti-Semitism. But what a vibrant, rich inner life they had. We have been drawing on the inspiration of this life for generations. Today there are about 30,000 to 40,000 Jews in Poland, 3,000 to 4,000 in Warsaw. They have one synagogue in Warsaw. On the Sabbath they get about twenty-five people, on the High Holidays several hundred. They have a kosher kitchen, they publish a newspaper, they can have Talmud Torahs for their children. But in a city like Warsaw, with a Jewish population about the size of our own community, there is not enough interest to have a school for their children.

The children of those who are leaders of Jewish culture know nothing of Jewish culture. Yiddish is as lost a language to them as it is to American children. The newspaper follows the party line faithfully. I spoke to the secretary of the Va'ad—the official association of religious communities—a doctor, not practicing his profession because should he do so, he would not be permitted to leave the country, and he was waiting to migrate to Israel or America. I visited the rabbi in his home—an old, sweet personality, feeble of body but quick of wit, dressed shabbily but with a sparkling temperament that belied the tragedy of his life. He had lost all thirteen of his children at the hands of the Nazis. Nowhere did I find a genuine light of hope.

We visited the site of the Ghetto, and here we had one of the greatest shocks of our trip. I knew that the Ghetto had been destroyed—building by building, room by room. I knew it had been reduced to shambles. I knew a monument had been built on the site in honor of the Ghetto fighters. I went to see it. There was the monument—but apparently after its dedication they stopped work on it. It was still surrounded by scaffolding, which made it almost impossible to see. I looked around for the ruins—they were nowhere to be seen. The Ghetto had been completely demolished; therefore, it was the first area to be rebuilt. Now all around were new big apartment houses. Only this one little unfinished square, with the unfinished monument, to mark the site. This was the ultimate tragedy: that a people could be destroyed, many of them buried in the ruins which are the foundation of those apartment houses—and now no trace of them lives. Life goes on as if they had never been. To summarize, Jewish life in Warsaw is now *a great, unmarked grave.*

We come now to Russia. It is so hard to summarize—there was such a multitude of impressions, each of them like an emotional hammer blow. It is so hard to weave it into a logical system and there is so little time tonight. Much I will have to leave for some future occasion. Some, I venture to predict, will find its way into my High Holy Day messages. We were in Leningrad and Moscow. We went to the synagogues, we spoke with people, we interviewed the community leaders, we visited with the rabbis.

I don't think I shall ever forget the Saturday morning service in Leningrad. I was given the honor of an *aliyah* [being called to the reading of the Torah]. There were about 400 people in attendance. The *gabbaim* [sextons] tried to sit us in a place of honor in the first row; their real intention was that we might not be in contact with others around. But the people found their way to me before the service and after the service and in the middle. I glanced up at the woman's gallery, and I saw Marcia similarly engaged. They were so eager for contact—to feel the bonds of unity with other Jews. "How is it in America?" they asked. "Do you have Jewish schools for your children there? Do you have synagogues? Do people come and pray?" As I told them, their eyes looked out in wonder and hope. A member of the choir came over to sit beside me. "Tell me," he said. "Is Yossele Rosenblatt still alive?"[3]

It might seem as if there is some hope among these people. But there are three hundred thousand Jews in Leningrad, and only this synagogue and four other little *shtiblach* [small synagogues] to serve them all. There was hardly a young person in the group. In Russia it is forbidden to have formal religious education for youth until the age of eighteen—by that time it is too late—even if the parents wanted it, and tragically most of them do not. There are no prayer books, no Yiddish papers, no Yiddish Theater, no schools. There are no religious supplies except for those smuggled in devious ways about which I cannot speak. People beg of you, not for money, not for clothes, but for a prayer book, for a Tallith [prayer shawl], for a *luach* [religious calendar] so they can know when the holidays come. They are willing to pay for them—fantastic prices if necessary—but they are unavailable.

Here is a book printed in Russia: the works of Sholem Aleichem, printed in connection with the hundredth anniversary of his birth. The Government gave publicity to it. It is interesting because the Yiddish is deliberately misspelled—to break off all connection between Yiddish and Hebrew. I carried a copy around with me as identification: "Sholem Aleichem" it said to whoever was able to read it. Surely no better greeting or identification could be found. Yet this book was unavailable in Russia. I bought eight copies in Czechoslovakia, and smuggle them in. The customs inspector found them, but fortunately he thought they were Arabic. I gave them away, and they were received as though they were worth their weight in gold.

---

3. Rosenblatt was one of the most celebrated cantors of the early twentieth century. His performing and recording career made him world famous.

(Yeshiva—if there is time).[4]

In Russia, the Iron Curtain for Jews is like *an iron paroches* [ark curtain] *preventing access to the Torah.* I spoke to one typical Jew about what the future might hold. "In another generation, if this continues, Jewish life will die," I said to him. "No," he answered, "it is already dead." Other spokesmen, whom I cannot quote, were more optimistic. They gave it as much as two generations— about fifty years—after which Jewish life will be no more.

"What can we do?" I asked one spokesman finally in desperation. "Tell the Jewish leaders in America," he said, "that when Khrushchev comes, they should plead with him to let the Jews out. There is no future for our people or our faith in a socialized state." On reading the papers on my return, I note that this is one subject that has been eliminated from the agenda of possible discussions between Jewish leaders and Khrushchev.[5] It might be embarrassing.

I must therefore, reluctantly, end as I began on a sorrowful note. We may pray for a miracle—and perhaps the miracle will come. More than once before this has happened in Jewish history. But we cannot count on miracles. In drawing up the balance sheet of Jewish life, we have lost six million at the hands of the Nazis, and virtually three million more are being lost under the reign of Communism. This realization evokes sorrow, and a sense of responsibility for us as American Jews. May we be equal to that responsibility.

---

4. This is what is in the typescript. Apparently a decision was to be made during the delivery about a quick vignette to be spoken extemporaneously.

5. Khrushchev's plans to visit the United States, in reciprocation for Vice President Richard Nixon's visit to the USSR in late July and early August 1959, were announced by President Eisenhower on August 3 and discussed by Khrushchev at a press conference in Moscow on August 5. During the month of August, the issue of Soviet Jewry was prominent in the American media. The *New York Times* reported World Jewish Congress charges that the USSR seeks to expunge its Jewish community (August 5, A54), an American Jewish Committee publication documenting the Soviet threats to Jewish religion and culture (August 9, A27), a reported indication by Khrushchev of willingness to meet with American Jewish leaders to discuss the status of Soviet Jews (August 11, A3), a Congressional request that the USSR permit full rights to Jews including the right to emigrate to Israel (August 12, A2), and a letter from a Moscow Jew disputing reports of antisemitism (August 26, A2). On August 31 (A4), it reported that, with the approval of the State Department, a special joint committee of 21 American Jewish organizations formally requested that the Soviet Embassy arrange a meeting with Khrushchev. Saperstein returned to the United States on September 4. Apparently in the negotiations about a meeting with Jewish leaders, the Soviets wanted to exclude the topic of emigration.

The Soviet Premier landed in Washington on September 15 and remained in the United States for 13 days, visiting New York, Los Angeles, San Francisco, Iowa, Pittsburgh, and Camp David. The issue of Soviet Jewry and antisemitism was raised frequently in the media during this period not only by Jewish spokesmen but also by journalists such as Harrison Salisbury and William F. Buckley, and by AFL-CIO President George Meany. President Eisenhower reportedly did bring up the status of Soviet Jewry with Khrushchev at Camp David, and was told that Jews were "treated like everyone else." There was no response to the request by the ad hoc committee of Jewish organizations for a special meeting with Khrushchev.

31

Moral Issues of the Eichmann Case
January 20, 1961

Prime Minister David Ben-Gurion's announcement to the Israeli Knesset on May 23, 1960, that Adolf Eichmann had been found, captured, and brought to Israel electrified public opinion in that country and among many Jews through-out the world. While not a universally recognized symbol of Nazism like Hitler, Himmler, or Goering, Eichmann was known to many Jews, especially those from Austria (where he took charge of Jewish affairs in 1938) and Hungary (where he arrived to assume responsibility for the liquidation of the Jewish community in 1944), as one of the Nazi figures most directly involved in the implementation of the "Final Solution." His "disappearance" from Germany at the end of the war left an unhealed wound in the memories of survivors. The realization that he would stand trial in Israel seemed to some a kind of poetic justice, to others an expression of divine providence.

From the announcement of his capture and throughout the period of investi-gation leading up to the trial, there were strong challenges from many sources about Israel's right to try Eichmann. Even some in the Jewish community raised issues about the propriety of Israel's abduction of Eichmann from Argentina and felt he should be tried elsewhere. The sermon below was the first of at least three delivered in 1961 on the subject; the second dealt with the moral implica-tions of the defense that he was just "following orders," while the third followed upon the verdict. The argument defending Israel's standing in this sermon was fairly typical of what was being said by its defenders at the time. More interest-ing is the claim that the Holocaust was being forgotten, not only in the general population but by Jews, and that the trial would serve "once and for all to put the facts of the Jewish tragedy under the Nazis on the record." While this was not widely stated to be the purpose of the trial at the time, many historians, in retrospect, believe that the renewal of interest in the Holocaust, both in Israel and in the United States, was largely triggered by this trial.

ON MARCH 6 IN JERUSALEM, AN HISTORIC TRIAL WILL BEGIN.[1] It will stand among the great trials in history that have played an important part in the working out of human destiny. It will be the trial of Adolf Eichmann.

The name of Adolf Eichmann has been much in the news since he was captured in Argentina last April and brought to Israel, where he is now awaiting trial under heavy guard. His own story has been published in *Life* magazine. A number of books have been written about him. We are ready, therefore, to say just who and what he was that makes this trial so important.

Eichmann was the person in charge of the program for the "Final Solution of the Jewish Problem." This was known as "Operation Night and Fog."[2] It involved three stages:

1. Deportation from Germany, Austria, Czechoslovakia and Hungary,
2. the gathering of these deportees in ghettos and concentration camps, and
3. their extermination through various means, including ultimately gas chambers.

If the Nazis had won the war, the figure of Adolf Eichmann would have had more than a distant academic interest to us, because he was destined to be the World Commissioner for the Global Extermination of the Jews, which means simply that it would have been his job to see that we too became the victims of gas chambers and fuel for the crematoria.

The arrest of Eichmann under the dramatic circumstances that surrounded it brought a thrill of excitement and satisfaction to Jews everywhere. We are human, and it is understandable that when the tables are turned, and he who was the hunter of our people is himself hunted down, it seems as if things are finally as they should be. However, ours should not be merely the satisfaction of vengeance. Understandable as such a feeling would be, it would still be unworthy of the high ideals of our faith. As Prime Minister Ben-Gurion said in a *New York Times* interview, "We are not out to punish Eichmann. There is no fit punishment for his crime. Ours is not the motive of revenge. How can six million

---

1. The opening of the trial was subsequently delayed until April 11, 1961.

2. This is not quite precise. *"Nacht und Nebel"* was the code word for Hitler's secret order issued on December 7, 1941, mandating that inhabitants of conquered lands in western Europe who "endangered German security" were to be seized and, if not summarily executed on the spot, were to be made to "vanish without a trace" in Germany. See William Shirer, *The Rise and Fall of the Third* Reich (New York: Simon and Schuster, 1960), 957–58. In the celebrated French documentary of Alain Resnais by this title, there is no emphasis on Jews as victims. Eichmann was not in charge of this program, but rather of transporting Jews to ghettos, labor camps, and death camps.

people be avenged?"[3] We feel, rather that there are moral issues involved in this case, and it is these moral issues that I wish to begin to discuss tonight.

The central moral issue will undoubtedly be dealt with in the trial itself. For it seems that Eichmann's defense in large measure will be based on the claim that he was merely doing his duty and following the orders of his superiors. I do not know how this defense will be handled in its legal context. I intend to discuss the problem from the moral point of view some Sabbath in the future, but prior to the case.[4] Let me now discuss three other issues:

1. Does Israel have the right to bring Eichmann before the bar of justice?
2. What purpose does Israel have in conducting this trial?
3. What moral and religious teaching is implicit in it?

First, as to Israel's right to try Eichmann. There are some who are deeply troubled by it. They feel it would be better if Eichmann were to be tried by an international court, or that he should be turned over for trial to West Germany.[5] They base their position on certain legal principles. A person should be tried for a crime in the jurisdiction in which the crime was committed. Neither the Jewish State, nor the law under which Eichmann is being tried was in existence when his crimes occurred. Thus, they conclude, he could not have committed any crime against a non-existent state, and it is not in accordance with justice to prosecute under an ex post facto law.

The problem with this reasoning is that it ignores the uniqueness of this situation. There is no precedent for this kind of crime. This is one case where there is a higher law—the law of morality and justice itself.[6] It cannot be considered in the category of an ordinary crime; this is a crime against humanity. The principles of humanity that were violated have not been created for this specific case. They have always existed. If this man is guilty of the crimes of which he is charged, there is no doubt in anyone's mind that these acts were evil and should be punished.

---

3. *New York Times*, December 18, 1960, Magazine, 62. Other arguments in the sermon are also drawn from this interview with Ben-Gurion.

4. This topic (the claim of following orders) was indeed addressed in a sermon delivered on February 10, 1961.

5. Among those who argued for an international court was the Zionist leader Nahum Goldmann; see Tom Segev, *The Seventh Million: The Israelis and the Holocaust* (New York: Hill and Wang, 1993), 329 and Gideon Hausner, *Justice in Jerusalem* (New York: Harper & Row, 1966), 455. As for Germany, French jurists claimed that only Germany was competent to try him (Hausner, 456). In addition, Joseph Proskauer, a New York attorney and honorary president of the American Jewish Committee, sent Ben-Gurion a letter arguing that Eichmann should be turned over to West Germany or some international body (Segev, 330).

6. This argument from the uniqueness of the crime was made by Ben-Gurion in his response to Goldmann (Segev, 329–30) and, later, by the Israeli Appellate Court following the verdict (Hausner, 440–41).

Furthermore, the simple fact is that there is no other court to which he could be turned over. Since the Nuremberg trials immediately following World War II when war criminals were brought to justice, there has been no international court for criminal cases. For ten years, Israel urged the establishment of such an international court. There were strong objections by the major nations, including the United States, which feared an invasion of their sovereignty. Such a court could not be convened again without bringing in representatives of both democratic and communist countries. It is very likely that instead of seeking justice, such a court would be used as a platform for each side to blame the other. Moreover, there does not seem to be any great desire to bring Eichmann before a new international court. At the meeting of the Security Council, called by Argentina after Eichmann had been abducted from that country and brought to Israel, not a single nation suggested that such a court be convened.[7]

How about Germany? But there is no single Germany; there is East Germany and West Germany. West Germany would not like to take over responsibility for this case, for it would imply that the Nazis represented only Western Germany. They have evidenced no interest in having the locale of the case moved there.[8] Moreover, if one says that Israel is unfit because it is an interested party, then Germany would be unfit for the same reason. This case might well be used by Germany to absolve itself of responsibility for the acts of the Nazis, although the German people and nation do carry a measure of guilt.

The fact is that there is no place except Israel that does not present more problems than it solves. Eichmann is being kept under heavy guard and in isolation, but he has a comfortable room and a private bath, he is permitted to dictate and write whatever he wishes, and he is free to publish anything he desires. He was permitted to choose his own attorney and to meet with this attorney as often as he wants. We can be sure the inmates of concentration camps were not treated so considerately. Every precaution is being taken for his safety—even to the fact that he will testify from inside a bulletproof glass shell. There is absolutely no evidence that Eichmann will not receive a meticulously fair trial. There is no popular or official clamor for his death. He has not been prejudged. Among other things, this public trial will prove to the world that justice in the State of Israel is a reality and not just a word.

Now to our second issue: What can this trial accomplish? It should be clear that we are not concerned solely with the fate of this one man. If that were so, he could have been charged with responsibility for the death of just a single Jew. This is an opportunity once and for all to put the facts of the Jewish tragedy under the Nazis[9] on the record.

---

7. On the Security Council meeting, see Hausner, 460–63.

8. Ben-Gurion in the *Times* Magazine interview, 7: "Why should Eichmann not be tried in Germany? The Germans do not ask this question. They can speak for themselves. They have never asked either that Eichmann not be tried here or that he be handed over to them."

9. In 1961, there was still no one accepted word to express the "Jewish tragedy under the Nazis." "The Holocaust" emerged as the dominant term during the next few years.

During recent years, there has been a tendency to underplay this subject. As we know, textbooks in Germany deal very gently with the deeds of the Nazi era. We can understand that. It is just as disturbing, however, to note that this era is treated equally gently in most American textbooks.[10] In most cases, modern history books deal with it in a cursory sentence or paragraph, stating in effect that Hitler did many evil things, including persecuting the Jews. The fact that millions of innocent people were murdered, including six of the sixteen million Jews living in the world, with the most horrible brutality, inhumanity, and cruelty, is not made clear. It has become popular to intimate that the figures are exaggerated, that the horrors are propaganda. Why is it important that the facts be established? For two reasons.

First, so that the nations of the world may come to realize the ultimate dangers of movements of prejudice, bigotry, Antisemitism and racial intolerance. If anyone had predicted in the early days of Hitler where his movement and his theories would lead, he would have been denounced as being insane. Antisemitism may for the time no longer be the large, pressing problem it once was. *Racial* intolerance, however, is as acute and intense as ever. Let us realize that those who cherish it are playing with fire. Failure to recognize other human beings as being fully human may well lead ultimately to brutality and violence. The Germans were a people of culture and civilization. Let the world take that lesson to heart.

But there is importance in this for Jews as well. We too have been overly ready to forget. We have not wanted to keep alive the memory of the catastrophe of our generation. A remarkable, dramatic and inspiring play like "The Wall" was ready to close its doors recently. Why? Because in New York, the success of a play depends in large measure on Jewish theater parties. And Jewish groups did not want to schedule it. They felt it was too somber. I am happy to report that due to gifts procured by Mrs. Isaac Stern, it is going to continue.[11] Our children should know these facts. We do not serve them well by sheltering them from reality. This happened in our generation. Let them know the suffering of our people, not merely as something from ancient times but as something recent, and real. Let them appreciate more the preciousness of our heritage because of the sacrifice demanded for its preservation.

Finally, it is good to see that accountability overtakes those who commit crimes against humanity. That has always been a basic tenet of our faith. But it does not always work out so clearly. Sometimes it takes time—many genera-

---

10. On this topic, see the essays by Walter Renn (Federal Republic of Germany) and Glenn Pate (United States) in Randolph Braham, ed., *The Treatment of the Holocaust in Textbooks* (New York: Columbia University Press, 1987).

11. "The Wall," written by Millard Lampell based on the novel by John Hersey, opened at the Billy Rose Theater on October 11, 1960. Its closing due to the lack of adequate audience was reported in the *New York Times* of January 10, 1961. Spearheaded by Mrs. Stern (the wife of the well-known violinist), who raised $20,000 to defray operating losses, the effort to keep the play running was reported in the *Times* of January 20, the morning the sermon was delivered. The play continued for another month, but its closing was reported on February 24.

tions. Sometimes we have to see it in the big picture of Jewish history over the ages. But our traditions have always dramatized this theme.

For example, we have the story of the Exodus, the preliminaries to which are set forth in this week's Torah reading. We read there the account of the final plagues: darkness and the death of the first born. The Rabbis describe it as *mida keneged mida*, "measure for measure," evidence of a moral law in the universe.[12] The Egyptians brought darkness to the world; they were afflicted with darkness. The Egyptians destroyed the children of the Israelites; their own first born were destroyed. We will stress it again some ten weeks from now when we celebrate Purim. Haman set out to destroy the Jews. He himself ended by being destroyed. There have been many Hamans through history, under different names. But Jewish history testifies that in the end, those who do evil go down in defeat, and those who are faithful, no matter how great may be their suffering and loss, cannot be destroyed as a people.

The fact that Eichmann will be brought to the bar of justice by a Jewish tribunal in a Jewish State is evidence that the mills of God may grind very slowly, but they grind exceeding fine. It is a case of unique and historic justice.

May God grant that out of this case and its attendant publicity, Jews will find a deeper devotion to their people and their spiritual heritage; that the nations of the world will find stronger commitment to the principles of humanity and deeper awareness of the dangers of intolerance; and that all mankind will come to see that justice—like truth and peace, as portrayed on the doors of our ark—is among the foundations of the world.[13]

---

12. Mishnah Sotah 1,7, B. Sanh 90a, and frequently in the rabbinic literature.

13. On the doors to the ark in the sanctuary were the three words (with accompanying symbols): *emet, din, shalom,* alluding to the statement in Mishnah Avot, "The world stands upon three things: truth, justice and peace." Compare the 1968 sermon on Vietnam.

New Frontiers in Catholic-Jewish Relationships
April 13, 1962

In early 1962, preparations were being made for the Second Vatican Council, which would open on October 11 of that year. It is difficult for many today to appreciate the transformation in the Roman Catholic Church during this period. The most dramatic changes instituted by the Council affected the worship service—a shift from Latin to the vernacular, the priest facing the congregation rather than the altar. But in addition to the internal reforms, the entire ambiance of relations between the Church and other religious communities was altered. Before this time, for example, Catholic churches would not participate in inter-religious community events, such as joint Thanksgiving services. Now the doors began to open.

The impetus for these changes came from the highest circles of Church leadership in Rome. But the view on the ground, on the grassroots level, is reflected in the description below. The following sermon identifies many different signals, both in the local community and on a broader level. The diagnosis is that something important is underway—something that would not become clear until some time later, but which showed all the promise of an exciting improvement.

IN FORMER AGES, THIS PERIOD OF THE YEAR was often a bitter and painful one for Jews. The Festival of Passover was approaching, which should have been an occasion for rejoicing. But this also meant that the Easter season was drawing near. This too should have been a joyous occasion for the Christian world, celebrating their faith in the resurrection of their Savior. But it was bound up too closely with the story of the Crucifixion—and the animosity against the Jews [rooted in the Gospel accounts often] erupted in physical attacks.

In medieval times, the basis for these attacks was often the false ritual murder accusation. Noting the care with which Jews prepared their matzah for the festival, and the use of red wine, the slander arose that Jews used the blood of Christians in their festival observance, particularly of Christian children. Interestingly, the same charge had been made against the early Christians by the Romans.[1] In the city of Lincoln in England, you can still see in its great cathedral the shrine of little Hugh of Lincoln—supposedly the victim of such a murder—whose story has been incorporated into Chaucer's *Canterbury Tales*, and thus became part of classical English literature.[2]

To anyone who knows the Jewish faith, the spirit of Jewish life and the abhorrence of blood even in the meat we eat, the ridiculous character of the charge is apparent. But this did not prevent thousands of Jews from being victims of the ferocity of mobs set in action by this accusation. For this reason, Jews found it wise at this season to remain as much as possible in their homes. And if a Christian child should have disappeared, their hearts were filled with foreboding. Readers of Heine's great novella, *The Rabbi of Bacherach*, will recall such a situation.[3]

I said that this was something from medieval times. Blind superstitions, however, live long in the minds of ignorant people. Some of you may remember the famous Mendel Beilis trial in 1911 in Kiev, Russia, in which the government, disregarding clear facts about the murder of a twelve-year-old boy by a gang of criminals, decided to prosecute it as a ritual murder.[4] Back in the 1920s at Massena in upstate New York, the death of a boy had the state police captain making the accusation that it showed the signs of a ritual murder.[5]

---

1. See E. R. Dodds, *Pagan and Christian in an Age of Anxiety* (New York: Norton, 1965), 111–12; S. W. Baron, *SRHJ*, vol. 1 (Philadelphia: JPS, 1952), 193. The accusations that Christians engaged in ritual cannibalism were apparently rooted in Christian claims about ingesting the body of Christ in the Eucharist.

2. See on this Joseph Jacobs, "Little St. Hugh of Lincoln: Researches in History, Archaeology, and Legend," in Alan Dundes, ed., *The Blood Libel Legend: A Casebook in Anti-Semitic Folklore* (Madison: University of Wisconsin Press, 1991), 41–71.

3. See Heinrich Heine, *Rabbi of Bacherach: A Fragment* (New York: Schocken, 1947), 5–6 and 16–17.

4. While the discovery of the dead child and the arrest of Beilis occurred in 1911, the trial was held in Kiev in 1913. Despite the blatantly antisemitic accusations, Beilis was acquitted. Older members of the congregation in 1962 may indeed have retained personal memories of the events fifty years earlier. It should be noted that the Vatican Secretary of State tried to help Beilis's defense by authenticating the papal bulls that had denounced ritual murder charges as libels. See Maurice Samuel, *Blood Accusation* (New York: Knopf, 1966), 242. On the reporting of the ritual murder charge in this trial by an influential Vatican periodical, see Charlotte Klein, "Damascus to Kiev: *Civiltà Cattolica* on Ritual Murder," in *The Blood Libel Legend*, 194–96.

5. See Morris Schappes, ed., *Documentary History of the Jews in the United States* (New York: Citadel Press, 1950), 616–17, citing *American Jewish Yearbook*, 5690, 1929–30, 348–352, and the *New York Times*, October 3,5,6,8, 1928. The event occurred in September 1928. Rabbi Berel Brennglass was interrogated by an officer of the state troopers at the suggestion of the Mayor of Massena, who implied that the four-year-old child who had disappeared might have been sacrificed by the Jews on the eve of Yom Kippur.

When I was at college [at Cornell University], I lived in a "Cosmopolitan Club" with members from different nations. One year at this season, a group of students were having a "bull session" in my room late at night. Among them was a close friend, Boyan Choukanoff, from Bulgaria. I had received a package from home; it contained Passover delicacies and I shared them with my fellow students. They were all crunching matzah and discussing philosophy, when somebody asked, "What kind of crackers are these?" "They're matzos for Passover," I said. Suddenly Choukanoff leaped from the bed where he had been sitting as though he had been shot, and with a wild look on his face he spat out what he had in his mouth. Recovering himself, with some embarrassment he explained that as a child his mother had told him that if he wasn't good, Jews would use his blood to make matzah.

These are extreme cases, but they are enough to make us realize why Jews were always troubled about Catholic attitudes. We felt somehow that Catholics preserved a greater measure of anti-Jewish prejudice than other non-Jewish groups. The attitudes of Catholic children whom some of us knew a generation ago, and the unwillingness of Catholic clergy to participate in interfaith activity, strengthened this impression.

Recently, however, there have been strong indications of a change in Catholic attitudes, and of new frontiers in Catholic-Jewish relationships. There seems to be a marked tendency on the part of the Church to combat prejudice and to bring about greater understanding. During the Nazi regime, Pope Pius XII was strongly anti-Nazi. He was instrumental in saving thousands of Italian Jews through the Vatican itself, and through the Church in various communities with the approval of the Vatican many more were saved.[6] The present Pope, John XXIII, has had no dramatic occasion for such heroic action. In many ways, however, he has worked to mitigate prejudice and intolerance. He has made several corrections in the official Catholic liturgy, eliminating phrases that were prejudiced or insulting to Jews.[7] Such changes are rare in Catholic liturgical history and mark a new attitude. Recently he received an official delegation from B'nai B'rith, and he used the occasion to comment on the wave of swastika incidents and denounce anti-Semitism. Such events, he said "are deeply painful not only because they are violations of the human rights of men, but because they divide the children of God."[8]

---

6. This image of Pope Pius XII's role in the Holocaust period, rooted in reports heard by Saperstein when he entered Rome as a chaplain soon after its liberation, and communicated in sermons given shortly after the war, would be modified a few years later. See the sermon on "The Deputy" below.

7. Reference is apparently to Pope John XXIII's removal of the term "perfidious" from the prayer for the Jews in the Good Friday liturgy. See John Pawlikowski, "The Teaching of Contempt: Judaism in Christian Education and Liturgy," in Eva Fleischner, ed., *Auschwitz: Beginning of a New Era?* (New York: Ktav and The Cathedral Church of St. John the Divine, 1997), p. 176.

8. This undoubtedly refers to a private audience, held on January 18, 1960, between Pope John XXIII and a small B'nai B'rith delegation led by its president, Label Katz. The *New York Times* account of the following day (A6:3), headlined "Pope Denounces

Apparently this was not intended to be just an isolated statement. There are many indications of this attitude penetrating into the lower levels of the hierarchy, apparently with official encouragement. In September 1960, a magazine called "Jubilee: A Magazine of the Church and Her People," had an interesting article called "Report from France." The author expressed deep concern over prejudice found in Catholic circles; she described the new awareness of this problem on the part of French Catholics and the program of self-purification they were undertaking. She admitted that the conscience of many Christians had been inoculated by the virus of hate as a result of theological teaching. She mentioned various new organizations that had been set up to deal with this problem.

Having made a study of catechisms and found the results to be sickening, these French Catholics were now trying to get educators and theologians to revise their thinking. They were working on new Bible editions and a new commentary on the missals—the prayer book of Catholic liturgy—eliminating those interpretations inclined to stimulate prejudice. The article spoke of the publication by a Catholic publisher of a French translation of the medieval Jewish classic *Hovot Halevavot*, by Bachya ibn Pakuda, "The Duties of the Heart," intended to evidence the high moral and spiritual character of post-Biblical Jewish literature. In this Catholic magazine for Catholic readers, the author stressed that the purpose was not missionary activity, but rather "to make a missionary movement for ourselves."[9]

Another Catholic weekly, "Ave Maria," recently had John J. O'Connor, chairman of the National Catholic Conference for Interracial Justice, write on prejudice in the schools. He described the amount of prejudice among young people of high school age. The article was a summary of a series of studies made by the Anti-Defamation League after the last batch of swastika incidents. His conclusion was that Americans—Catholics no less than others—must correct the ignorance and stereotyped thinking of their youth. "We need a reformation of our textbooks."[10]

Anti-Jewish Bias," states "It is a Vatican rule not to allow the Pope to be quoted when he speaks in a private audience, so there is no record of what the Pontiff said," but that "Vatican sources said the Pope had been positive and outspoken in his condemnation of anti-Semitism in all its manifestations." Saperstein's account must be based on a different source, of which I am unaware.

9. Claire Huchet Bishop, "Report from France," *Jubilee* 8:5 (September 1960), 2–5. The author wrote, "This French movement is totally removed from all thought of converting the Jews. That is its distinction and possibly what makes it unique in the history of Judeo-Christian relations so far. If the participating Christians have any missionary spirit at all it is turned upon themselves." Compare this author's later book-length study, *How Catholics Look at Jews* (New York: Paulist Press, 1974).

10. See John J. O'Connor (not the one who became Cardinal Archbishop of New York, who was a chaplain in the Navy at the time), "Prejudice in the Schools," *Ave Maria* 94:12 (September 16, 1961), 5–8. The studies summarized, published by the Anti-Defamation League following a wave of swastika paintings on American synagogues, were entitled

On January 25 of this year, the press reported a sermon delivered at St. Patrick's Cathedral by Rev. Robert W. Gleason, chairman of Fordham University's Department of Theology, in which he stressed the Jewishness of Jesus. Christ, he stated, was a Jew from a Jewish culture. His mother was a Jewess, his family were Jews, his disciples were all Jewish. "He worshipped in synagogue and Temple, he kept Jewish festivals, he drew his prayers from the prayers of the Jewish people. The man who looks down upon Jews is an apostate from the Christian faith," he concluded. "Prejudice is Christian spittle in the face of the Jewish Savior." Remember that this is a Catholic priest and professional preaching in a great Catholic cathedral.

A few months ago, some of you may have tuned in on a television play called "The Chosen People." It told the story of a Christian High School girl who learns that the community club where the Senior Prom is to be held does not admit Jews, so that some of her classmates cannot attend. In seeking the reasons for this exclusion, she and her friends discover irrational prejudices in their own community. She doesn't say, "It's none of my business." Instead, encouraged by her father, she influences her friends to recognize their moral responsibility and to take action against injustice. This program was one of a series in a similar vein, the previous one having dealt with prejudice against Negroes. Who sponsored it? Not the Anti-Defamation League, or the "Eternal Light." It was the NBC "Catholic Hour," sponsored by the National Council of Catholic Men.[11]

In our own community, we have seen manifestations of this new outlook. For many years, outside of personal friendships, there had been no official relationship between the Catholic and Jewish religious communities. Catholic clergymen ignored invitations to programs of interfaith understanding. Several weeks ago, however, I received an invitation to a program presented at St. Raymond's Catholic Church in East Rockaway. The speaker was Leon Paul, and his subject was "The Jewish Background of Catholicism." Together with a small group of our members, I attended. Mr. Paul is a convert from Judaism, which made me naturally a little apprehensive about his motives. However, I found nothing objectionable in his presentation, and later discovered that he had given a series of lectures on this same subject at an adult education program sponsored by Molloy College in Rockville Centre, and a similar one in New Jersey. This course was directed not to public relations but to Catholics.

A week later, I received a call from a Catholic lay leader in the community, who said he didn't think it was right not to follow up our beginnings and invited a group of our people to an explanation of Catholicism at the church. We went, were most graciously received, and had a most interesting evening. We promised to reciprocate; several days later I received a follow-up call to fix a date

---

"Swastika–1960," "What High School Students Say," and "The Treatment of Minorities in Secondary School Textbooks."

11. "The Catholic Hour," which began on radio in 1930, premiered on NBC television in September 1951. During the 1961–1962 season, it was shown on Sunday mornings, rotating with "The Eternal Light" and "Frontiers of Faith."

when their group might visit us. They did so last Thursday evening. Their priest accompanied them, and they all listened attentively while I explained Judaism.

What does this all portend? Frankly, I'm not sure. Some of my colleagues have said, "Don't be taken in. This is merely another approach. The purpose of the Church is to win the world to Catholicism. The new frontiers of which you speak are just a new gate to conversion." I am not disturbed. I know that by its very nature, Catholicism must be a missionary faith. I know they would like to win the world. But I have enough confidence in Judaism to feel that it can hold its own in objective comparison. I do not fear that either I or members of our congregation will be lost to us by coming to understand the religion of our neighbors.

On the other hand, I do think it a good portent for the future that people come to understand each other, to know something of each other's faith, to respect each other's observances and convictions. Our Catholic neighbors have opened up a door that has long been closed. I certainly will not close it again. The hope of the world lies in open, not closed, doors—in greater knowledge and understanding rather than less. Where the light of truth is allowed to shine in, the vermin of prejudice scurry away or perish. In Micah's great prophecy of peace, in which he echoes Isaiah's words about beating swords into plowshares and not learning war any more, he adds the sentence, "For let all the peoples walk each in the name of its god, but we will walk in the name of the Lord our God for ever and ever" (Mic. 4:5). Peace and understanding do not require that we surrender our faith or call upon others to surrender theirs. The new frontiers of interfaith understanding have room for all faiths—side by side.

33

The American Dream, In Color
September 6, 1963

On August 28, 1998, at a ceremony on the 35th anniversary of the "I Have A Dream" Speech by the Rev. Martin Luther King Jr., President Clinton described his own reactions to that experience in the following words:

> *Most of us who are old enough remember exactly where we were on August 28, 1963. I was in my living room in Hot Springs, Arkansas. I remember the chair I was sitting in. . . . I remember exactly the position of the chair when I sat and watched on national television the great March on Washington unfold.*
>
> *I remember weeping uncontrollably during Martin Luther King's speech. And I remember thinking, when it was over, my country would never be the same and neither would I.*
>
> *There are people all across this country who made a more intense commitment to the idea of racial equality and justice that day than they had ever made before. And so in very personal ways, all of us became better and bigger because of the work of those who brought that great day about. (New York Times, Aug. 29, 1998, A10)*

The impact of the gathering and of King's eloquence was not limited to impressionable teenagers. The following sermon shows mature leaders felt it as well.

Yet between the March on Washington and the first Friday evening following Labor Day (customarily the first time Saperstein delivered a formal sermon), events at home had raised a difficult touchstone for the relationship between lofty aspirations for civil rights and racial harmony in the South and wrenching conflict in one's own northern community. As these events are addressed at the end of the sermon, a little background is necessary to understand the issues.

The Union Free School District Number 12 encompassed a substantial part of the population in the village of Malverne, a portion of northern Lynbrook, and the unincorporated village of Lakeview. There was an elementary school in each of these areas, and a centrally located junior and senior high school. As the population of Lakeview became increasingly black during the 1950s, due to the movement of mostly professional black families from New York City into an attractive middle-class suburb, the Lakeview elementary school became about 75 percent black, while the other two elementary schools, because of existing housing patterns, were entirely white. Aided by the NAACP, the Lakeview community filed a complaint with the State Commissioner of Education that the school was racially imbalanced due to "de facto segregation" in housing patterns, and sought relief. This was considered an important test case of pure de facto segregation as there was never any allegation of gerrymandering to segregate black students.

On June 14, 1963, Commissioner James Allen issued a decree, based on the report of a committee he had established to study the Malverne situation. It mandated that all local school boards in the state with racially imbalanced schools file a report by September 1 of plans to eliminate that imbalance, and that the Malverne School District must put the committee's recommendation into effect by the opening of school in September. The Committee considered the most effective solution to be the "Princeton Plan," whereby all children from kindergarten to third grade would attend either the Malverne or the Lynbrook school, and all children in fourth and fifth grades the Lakeview School. After weeks of divisive protest and counter-protest, the School Board voted to implement a compromise modified version of the Princeton Plan, whereby children in kindergarten and first grade would attend their neighborhood schools, while children from the next four grades would be bussed to equalize the racial distribution in the three schools. But on August 19, a taxpayer's suit was filed to block implementation of this plan. The School Board decided to wait for a legal resolution, and accordingly, the schools opened on Wednesday, September 4— three days before the sermon—the same way they had closed in June, except that a substantial percentage of the black students boycotted the public schools and attended a new, temporary "freedom school" established by the Lakeview leadership.

Temple Emanu-El was located in Lynbrook, but Saperstein himself (along with many of the Temple's members) lived in the adjacent village of Malverne. His two sons attended the public schools there, and his wife, Marcia, was an active leader of the effort to achieve racial balance in the elementary schools. With the community so divided, he apparently felt that it would be hypocritical to limit his sermon to the March on Washington and avoid the issues in the Temple's own neighborhood. The discussion at the end brings the sermon down from the heights of inspiration to the smaller but more ambiguous and tougher issues in the North. Most Jews (though certainly not all) were on the side of the black community in this one. The issues that would begin to create a wedge were not long in coming.

WE AMERICANS HAVE A DREAM. Its sources go back to the Bible. There Moses cried before Pharaoh, "Let my people go that they may serve me" (Exod.

7:16). There the Torah commands us, "Proclaim liberty throughout the land, unto all the inhabitants thereof" (Lev. 25:10). There the prophet Malachi proclaimed, "Have we not all one father? Hath not one God created us?" (Mal. 2:10). That dream of freedom and equality is echoed in our Declaration of Independence and our Bill of Rights, in the words of Thomas Jefferson and Abraham Lincoln, in the history of the America Revolution and the Civil War.

The Emancipation Proclamation, issued in 1863, was intended to bring that dream to fulfillment. A hundred years have passed since then. Something has gone wrong. Just as we have had dreamers of dreams, so, in Lillian Smith's phrase, we have had "Killers of the Dream."[1] There are those in America who, for whatever reason, cannot bring themselves to accept the principle that the color of the skin is not the measure of the man. With all the resources of their strength they seek to crush the burgeoning dream. And so the anguished cry of the Negro is heard echoing the words of Moses: "Let my people go!" "We want freedom now!"

On August 28, just nine days ago, the Freedom March on Washington took place. I'm sure you read about it in the papers or saw it on television. I had the privilege of being there—and I am proud to say several of the young people of our congregation were there as well, as an expression of something they felt to be their moral obligation. I believe it will go down in history as one of America's great days of glory.

Let me tell you about my own experience that day. Most of those who attended traveled by train or bus. I flew down that morning. Those who did travel by bus told me of the experience of driving through the Negro sections of cities like Baltimore. Negroes standing the curbs waved to them as they went by. "You tell them for us," they cried, and the light in their eyes expressed their thanks. It made me think of the end of the summer nineteen years ago, 1944, when we had come into France on the southern invasion and we drove up from the Riviera through the mountains to Grenoble.[2] As we came through each French mountain town, the people lined the roads to wave to us in greeting: we were Allies, on the road to victory.

Coming from the airport toward the site of the demonstration, the streets were empty of traffic. Our taxi driver commented that not even on Sundays or holidays had he ever seen it so empty. Then we came into the shadow of the Washington Monument, left the taxi, and suddenly we were caught up in a great stream of humanity. Down the road came a procession of buses, one after another, from near and far, each filled with people, white and black, who had come to join the demonstration. The sidewalk was crowded with people all moving toward the Washington Monument mall. I was swept along with them.

---

1. A reference to Lillian Smith's powerful study of Negro social conditions in the American South, *Killers of the Dream* (New York: W.W. Norton, 1949, reprinted in 1961 and 1963). Saperstein would use this phrase at a climactic moment of the following sermon.

2. See the Rosh Hashanah sermon from 1944, above.

Our Reform Rabbis had planned to meet near the backstop of the baseball field. There I found them, and it was a great feeling. Long Island was perhaps better represented than any other area, but colleagues had come in from as far away as Chicago just to be there that day.

The crowd kept increasing—one group had marched all the way from New York, some came in from California—until it eventually reached more than 200,000. They represented all kinds of groups: religious, labor, educational, political. The march from the Washington Monument to the Lincoln Memorial is little more than half a mile. It was supposed to begin at 12 noon. But before any formal announcement was made, it began spontaneously. Suddenly it seemed that everybody was moving toward Constitution Avenue. They filled the street from side to side. It wasn't an organized march—nobody tried to line up or to get in step. We just strolled along, an informal army with banners.

After we reached the Lincoln Memorial area, I stood for a while along the road and watched the others coming. Some groups were singing, some were chanting, but all had a spirit about them: they were there for a purpose, and they were lifted up by that purpose. The steps of the Lincoln Memorial were crowded with speakers, television apparatus, and special guests. Through the majestic rotunda could be seen the great sculptured figure of the Emancipator, seated as through the weight and hopes of the world were upon him. For several hours a program continued, with fine singers and speakers. Everyone was in a kind of holiday mood, many taking out their lunches and sitting on the grass as if they were on a picnic.

At two o'clock the formal program began. There were moving moments of rare intensity. Marian Anderson got caught in traffic and arrived too late to sing the Star Spangled Banner, but she sang her heart out with the spiritual, "I've Got the Whole World in my Hands." Mahalia Jackson swayed the vast crowds with "When the Saints Come Marching In." There was a moment of silent prayer for Dr. William E. B. DuBois, pioneer of the movement for Negro freedom, who had raised his voice in protest at the turn of the century and had died at the age of 95 just the day before. There was a speech by Rabbi Joachim Prinz, president of the American Jewish Congress, which seemed particularly appropriate because, as he explained, he had been the rabbi of the Jewish community of Berlin under the Hitler regime.[3] But the highlight of the day, the speech which really electrified the crowd, was that by Dr. Martin Luther King, Jr.

This was his great day. He was introduced as the conscience of America, and in a very real sense, that is what he has become. He is a disciple of Tolstoy and Gandhi, an advocate of [non-violence and] passive resistance. He is also a great orator. As he was introduced, the people sitting on the grass, relaxing from the long, long program, jumped to their feet in a spontaneous tribute. If he had been another kind of leader, he could have caused a riot. He could have transformed the demonstration into an invasion. Instead, he articulated the theme of the day

---

3. Prinz was arrested by the Gestapo and expelled from Germany in 1937. He became rabbi of Temple B'nai Israel in Newark, New Jersey, and was president of the American Jewish Congress from 1958–66.

in terms that no one who heard them will ever forget. He reached the great climax of his speech in that wonderful passage, "I have a dream." Again and again he used that phrase, and each time, the crowd went wild as the mood was lifted to greater and greater exaltation. "I have a dream," he said,

> that one day this nation will rise up and live out the true meaning of its creed: "We hold these truths to be self-evident, that all men are created equal."
>
> I have a dream, that one day on the red hills of Georgia, the sons of former slaves and the sons of former slave-owners will be able to sit together at the table of brotherhood.
>
> I have a dream, that one day even the State of Mississippi, a state sweltering with the heat of injustice, sweltering with the heat of oppression, will be transformed into an oasis of freedom and justice.
>
> I have a dream, that my four little children will one day live in a nation where they will not be judged by the color of their skin but by the content of their character.
>
> I have a dream, that one day every valley shall be exalted, every hill and mountain shall be made low, the rough places will be made plain, and the crooked places will be made straight, and the glory of the Lord shall be revealed and all flesh shall see it together.[4]

As Dr. King concluded with a quotation from a Negro hymn, "Free at last, free at last, thank God Almighty . . . ," the crowd, recognizing that he was finishing, roared once again.

How shall we summarize the impact of this event? First, I believe it was testimony to the fact that the Negro minority of America has come of age. This was not something that had been done for them; it was a project of responsible Negro leadership, and the great majority of the participants were Negroes. The planning, the logistics, the details were all done carefully and well. Despite the apprehensions of some, the participants conducted themselves with dignity, with rare courtesy and good humor. This event changed the image of the Negro in the eyes of many—people who were there, who read about it, or saw it on television. In particularly, it must have changed the image of the Negro in his own eyes. I could not help feeling a tinge of envy: If only we Jews had had the courage and strength to do something on that scale when millions of Jews were being slaughtered at the hands of the Nazis.

Second, it was significant that though the Negroes were in the majority, they were not alone. Approximately 30 percent of the marchers were white. This was not a matter of white and black; we were there as Americans, and ultimately as human beings. Some of the placards had quotations from the Bible in Hebrew; they elicited great interest, as evidence of our common spiritual roots. Rabbi Joachim Prinz, in his moving address, pointed out that under the Hitler regime he learned that bigotry and hatred are not the most important problems. The most disgraceful problem, he said, was silence. A great people had become si-

---

4. This passage was not written into the text of the sermon; it was quoted from a newspaper report that was used along with the typescript.

lent onlookers, remaining silent in the face of hatred, brutality and murder. America must not become a nation of onlookers. "We must not be silent," he said, "not for the sake of the Negro, but for the sake of America."[5]

Thirdly, the demonstration was a great tribute to American democracy. In other countries, governments have always attacked [protest] marchers. Here the government aided the march, and the President received its leaders respectfully and sympathetically.[6] These Negroes were not in rebellion against the United States. They were demanding their legal rights under the government of the United States. This was not a defiance of democracy but an expression of it.

Some reactionaries, like David Lawrence, the political commentator, and Senator Strom Thurmond of South Carolina, called it a day of disgrace.[7] They claimed that because it was televised to Europe, it would hurt our image abroad; that the spectacle of 200,000 people demonstrating for freedom and equality would give the impression that these were absent here. I believe the contrary was true. It is indicative that after first planning its presentation, Russia decided against exhibiting it on television. Apparently the Russian authorities feared it might suggest techniques to their own people. Certainly it is impossible to conceive of such a demonstration in Moscow's Red Square.

Fourthly, the demonstration should make us realize that words and feelings are not enough. The theme was expressed in two words: FREEDOM NOW. One hundred years is too long to wait. The central lesson is that you cannot solve a problem by ignoring it. The longer you postpone redress of grievances, the harder it becomes. We cannot get by like the false prophets of old, crying *Sholom, sholom, v'ayn sholom*, "'Peace, peace,' when there is no peace" (Jer. 6:14). If we had done something about Negro schools, and housing, and jobs one

---

5. Excerpts from Prinz's speech, including this passage, were printed in the *New York Times*, August 29, 1963, A21, col. 2. The full text reads, "The most urgent problem, the most disgraceful, the most shameful and the most tragic problem, is silence. A great people [the Germans], which had created a great civilization had become a nation of silent onlookers. They remained silent in the face of hate, in the face of brutality and in the face of mass murder. America must not become a nation of onlookers. America must not remain silent. . . . It must speak up and act, from the President down to the humblest of us, and not for the sake of the Negro, . . . but for the sake of the image, the idea and the aspiration of America itself."

6. Kennedy, who was originally not in favor of the March for tactical reasons, did not address the crowd, but he met with ten of the March leaders and urged support of the administration's civil rights legislation, which was indeed one of the purposes of the March.

7. I have not found the term "day of disgrace" cited from either of these men. David Lawrence was editor of *U.S. News and World Report* from 1959–73. His editorials before and after the March express a clear lack of enthusiasm for the civil rights agenda and the technique of "'demonstrations' on the streets," as well as a strong distaste for the prominent role of religious leaders in the effort to influence public opinion and Congress on behalf of specific legislation (August 19, September 2, 9, 23). In the weeks before the March, Strom Thurmond denounced King from the floor of the Senate for "inciting and organizing the riots" and for the alleged communist sympathies of men (especially Bayard Rustin) in King's top circle.

hundred years ago—or ten years ago, or even one year ago—we would not have the serious problem we have on our hands now. When I heard Dr. King speak about his sons, I thought of my own sons. How would I feel if instead of taking opportunity and freedom for granted, they would have to fight just to be accepted as human beings? James Baldwin put it succinctly when he said, "This day was important in itself. And what we do with this day is even more important."

We are interested in passing the Administration program on civil rights.[8] We know that law cannot change the hearts of men. But it is the beginning. It can at least help to control those who are heartless. But it is not with Washington alone that we must be concerned. We have our problems right here, in our own community. I had originally not intended to speak about the local school situation at this time. But the other day, I went over and look at the faces of the people standing at the barricades at the Davison Avenue School in Lynbrook.[9] They were like pictures I have seen of people in Little Rock and Birmingham. There was hate in these eyes; one sensed that not far beneath the surface there was a residue of bigotry, which might at any moment erupt into violence. Looking at them, I felt fear.

I do not have any ready-made solution to the perplexing and difficult problem of this school district.[10] Many people have spent many hours grappling and struggling with it. I do know one thing: that segregation is evil, and that we must strive to correct that evil. This does not mean that I agree in every respect with the pressure groups working to promote integration. I do not agree that the educational program must be ruthlessly subordinated if necessary to the achievement of this end, or that children should be cavalierly moved for long distances. But I do believe that we must be ready to make sacrifices and accept inconvenience to achieve this goal. Otherwise, our protests are nothing but hypocrisy.

Speaking for myself alone, I was favorably impressed by the plan set forth by the District School Board—a modification of the "Princeton Plan" proposed by Commissioner Allen.[11] It had imperfections, but it achieved the purpose: it

---

8. The Kennedy administration proposed its omnibus civil rights legislation, including a prohibition of discrimination in public accommodations, on June 19, 1963, and it was acrimoniously debated in the Congress during that summer. With strong support from President Johnson, it was finally passed and signed into law in June 1964.

9. See introduction. Because of the School Board's decision to maintain the status quo on opening day (Wednesday, September 4—"the other day" mentioned—) pending court resolution of the taxpayer's suit to block introduction of the "modified Princeton Plan," black families organized picket demonstrations at the Lindner Place School in Malverne and the Davison Avenue School in northern Lynbrook. Angry white parents and taxpayers gathered behind police barricades to watch the demonstrators. The mood turned ugly, and seventeen arrests were made during the first week of classes.

10. See introduction for the background.

11. See introduction. The phrase "speaking for myself alone" may have been intended to signal that he was not claiming to represent the Temple on this divisive local issue. Alternatively, it may hint that his wife did not agree with him and thought he was being too moderate on this matter.

integrated our schools, while avoiding some of the extreme movement [of small children] that the original plan required. I am sorry that neither group was willing to accept it, that each wanted its own way, all the way. I am more sorry that the Board did not have the moral conviction to go ahead with it anyway. I am given to understand that no legal obstacle prevented them from doing so.

I would have had greater admiration for them if, instead of retreating to the status quo, they had said, "We could, if we wished, find an out; we could, if we wished, stall around until this legal rhubarb is settled, which may take years. But we're not going to. We're going to put this plan into effect because we feel it is fair and right, because it achieves the goal of desegregation to which we have committed ourselves. Whether the law makes us do it or not, we're going to do it—because this is the American Dream."

The American Dream: liberty and justice for all. For too long it has been a dream in black and white—or more truly, a dream for whites and not for blacks. The time has come when this dream must be a dream in color, a dream that embraces Americans of all races and national backgrounds and faiths. To the fulfillment of such a dream, let us dedicate ourselves.

34

Martyr for the American Dream
November 22, 1963

The news of President Kennedy's assassination was broadcast on the East Coast during the lunch hour on Friday, November 22, 1963. From that time on, America came to a virtual standstill. Those who lived through it will vividly recall the sense of almost paralyzing bewilderment and numbing grief; those who did not can only imagine a nation in a sudden state of collective trauma.

Among those who were affected in an unusual way were rabbis who were preparing their sermons for the Friday night service. Not only did work on the sermon come to a stop; whatever the topic the sermon addressed, it now seemed totally out of place. In a matter of hours, Jews would be streaming into their synagogues as on the eve of the New Year. They needed to hear something that would articulate their feelings of loss, something that would put the shattering events of the day in context and perspective.

In the Lynbrook Temple, partition doors at the rear of the sanctuary were opened and extra seats hurriedly set up. Some 800 came to the service, almost three times the usual number of Friday night worshippers.

Characteristically, Saperstein's message included his own deliberations about what to do, and then—disclaiming a "formal sermon" or a "formal tribute"—goes on to give a tribute that is not without rhetorical effect. Perhaps the high point was the reference to Lillian Smith's Killers of the Dream, *a book on which he had spoken several years before. Now the title is reversed: "My friends, you can kill men, women and children. But you cannot kill a dream."*

There are some who were in the congregation that night who still remember the sound of those words.

WE COME TOGETHER TONIGHT WITH HEAVY HEARTS. The joy that the Sabbath brings each week is clouded over by the shadow of tragedy that has fallen on our land. A noble heart has been stilled. A heroic life has been snuffed out. The leader of our country has been assassinated. All of us are plunged in grief.

I had prepared a sermon for this evening on Jewish books. When the tragic news came, I told myself that I must go on and preach the sermon that I had planned. But my heart was not in it. The sermon is here. I'll bring it to you some future time.[1] Tonight, I have no formal sermon to preach. Our prayers, in a sense, are my sermon—for they are the expression of the faith that lifts us up over our grief. I have no formal tribute. The sorrow we share as we gather together is the expression of our tribute.

The evaluation of the life of John F. Kennedy will be made by countless writers and speakers in the course of the next week and by historians in the course of the years to come. He was, perhaps, not one of the greatest of our presidents. But he stood for something as real and essential to our country as anything could be. His program was the "New Frontier."[2] Disagree some may on details or on emphasis. But his "New Frontier" was really the old eternal American frontier in new perspective.

What was the essence of his program? It was that men are more important than things, that peace is more precious than war, that justice and freedom are more to be prized than political advantage. His was the spirit of America. He wrote a book called *Profiles in Courage*. His own story could be added as the chief chapter of that book.

John F. Kennedy was a devoted, loyal Catholic, but he took a courageous stand on the separation of church and state.[3]

He was a man of great wealth and privilege, but his heart went out to the needy and underprivileged in our country and all over the world.[4]

---

1. The text of this sermon, entitled "The Heartbeat of Jewish Books," is dated "Nov. 23, 1963." It was actually written after the news of the assassination, which it acknowledges in the first two paragraphs, then makes a transition about the need to rise above the destructive power of hatred through the traditional Jewish value of study. Later, apparently in the middle of the afternoon, Saperstein decided to replace it with the present text. The original sermon was delivered two weeks later.

2. This was the theme set forth in Kennedy's acceptance speech at the Democratic National Convention in Los Angeles on July 15, 1960 ("We stand today on the edge of a New Frontier—the frontier of the 1960s—a frontier of unknown opportunities and perils—a frontier of unfulfilled hopes and threats. . . . It sums up not what I intend to offer the American people, but what I intend to ask of them."). The phrase was used for the legislation proposed to Congress by the new Administration.

3. The preacher and listeners were likely thinking here of candidate Kennedy's address to the Greater Houston Ministerial Association on September 12, 1960, in which he responded to the attack of more than 100 traditional Protestant clergymen and lay leaders. This included the statement, "I believe in an America where the separation of church and state is absolute." See *"Let the Word Go Forth": The Speeches, Statements and Writings of John F. Kennedy*, ed. Theodore Sorenson (New York: Delacorte Press, 1988), 130–34.

4. As expressed, e.g., in his Inaugural Address: "To those people in the huts and villages of half the globe struggling to break the bonds of mass misery, we pledge our best

He was young, but he was concerned about legislation for the security and medical care for those who are old.[5]

He was a war veteran, but he made the first great strides in the pilgrimage of peace for humanity.[6]

He was white, but he fought for civil rights for people of all races.[7]

Not knowing what prompted this tragic crime, I shall not draw any moral from this sorrowful event. This much we know, however: that it was evidence of the corrosive power of hatred—poisoning the spirit and corrupting the mind of human beings.

It was this spirit that destroyed six million Jews in Germany.

It was this spirit that took the life of Medgar Evers in Jackson, Mississippi— a man who didn't want to harm anybody, but only to help awaken people to the moral challenge of the hour.[8]

It was this spirit that bombed the church in Birmingham and took the lives of four innocent children, whose parents mourned them as we would mourn the loss of the lives of our own children.[9]

It was this spirit that has taken the life of the President of the United States of America—and brought grief to his loved ones, sorrow to our nation, and shame to our country.

Some years ago, there was a book by Lillian Smith called *Killers of the Dream*. My friends, you can kill men, women and children. But you cannot kill a dream. Perhaps we needed this tragic event to make us realize the danger of harboring hatred, to turn our country and its people with revulsion against this spiritual disease—to make us realize that to harbor hatred of your fellowman is a vicious betrayal of humanity.

The President of the United States is dead. He has fallen in the midst of his labors.

---

efforts to help them help themselves. . . . If a free society cannot help the many who are poor, it cannot save the few who are rich."

5. Kennedy showed leadership in this area while still in the Senate, presenting his Ten Point Program on Old Age (the "Bill of Rights for the Elderly") in August 1958. Medical insurance was third on this list. The administration's Medicare bill was presented to Congress in February 1961, and Kennedy tried to generate support at events such as a Madison Square Garden rally of 20,000 in May 1962. Medicare was not passed by the Congress until 1965.

6. Perhaps alluding to the establishment of the Peace Corps, or the address to the United Nations General Assembly delivered just two months earlier, on September 20, 1963 (*"Let the Word God Forth,"* 299–305).

7. Kennedy presented his "Civil Rights Act of 1963" in a special message to Congress on June 19, 1963: "The legal remedies I have proposed are the embodiment of this nations; basic posture of common sense and common justice. They involve every American's right to vote, to go to school, to get a job, and to be served in a public place without arbitrary discrimination."

8. Evers, an NAACP organizer, was killed outside his home in Jackson, Mississippi, on June 12, 1963.

9. The Birmingham church bombing occurred on Sunday, September 15, eighteen days after the March on Washington.

He was a martyr for the American dream as truly as was Abraham Lincoln. He gave his life for his country as truly as anyone who fell on the field of battle. Perhaps even in death, he will continue to help achieve the goal to which his life was dedicated. Sometimes death is the price that must be paid for the victory of an ideal.

Lord Byron put it in this poem:

> They never fail who die
> In a great cause. The block may soak their gore;
> Their heads may sodden in the sun; their limbs
> Be strung to city gates and castle walls—
> But still their spirit walks abroad. Though years
> Elapse, and others share as dark a doom,
> They but augment the deep and sweeping thoughts
> Which o'erpower all others and conduct
> The world at last to freedom.[10]

Moses walks with us, though he never set foot in the Promised Land, so long as our faith endures.

Lincoln walks with us, though he died before he could see the fruits of victory, so long as our nation is united.

Herzl walks with us, though he died with his task unfulfilled, so long as the State of Israel remains the fruition of his dream.

President Kennedy will walk with us—if we will but carry on to make the American dream ever more real.

---

10. The passage is taken from Byron's play, "Marino Faliero," Act. II, sc. 2, lines 93–101. See Byron, *Complete Poetical Works*, ed. Jerome McGann, 5 vols. (Oxford: Clarendon Press, 1986), 4:356–57. It was found by Saperstein in *Masterpieces of Religious Verse*, ed. James Dalton Morrison (New York: Harper and Brothers, 1948), 595.

35

"The Deputy"—Where Does the Guilt Lie?
March 20, 1964

Saperstein's army service in the European Theater during the Second World War left him with a rather positive attitude toward the behavior of the Catholic Church in Italy and France during the period of German occupation. For one thing, as an American chaplain he had been given a brief audience with Pope Pius XII, and was moved by his dignity and demeanor—particularly the Pope's decision not to hold out his ring to be kissed when he noticed the insignia of a Jewish chaplain. References to Italy can be seen in the sermon below. As for France, I cite from a letter dated September 12, 1944:

> *A special word of commendation must be given to the Catholic Church. As in Italy, so in France, sanctuary was given to Jews in churches, monasteries and seminaries. Particular children were given refuge and the church was thus instrumental in saving many lives. Official instructions were apparently passed down to every parish priest to do everything in his power to save Jews from destruction. The picture fits in so closely with that which prevailed in Italy that I have no doubt that in back of it is the Pope himself, although no definite political statement has been made in this regard.*

The reaction to the powerful condemnation of the Pope and the Church leadership in Rolf Hochhuth's play The Deputy *was therefore nuanced, as reflected in the four answers to the questions that structure the sermon: "Yes, but . . . ; No, but . . . ." The end of the sermon is a rather stunning turnabout, as criticism for behavior during the Holocaust period is directed elsewhere. Following the rhetorical technique of Amos's first two chapters, the rebuke at first appears to be aimed far away, but then it comes closer and closer, until it finally is leveled at the listeners themselves. While the primary guilt was of course focused on the Nazi perpetrators, the leaders of the Catholic Church were not the only*

bystanders who might have diminished the tragedy had they chosen to act dif-
ferently.

NO DRAMA IN RECENT YEARS has caused as much discussion and excitement as "The Deputy." It was written by a young German playwright, thirty-three years old, Rolf Hochhuth, under the German name *Der Stellvertreter*. His first published work, it has now been shown in many of the leading centers of the Western world. In some, it aroused jeers and cheers. In others, eggs and fruit were thrown at the actors. In others, physical violence broke out. In many, there were repeated demonstrations. In the United States, newspapers, magazines and radio-programs have been filled with discussion for and against. I have a large file of material on the subject; I have read everything I could get my hands on; I have seen it, and twice read the acting script of the play, which I have here. To-night I want to share some of my thoughts and reactions with you.

I am sure that by this time you all know what it is about. Let me summarize the story in a few sentences. A young Jesuit Priest, Riccardo Fontana, is visiting the Papal Nuncio in Berlin. The year is 1942. Into the room bursts an SS officer named Gerstein. His character is based on an actual person. An anti-Nazi, he had volunteered to serve in the SS in order to see if rumors about the extermination program against the Jews were true. Now he hysterically informs the churchmen that Jews are being slaughtered—tens of thousands each day. He has come to tell them what he has seen, so that they may report it to the Pope, who will lift his voice in denunciation.

The Papal Nuncio explains that nothing can be done. But Father Fontana finds himself drawn to Gerstein. He seeks him out and ultimately takes it upon himself to appeal to the Pope for his word and action concerning the indescrib-able deeds of inhumanity that are being perpetrated. Using the influence of his father, an important Catholic layman and investment advisor to the Vatican, the young man comes into the presence of the Pope. By this time, the Nazis are de-porting Jews from the streets of Rome, seized under the very windows of the Vatican. Fontana pleads with the Pope to speak out. The Pope refuses—it is not expedient to do so. Ultimately he issues a statement, so general as to be mean-ingless. Father Fontana takes a yellow star, pins it on his robe over his heart where all Jews must wear it, and joins the Jews on their forced pilgrimage to death at Auschwitz.

This is the main plot of the play. The aspect that has caused all the excite-ment is the implied accusation that the Pope could have done something to save the Jews and did not, and that he therefore failed to fulfill his role as the *Stell-vertreter*, the Deputy of Christ and God to man.

We are approaching the Passover season, with the Seder and its four ques-tions. Let me then ask and try to answer four central questions about this play.

First, is it a good play? My answer is, "NO, but. . . ." I am not basically con-cerned here with literary evaluations. But it is a play, and we must measure it first in terms of that medium. And I must say that viewed as such, it falls short. True, it has powerful impact. But that is primarily because we are emotionally implicated—it touches a raw nerve on the part of Jews and Christians alike. If we could see a play like this from a position of historical objectivity, as we see a play of Shakespeare, I don't think it would stand up on its dramatic merit. Its characters are two-dimensional. They are more caricatures than characters. It does not have the inner tension of character we find in *Macbeth*, or *Othello*, or *Hamlet*. In other words, it is not a great masterpiece.

Yet I feel strongly that this play should be shown and that people should see it. For it opens up a festering sore of modern history, the most crucial moral problem of our times: How could the world have allowed six million human beings, men, women and children, to be crushed, dehumanized and murdered, when all the world turned aside as though this was not a problem for mankind because the victims were Jews. For sixteen years after the war, the problem was shunted aside. People preferred not to look at it too closely. It was too uncomfortable. Then the Eichmann trial brought it out into the open. And now this play focuses a spotlight upon it. The problem must be faced. Whether we agree with the play's message or not, it is high time for Jews and the world to break away from this conspiracy of silence.

There are those who say that the time is not propitious for bringing this problem to the surface. A new era of interfaith relationship is just beginning. The Catholic Church is just about to issue its ecumenical statement against anti-Semitism, lifting the charge of deicide from the Jews. We don't want to upset a delicate situation. This does not concern me. The issues must not be intermingled. If Catholicism has something to say about Jews and anti-Semitism, let them speak the truth. And if we have something to say about the Pope and Catholicism, let us speak the truth. Let us not degrade ourselves by trading favors. Good will that has to be bought is not worth the name. And so I say, see the play.

My second question: Is the charge of the play true? My answer is, "YES, but. . . . " It is unfortunately and tragically true that the Pope did not speak out against the Nazi atrocities and barbarisms against the Jews. Defenders of the Pope have sought to counter the charge by citing statements that the Pope did make expressing sympathy for those who suffered. The simple fact is that in every case, the statement was so general and vague, so covered over with diplomatic and theological verbiage, that it had no bite.[1] For all practical purposes, we can say with accuracy that the Pope was silent in this great hour.

In his written version of the play, which incidentally is almost three times as long as the stage version, Hochhuth adds about fifty pages of documents to substantiate the historicity of his material. He has done his research. He makes a valid case. And all the efforts of the champions of Pope Pius XII to refute it, all

---

1. The statement generally cited both by critics and defenders of the Pope's policy came near the end of the Christmas Message of 1942, referring to "the hundreds of thousands of persons who, without any fault on their part, sometimes only because of nationality or race, have been consigned to death or to a slow decline." Critics, including some at the time, noted that it did not specify the Jews as primary victims, or the Nazis as perpetrators, or the act of systematic mass murder.

the way up to the present Pope himself, cannot negate the fact that the Pope remained silent.

But there is another side of the picture, equally true, to which Hochhuth does not do justice. That is what Pius XII *did* do, a story out of which another playwright might have made another play in which the Pope was the hero. Yes, Hochhuth refers to the fact that the Pope instructed the Church to help the Jews, that Jews were taken into Catholic institutions, that the Vatican paid out money to redeem Jews. But he passes this off as if it was piddling detail compared with the duty to speak out. And I feel that as Jews, we must not brush off so lightly the positive things the Pope did.

I speak here from personal experience. I came into Rome three days after its military liberation [by the American Armed Forces, on June 4, 1944]. I went immediately to see Rabbi Zolli, the chief Rabbi of Rome.[2] Some may suspect his word because he subsequently became a convert to Catholicism, and spent the rest of his life in the Vatican. But what he told me was corroborated by others in the Jewish community. "How did you survive?" I asked. "I was taken during the period of Nazi occupation into the Vatican itself, where many of us were given sanctuary." He went on to tell me how, when the Nazis came into Italy, they had demanded a ransom of 50 kilograms—110 pounds—of gold from the Jewish community, otherwise 300 Jews would be taken and deported. The Jews could raise among themselves only about 75 pounds. The Chief Rabbi went to the Pope and received from him 35 pounds of gold—worth between $15,000 and $20,000—to make up the remainder of the ransom.[3]

I drove into the Ghetto of Rome. People seeing the Star of David on my jeep crowded around me. "How did you survive?" I asked. "The Pope gave orders to the churches and the monasteries to take us in," they said, "and they did, and saved our lives."[4] Later, after VE day, I came into Belgium and found there Fa-

---

2. Saperstein described his meeting with Zolli at length in a sermon entitled "Flight From Fear," delivered on February 15, 1946 (one of his first sermons after returning to Lynbrook; see also the published sermon above from February 8, 1946), which was one year after Zolli's conversion to Catholicism. There he refers to his notes on the meeting, which are apparently no longer extant.

3. Zolli himself described this in his book *Before the Dawn: Autobiographical Reflections* (New York: Sheed and Ward, 1954), 160–61, where it is clear that the fifteen kilograms was to be a loan, as he quotes himself as saying "As for repayment, I myself shall stand as surety, and since I am poor, the Hebrew of the whole world will contribute to pay the debt." On this incident of Nazi extortion and the Vatican response (in late September, 1943), see Susan Zuccotti, *The Italians and the Holocaust* (New York: Basic Books, 1987), 109–13, confirming the fifty kilograms of gold, giving the number of Jews held ransom as 200, and concluding that the Vatican offer—whether at its own initiative or in response to Jewish requests, whether as a gift or as a loan until the Jews could raise the full amount, was ultimately not needed, as the Jews raised the fifty kilograms from other sources.

4. The following is taken from a letter describing experiences in Rome after the liberation, written by Saperstein in June 1944: "It is an interesting fact that the clergy was very sympathetic with the Jews. They took them in and gave them sanctuary and refuge in the churches. Some were given refuge in the Vatican City. In September [1943] the Fa-

ther André, to this day my cherished friend, with a house full of Jews to whom he had given refuge at risk of his own life during the Nazi occupation. "Why did you do this," I asked him, "placing your own life in danger?" "I did this," he said, "because we have one God and we are all brothers, and the Holy Father instructed that we should do all possible to aid our Jewish brethren."[5]

No one can say exactly how many Jews were saved by the Church. True, against six million, it is a relatively insignificant number. But the Talmud says that he who saves even a single life is as one who saves the world.[6] The Pope did not have to do this. He could have washed his hands of the whole problem.[7] He did choose to do it, and it must be considered as part of the record, and not just brushed off as an unimportant incidental detail.

Now for our third question. Is this play fair in its treatment of the Pope? My answer is, "NO, but. . . ." You see, as I pointed out, the *facts* are there. It is in the depiction of the *motives* of the Pope that I feel Hochhuth was unjust and unfair. The Pope he presents is not a personality but a caricature.

The play gives three possible reasons for the silence of the Pope. The first is indifference. This is reflected in an implied accusation of financial greed, placing the material welfare over the Church above the welfare of human beings. In a painful scene just before the Pope refuses to take action to save the Jews, he is shown discussing with great interest and concern the Vatican's financial investments. This I consider to be an unjust, unworthy and unfair innuendo, for which there is no historical warrant. The Pope was cautious. He was not indifferent.

The second reason stressed in the play is political expediency. Again and again it is stated or implied that the Pope was concerned primarily about the struggle between east and west, the fight against communism. He looked upon communism as a greater menace to the Church than Nazism. He did not want to undermine the Germans in their struggle against the forces of communism. Germany had to remain as the balance of power.

There is a certain amount of validity in this issue. I cannot justify the weighing of human beings in terms of tactical manipulation. But I think we should try to understand the position of the Pope a little more clearly. It is not

---

Jews had been ordered to provide fifty kilograms of gold. People gave their jewels, but still they were some kilograms short. The balance was made up by the Pope, although this cannot be told publicly. Some of the local priests told me about these things first. I tended to discount them. Then Alexander Uhl of P.M. [??] told me substantially the same story. Finally, in Rome one of the Jewish people I met told me that her family had found safety in the period of terror in one of the churches which was opened for them by the priest."

5. Saperstein's report of the life-saving activities of Father André was carried by the *New York Times* on December 28, 1945. See the introduction to "The Voice of Joy and Gladness" (1945) above.

6. Mishnah Sanhedrin 4,5.

7. This may allude to a particularly controversial scene in the play when the Pope, after insisting on his policy of neutrality, actually washes his hands in a special basin, in an obvious allusion to Pontius Pilate. See Hochhuth, *The Deputy* (New York: Grove Press, 1964), 219–20, and the author's discussion of the scene on 350–51.

quite so simple as Hochhuth makes it. The Pope is the spiritual leader of 500 million Catholics, it is true, and therefore ideally should speak for the conscience. But the Pope is not a prophet. He is a priest. He is responsible also for an *organization* of 500 million people. We must not condemn him too readily if, to paraphrase Churchill, he should say, "I did not become Pope to preside over the dissolution of the Catholic Church." He could have excommunicated Hitler. He could have refused the sacraments to the Catholics of Germany. But he undoubtedly remembered that the Reformation began in Germany, and to force the issue might break the Catholic world in two. We do not condone his silence. But we must try to understand it.

The third reason given in the play is stated in his own words: to avoid greater harm. This, in my mind, is the only reason that carries any moral weight. And I think that in truth it was an important consideration. Hochhuth implies that if the Pope had spoken, the Nazis would have stopped or slowed down their extermination program and countless Jewish lives would have been saved. That is a matter of conjecture. We may be inclined to overestimate the power of the Pope. The Pope himself had fears that action on his part might have had the opposite effect—it might have intensified the program against the Jews and against Catholics as well. There are arguments and testimony on both sides. The fact is that he also took no [public] action regarding the 3,000 priests and many more thousands of Catholics who met their deaths in concentration camps.

I would have liked the Pope to speak out even if it did no good—because of moral principle. That is what Father Fontana does at the end of the play: he goes to his death even if only God will be aware of his sacrifice. But to do that, we need a hero. Pius XII was no hero. But that does not mean he was a villain, or a criminal. I think this was a matter of judgment. I believe, as the play does, that he judged wrong. But the play condemns, and I am not so quick to condemn.

My final question: Is there a moral message in this play for our times? My answer is, "YES, but. . . ." Let me explain the "but" first. This play points the finger of accusation at one man: the Pope. Yes, there are incidental references in the play that the Germans are primarily guilty, and Hochhuth and Shumlin the producer have stated in defense that the play is not anti-Catholic but a challenge to everyone. But let us not quibble; let us be honest with ourselves: the play condemns the Pope and leaves the idea that the silence of the Pope was responsible for the death of many Jews who otherwise might have survived.

I think that Hochhuth asks the right questions, but he gives the wrong answers. I point the finger of accusation not at the Pope, but at humanity. And I start first with the German people. Let us not be shunted off onto a sidetrack: it was not the Pope who killed the six million, it was the German people. I did not say "the Nazis," I say "the German people," because it was they who chose Hitler, who supported the Nazis, who yelled "Sieg Heil" like crazy while they were on top of the world, and—if they did not participate in the extermination program—chose to look the other way. No one yet, out of all the young, repentant, guilt-laden Germans about whom we hear so much, has written a play about the guilt of the German people.

Why doesn't Hochhuth try his hand at that one? Let him begin with his father and mother, and let him say, "Damn my father and mother, who sent me into the Hitler Youth organization when I was a boy, so that if the Nazis had won, I would have grown up to be a good respectable Nazi. They should have gone to their death and let me die before they did that." If he is looking for heroes, why doesn't he begin with his own family?

And let him turn the finger of accusation against himself. Before he wrote this play, as editor for a publishing company he prepared the two-volume *Works* of Wilhelm Busch, a nineteenth-century satirist whose material contains many anti-Semitic stories. Oh, I've heard him defended: "He was an editor; if a man is editing the works of Charles Dickens, you don't expect him to leave out *Oliver Twist*." True, but the situation is different. If a man is an alcoholic, you don't give him a bottle of whiskey. Just fifteen years ago, German had perpetrated a bloodbath, justified by anti-Semitic propaganda. You don't feed such a people anti-Semitic literature. Hochhuth did not have to take that job. But it meant a good living, and he did. If he's looking for heroes, let him begin with himself.[8]

And I would point the finger of accusation at humanity:

— At the Evian Conference for Refugees in 1938, where everybody spoke words of sympathy and nobody opened their doors.[9]

— At the British government that guarded the gates of Palestine with armed forces when Jews seeking refuge there were drowning in the sea.

— At the great leaders of our war effort, who couldn't afford a single bomber to drop a bomb on Auschwitz because it was not strategically practical.

— At people here in our congregation, who in 1938 could have saved a life when I pleaded with them to sign affidavits for refugees, but preferred not to

---

8. This passage apparently reflects a contemporary debate that I cannot trace. That Hochhuth worked for the Bertelsmann Verlag, a large German publisher, and edited a new edition of the works of Wilhelm Busch, appeared in the *New York Times* biographical sketch on Sunday, March 1, 1964 (Book Review section, 31). The question of the antisemitic character of the material is more complex. Busch (1832–1908) was well known as a poet, artist, and cartoonist; his most famous creation, *Max und Moritz*, became the basis for "The Katzenjammer Kids" in the United States. One chapter of one of his works, *Plisch und Plum* (chap. 5), does feature an antisemitic caricature: in the description of an American critic, "a rumpled, curly-all-over, baroque-nosed, shuffling ol'-clothesman" named Schmulchen Schivelbeiner. The critic considers this to be a satire, a *reductio ad absurdum* of the "nasty-genteel" anti-Semitism circa 1880. See Walter Arndt, *The Genius of Wilhelm Busch: Comedy of Frustration* (Berkeley: University of California Press, 1982), 4. Busch was not known as an antisemite, nor is he discussed in the common scholarly treatments of nineteenth-century German antisemitism. The condemnation of Hochhuth for editing his works as analogous to a bottle of whiskey to an alcoholic appears to me to be rhetorical overkill.

9. On the Evian Conference, see the 1974 sermon below, n. 13.

do it, because it might have involved an unwelcome financial responsibility.[10]

This is the moral message of the play. We must take a deep look at what went on under Hitler. The world was guilty of the sin of silence in the time of Hitler. Millions of good people, by their indifference, share responsibility for that tragedy. And then we must take a deep look at our own times, and ask, "Where am I? Where do I stand? Why am I silent?" Some day, a young playwright will write a drama about the moral struggles of our own time and ask what *we* said and did in the face of man's inhumanity to man.

De te fabula narratur: this story is told concerning *you*. "Do not send to know for whom the bell tolls. It tolls for thee."[11]

10. For the rhetorical model of this passage, see introduction. Saperstein was fond of teaching these chapters from Amos in terms of audience response: the speaker arouses satisfaction in his listeners by condemning their enemies, but then they become more and more uneasy as the same pattern of condemnation is applied closer to home, and finally to the listeners themselves.

11. John Donne, *Devotions upon Emergent Occasions*, Meditation XVII. A sermon delivered in early January 1940 was entitled "For Whom the Bell Tolls." It discusses Hemingway's book and cites the full passage from Donne's Devotion, taken from the book's foreword, applies the theme to Moses's decision to stand up for the underdog, and leads to the conclusion that—while America should stay out of the war—Americans should not be isolationist but should give to Britain and her allies "every assistance that we can give," for "the bombs falling across the seas are hammering out our destiny and the destiny of civilization."

36

The War on Poverty
March 26, 1965

While the immediate inspiration for this sermon was the conference described in the first paragraph, it also responded to a growing issue of national concern in the 1960s. A major factor in bringing poverty to the political agenda was Michael Harrington's book, The Other America: Poverty in the United States, *first published in 1962 and then reprinted in a popular Penguin edition in 1963 and often afterward. Filled with data and facts, it also made a powerful moral appeal. President Kennedy, who read the book shortly before his death, approved the planning of programs for a "war on poverty," and President Johnson continued to make this a priority, with a public proclamation on March 14, 1964. The Economic Opportunity Act of 1964, part of the Johnson Administration's "Great Society" legislation, set as its goal "to eliminate the paradox of poverty in the midst of plenty in this Nation." An Office of Economic Opportunity, headed by Sargent Shriver, established many training and educational programs including VISTA (the "domestic peace corps") and Project Head Start.*

The religious communities had not taken the lead on this issue, but they were galvanized to take action in support of these programs. The Reform Movement's Union of American Hebrew Congregations published a 130-page booklet entitled There Shall Be No Poor . . . , *written by Rabbi Richard Hirsch, director of the movement's Religious Action Center in Washington D.C. In a sense, it was a liberal Jewish version of* The Other America, *with a chapter on "Judaism in Pursuit of Economic Justice" and other citations of specifically Jewish texts to supplement the data and graphs. (While the booklet actually appeared somewhat after the sermon, Saperstein heard Hirsch use material from the pamphlet in the address he delivered at the conference described at the beginning of the sermon.)*

Poverty was bound to be somewhat distant from the experience of most congregants in a solidly middle- and upper-middle-class Long Island Reform Tem-

ple, as Saperstein concedes in his second paragraph. A central function of the sermon therefore had to be educational, presenting facts to make the case that, despite growing national prosperity, this was indeed a serious problem with a claim to the conscience of suburban Jews. Saperstein used the Harrington book and material from the conference for his data. The moral appeal to support the new government agenda comes after this foundation has been carefully established.

ABOUT A MONTH AGO, I WENT DOWN TO WASHINGTON to represent our congregation at a conference called by the Religious Action Center of the Union of American Hebrew Congregations.[1] From time to time such conferences are held, bringing together Reform Jewish representatives from all over the country to discuss vital current issues, meeting together with authorities in the field and with leading government officials. Again and again, one becomes aware of how valuable it is to our movement to have this Center for social action in the nation's capital.

The issue that concerned us this time is that which I have taken for my theme tonight—the war on poverty. It may seem like a strange issue to be focusing on in these times. This problem does not affect us directly. In fact, many religious leaders have been concerned with the dangers of affluence upon our group life. Nor does it seem urgent. Our future seems to be involved with fighting far across the seas, and the demonstrations for voting rights. To most of us, poverty seems a minor and distant issue. And yet it is a major, terrible blight upon American life, and it may well be bound up with these others in determining the future destiny of our nation.

How big a problem is it? That depends, of course, on where we draw the line. What level [of income] makes a person poor? There have been various definitions, and of course it is impossible to draw a precise line, among other things because of individual differences. The Bureau of Labor statistics calculated that an individual person must have a total income of $1,500 per year, and a family of four about $6,000 per year, to live modestly but adequately. More than half the population of America would be below that level. Take the other extreme: figure $500 for an individual, $2,000 for a family: there would still be 20 million Americans below that threshold. Or let's compromise: say $1,000 for an individual—about $20 a week gross—and $3,000 ($60 a week) for a family of four. Twenty percent of American families—about 36 million people—would have to be classified as poor.[2]

---

1. The "National Conference on Poverty," held on March 2 and 3, 1965, had the theme "Judaism in Pursuit of Economic Justice." Major addresses were given by Sargent Shriver, Director of the Office of Economic Opportunity, and Francis Keppel, Commissioner of the U.S. Office of Education. The director of the RAC was then Rabbi Richard G. Hirsch, who also addressed the conference. (Saperstein's son David, who heard this sermon as a high school senior, became director of the Center in 1974.)

2. For a roughly contemporary discussion of income criteria for the definition of poverty and numbers of Americans who fit this definition, see the Appendix to Michael Har-

It's hard to believe, isn't it, when our economy is burgeoning, our national productivity increasing, the stock market hitting new heights, and most of us making more money than we ever did before. That is one of the insidious aspects of poverty today: it's largely invisible. In part it's invisible because of the fallacy of averages. The fact is that these are prosperous times if we look at the average figures. But if you take two people—one family makes $50,000 a year and their maid who makes $4,000 a year—their average income would be $27,000 a year. That is mathematically correct, but it doesn't tell the truth.

Poverty is invisible secondly because it doesn't appear in people's clothing the way it used to. American society has informalized the clothes of the rich, and mass-produced cheap clothes for the poor, so that the poverty you might pass in the street doesn't necessarily hit you in the eye. Thirdly, there was a time when people of all economic levels lived in the same community—the poor on the other side of the tracks, perhaps, but still visible and in the awareness of others. Now the affluent move away from the downtown cities, which become transformed into ghettoes of the poor. We go through them in trains, busses and subways, but we don't see them. Occasionally we drive through sections like Harlem and wonder why so many men are standing around purposelessly in the middle of the day, but it is another world, and we go about our business.[3]

This is obviously different from the poverty back in the big Depression of the '30s. Then economic decline hit everybody.[4] It may have been the loss of paper profits in the stock market to some, but it made everybody aware of the fact that times were hard. Moreover, you could see the evidence. People were selling apples on the streets. I remember when my father went out desperately peddling neckties, three for a dollar. I recall bread lines on Times Square. I was then a student, majoring in economics, and I went down and lived for three days on the bread lines in the Bowery to see what it was like.[5] Today it's different: poverty is an invisible reality underneath the surface of an affluent society.

Who are these poor who do not make enough to live at a minimum standard of health and decency? Many have a tendency to identify the poor in terms of moral judgment. It is implied that it's the people's own fault if they don't make a decent living. They must be lazy, shiftless, lacking in ambition.[6] They want to

---

rington, *The Other America* (Baltimore: Penguin Books, 1963), 171–186. Harrington concludes, "somewhere between 20 and 25 per cent of the American people are poor. They have inadequate housing, medicine, food, and opportunity. From my point of view, they number between 40,000,000 and 50,000,000 human beings" (178). Compare Richard Hirsch, *There Shall Be No Poor . . .* (New York: Union of American Hebrew Congregations, 1965), 30.

3. The "invisibility" of poverty is discussed in the first chapter of Harrington, 11–14.

4. The contrast between poverty in the 1930s and contemporary poverty is made in Harrington, 15–16 (drawing from John Kenneth Galbraith), and Hirsch, 28–29.

5. Saperstein wrote a paper about his experience on the bread lines that remained in his files throughout his career.

6. Compare Hirsch, 1–3: a Gallup Poll taken in March 1964 revealed that 54 percent of Americans believed that a person's poverty is due to "lack of effort on his own part."

get a free ride and live on relief. Some times the argument is turned around, as if the poor people ought to be glad they are poor. They probably don't know anything better; they're happy as they are; they don't have the worries and tensions of those in the upper brackets of the economic structure.

People who say such things need to learn some of the basic facts of life. Sholem Aleichem reminded us that poverty is no shame, but it's no honor either.[7] Whatever it is not, poverty is misery and suffering and degradation and despair. It is like a trap, which swallows up certain segments of the population with little regard to individual character and innate worth.

What are these segments? First, there are those who are industrial outcasts, who have had the bad luck to be tied up with an industry that is dying or has become automated. Take the Appalachian region. In areas where mining once gave employment to thousands, now a few hundreds with modern equipment can produce the same amounts.[8] In other industries, as machines do more and more of the work, the unskilled jobs are eliminated. We thus find that the poorest people to begin with suffer the most. They occupy an upside-down role in the economy. The same forces that expand the economy of industry and increase the prosperity of the country drive them out and prevent them from sharing in that prosperity.

Second is the problem of the aged. Advances in health and hygiene have increased the life span. The proportion of aged people in our population has skyrocketed in recent years. But we have done something that is in essence cruel: we have given them meaningless years to live out, because we have not increased the opportunities for living with the increase in the span of years. Sixty percent of the people over sixty-five in our country receive an annual income of less than $1,000. Half the aged—about eight million—can't afford decent housing and nutrition and health care. One and a half million live alone on less than $600 a year. We have kept them physically alive, but we have made them humanly obsolete.[9]

The third group is the farmer. The folk image of America has always idealized the farmer, in terms of self-reliance, hard work, innate dignity. Today, the farmer is the poorest element of the population. New techniques have favored the large, mechanized farm. The small farmer can no longer make a living; there is no need for him any more. Fifty years ago, one farmer was needed to raise products consumed by seven people. Today one farmer can raise the greater amount of consumption for twenty-four people. Migrant farm workers average $1,000 per year; 56 percent don't have enough to eat. As a result, a million people a year are being squeezed off the land, pouring into the city slums, where

---

7. A Yiddish proverb (*Orem iz keyn shand, ober oykh keyn groysser koved nit*): see Joseph Baron, *A Treasury of Jewish Quotations* (New York: Crown Publishers, 1956), 365b, 366b.

8. Compare Harrington, 44–47, on the Appalachians.

9. On the elderly poor, see Harrington, 101–18. The 60 percent at $1,000 is a Bureau of Census figure for 1958 (Harrington, 104); the eight million figure is on p. 102.

they are equipped only for the most menial type of industrial labor—the very areas where opportunities are diminishing at the most rapid rate.[10]

The fourth group is the Negro. They suffer from all the other factors with a special burden, because of their color. Negroes in industry suffer more from displacement; mostly unskilled, they are invariably the first to be fired. Negroes in agriculture suffer more than others. Forty percent of them earn less than $1,000 a year. They are squeezed out as sharecroppers and as small farmers, scratching the earth for an ever more meager living and going ever deeper into debt.[11]

It all becomes a vicious cycle. Poverty breeds poverty. The poor suffer more from illness, limited education—and so they sink deeper and deeper into the morass of poverty. Those who are crushed in industry and agriculture during their productive years can look forward only to a more miserable old age. Those who are poor are forced to live in slums under conditions of degradation which destroy their morale, their motivation, and their hope. In his book *1984*, George Orwell described the poverty-stricken workers whom he called the "proles." They are the poor who had lost all hope. Crushed and defeated, they can no longer envision revolution or reform. Are we—not by purpose or intent, but because of unawareness and insensitivity—creating a society of the affluent on one side, and the "proles" on the other?

But why is this our problem? First, let me give you some practical considerations. Poverty affects us economically. Poor people cost society money. They require more social services than others do. They consume a good part of our budgets. It has been estimated that poverty costs us about $50 billion a year in direct payments, not counting losses in human values. If we can diminish this problem by the expenditure of some billions of dollars, it is not a handout, it is a practical investment.

Second, it is important in our fulfillment of the world role we envision for ourselves. The struggle with communism is, in the final analysis, to be determined not by the accumulation of armaments, or competition in the space race, but by the character of the societies we produce. The poor who make up this "other America" may be invisible to us; they are not invisible to the communists or to those who are in the middle, comparing our way of life with that under communist rule. The 80 percent who make up the affluent segment of society assume that it is the same for all. From distant lands, they discount the 80 percent and concentrate on the submerged 20 percent.

But most important, poverty is a moral and religious problem. We speak about the dignity of man, of responsibility for each other. If these facts are true, it is an intolerable and monstrous example of unnecessary suffering. It is a challenge to the conscience of us all. Perhaps some of the figures I have presented—taken from reputable sources—may be unduly weighted. But we must not quibble over percentages. We must face the problem.

---

10. Compare Harrington, 47–59, Hirsch, 101.
11. Compare Harrington, 63–82.

This is not a matter of philanthropy. It does not call for charity in its usual sense. It does call for charity at its highest level, as envisioned by Maimonides—the charity that will make charity unnecessary because it enables people to help themselves.[12] Significantly, at our conference in Washington, Sargent Shriver, Director of thè U.S. Office of Economic Opportunity, cited this passage from Maimonides.

What can we do? We can first give support to our nation's War on Poverty. A complex program, including the Job Corps, work-training and work-study programs, investment incentives, volunteer services, and many others, is being put into effect. The problem is so great in scope that it needs the federal government. But effective action requires understanding and support on the part of the people. This is one reason I chose to speak about it tonight.

Second, the program includes community action projects.[13] The federal government will give major financial support to local projects involving education, job training, health services, vocational rehabilitation, and so forth. We must be alert to possibilities within our own communities. And when they arise, be quick to give them effective moral support.

Third, we must endeavor to remove the blinders from our eyes, and the dampers from our consciences. We must be alert to do what we can personally to remove this blight from our nation's conscience, to keep ourselves from strengthening the [negative] pattern in our own relations with others, including employees, to be prepared constantly to favor such legislation and government action as will contributed to the improvement of the situation.

Aristotle, in his *Politics*, accepted the institution of slavery, prevalent at that time. But he envisioned that under one circumstance slavery would no longer be necessary: if inanimate objects could by intelligent design be made to do things—if, for example, the statues of Daedalus were to come to life.[14] We today are seeing that vision realized. But, like all material achievement, our new technology can be used for good or evil—to increase misery, or to bring an end to poverty; to crush the spirit of people, or to usher in the new Great Society. This is, in the final analysis, a moral decision. The American people must give the answer.

---

12. Maimonides, *Mishneh Torah*, "Laws of Gifts to the Poor," 10, 7; *A Maimonides Reader*, ed. Isadore Twersky (New York: Behrman House, 1972), 136–37.

13. The Community Action programs, some of which attempted to empower the poor by organizing them for political action, were among the most controversial components of the "War on Poverty."

14. Aristotle, *Politics* 1, 3 (*The Basic Works of Aristotle*, ed. Richard McKeon [New York: Random House, 1941], 1131): "If every instrument could accomplish its own work, obeying or anticipating the will of others, like the statues of Daedalus, or the tripods of Hepaestus, which, says the poet, 'of their own accord entered the assembly of the God;' if, in like manner, the shuttle would weave and the plectrum touch the lyre without a hand to guide them, chief workmen would not want servants, nor masters slaves."

37

On the Freedom Trail in Alabama
September 10, 1965

*The experience in Alabama during the summer of 1965 was one of the most ex-
hilarating and poignant of Saperstein's career. Without fully knowing what they
were getting into, Harold and Marcia Saperstein volunteered for voter registration work in Lowndes County, Alabama, as part of an effort to demonstrate the
solidarity of northern clergy with the civil rights movement. They found a black
community that welcomed them warmly within a larger environment of fright-
ening external tension, even of danger. Two years later, in a letter dated June
11, 1967, after describing the sound of Jordanian mortar shells heard from the
Hebrew Union College building abutting no-man's land in Jerusalem, Marcia
Saperstein wrote,*

> Yet we never had the sense of personal threat that we had riding along the
> dirt roads of Lowndes County in a car driven by Stokely Carmichael at 90
> miles an hour, making U-turns as we approached road blocks and being
> chased by a car filled with red-necks, a rifle rack in its back window and a
> man next to the driver pointing a rifle out the front window.

That aspect of the experience was not included in the sermons given back home.
*Two consecutive Friday night sermons were devoted to reporting about the
time in the South. The first sermon, which appears below, was largely informa-
tional, explaining the purpose of the time spent in Alabama, describing some of
the experiences, and communicating what had been learned. The following
week, deep pain and visceral anger accompanied the information presented
from the pulpit. That sermon, entitled "Murder on the Roads of Alabama," described Jonathan Daniels, the Episcopal Divinity student with whom the Saper-*

steins had worked, who was shot to death not long after they returned to the
North. It was a period in the struggle for equality and fairness when good and
evil seemed as unmistakably clear as they had during the Nazi era, and when the
inspirational power of rhetoric was palpable throughout the civil rights move-
ment. In future years, Saperstein would frequently return to the memories of
those days (see "An American Tragedy," and "Days I Remember").

MARCIA AND I HAVE RETURNED MANY TIMES after the summer, eager to share with you memorable experiences that have inspired us and sometimes brought us sadness. Few summers have been as unforgettable as the one now ending. It included, first, the opportunity of sharing with some of our members a wonderful pilgrimage to Israel and Europe. In future weeks, I hope to share with you some of the enthusiasm and joy we found on that trip. We had returned only a few days when we continued our journeys, this time to Selma, Alabama. There we had one of the most inspiring, uplifting, exciting, heartwarming, and ulti-mately tragic experiences we have ever known.

Let me answer, first, a question I know is in many of your minds. Why did we go to Selma? What were we seeking to do? After all, Selma is just a typical southern town, with a population of less than 25,000, in the midst of a fertile agricultural area known as the black belt, supporting several industrial plants. There are many towns like Selma throughout the South. But somehow Selma has become a symbol—a milestone on the Freedom Trail. The famous March from Selma to Montgomery has become a truly glorious page in the history of the struggle for human freedom.[1]

For a few days, Selma was in the spotlight. Thousands of people converged upon it to demonstrate for freedom and equality. It had its hour of glory. The march was held. A few civil rights workers were killed. And then the excitement was over. The goal had not yet been reached; the work was not yet completed—it had really just begun. Except for a handful of civil rights workers, the Negroes of Selma were virtually forgotten. But not completely.

One of those who had been killed during the demonstrations was the Rever-end James Reeb, a Unitarian-Universalist minister, clubbed down from behind as he passed the "Silver Moon Cafe" near the center of town.[2] The Unitarian church decided they were not going to pull out. They established what they called a "religious presence" in Selma. This meant merely that they would have a clergyman there constantly to show that religious leaders were still concerned.

---

1. The March began in Selma with 3,200 participants on March 21, 1963, and ended in Montgomery on March 25 with about 25,000 (including the present editor, represent-ing the Harvard-Radcliffe Hillel Society). See Juan Williams, *Eyes on the Prize: Amer-ica's Civil Rights Years, 1954–1965* (New York: Penguin Books, 1987), 251–85.

2. Reeb, of Boston, was attacked in Selma on March 9, 1963; brought to a hospital in Birmingham, he died two days later at age thirty-eight. The Rev. Martin Luther King Jr. delivered a eulogy at a memorial service in Selma on March 15. Defendants in his murder trial were acquitted on December 10.

The report of this project caught the imagination of an interfaith civil rights meeting and it was decided to enlarge it to include participation of clergymen of all faiths. Unfortunately, it never quite got off the ground. Marcia and I were the only Jewish representatives who participated.

What did we do there? We were not committed to any particular organization or project. We were free to work in any area to which we felt drawn. We soon made contact with all the civil rights organizations working in Selma. For example, one group of young people from the State College of San Francisco had organized the Selma Free College. They gathered a library of 17,000 books, the best library in that part of Alabama.[3] They wanted to donate it to Selma University, a junior college for Negro teachers, but for reasons which I do not have time to explain it was not accepted. So they had to set up their own library. Marcia and I helped them move the books from the church attic where they were stored to the bare building someone had rented for them. I live with books all the time. This was the first time my work consisted of moving them physically.

One morning we taught classes in their Freedom School. I taught a group of Negro children a class in geography. There were not enough chairs, so most of them sat on the floor. None of them had ever been more than a few miles from Selma. I tried to give them some idea of the greatness and variety of America, and I will always remember the light of excitement in their eyes as I told them about their country.

One afternoon, we joined with several doctors from the Medical Committee for Human Rights at a meeting in a church. At this meeting, we laid the foundation for a Negro health organization that would try to meet the unique medical needs of Negro children.

I made four public addresses. Two were at mass meetings in Selma, sponsored by the Dallas County Voters' League. The Negro mass meeting is a strange new development, combining religious and political activities. They may include prayers and Bible readings, freedom songs and speeches. We were there at a crucial time: when the voting bill was approved by the President and federal registrars were sent to those counties where the record of suppression of Negro voting was worst. These included Dallas and Lowndes counties, where we were working.[4] The spirit of these meetings was fever high: a spirit of victory and

---

3. A mimeographed two-page statement kept by Saperstein, entitled "Selma Free College: A Brief Introduction," was written by the "General Coordinator" about a month after the arrival of the San Francisco students on June 19, 1965. It states, "Classes are being held under its auspices in art, English, French, Negro history, Negro literature, dramatics and federal laws. . . . Nearly 200 children, teens and adults of Selma's Negro community are participating in more than 60 hours weekly of activities. As awareness and demand grows, the program is being modified and expanded to keep up. The College library presently numbers 18,000 volumes, rivaling in size any in western Alabama and easily bettering them in quality." On July 12, the Library was moved to the Green Street Baptist Church, from which apparently it had to be removed a few weeks later.

4. See Stokely Carmichael and Charles Hamilton, *Black Power* (New York: Vintage Books, 1967), 104: "From March to August, 1965, about fifty to sixty black citizens made their way to the courthouse to register and successfully passed the registration

exuberance. They invariably ended with the singing of "We Shall Overcome." Marcia and I were the only white people at one meeting. As we grasped hands and sang, neither of us could refrain from weeping.

One speaking experience was unique. We attended a Negro Baptist revival meeting. Again, we were the only white people present. We had come to observe. It was a fantastic experience, with spiritual singing in which the people poured forth their faith, hope and yearning. The preacher, like an old Jewish *maggid* [popular preacher], started slow and then whipped himself into a frenzy as he chanted and shouted. Near the end of the meeting, the minister recognized me and called on me to speak. I doubt whether many rabbis have had that experience. Let me say that it is going to be hard to get used to our comparatively sedate and reserved congregations. Negro audiences respond unselfconsciously. They interact with the preacher. When they agree with you, you hear them call out, "Amen," "that's right," "speak to us."

We interviewed many people. These included leaders of the Negro community, white officials—like Bob Frye, FBI director in Selma, and Wilson Baker, director of Public Safety. We met also with the leaders of the Jewish community. I can understand their predicament. Some of them have my sympathy: they are torn between principle and economic necessity. Some have my contempt: they justify their failure to act, reflecting the poisoned prejudice of their environment.[5] Some time in the future I will analyze their problem in greater detail.

Among our most exciting experiences was work with SNCC, the Student Non-Violent Coordinating Committee, out "in the counties." This phrase refers to the rural areas. We were working on voter registration in Lowndes Count, one of the toughest counties in the South, where the population is 80 percent Negro but where before this year not a single Negro has been registered.[6] We went from farm to farm. We visited the county seat in Hayneville, later to be the scene of tragedy to one of our group.[7] We attended the second Negro mass

---

'test.' Then, in August, the 1965 Voting Rights Act was passed and federal 'examiners' or registrars came into the county. No longer did a black man face literacy tests or absurdly difficult questions about the Constitution or such tactics as rejection because one 't' was not properly crossed or an 'i' inadequately dotted. The voting rolls swelled by the hundreds." The Voting Rights Act was signed into law by President Johnson on August 6, 1965; in a new conference of August 25, Johnson announced that the number of Negroes registered in Mississippi had doubled since passage of the new law.

5. Compare the statement in the 1957 sermon to the CCAR above: "I shall not speak at length of those in our day who succumb to the force of expediency. It is in poor taste for those who do not stand on the combat line of the integration problem, for example, to pass judgment upon the conduct of colleagues who do."

6. The *Washington Post* of March 26, 1965, in an article on the murder of Viola Liuzzo, stated, "Lowndes County is one of the targets of the voter registration drive started in Selma in January and extended later into other counties of Alabama. The County, with a population of about 15,000, has four Negroes to every white resident but only two Negroes registered to vote. Both of them were added to the voting list this month [March] after the civil rights struggle was under way."

7. The reference here, and at the end of the first paragraph, is to the murder on August 20 of Jonathan Daniels, a student at Episcopal Theological School in Cambridge,

meeting ever to be held in Fort Deposit, where I was one of the speakers. And we ended up attending the Southern Christian Leadership Conference convention in Birmingham.[8]

Did we accomplish anything? It is hard for me to evaluate this. Certainly, we did not play any crucial role. We did not achieve anything that wouldn't have been achieved if we had not been there. And yet I think that few things I have ever done have been so valuable. For one thing, I like to think that our presence had an effect on some of the civil rights workers. Many of the white ones are Jewish. Whatever their religious commitment, a rabbi to them, as to men in the Army during the war, is a link with the more stable universe they had left: a bond with home and roots, a reminder that they have not been forgotten. One sweet girl from San Francisco said, as we were leaving, "We're so sorry you can't stay. You're good for our morale."

I like to think that the things I said at mass meetings meant something to the audience. I spoke as a white, a Jew, a rabbi, and assured them that their problem was our problem because we are all human beings. I felt the warmth of their response. I hope I may have touched their hearts and brought them a little extra strength and hope and faith in America.

I like to think also that our presence there shook up some of the white community. You see, we lived among Negroes. When white cars would pass and see us walking in that section, they would swing around to look at us. There was hatred in their eyes, but there was also a bit of puzzlement. We didn't fit their stereotypes; we were obviously not beatniks or wild kids. The Jews to whom we spoke were frightened and a little annoyed by our presence, but also I think a little troubled in conscience. I hope we opened up at least a tiny chink in the armor of their self-righteousness.

I think we did some good just by being there. Marcia and I were the only husband and wife team in Selma. Except for the doctors and the Unitarian minister, we were the only middle-aged workers on the scene.[9] We had no car, and so we walked a great deal in Negro areas. We were always carefully and soberly

---

Massachusetts, who had been working in Selma throughout the spring and summer of 1965. He was mortally wounded by a shotgun soon after his group was unexpectedly released from the prison in Hayneville. (Carmichael refers to this in the continuation of the passage cited above: "The whites of Lowndes moved swiftly with the old weapon of terror: some two weeks after the registrar's arrival in Hayneville, the county seat, civil rights worker Jonathan Daniels was shotgunned to death and his fellow seminarian, Richard Morrisroe, critically wounded in Hayneville.") Thomas Coleman, the shooter, claimed self-defense and was eventually acquitted. Saperstein's sermon of the following week, September 17, entitled "Murder on the Roads of Alabama," was devoted to Jonathan Daniels' violent death and funeral. See also below, "An American Tragedy," and "Days I Remember."

8. The annual convention of the Conference was held that year from August 11–13. For more on Saperstein's experience at the convention, see "An American Tragedy," below.

9. Harold Saperstein was fifty-four years old, and Marcia forty-five, during the summer of 1965.

dressed. We greeted the Negroes who passed us in the street or who sat on their porches in friendship. This is very rare. It meant a great deal, and word about us got around. We would call a cab—a Negro cab, because you have to decide which it will be. The driver, seeing us emerging from a Negro home, would be surprised, and then he would say, "You must be the couple that's been walking around. I heard about you."

We felt it particularly when we went down to the Federal Building in Selma. The federal registrars had just come in to supervise voting registrations. The line consisted of hundreds of Negroes, it stretched back and forth through the corridors and down the staircase. The white employees walked past them as though they didn't exist. But we already knew many of them, and we walked up and down the corridors, greeting people. I was deeply moved and had to fight back the tears. I would smile and say, "It's a wonderful day. Good luck!" I could hear the people in back asking, "What did he say?" And I could hear them repeating, like an echo, "He said, 'It's a wonderful day. Good luck!'" Just those few words, but their eyes brightened.

Most of all, this was worthwhile to us because we learned so much. There are things in life one cannot learn from books. The facts are there, but only through experience can one see them in true perspective, in their full dimensions. I came away with a real admiration and respect for the civil rights workers. Some of them may very well be confused kids, some may be looking for excitement, some may be what we would call beatniks, but by and large they are as fine and idealistic a group of youngsters as I've met anywhere. Most of them receive no compensation. Those on the regular staff of organizations like SNCC or SCLC or CORE[10] get about $10 a week for maintenance. They live in crowded rooms, many of them without beds. They don't get enough to eat; it's a big deal when they are invited to dinner by one of the Negro families.

They are often worried and frightened; many of them suffer from the occupational malady of ulcers. Some of them know what it is to be beaten with sticks, and burned by cattle prods, and threatened with guns, and crowded into jail cells. But they are there—some of them having interrupted brilliant academic careers—and they are working. And I say that America can be proud that out of our affluence we've been able to produce such idealism. They are our greatest hope for the future.

We learned also how little communication there is between Negro and white in the South. The southern white deceives himself that he knows and understands the Negro. "We get along with our Negroes," they say, "if it wasn't for all this outside agitation. We've lived with them for generations; we know how to treat them; we know what they want themselves." It may seem presumptuous for me to say after so brief a visit, but I am convinced that southern whites don't have the slightest idea of what the Negro really feels and thinks. Over the centuries, the Negro has developed the art of playing the role the white in the south

---

10. SCLC = Southern Christian Leadership Conference; CORE = Congress of Racial Equality.

expects him to play. It has been their *modus vivendi*. We had the privilege of seeing the Negroes from the inside. During our stay, we were part of their group. And talking with whites, we found that we had to tell them what was going on in the Negro community. The great need is to open up channels of communication.

We learned too that what is going on is a real revolution, a revolution that implies not merely external change but a change in the fundamental patterns of life. This explains why it is so deeply resented by southern whites. It is the end of an era. It has its *economic* side. The Thomas Jefferson Hotel in Birmingham, where most of the Negroes stayed during the SCLC convention, has only recently been integrated. Negroes are now accommodated. But the Negro elevator operators receive a salary of $35 every two weeks. The woman whose home we shared is a practical nurse. She tends an aged millionaire invalid woman of the old south, living in a faded mansion. She is on duty sixteen hours a day. And she receives $5 a day, with no vacation. That kind of economic exploitation has got to end.

The revolution has its *political* aspects. For months, Negroes in Selma had been trying to register to vote. Hundreds would line up. No one could get out of line to eat or to relieve themselves. They stood there all day. The local registrars would take an hour and a half for each interview. At the end of the day, they would have seen six individuals, and the rest would be sent away, to return the next registration day two weeks later. In Lowndes County, I spoke to an elderly, fascinating, brilliant blind preacher, Reverend McCall.[11] "I can read Braille better than most of them can reading printing," he said. "The first time I went they read me the wrong question, so I gave them the wrong answer. Then the federal government said they could ask only personal questions, so they asked me my name and address and how old I was and whether I was married. I must have given the wrong answers again, because they failed me a second time. But now the federal registrars are there, and I'm going down tomorrow and this time I'm going to register!"[12]

But most important, it is a revolution in terms of human dignity. The Negro wants not merely to educate his children, to earn a living, to vote; he wants to be treated like a man. The signs are down in the waiting rooms and rest rooms of the South. But if you look at the Selma phone book, you will notice that some women's names have a Mrs. or a Miss, and some have no title—just the name. The Mrs. or Miss designates a white woman; its absence means that she is a Negro. As we were leaving Selma, we met some teenage girls who had been present at a mass meeting the night before. We walked along and talked with them. They were thirsty and started to go into a refreshment stand. Suddenly

---

11. For more on this blind preacher, see "The Dilemma of Vietnam" and "An American Tragedy," below.

12. Again, Carmichael and Hamilton, *Black Power*, 104: "The *act* of registering to vote does several things. It marks the beginning of political modernization by broadening the base of participation. It also does something the existentialists talk about: it gives one a sense of being."

they veered. "Why didn't you go in?" we asked. "There were too many white people there," they said. "We'd get our heads bashed." They don't necessarily want to be loved. But they do want to be respected and treated like human beings.

From everything we could see, despite centuries-long provocation, the southern Negro does not hate the white. The hatred is on the other side. In all our conversations, in all the meetings we attended, we never heard hatred expressed. I think it is due to the religious orientation of the civil rights movement in the South. Unlike the North, civil rights in the South is a church-centered movement. It speaks in terms of faith and love. It has made a virtue of non-violence. I don't know how long it can continue that way. There are those who are getting impatient. But thus far, the struggle of the Negro in our southern states for freedom has been one of the great spiritual achievements of American history. It is worthy of the American dream.

There is much more that I could say. But time has passed, and I have already spoken longer than usual. Let me therefore conclude. There will be setbacks, and there will be resistance, there will be outbreaks of violence on both sides, and lives will still be lost. But the die is cast. There is no turning back. A new day is dawning, a day when the words our nation has spoken—freedom, equality, justice—those words which have been the glory of the American dream, will come close to reality. And when they sing "We shall overcome," they do not mean that one group shall triumph over another. They mean that "black and white *together*, we shall overcome"—we shall overcome the hatred and prejudice which have blighted the American dream; we shall overcome the poverty and injustice which have crushed the hopes of so many in our country; we shall overcome the shame of a nation that has betrayed its own ideals.

Together we go forward. With God's help, "deep in my heart, I do believe, we shall overcome some day."

38

The Dilemma of Vietnam
June 10, 1966

All members of the American clergy must have agonized over the American in-
volvement in Vietnam during the late 1960s. And whatever their own private
position on the issue might have been, a second question was whether they had
the right—or the obligation—to express that view from the pulpit. The relation-
ship between religion and politics was fluid during this tumultuous period; just
as it was tested and clarified in the context of the civil rights movement, so did
the Vietnam War push sensitive religious leaders to articulate, for themselves
and for others, positions they might not have imagined a few years before.

As we have seen, Saperstein's position on war shifted dramatically over the
years—from a fervent pacifism in the 1930s to support of the war against Nazi
Germany after 1939 to active participation in the American war effort as a
chaplain, enthusiastic endorsement of Israel's battle for survival in 1948, and a
willingness to return to uniform, if necessary, to combat militant communism in
Korea. The patriotic identification with the United States and pride in the
American Army uniform continued well into the 1960s. But Vietnam raised un-
easy questions once more. The introduction to the sermon expresses, perhaps
instinctively, an old rhetorical topos of late medieval Jewish preaching: the rea-
sons why it might have seemed preferable to remain silent, outweighed by the
factors that compel the preacher to speak.

The opposition was based not on a renewed pacifism, but on an attempt to
define a kind of "just war" ethic. This was formulated by appeal to the state-
ment from the Mishnah Avot that "the world is founded on three things, truth,
justice, and peace." The three Hebrew words, emet, din, shalom, were inscribed
on the doors of the ark in the Lynbrook sanctuary, together with the accompa-
nying symbols: an open book, a set of scales, and a dove. This provided both a
structure for the sermon and a strong rhetorical foundation, appealing to the
self-image of the congregation. These are values we all treasure, the argument

implies; we look at them every time we worship. American involvement in the war undermines all three.

THIS IS ONE OF THE MOST DIFFICULT SERMONS I have ever grappled with. For many months, the dilemma of Vietnam has troubled my days and tormented my nights. Again and again I have planned to preach on it. Each time I have backed away—not because of fear but because of confusion in the face of the complexity of the problem. Finally, as I approach the end of the preaching season, in simple self-respect, I felt compelled to confront the problem.

There are those who maintain that clergymen have no right to pass judgment on specific problems like this. They maintain that it is the function of the religious leader to proclaim the ideal—in this case, to talk about the importance of peace—but to leave practical solutions to the political leaders. This position is based on an assumption that ideals are simple, but reality is complex. To deal with it, you must have specialized information. The religious leader knows no more than any concerned layman. How, then, can he speak with authority?

I recognize the pertinence of this criticism, but not its validity. Granted that there is a danger of the lack of political expertise, and an ignorance of inside information that may be available to responsible public officials. If we are to say that this means we must leave all decisions to public officials, and accept them passively, the very foundation of democracy is undermined. The rabbi speaks with authority on moral issues. And problems as vital as Vietnam cannot be separated from moral issues. Granted that these moral issues must be weighed in the arena of reality. I would rather take my chance on being unrealistic than to abrogate my responsibility as a moral and spiritual leader.

There are those who would denounce any criticism on Vietnam—in view of the fact that our nation is fighting a war there, though undeclared—as unpatriotic. Anyone who speaks negatively about government policy is undermining our war effort, betraying our men who are fighting and dying in the jungles, they contend. I take issue with this very strongly. If we were to accept this thesis, all dissenting opinion would be precluded. We would have a nation of moral robots. We would lose more than we would gain. I do not agree with those who burn their draft cards or try to obstruct troop convoys. But I admire the courage and defend the right of those who dare to speak out in criticism often at great sacrifice to themselves.

In doing so they have good precedent. In 1848, Abraham Lincoln made a powerful attack in the House of Representatives upon the Mexican War then in progress as being unnecessary and unjust.[1] In a recent issue of the "Saturday Review of Literature," Theodore Sorenson pointed out that our country "is not so rich in intellectual and inspiration leadership, or so certain of its course in the

---

1. For Lincoln's anti-war speech, delivered on January 12, 1848 soon after his arrival as a freshman Representative from Illinois, see Carl Sandburg, *Abraham Lincoln: The Prairie Years* and *The War Years* (New York: Harcourt Brace, 1954), 95–96.

world . . . that it can afford the suppression of any thoughtful view. . . . We cannot afford to listen merely to the spokesmen for the state and the status quo."[2]

Before I continue, let me make clear that I do not condemn our national
leaders as warmongers. I do not divide people between hawks and doves as
though it were a division between black and white. I can appreciate the agonizing position of those who are responsible for policy decisions. I know they want
peace even as all of us want peace. But I am convinced that however they may
speak in terms of humanitarian ideals, and human freedom, and moral commitments, these are merely rationalizations.

Our foreign policy in Vietnam is dominated by one basic objective: the con-
tainment of communism. To achieve this objective, our leaders are willing to
subordinate every other consideration. It is my contention that the policy we are
following may or may not stop communism. I am very doubtful about it myself.
But it definitely is violating moral principles. And this, I am convinced, will—if
allowed to continue—destroy our soul and, in the final analysis, weaken rather
than strengthen our position in the world.

What are the moral considerations with which we should be concerned in
Vietnam? We are gathered here in our Temple. We take pride in it and avow
allegiance to the principles for which it stands. Here on our ark is a symbolic
representation of a famous Rabbinic passage: "The world endures by three
things: truth, justice and peace," *emes, din ve-sholom*.[3] I think our Vietnam policy is destroying all three of them.

In any critical international situation, **truth** is invariably the first victim. I
would like to feel that although communist governments feed their people
propaganda and distort the facts, our government gives us the truth in the spirit
of democracy. Unfortunately, the record of recent years does not warrant this
assumption. I could cite innumerable examples as evidence. Remember a few
years ago: Powers and the U-2 incident. Our officials were caught in a trap and
were exposed in one lie after another.[4]

In April 1965, congressional leaders were called to an emergency meeting at
the White House and told that the revolution in the Dominican Republic was out
of control, that American lives were in danger and Marines were being landed to
protect them. Four months later, the Senate Foreign Relations Committee revealed that the major reason for our action was our determination to defeat the

2. Theodore C. Sorenson, former special assistant and counsel to President Kennedy,
in "The New and Future Clergy," *Saturday Review*, April 30, 1966, 24 (an editorial). A
similar position had been expressed by Sorenson in "The Rate of Dissent," an editorial in
the April 2, 1966 issue, his first contribution as a *Saturday Review* Editor-at-Large.

3. M. Avot 1, 18.

4. Francis Gary Powers was shot down over Soviet territory on May 1, 1960. After
the incident was announced by Khrushchev on May 5, Powers was first identified by the
Americans as the pilot of a NASA weather observation plane, then the State Department
admitted it was an intelligence plane but denied that Washington had authorized a flight
across the Soviet border. Eventually, after Powers confessed, the U.S. Government admitted that President Eisenhower had authorized the policy of U-2 overflights.

rebel forces whose victory seemed imminent.[5] When Arthur Schlesinger was asked last Thanksgiving by the *New York Times* why his published account of the Bay of Pigs incident contradicted the story he had given the press at the time as the official government spokesman, he remarked simply that he had lied.[6]

The facts that we are fed about our purposes in Vietnam and about the progress of the war are equally suspect. David Halberstam was awarded a Pulitzer Prize for his coverage of Vietnam as a correspondent for the *New York Times*. In the January 1965 issue of "Commentary," he points out the efforts of our government to present an over-optimistic picture of the war—and the obstacles placed in the way of those who wanted to present the facts.[7]

Coupled with the stifling of truth is the confusion of moral issues [leading to the abandoning of **justice**]. If you were to listen to our official statements, it would seem that we are in Vietnam at the request of the people of Vietnam and in fulfillment of a sacred obligation we have made to them. We are concerned with protecting them from communist aggression, with defending their liberty and their right to self-determination.

Thus it is that the realists talk in terms of moral values. And so we who are moralists and idealists must talk in terms of the real situation. What are the facts? First, a little historical background. I am convinced that Ho Chi Minh, leader of North Vietnam, is a communist. But his program is not one of simple communist aggression. He has been leading a national revolution since the beginning of World War II. At that time, we were glad to help him in his resistance against the Japanese.[8]

After the war, he fought the French in their effort to reestablish their colonial empire. Now we turned around and poured more than a billion dollars of military aid to the French before they were ignominiously forced out of the area.[9] In 1954, the Geneva Agreements were reached dividing Vietnam temporarily into two sections, providing for free elections in 1956. Ho Chi Minh at that time

---

5. Both considerations—protecting the lives of Americans in the Dominican Republic and concern that the rebels might succeed in bringing a communist-sympathizing government to power—were communicated to Washington in the period leading to American intervention, but only the first was mentioned by President Johnson in his television announcement on April 28, 1965, shortly after he had briefed leaders of Congress. The Senate Foreign Relations Committee opened its hearings on July 14, 1965. For different assessments of American motivations, see Abraham Lowenthal, *The Dominican Intervention* (Cambridge: Harvard University Press, 1972), 132–36.

6. For the "published account," see Arthur M. Schlesinger, Jr., *A Thousand Days* (Boston: Houghton Mifflin, 1965), 232–97.

7. David Halberstam, "Getting the Story in Vietnam," *Commentary* 39 (January 1965): 30–34. "Those who wanted to present the facts" refers to the press corps in Saigon.

8. "Some scholars have suggested that Ho's revolutionary army even received financial and military support from the OSS and that he himself was an 'official agent.'" *Encyclopedia of the Vietnam War*, ed. Spencer C. Tucker, 3 vols. (Santa Barbara: ABC-CLIO, Inc., 1998), 1:287.

9. Following their defeat at Dien Bien Phu in May 1954.

could have taken over all of North and South Vietnam. He accepted the agreement, however. We are not a signatory to that agreement, but we gave our pledge that we would not interfere or hinder the right of self-determination.

A year later we took over the throne of colonialism left vacant by the French. It was we who set up Diem as a puppet ruler. It was we who encouraged him to deny the national elections because we were convinced that the party of Ho Chi Minh would have won them, in violation of the central condition of the agreement.[10] Since the murder of Diem, we have set up a succession of nine different rulers—not one of whom really represented the South Vietnamese. The lack of enthusiasm of the South Vietnamese for the war is quite apparent. In the last six months, some 100,000 of them have deserted.[11]

In the hope of forestalling communism, we seem to have a penchant for giving our support to anti-democratic leaders here as in other areas. We like to think of ourselves as the Sir Galahad of modern history—the knight in shining armor. Let us not be surprised, however, if we present a different image in the eyes of many of the people in the countries we are aiding. In the newly emancipated nations, this tendency lends an aura of credence to the communist propaganda that we are the Al Capone, the capitalist [gangster and] exploiter.

Thirdly, the ideal of our faith has always been **peace**. I do not speak now as a pacifist. I once was—between the two world wars. I faced that problem when I enlisted as a chaplain. I believe that there are occasions when one must fight against evil. If another Hitler should arise, I would want to be among those who stand up and fight to destroy him and the evil he would represent. I recall now a fascinating debate in Lowndes Country, Alabama, between an elderly, blind Negro preacher and my friend, Stokely Carmichael—now the national chairman of SNCC—on non-violence.[12] Stokely, now one of the most militant of Negro civil rights leaders, was then an advocate of non-violence. I was on the other side, believing that there are times when violence is necessary.

This is in accordance with Jewish tradition, as applied to war. That tradition distinguished between *Milchemet reshut*—a war of choice—and *Milchemet mitzvah*—a war of obligation. Participation in the first depended upon [the Sanhedrin's] judgment. In the second, it was a duty.[13] The war against Hitler was a *Milchemet mitzvah*. I cannot place the war in Vietnam in the same category.

---

10. Ngo Dinh Diem was appointed Prime Minister in June of 1954, and declared himself President of the Republic of Vietnam on October 26, 1955. He served in this capacity until, following a successful coup on November 1, 1963, he was killed while attempting to flee the country. "The agreement" refers back to the Geneva Accords of 1954.

11. From the ARVN (the Army of the Republic of Vietnam).

12. The blind preacher is mentioned in "On the Freedom Trail in Alabama" above; also also the reference to this debate in "An American Tragedy," below. For Saperstein's continued support of SNCC in 1966 despite Carmichael's "Black Power" policy, see Arthur Hertzberg, *The Jews in America* (New York: Simon and Schuster, 1989), 366.

13. The distinction between these two categories of war is based on Mishnah Sotah 8,7; B. Sotah 44b; Maimonides, *Mishneh Torah*, "Laws of Kings" 5, 1–2. It was argued at length by Jews during this period; see, for example, the essays in *Judaism and World Peace: Focus Viet Nam* (New York: Synagogue Council of America, 1966).

Our national leaders believe that the successful conduct of this war is the best way of bringing peace. I am not a military expert, but most of the experts are in agreement that this war cannot be won at all, or at best will take many years. We started out giving material and military counsel, we proceeded to send token combat troops, and we have escalated it until we now have almost 300,000 fighting men in Vietnam. The prediction is that we will need 200,000 more to achieve our objective of closing off the North Vietnamese border.

Predictions are that within a year we will have a million men under arms. Despite our regular claims of destruction of more and more North Vietnamese, they seem to be gaining in strength. One day the reports will show a great victory, a couple of months later the same area is being fought in again. Escalation and bombing seems to drive the South Vietnamese to the Viet Cong, the Viet Cong to the North Vietnamese, and the North Vietnamese to Communist China. I cannot see this as a way to achieve peace.

True we have offered to negotiate. I believe we were sincere. But our offer has too often been bound up with impossible conditions. On several occasions Hanoi also has made overtures to us for discussion and negotiation. In each case, they have been ignored or refused. Incidentally, this information was never stressed in the American press, but is based on reports in the "Manchester Guardian," a usually reliable news source.

In the meantime, the fighting goes on and we become more and more accustomed to it. In 1937, the Germans committed the first act of saturation bombing in Spain. The world reacted in horror, and Picasso portrayed the nightmare in his great mural.[14] Last night, there was a program showing documentaries of the war in Poland. Hitler ironically announced, "Germans do not fight women and children." Gradually we became accustomed to it. We took Hiroshima and Nagasaki in stride. And now we take it for granted in Vietnam. It is this *dehumanization* that brings over us the threatening cloud of the possibility of nuclear warfare.

These are the moral principles at stake. And this is the dilemma of Vietnam: what shall we do? Let me state it very briefly. We cannot reverse history. We cannot end the fighting and pull out. We can, however, end the bombing. We can reverse the process of escalation. We can continue to seek to negotiate with everybody concerned, without exceptions. We can prepare to withdraw our troops and bases if and when they can be replaced by adequate international forces. We can utilize our vast economic resources for fighting *not people, but poverty and injustice*, in our own country and all over the world. We can strengthen the United Nations as the international medium through which tyranny shall be thwarted and international reconciliation brought about.

In the Bible reading for this week,[15] we read of the spies who returned to report on the land of Canaan. They saw the same things, but they came back with two different reports. The realists were in the majority, but if their advice

---

14. "Guernica."
15. From the lesson "*Shalah*" (Numbers 13–15).

had been followed, we would not be here now. The idealists were few, but theirs was the hope of the future. So may it be in our day.[16]

---

16. For a more extensive homiletical treatment and application of this biblical motif, see "Keepers of the Keys," below.

39

A Great Miracle Happened There
September 8, 1967

Temple Emanu-El arranged an eight-month sabbatical leave for Saperstein be-
ginning January 1, 1967. The first two months were spent in travel, including a
first visit to countries in Southeast Asia. From March to June the Sapersteins
were in Jerusalem, where they lived at the Hebrew Union College building and
studied Hebrew and archaeology. This was before the HUC–JIR required all
students to spend their first year in Israel, but there was a group of rabbinical
students who were there on leave. The College, headed then by the renowned
archaeologist Nelson Glueck, also hosted a number of archaeologists and Bibli-
cal scholars from American universities.

As the tension between Israel and its Arab neighbors mounted in the second
half of May, Saperstein's attitude toward the American academics began to
sour. In a private letter dated May 21, he wrote,

> *If a crisis comes, I think most of the youngsters and certainly the Christian*
> *professors around here will take off. It's understandable but a little disap-*
> *pointing. [We] have decided that if things break, we're sticking around.*
> *Don't know what we can do (certainly they won't need chaplains), but there*
> *should be some way we can be helpful. Apparently most of the world would*
> *sit by complacently as they did for the six million. There are strange psy-*
> *chological forces at work here. Most educated non-Jews would disclaim*
> *anti-Semitism but few of them would grieve if Israel were wiped out. I must*
> *admit that the majority of the Christian fellows here are strongly pro-Arab.*
> *I'm still waiting for one of them to utter a word of criticism of anything the*
> *Arabs do. Living with them, [we] have come to realize more strongly than*
> *ever the great difference there is in the way Christians and Jews think and*
> *feel.*

That sense of disillusion and frustration, vulnerability and isolation, communicated in at least one sermon following his return to Lynbrook in September, would color some of the positions taken in the 1970s.

This was not, however, the message he brought in his "Welcome Home Service." Here the tone was entirely upbeat, emphasizing the extraordinary sense of deliverance from peril that made all who experienced it sense a kind of providential presence, subsumed under the organizing theme of "miracle." The events of the Six-Day War were, of course, known to all in the audience. But this was the first time most of them would have heard these events from the perspective of their rabbi, who had been there, and was now sharing his sense of what it was like, and what it meant. More than thirty years later, the heartfelt praises of the Israeli population, its unity and idealism before, during, and after the war, and the negative depictions of the Jordanians and Egyptians, seem curiously distant. This makes it all the more important to appreciate how they evoke the transforming exhilaration of a unique moment in modern Jewish history.

BARUCH *[ATAH ADONAI, ELOHEYNU MELECH HA-OLAM]* shehechyanu *[ve-kiymanu ve-higiyanu la-zeman ha-zeh.* Blessed are You, O Lord our God, King of the universe, who has] kept us alive, watched over us, and brought us to the joyous reunion.[1]

It is so good to be back. Our sabbatical year has been for both Marcia and myself a wonderful, inspiring, unforgettable experience. Yet for eight months, I have been looking forward to this hour, when once again I might stand in this pulpit. For this, in a very real sense, is my life. Perhaps I should warn you, however, that sabbaticals get to be a habit. I waited thirty-four years for this, and now I give formal notice that thirty-four years from now, I shall expect another.

It is significant that in the observances of our faith, there is only one festival bound up specifically with military victory. That is the festival of Chanukah, where the motto was formulated, *nes gadol hayah sham* ["a great miracle happened there"]. The miracle was twofold: first, in triumph on the field of battle against crushing odds, and—more important—in the ultimate triumph of spiritual values: "Not by might nor by power but by my spirit, saith the Lord" (Zech. 4:6).

Ours is a sophisticated generation. The concept of miracles embarrasses us. We associate it with an ancient, pre-scientific era. And yet I cannot help recalling a statement by the first president of Israel, Dr. Chaim Weizmann, a renowned scientist, who said, "A good Jew must believe in miracles if he is a realist."[2] It is my sincere conviction that Marcia and I were privileged to have par-

---

1. The words outside the brackets are what appear in the typescript, with dots of ellision; the full paragraph is what was said.

2. Compare the end of "Birth of a Nation," above. I have not found the exact source of this quotation; it may be a transformation of his witticism, "To be a Zionist it is not necessary to be mad, but it helps." See Amos Elon, *The Israelis: Founders and Sons* (New York: Holt, Rinehart & Winston, 1971), 139, 188.

ticipated in a modern miracle, surpassing in scope that of the days of the Macca-bees. We too have seen the soul of a people galvanized by circumstances into gallantry and welded into unity. We too have seen the triumph of the few over the many. We too have seen the ultimate victory of the spirit. We have seen Is-rael's war, and again I say, *nes gadol hayah sham.*

To properly understand this miracle, we must first see the war in its practical context. Here I must admit that, fortunately, I proved to be a very poor military analyst. With my experience as a combat army chaplain in World War II, I con-sidered myself something of a *mayvin* [expert] in military affairs. And I was not nearly as sanguine about an easy victory as many others were, or at least claim to have been. I knew Israel had a magnificent, well-motivated, well-trained army. But I was a realist. And I looked at the map. Anyone who has toured through Israel will recall how at almost every turn your guide would point out: Over there, within eyesight, almost within an arm's reach, is enemy territory.

On the map Israel was a tiny speck of some 8,600 square miles in a vast Arab world of a million and a half square miles. In population it had a little over two million Jews surrounded by a hundred million Arabs sworn to their destruc-tion. From Sinai airfields it was barely six minutes by plan to the very heart of Tel Aviv. I knew that for ten years the Soviet Union had been pouring into these Arab countries two billion dollars of the most modern military equipment. Fac-ing the firepower of modern weaponry, even in the hands of less-than-perfect soldiers, could (I was convinced) prove very costly.

Furthermore, we had been reading and hearing a great deal about the chang-ing spirit of the Israeli people. Truthfully, we thought we had seen evidence of it. The idealism and sacrificial spirit and dedication of the early days were gone. The people had become materialistic. Internal dissension was widespread. Moreover, one had merely to look around to realize that the majority of the Is-raeli population was now made up of Oriental Jews, many of whom in outward appearance seemed little different from the enemy they would be confronting on the field of battle.

I recognized the importance of skill, courage, and motivation. I was con-vinced that Israel could beat any one or perhaps two of the Arab countries. But when I saw it would have to be a multi-front war, and when I realized that Israel would have to go it alone, I wasn't so sure. I was convinced that only a miracle could bring victory. And I did not believe in miracles. It was in that framework that Marcia and I decided that, despite the urging of the American consul, we had to stay. As I wrote in a letter to some of you, Jews have been running long enough. In Israel, they stand. And if it was our *zechut*, our privilege, to be in Israel at precisely that moment, we would stand with them. But the miracle did happen.

The miracle was actually threefold. First, there was the period of crisis lead-ing up to the war. I must honestly say that this was the hardest of all. Tension grew from day to day. Each night one went to bed with apprehension, each morning one awakened with a start not knowing what the night had brought. I attended a press conference held by Abba Eban in which he explained that Israel was investing time in the hope that the nations of the world would guarantee its right of free navigation in international waters.[3] One reporter asked him, "How long will you wait?" He answered with the magnificent eloquence of which he is so uniquely capable, "I cannot give you an exact timetable, although it is inscribed on the tablets of my heart. But this I can tell you: it may be days, it may be weeks, but other denominations of time you can eliminate from your vocabulary."

Many thought that days or weeks were too much, that their leadership had betrayed them out of timidity, that by delay they had lost their chief hope: of catching the enemy off balance. There was a brief letdown in morale; as the situation deteriorated there was panic buying in all the food stores. And then something wonderful happened. As the prospect of life-and-death struggle became imminent and inescapable, the people changed. As many were mobilized, buses were fewer, service everywhere was poorer, people became considerate of each other. They didn't crowd on queues. The stopped their cars to give you a lift on the street. Political parties stopped carping at each other. The religious parties dropped the autopsy issue, which had become so acute it had actually led to physical violence.[4] There was a new sense of national unity.

The students of the Rabbi Kook Yeshiva were called up in the emergency on the night of the Sabbath. They asked their Rabbi [Zvi Yehudah Kook], son of the late Chief Rabbi [Abraham Isaac Kook], if they were permitted to go. He answered that this was *pikuah nefesh* [saving of life]. When human life was at stake, not only was it permissible to go, but they were permitted to carrying their *tefillin* with them on the Sabbath.[5] Up in Meron, one of the great Orthodox strongholds of Israel, where the tomb of Rabbi Shimon bar Yochai is venerated, the Rabbi called his students immediately after Sabbath morning services to work filling sandbags and digging trenches. These may seem like petty concessions. But to anyone who knows the Israeli scene, they are major developments.

---

3. Through the Egyptian-blockaded Strait of Tiran, providing access to the Israeli port of Eilat.

4. Autopsies had become a tinder-box issue in the first half of 1967, with Israeli rabbis (including the Chief Rabbinate), elderly American rabbis living in Israel, and the National Religious Party leading the campaign against the practice in Israeli hospitals. "By the late spring of 1967 the antiautopsy campaign had reached a fever pitch. Billboards urged the Orthodox to support to fight against autopsies. Pictures of dissected bodies and horror stories about the treatment given to bodies were circulated. Pathologists were threatened. Public prayers and fasts were held. At a meeting organized by the Committee for Safeguarding Human Finally a riot occurred and police were stoned. . . . Just as the controversy reached a boiling point, the battle over autopsies was suddenly suspended as problems of security, the Six-Day War, and its aftermath took national precedence." Norman Zucker, *The Coming Crisis in Israel* (Cambridge: MIT Press, 1973), 168–69.

5. I have not found reference to this specific decision of Rav Kook. But a few weeks before the outbreak of the war, when asked by his students if it was permissible to view the military parade in Jerusalem scheduled for Israel Independence Day, he is reported to have said, "Of course; know that this is the army of Israel that will liberate the Land of Israel." Ian Lustick, *For the Land and the Lord* (New York: Council on Foreign Relations, 1988), 36.

That week Marcia and I went to the Magen David Adom to give blood. We were numbers 216 and 217 and had to wait several hours. As we looked around, we saw the whole cross-section of Israel's population: soldiers, yeshiva *bochurim* [students], old and young, Sephardim and Ashkenazim—all waiting to give their blood. And looking back, I say, *nes gadol hayah sham*, "a great miracle happened there."[6]

Then came the actual war. We had been in Ramat Gan, near Tel Aviv, on Sunday evening, where Marcia spoke to the Sisterhood of the congregation where I had been preaching in the absence of its rabbi, who was serving as a gunner on a tank near the border of Sinai. We got home about 2:30 in the morning. Monday morning, one of those things happened which can be designated as "only Israel." On Sunday, the newspapers announced the signals in case of an air raid. A wavering signal on the siren was an alert; it meant take cover. A long, straight signal would be the all clear. About 8 o'clock we were awakened by an all-clear signal. Someone had pushed the wrong button. We looked out, people were going about their business, busses were running, we assumed it was just a test. So I went to the school where I was serving as a volunteer English teacher. My first class that morning was scheduled to read—of all books—*Little Women.* I reached school, and everything was strangely quiet—until I found the children in the air-raid shelter and was informed that the fighting had finally begun. On the radio, the final units were being called up by code names.

By the time I got home the fighting in Jerusalem had started. At first there was just desultory small arms fire. It became heavier during the afternoon, and by night the bombardment was in full swing.[7] We didn't go down to the shelters. We stayed up where we could see what was going on. Sleep that night was interrupted by the crackling of small arms, the whistling of mortars, the explosion of shells. The sky was lit up with tracer bullets and flares like a gigantic fireworks display. We listened to the radio, to the martial music that substituted for all programs between news broadcasts.

All week long we had been listening to the Jordanian radio. The Arabic broadcasts, translated for us by some of our Semitics scholars, screamed the call for the *jihad*, the holy war. "The hour has come. Our honor will be redeemed. Go forth to fight and kill for Allah. The enemy will be destroyed: men, women and children." The English broadcasts, intended for people like us, warned us to go home, threatening that otherwise we would have to accept our fate with all the others in Israel. During the first day of fighting, the Arab broadcasts pro-

---

6. For a discussion of the high level of morale and cooperation in Israel in the days leading up to and immediately following the outbreak of war (without, however, mentioning the role of the orthodox), see Walter Laqueur, *The Road to Jerusalem: The Origins of the Arab-Israeli Conflict, 1967* (New York: Macmillan, 1968), 128–33; Golda Meir, *My Life* (New York: Putnam's Sons, 1975), 359–60. Sachar emphasizes a "grim mood . . . of impatience and frustration" (631).

7. Namely, the bombardment of Israeli west Jerusalem by Jordanian forces in east Jerusalem.

claimed one victory after another. They were on the way to Tel Aviv. Haifa was in flames. They had downed a hundred Israeli planes. They had taken Mt. Scopus. They were advancing on every front. In the meantime, the Israeli radio gave only routine, conservative reports. We listened, wondering what was really happening. Then, in the middle of the night, came the electrifying news. We had caught the Arab Air Forces on the ground, and in the first few hours of fighting had broken the back of their air power, destroying more than 300 planes. Our forces were on the way to Gaza, and already deep in Sinai. Then the avalanche of victory swept on: on the Egyptian front, the Jordanian front, the Syrian front. You who were glued to the television know the story as well as I do.

What brought about this astounding victory, which has virtually no parallel in all of military history? Despite its speed and scope, wars are never easy, and victory never comes cheap. In many places there was bitter fighting. Lives were lost and blood was spilled. Part of the explanation lies in the remarkable skill, daring and dedication of the Israeli forces and their leadership. It is instructive to compare the low percentage of officer casualties among the Arabs as against the high percentage, more than one-third, of officer casualties for the Israelis. They took amazing risks. When you cut through and around an enemy and attack him from the rear you've got to carry it through, because if you can't you have no place to retreat. Remarkably, despite the danger, everyone wanted to get into the battle. Old men wept because they volunteered as veterans and were told they could serve better staying home. On our custodial staff [at the Hebrew Union College] was a young, sweet Yemenite boy, who postponed his wedding because of the crisis. He was a paratrooper and each day he pleaded with the authorities to call him up. They told him to bide his time. The day he was called and he came to say good-bye, his face was radiant—he would be able to defend his country. I have never seen this kind of spirit anywhere else.

Part of the explanation lies in the ineptitude of the Arabs. You all know how the [Egyptian] Air Force was caught napping when the Israeli planes flew out to sea and came in from behind. At Shechem [on the West Bank], the Israelis circled around and came down from the north. The Jordanian tanks were waiting for them facing south. Civilians welcomed the Israelis with cheers, thinking they were reinforcements from Iraq. In the Sinai desert, the Egyptians dug their tanks in, losing the mobility that is the chief virtue of the tank as a weapon, and transforming it into a fixed gun emplacement. The Saudi Arabians sent up eight jet planes to reinforce the Egyptians in Sinai. They had not learned that the airfield was already taken, and they were guided in by an Arabic-speaking Israeli, and then captured.

But there was something else, something ineffable and mysterious, which brought about the coincidence and effectiveness of all these factors. After all the military analysis is over, only the concept of miracle can explain what happened. And so again I say, *nes gadol hayah sham.*

But the greatest miracle of all was the fact that Israel fought and won a war without being corrupted by it. Israel remains a non-military nation, and its army remains an army of civilians. They don't look like soldiers, they don't act like soldiers; they only fight like soldiers. A few days before the fighting began, we visited the great Israel Museum in Jerusalem. There were hundreds of soldiers in combat uniform going through, examining the archaeological exhibits. Where but in Israel, where but among Jews, would soldiers on the eve of battle use their few hours of freedom to visit an archaeological museum? That week, along the main streets of Jerusalem, I noticed people building booths. I asked what they were for, expecting that they must have something to do with recruitment and preparations for the war. I was told that they were for the annual book fair, always held at that time of the year. Where but in Israel, among Jews, would a people facing the crisis of life and death concern itself with books?

Saturday night, while the last fighting was still going on at the Syrian front, a great victory celebration was held. It took the form of a concert. As we came into the magnificent concert hall, we walked past the billets of soldiers, bivouacked on the floor. Some were already asleep. Many of those who were awake came and stood in back to hear this music. The gifted Indian conductor Zubin Mehta started with "Hatikvah." With the first strains, he turned to the audience and, like magic, every voice swelled into a magnificent chorus. I have never heard "Hatikvah" sung like that. Where but in Israel, among Jews, would a victory be celebrated by an orchestral concert?[8]

On that wonderful Wednesday, when the Old City was taken, people poured out into the streets [of Jerusalem]. We went to the Mandelbaum Gate[9] and saw the military cars carrying the Ashkenazi Chief Rabbi Unterman and the Sephardic Chief Rabbi Nissim, carrying a Torah in the same automobile—truly this seemed like *Meshiach zeiten* [messianic times]—and leading government officials passed through the cheering crowds. They were on their way to the Western Wall. This—not booty, not territory, not vengeance—this was the ultimate meaning of the victory to the people in Israel. That day, everybody greeted each other with the phrase *Chag Sameach*, "happy holiday," as thought it were a religious festival. Never once did I hear anyone gloating over the defeat of the enemy.

Never once did I hear people speak exultantly of revenge in the light of their overwhelming victory. Instead, even the secular Israelis would say, "How privileged we are that our generation has seen the fulfillment of a two-thousand-year-old prayer. What a wonderful thing it is that at least Jerusalem is united, that we can visit the *Kotel ha-Ma'aravi*, the Western Wall, and all the other sacred places." A people that can fight and win and not lose its sense of values, a people that even in war can place religious ideals above all else, is a great people. That this could happen in our day justifies saying once again, *nes gadol hayah sham*, a great miracle happened there.

---

8. On this Saturday night concert, featuring as soloists Daniel Barenboim and Jacqueline du Pré, see Martin Gilbert, *Jerusalem in the Twentieth Century* (New York: John Wiley & Sons, 1996), 292–93.

9. This had served as the checkpoint for passage between east and west Jerusalem during the period when east Jerusalem was under Jordanian control.

But miracles in Jewish life are not the repudiation of human responsibility. They happen only to people who are worthy of them, and they impose responsibilities on those who have benefited by them. The modern miracles of this victory were made possible because Israel had prepared for it—not merely by nineteen years of statehood, but by 4,000 years of love for a land and commitment to an ideal. After the victory of Chanukah, it was decreed that we should kindle lights, so that we might never forget the miracles of the Maccabees. We too should kindle lights in our hearts: to remember the valor of our people and the glory of our faith. We who serve that faith have a role to play as important as that of the soldiers who fought on the battlefields. May the memory of these miracles inspire us all to dedicate ourselves anew to our people and to our heritage.

40

An American Tragedy
April 5, 1968

The assassination of President Kennedy occurred around lunchtime on a Friday, leaving little time to prepare a formal sermon in response to the psychological trauma of that event. The assassination of the Reverend Martin Luther King, Jr., coming on a Thursday night, left all of Friday—the day Saperstein generally devoted to preparing his Friday evening sermon—to formulate some reaction to the devastating shock and the almost paralyzing grief following the news that once again one of America's most gifted and inspiring leaders had been brutally cut down in his prime. As on the Friday night of November 23, 1963, Jews thronged to synagogues to be together, to vent inchoate feelings in rituals of mourning, to seek an articulation of what it all meant for them.

Not surprisingly, Saperstein drew from the personal experience we have encountered in two previous sermons, describing the "March on Washington" in August 1963 and the voter registration work in Alabama during the summer of 1965. It is a personal statement, of the kind that relies for its effectiveness upon bonds long established between rabbi and congregants, evoking experiences they may recall having heard recounted, now shared in a context where the optimism of the past has become painfully problematic. There is also an element of criticism: at one point, after asserting that many bigots in the South share the blame for this murder, the preacher suggests that there are those in the North, indeed in his own congregation, who harbor prejudice and share in the responsibility. Characteristically, however, the sermon turns to a note of comfort and reaffirmation of hope, in the theme that ideals and dreams transcend the limitations of a single human life, and can be perpetuated by others who continue their work.

I FELT COMPELLED TO CHANGE THE THEME OF MY SERMON TONIGHT. I had planned to talk on "The Passover Plot," a book dealing with a great tragedy that occurred in the land of Palestine almost 2,000 years ago.[1] Instead I shall speak of an American tragedy, which occurred in our land in the city of Memphis, Tennessee, last night—the murder of the Reverend Martin Luther King. I speak with shame and with sorrow, yet with hope.

I say first that I speak with shame. I want to be proud of my country. I like to think of America as symbolized by the Statue of Liberty, proclaiming, "Give me your tired, your poor, your huddled masses yearning to breathe free."[2] I like to think of America as symbolized by Abraham Lincoln's "With malice towards none, with charity for all, with firmness in the right as God gives us to see the right, let us strive on to finish the work we are in."[3] I like to think of America as that great outpouring of people of all religions and all races who gathered in Washington in the famous March in 1963 to affirm their dedication to the cause of human rights, human freedom, and human dignity.[4] This is the America I love.

But there is another America that we do not like to acknowledge, but the reality of which forces itself upon us. What is it in America that makes for these outbursts of violence that fly in the face of all reason and negate the spirit of humanity? No monarch in England has died by violence in many centuries. In our national history of less than two hundred years, how many Presidents have died at the hands of assassins? We speak of America as the land of "liberty and justice for all." How many Americans, white and black, who stood up to make these ideals real have died at the hands of brutal bigots? With shame for my country, I add to their roster the name of Martin Luther King.

True, you may say that these acts are committed by individuals with perverted minds. But there must be something in the climate of our country of our country that encourages this kind of brutal, violent destruction. It was not only the hand of Lee Harvey Oswald that assassinated President Kennedy. It was the spirit of hatred and bigotry, which seethed through Dallas and other cities of our country, that gave impetus to that historic crime. It was not the sick mind of an unbalanced racist that conceived the murder of Dr. King. It was the deep, sometimes unspoken feeling on the part of many, not only in the South but in the North as well, which, however camouflaged, resents the liberation and the equality of their dark-skinned fellow citizens.

---

1. Hugh J. Schonfield, *The Passover Plot: New Light on the History of Jesus* (New York: Bernard Geis Associates, 1965), a provocative and controversial book arguing that Jesus contrived to be arrested and crucified, planning to fake his "death" so that he would be "resurrected" in fulfillment of messianic prophecy.

2. Compare the beginning of "I Lift My Lamp" from 1952, above.

3. Abraham Lincoln, Second Inaugural Address, now readily accessible in William Safire, *Great Speeches in History* (New York: W. W. Norton, 1992), 441.

4. See above, "The American Dream, In Color," 1963.

When we were down in Selma, Alabama in the summer of 1965,[5] we saw this hatred and this lust for violence in the eyes of the men who followed our car with shotguns in the back window of theirs—one of them the man who barely a week later was to commit the cowardly murder of Jonathan Daniels, a brilliant, dedicated young seminary student, who was riding with us that day. We heard it in the bitter hatred in the voices of those who tried to run us down as we walked across the driveway of a motel, and as we jumped aside shouted at us, "Nigger lovers!" I sense it in the people who tell me, "I don't have anything against Negroes, but if they move in, property values are going to go down," or "I'm for equal rights, but they want to get it too fast. They're not ready for it."[6]

That summer in 1965, Marcia and I were with Stokely Carmichael, working on voter registration in Lowndes County, the toughest country in the South. Stokely wanted me to meet an old Negro preacher, now completely blind. The old preacher insisted that the only thing a bigot would respect is a gun, and the only way to meet force is by force. Stokely defended non-violence and insisted that the only thing force would prove was who had the bigger gun. The old preacher turned to me and asked, "Rabbi, are you one of those non-violent fellows?" I answered that while I admired the moral idealism of non-violence, there are times when you must stand up and defend yourself, citing the example of the Jews in Israel. And so we argued the issue.

What made Stokely change? What turned him into the advocate of violence and Black Power? Did Jonathan Daniels' brutal murder have something to do with it? And if I were to meet him now, what could I say to him in the face of this tragic event?[7] When violence rears its head in the Negro world, is it not because we have failed to control or even to punish violence in the white world? It is part of the American tragedy that we kill our noblest sons.

I speak, secondly, with sorrow, because so much has been lost in the death of Martin Luther King. I heard him a number of times, but three stand out in my mind. One was at the Freedom March in Washington, to which I alluded before. There he spoke for the American people because his dream was the American dream. I heard him at the convention in 1963 at Chicago of the Union of American Hebrew Congregations, where he gave the main address at the closing banquet. He could have given a fatuous talk about brotherhood, and made everyone feel self-satisfied. Instead, he stirred the conscience of the thousand delegates there, reminding them that civil rights are human rights, that the struggle for them is everybody's struggle, and their denial is everybody's guilt.

And I remember his talk at the closing meeting of the Southern Christian Leadership Conference in Birmingham in August of 1965. We met Jon and Stokely there again. The audience there was largely Negro. Not long before, a bomb had been thrown into a church in Birmingham, and four little Negro children had

---

5. See above, "On the Freedom Trail in Alabama," 1965.

6. On this passage, see introduction.

7. Saperstein never did meet Carmichael again. He changed his name to Kwame Ture in 1968, and began to espouse militantly anti-Israel positions. He died on November 15, 1998.

been killed.[8] Only a week before, the Voter Registration Bill had been passed in Congress, and we were heady with victory. It was a perfect opportunity for demagoguery. King could have appealed to his audience, roused their emotions—they were ready to respond to anything he said. Instead, he spoke about Vietnam. He pointed out that it diverted effort from the home tasks, but more important that it was a denial of basic moral principles. He spoke not just as a Negro leader, but as an American prophet.

Martin Luther King dared to apply his religious principles literally. Some of the more extremist elements in the Negro world condemned him as an Uncle Tom, which to them is the ultimate insult. They felt he was not militant enough. The fact is that Martin Luther King was extremely militant. His non-violence did not mean passive acceptance of wrong. He stood up fearlessly against discrimination, against denial of civil rights—for freedom and equality. And in this struggle he was attacked, and beaten, and jailed—but he insisted for himself and for his followers that they would not strike back. And on this basis, he won battle after battle: the right to sit in buses wherever there was a seat, the right to sit at lunch counters, the right to use municipal swimming pools, the right to attend public theaters.

Like Gandhi in India, non-violence became an example of the power of the spirit. But it works only where the people against whom you stand have a basic sense of humanity. It seemed to be working here. But now this comes—and one wonders. It was such a meaningless, destructive act. Martin Luther King was the leader of the forces of moderation in the Negro world. Men like him inspired hope that our problems could be solved without bloodshed. If his murderer had wanted to stimulate rioting and violence, he could not have chosen a more effective way.

Dr. King did not hold back. In a tragic hour in our community some weeks ago, I used a story by the South African novelist, Olive Schreiner, called, "The Artist's Secret." It tells of an artist whose work was distinguished by a strange shade of red: lifelike, pulsating. Others tried to copy it, without success. He went on painting picture after picture, all with that same glowing color. As time passed, he became pale and weak, but he continued relentlessly at his work. One night, he died. His colleagues searched his studio, hoping they might find the mystery of the Artist's Secret, but they found nothing. The author concludes, "If they had examined his body, they would have seen beneath his heart a fresh wound, now closed in death. He had been painting with his life's blood."[9] Dr. Martin Luther King painted with his life's blood, giving his life for his cause. His loss is part of the tragedy and sorrow of America.

---

8. Saperstein misremembered the chronology here; the Birmingham church bombing occurred on Sunday, September 15, 1963 and he referred to it in his sermon following the assassination of President Kennedy.

9. This story was clearly a favorite with Saperstein, although he was careful not to over-use it. Compare the conclusion of his eulogy for Rabbi Stephen S. Wise above (1949), in which he refers back to his citing of the story in a tribute to his uncle and predecessor in Lynbrook, Rabbi Adolph Lasker (d. 1933).

But finally, I speak tonight with hope. Like Anne Frank, who wrote, "Despite everything, I still believe that man is good at heart,"[10] I say, despite everything, I still believe that the American dream is not a fantasy. It hurts so much to realize that he was only thirty-nine years old. Truly this is an example of an unfinished life. And yet is this not the destiny of all idealists? The great tasks of mankind are continuous—they must be carried on by generation after generation. Each advances the cause as far as time and strength permit, and then passes on, finding comfort in the realization that others will continue.

Was Abraham Lincoln's life unfinished?[11] He had spent four crucial years leading his country in a terrible war to preserve the Union and to emancipate the slaves. He died before he could see the fruits of his labors. Decades were to pass while his dream remained a dream. But whatever progress has been made in our day toward human equality is the continuation of the work of Abraham Lincoln.

Was the life of Theodor Herzl unfinished? For eight years, he burned himself out to gain a homeland for his people. He met bitter opposition from within and without. Finally he died [at the age of forty-four], his work unfinished. But the living State of Israel today is the continuation of the work of Theodor Herzl.

Was the life of Moses unfinished? Forty years he spent guiding his people in the wilderness. And then he died on the far shore, never privileged to set foot in the Promised Land, which was his goal. But wherever the Jewish faith and people live today, the spirit of Moses lives on with them.

Dr. King had a premonition of his death. Just the day before, in Memphis, he had said, "Like anybody, I would like to live a long life. [. . .] But I'm not concerned about that now. I just want to do God's will. And He's allowed me to go up to the mountaintop. And I've looked over and I've seen the promised land. I may not get there with you, but I want you to know tonight that we as a people will get to the promised land. [. . .] I'm not worried about anything. I'm not fearing any man. Mine eyes have seen the glory of the coming of the Lord."[12]

The ancient Rabbis understood it when they said, *Lo alecha hamelacha ligmor, ve-aincha ben chorin lehibatel mimenu*, "It is not for you to complete the task. Yet you are not free to desist from it."[13] He followed that principle. And so must we.[14] If we are sincere in our outrage and sorrow at this murder, we must

---

10. Perhaps the most widely quoted statement from Anne Frank's *Diary*.

11. At this point, Saperstein reprises the final sentences of the 1963 Kennedy sermon, developing the well-known examples of unfinished tasks in the lives of great figures in our history.

12. The full text of King's final sermon, to which this passage is the conclusion, is now conveniently accessible in *American Sermons: The Pilgrims to Martin Luther King Jr.* (New York: The Library of America, 1999), 876–85.

13. M. Avot 2, 16.

14. In the typescript, there is an arrow drawn at this point to the following paragraph clearly written after original text was completed:

I remember in Jerusalem, the day the Old City was liberated [June 7, 1967]. We had gone down to the Mandelbaum Gate to welcome the returning soldiers. Then we came back to our building [the Hebrew Union College]

vindicate this life so tragically cut short by strengthening the cause of human love, of brotherhood, of equality and justice, of peace and goodwill, which he served with such utter dedication. This is the task. And this is our hope. If this task is to be stifled and this hope crushed by a bullet from a gun, then all is lost and America is lost—and it will not be worth saving. His dream must be our dream, and we must make that dream real. Let us hear it in his own words once again, as I heard it on that unforgettable day in Washington almost five years ago:

(TAPE RECORDING—I HAVE A DREAM)[15]

---

where the border police had been quartered with us during the fighting. It was a great and historic hour. Suddenly we realized that the five of us, all Americans, wanted to proclaim that we shared this time of destiny as Americans. As we came up the steps, almost instinctively, we reached out, grasped each other's hands, and entered the building singing, "We Shall Overcome." A song of the Civil Rights Movement, first made popular by the followers of Dr. Martin Luther King. Somehow we felt that this was the spirit of America, the expression of the eternal hope and faith of our country.

(On the visit to the Mandelbaum Gate, compare the 1967 sermon, above, at n. 9). Coming as something of a diversion at this point in the present sermon, I doubt that this passage would have actually been said from the pulpit; I suspect rather that Saperstein would have used the tighter conclusion as originally written.

15. Written this way in the typescript. The sermon obviously ended with King's words.

41

Portnoy's Complaint, And Mine
March 28, 1969

Philip Roth's novel, Portnoy's Complaint, *was an immediate literary and cultural sensation. Published on February 21, 1969, it sold 420,000 copies in hardcover within a year. It was praised by some critics as "the book of the present decade and as an American masterwork in the tradition of* Huckleberry Finn*" (*Life Magazine, *February 7, 1969), or "the most important book of my generation" (*Washington Post, *February 10, 1969), and excoriated by others as immature, exhibitionist pornography, or a mere collection of gags. It evoked tumultuous feelings, and it was impossible to ignore.*

In deciding whether to discuss this book from the pulpit, rabbis who occasionally devoted sermons to popular and controversial books, films, or plays, faced a dilemma. On the one hand, its Jewish content was undeniably crucial to the book. It clearly raised issues of importance to American Jews in working out their relationship with gentile society. On the other hand, while few questioned the literary virtuosity of the author, some rabbis felt that the book's content and style made it inappropriate for serious discussion in the context of a worship service. Some were even reluctant to admit publicly that they had read it.

Announcing a sermon on Portnoy's Complaint *a little more than a month following its publication was thus to negotiate a potential mine field. As it was clearly of interest to his congregants, this was precisely the kind of challenge that Saperstein rarely avoided in his choice of sermon topics. In front of an unusually large assembly of Friday night worshippers—most of whom, he notes, had probably read the book—he set out his own "complaint" about the book, characteristically divided into three components. The treatment of the explicit sexuality and of the book's presentation of Judaism and Jewishness—two themes that come together in the protagonist's fixation upon gentile women as sexual objects—was not surprising. Less common in other reviews was a critique of the caricature of the Jewish mother, discussed in the second section of the sermon.*

Though it does not come out explicitly, Saperstein seems here to have been drawing from memories of his own mother, a very different personality from Mrs. Portnoy.

MY SERMON TONIGHT IS ABOUT THE MUCH DISCUSSED BOOK by Philip Roth, *Portnoy's Complaint*. Rarely has a book evoked such intense and contradictory responses. It immediately jumped to the top of the best-seller list. It was reviewed on the cover page of the Sunday *Times* Book Review Section. The author got his picture on the cover of the "Saturday Review." The book has been discussed in countless magazines, radio interview programs, coffee klatches and commuter trains.

I said that the reception was contradictory. Most of the general public who rushed to buy the book and read it reacted with the conclusion that it was disgusting, prurient, pornographic. Many people have told me they couldn't finish the book because it made them sick. On the other hand, many of the intellectuals have welcomed it with paeans of praise. One of the most gifted exponents of Jewish theology, Rabbi Eugene Borowitz, professor at the Hebrew Union College in New York, calls it "one of the great moral documents and Jewish books of our time."[1] I think I understand what both sides are getting at, but I disagree with them both.

It is true that the book contains language which has only recently become acceptable in mixed society and which most of us are still rather uncomfortable about using. I can remember some thirty-three years ago when one of the officers of our Sisterhood tore a page out of a book by Hemingway in our Temple Library because it contained one four letter word that she feared might contaminate the good ladies of our organization. And it is true that the book deals quite explicitly with sexual experience—from adolescent masturbation to mature impotence—with all kinds of usual and, shall I say, unusual forms in between. This kind of freedom of description has usually been associated with overt pornography.

Yet I do not maintain that this is a dirty book. Rather, it is a sad book. The central character, Alexander Portnoy is pretty much of a heel, but he is not really bad. He is rather a sick and pathetic man. The essence of his problem is expressed in a kind of foreword to the book which pretends to be a page from a medical manual in which a definition of his illness is given by Portnoy's psychiatrist, Dr. O. Spielvogel. "Portnoy's Complaint: a disorder in which strongly felt ethical and altruistic impulses are perpetually warring with extreme sexual longings, often of a perverse nature. However, neither fantasy nor act issues in genuine sexual gratification." This is serious business, even though the technique adopted by the author is humor and caricature.

---

1. Alan Cooper, in *Philip Roth and the Jews* (Albany: SUNY Press, 1996), p. 116, cites this phrase; the source seems to be Borowitz, "Portnoy's Complaint," *Dimensions* (Summer, 1969), p. 48–50. This was printed too late for it to be the source used in the sermon; Borowitz may have used the phrase in a talk given in the spring of 1969 heard by Saperstein or reported in the local media.

On the other hand, I cannot agree with those who acclaim this book as a great moral document. Borowitz insists that the book is obsessed with morality. I believe it is obsessed with a hatred of morality. Borowitz indicates that Portnoy sees his Jewishness as the central means to his humanization. I believe he sees his Jewishness as the denial of, the obstruction to, his humanization.

I assume that most of you have read the book or heard enough to know what it is about. For those of you who have not, let me summarize its content in a few sentences. Alexander Portnoy has been a brilliant child and a successful attorney, and he has now been appointed as Assistant Commissioner of Human Opportunity in New York City. But Portnoy is an unhappy man, and the book finds him on a psychiatrist's couch. The content of the book is a kind of psychoanalytical monologue, in which the patient probes into himself, dredges out of his memory experiences that have molded him, and cries out his resentment against those influences that he feels have stifled him and denied him happiness.

Three elements are central to the development of the story. The first is the emphasis on sexuality, the second is the excoriation of his mother, the third is the negation of the moral heritage of Judaism. It is a kind of combination of Kinsey and "How to Be a Jewish Mother," written in a spirit of self-hate.[2] And this is where I take issue with Roth and prepare to articulate what I shall call, "Saperstein's Complaint." In doing so, let me make it clear that I do not deny his right to write a book like this. Roth is a creative artist; this is apparently what he knew, what he felt, this is his set of hang-ups, and this is what he wrote about. Secondly, I have no justification or competence in denouncing this as a novel. Let me say that in my judgment, Roth is a brilliant writer, with flashes of amazing insight and uncanny craftsmanship. He also has a rich sense of humor—humor usually of mimicry and exaggeration, humor that is sometimes a little painful, what we might call "black humor," but unusually funny nevertheless. But in writing this book, Roth also had a message to convey. He has set himself up as a moralist and has made clear value judgments. And here, as a rabbi, I do claim some competence. It is on this basis that I take issue with him.

First, about Roth's emphasis on sexuality. I am not a Puritan about these things. There is no doubt in my mind that man is at least in part a sexual animal, and that the most saintly human beings are subject to sexual fantasies and impulses which would be out of place in a Sunday School textbook, and which we have long hesitated to admit. Roth's description of adolescent sexuality, for example, rings true to me. It reveals a marvelous recall of things that most people have forced themselves to forget. There is perhaps some therapeutic value in facing up to the truth.

But truth that is one-sided and distorted ceases to be the truth. And as Portnoy goes on through the years with sex as his central preoccupation, using women not out of love but out of hate, he ceases to represent the universal hu-

---

2. A reference to *Sexual Behavior in the Human Female*, by Alfred Kinsey's Institute for Sex Research (popularly known as "The Kinsey Report") (Philadelphia: Saunders, 1953), and Dan Greenburg's *How To Be a Jewish Mother: A Very Lovely Training Manual* (Los Angeles: Price, Stern, Sloan, 1965).

man condition, and he becomes instead an example of psychic illness. His gutter vocabulary may be a breakthrough in respectable literature, but deep down it is a mark of adolescent exhibitionism. You may say that Roth is simply describing his character, who is a sick man. But in describing any character, there are always other perspectives than the toilet-seat view of life. The creative artist, in painting a picture, does not need to put in every line that he sees. He suggests the total expression rather than depict it in every detail. Thomas Mann also wrote a book about a sick man, in his case, afflicted with tuberculosis, which he called *The Magic Mountain.* He did not need to describe in detail every appearance of the bloody sputum to make his point. Sex is part of life, but it is only part. If Roth wants to write about this, that is his privilege. But let him not pretend and let us not be conned into believing that he is giving us the full picture, the real picture, that he is "telling it like it is."

Secondly, I would like to complain about Roth's portrayal of Jewish motherhood. His mother represents all the things we have come to denounce in maternal influence. She is domineering, castrating, over-protective, self-pitying. She forces him as a child to eat by threatening him with a knife. She disciplines him by locking him out of the house. She makes him comply by pretending to withdraw her love. Even when he is grown up, she compels his reluctant loyalty by exploiting his sense of guilt.

It is obviously an exaggeration. But there is an element of truth in it, which all of us recognize. This has been the theme of innumerable Jewish jokes. But while Roth writes with barbed humor, it is more than a joke to him. It's deadly serious. As Portnoy says, "Doctor, this is my life, my only life, and I'm living it in the middle of a Jewish joke. I'm the son in the Jewish joke. Only it ain't no joke." He summarizes his attitude toward manipulating Jewish mothers in the story of Ronald Nimkin, the good boy who obeyed his mother and gave promise of becoming a concert pianist. When he hanged himself at the age of fourteen, he left a note, "Mrs. Blumenthal called. Please bring your mah-jongg rules to the game tonight." Obedient and devoted to the very end!

There may well be mothers like Portnoy's. What annoys me is Roth's intimation that this is the standard Jewish mother, that those who differed were the exceptions. Now I've known lots of Jewish mothers, in addition to my own. They were sacrificially and fiercely protective. They were inordinately concerned about the success of their offspring. But I am convinced that most of them were genuinely unselfish, and that their influence upon their sons was constructive rather than destructive.

My criticism of Jewish mothers like Portnoy's is different from Roth's. I am unhappy about them not because they were demanding but because they were not demanding of the right things. Not because they were "Jewish," but because they weren't Jewish enough. Portnoy condemns his parents for foisting Judaism on him. But there is no evidence that they even tried to transmit to him as he grew up any real understanding of his heritage, anything of the warmth and beauty of Jewish observance, any memories that would be inspiring and heartwarming. Portnoy—or rather we might say Roth—does not seem to be even aware of this failing. But this is Portnoy's mother's real failure. And here we have a lesson for all Jewish mothers.

My third complaint about Roth has to do with his Jewishness. I said it about *Goodbye, Columbus* and I say it now: Roth is a classic example of Jewish self-hate.[3] In this respect, I think he is typical of many Jewish intellectuals of our day, and it is a painful thing to admit. It evidences the failure of our Jewish education during the last generation. I see indications of it in some of our teenagers. They come up to me after a confirmation class, "You always say good things about the Jews. Why don't you say bad things once in a while."

I have never hesitated to say "bad things" about Jews when the facts indicated that this was called for. But whatever one can say about the behavior of Jews, I have great respect for the Jewish heritage. While Roth uses Jewish characters and draws on his Jewish experience, however, he has only contempt for Jewishness. He takes delight in condemning and mimicking a rabbi as a bore and a hypocrite. He describes Portnoy's rebellion against going to the synagogue on Rosh Hashanah at age fourteen with a kind of pride. He portrays Judaism as a set of meaningless, primitive laws, dealing mainly with *milchigs* and *fleishigs* [dairy and meat foods or dishes], which Portnoy insists were at the root of all his troubles.

He sees Judaism as a deterrent to the full and happy life. "To be bad, mother," Portnoy says on his psychiatrist's couch, "that's the real struggle. To be bad and enjoy it. That's what makes men of us boys, mother. Let's put the Id back in Yid."

He speaks about the hatred that Jews were supposedly taught to feel for non-Jews. "The first distinction I learned," Portnoy says, "was not night and day, but goyish and Jewish. Jew, Jew, Jew: It's coming out of my ears already. I happen also to be a human being." He speaks about the sense of moral superiority which was instilled in the hearts of Jewish children: "We were superior because we were Jewish." And he describes the longing in all swarthy Jewboys for those blond exotics called *shikses*.

I can only say that this is a reflection of something very wrong—not in Judaism but in Roth. Of course Judaism stands for moral values. But the concept of original sin did not emerge in Judaism. Judaism is basically a life-accepting, not life-denying, religion. One who wants to know the joy of life need not negate Judaism. Only one who wants to live without any standards at all must do so. The bitter point is that even if such a person succeeded, he would not know true joy.

---

3. On this theme it is interesting to compare a review published by Gershom Scholem, the great scholar of Jewish mysticism, in the Israeli newspaper *Haaretz* in late May, 1969 (several months after this sermon), and translated in the *CCAR Journal* of June, 1970), which includes the following: "Here in the center [of the book] stands the loathsome figure whom the anti-Semites have conjured in their imagination and portrayed in their literature, and a Jewish author, a highly gifted if perverted artist, offers all the slogans which for them are priceless. . . . This is the book for which all anti-Semites have been praying" (56–57). This point had already been made by Marie Syrkin, writing in *Midstream*, April, 1969; see Cooper, 109.

Like most of you, I was brought up in the same general kind of world as was Roth. I was taught to be loyal to Jews and Judaism, but I was never taught to hate the non-Jew. Sometimes they attacked us because we were Jews. When we had to, we fought in self-defense. But never to my recollection in hatred. Nor did I find myself lusting after blond-haired *shikses*. I'll admit in my fantasy there were some blondes among the others, and some of them may not have been Jewish. But it was not their "*shiksekeit*" ["Gentileness"] that made them desirable. It was just that they were pretty girls.

These are Saperstein's complaints: about Roth, and Portnoy, and preoccupation with sex, and un-Jewish Jewish mothers, and Jewish anti-Semites. But read the book yourself. Don't go to it to be shocked or titillated. Go to it rather to enjoy it, but at the same time to be critical. Its success is assured. I only hope that Roth will contribute some of the money he makes from it to worthwhile Jewish causes.[4]

---

4. According to an article in the February 7, 1969, issue of *Life*, Roth had earned "almost a million dollars prior to the first press run" from book club contracts and advances on paperback and movie rights. Quoted in Cooper, p. 106–7.

- 42 -

The Ordeal of Soviet Jewry
December 29, 1970
Hillcrest Jewish Center, Queens, New York

On the evening of December 24, 1970, news media in the United States were filled with the verdict in the "Leningrad Trials," which had begun on December 15. This was given front-page coverage in papers the following day, and the news of the subsequent days was largely dominated by a fire-storm of protest coming not only from American Jewish circles but from political figures and religious leaders throughout the world. The Soviet authorities explained the death sentence as appropriate in that the penal code defined the attempt to flee the country as an act of treason. But outside the Soviet Union, the two Jews sentenced to death became symbols of the "Refusenik": Soviet Jews who had re-discovered their Jewish identity, decided to try to leave the land of their birth for their ancestral homeland, were denied permission and subjected to harassment and persecution, and resolved never to accept the Government's decision. More than just persecution of Jews, this became an issue of the fundamental human right of free travel.

Saperstein, who had been elected to the presidency of the New York Board of Rabbis in February of 1970, was identified in the media as one of the "leaders" of New York Jewry. His call for a national day of prayer and protest on behalf of the defendants was carried by the general as well as the Jewish news services (AP, UPI, JTA). The address he delivered at a protest meeting held at a large Queens synagogue on the last night of Chanukah provided an opportunity for him to share with a wider audience material based on his three visits to the Soviet Union that had been incorporated into earlier sermons to the Lynbrook congregation.

FIVE DAYS AGO, AS WE WERE PREPARING TO KINDLE the third light of the Chanukah Menorah and the Christian world was preparing to celebrate the eve of Christmas, a Soviet Court in Leningrad announced its sentence on eleven defendants, nine of whom were Jewish, accused of attempting to hijack a Soviet airliner. Today, these men and women languish in a Soviet prison—two of them, Mark Dymshits and Eduard Kuznetsov, sentenced to death, the others to prison terms of four to fifteen years. Meanwhile, more than twenty other Soviet Jews, arrested on the same day, await trial for treason.[1]

It is this blatant desecration of justice that has brought us together tonight. There are some who may question the desperate urgency of our concern. In a world of turmoil and tragedy, they might say, where tens of thousands have met death in Vietnam, where hundreds of thousands dwell in the shadow of danger in Israel, where violence stalks the streets of America, why make such a fuss over a handful of individuals?

I think we would all agree that such an attitude denies a fundamental principle of the Jewish heritage. Justice and morality are not measured by numbers. To lose sight of the sanctity of human life, even in this age of general destructiveness, would be the ultimate tragedy. Judaism has taught us that "He who saves the life of even a single human being is as though he had saved the entire universe."[2] We are determined that no effort on our part will be too great to see that Dymshits and Kuznetsov shall not die.

But important though these individuals are in our eyes, our concern is not confined to them. Through centuries of survival in the face of persecution, of constant vulnerability to attack, we Jews have developed a sixth sense for danger. We recognize the threatening symptoms. We smell the foul odor of anti-Semitism. We have reason to suspect that the ground is being prepared for an all-out attack upon the Jews of the Soviet Union, and indirectly upon world Jewry.

The technique is an old one. In the Middle Ages, all that was necessary was to concoct a charge of desecration of the host or ritual murder. The prejudices of the populace were aroused and Jews were massacred. Thus a dual purpose was served: one, the financial resources of the Jews were confiscated, and two, the resentment of the people against their own bitter lot was diverted.[3]

The Nazis used this technique to great advantage. The Reichstag fire in February of 1933 was planned and executed by the Nazis themselves. The Communists were charged with the crime, and a terror-stricken country cravenly en-

---

1. See the extensive coverage in the *New York Times*, starting on December 25, 1970, through December 30, the day following the occasion of the sermon's delivery (summarized in *New York Times Index*, 1970, p. 1946.

2. M. Sanhedrin 4,5; compare the 1964 sermon on *The Deputy*, above.

3. It is worth noting that some of the medieval popes condemned the ritual murder charge as a libelous "pretext so as to rob them [the Jews] and seize their property." See Innocent IV, letter of July 5, 1247, in Solomon Grayzel, *The Church and the Jews in the XIIIth Century* (New York: Hermon Press, 1966), 271; see also Gregory X, papal bull of October 7, 1272, in Grayzel, *The Church and the Jews in the XIIIth Century*, vol. 2 (Detroit: Wayne State University Press, 1989), 118.

trusted to Hitler the authority to suspend all civil rights.[4] In 1938, the desperate act of seventeen-year old Herschel Grynspan—half crazed with worry over the fate of his parents exiled into No-Man's land—in shooting some minor assistant from the German Embassy in Paris was used as a pretext for the terrible Kristallnacht, which ended all illusion about the ultimate purpose of the Nazis.[5]

The Russians themselves had long experience in the use of this technique. Under the Czars, where a pogrom was desired it was merely necessary to spread vicious rumors of Jewish villainy among the people.[6] Stalin gave a prime demonstration of the way it could be used with his infamous "Doctors' Plot" of 1953. Coming in the wake of the campaign against "cosmopolitanists" and "internationalists"—which really meant Jews—the charge that Jewish doctors were plotting to murder the leaders of the Soviet Union was the springboard for the arrest and execution of many of the leaders of the Jewish community, forcing Jews out of prominent positions and crushing all Jewish cultural enterprises.[7]

In order to understand the events of these past few days, we need to place them in the proper context. Since the death of Stalin, persecution has not been so blatant. Yet the Soviet government has imposed a systematic policy toward its Jews of that can only be called spiritual genocide. The idea was that if they could crush Jewish loyalty and prohibit Jewish education, the Jewish community would soon disappear. It looked as if this ruthless policy was effective.

I have made three visits to the Soviet Union, observing what I could of Jewish life there. After the first two, in 1959 and 1961, I came back extremely pessimistic. My conclusion was that after having said Kaddish for six million vic-

---

4. On the Reichstag fire and its exploitation by the Nazi regime to promulgate emergency decrees that spelled the end of the Weimar Republic, see William Shirer, *The Rise and Fall of the Third Reich* (New York: Simon and Schuster, 1960), 191–95.

5. On Grynspan and Kristallnacht, see Saul Friedlander, *Nazi Germany and the Jews*, vol. 1 (New York: Harper Collins, 1997), 267–79. Grynspan's parents, together with other Polish Jews living in Germany, were forcibly deported over the border with Poland in late October 1938; the Polish government, which had cancelled the passports of such Polish Jews, refused to allow them to enter Poland. A letter describing the plight of the refugees, reaching Grynspan in Paris, apparently triggered his decision to attack an official in the German Embassy.

6. See Salo W. Baron, *The Russian Jew Under Tsars and Soviets*, 2nd ed. (New York: Schocken, 1987), 44–45.

7. On the "Doctors' Plot," see Baron, 277–78 and, for extensive analysis, Louis Rapoport, *Stalin's War Against the Jews: The Doctors' Plot and the Soviet Solution* (New York: Free Press, 1990.

Pages 3 and 4 of the sermon typescript were apparently lost at some point (Saperstein's recollection is that he gave them to a reporter in an effort to ensure an accurate version of what he had said), and replaced by Saperstein with half a page of outline notes. I have reconstructed the following six paragraphs, using another unpublished sermon, from Kol Nidre 1959, which describes in detail the concert in Leningrad, to flesh out paragraphs 3 and 4. The fifth paragraph is based on a sermon entitled "Anti-Semitism—Soviet Style," dated April 24, 1964.

tims of the Nazis, we would in the next generation have to say Kaddish for three million more in the Soviet Union, who had lost the will to survive as Jews.[8]

I will never forget a Sunday evening in the great synagogue of Leningrad, 1959, when a new cantor was welcomed by the community. Backed by a magnificent choir, he gave a special concert, a sermon in song, expressing a message that he would not have dared to say openly. He sang the Biblical verse, *mah nora ha-makom ha-zeh, ein zeh ki im beit Elohim, v'ze shaar ha-shamayim,* "How awesome is this place, This is none other than the house of God, this is the gate of heaven" (Gen. 28:17). These are the words that Jacob said upon awakening from his dream of a ladder rising to heaven. The song continued to tell of the synagogue as the place of refuge, where Jews can come to pour out their sorrows, to be near to their God. "This is none other than the house of God."

And then he continued with a musical setting of the famous passage from the Mishnah, "These are the things whose reward is without measure: honoring father and mother, performing deeds of kindness, visiting the sick." And the elderly Jews in the congregation began to weep, because they knew the conclusion of the passage, *ve-Talmud Torah ke-neged kulam,* "and the study of Torah is equal to them all."[9] They wept because they were forbidden to study Torah and to teach Torah to their children, and they knew that our greatest weapon, our strongest defense, had been taken from them: the power of transmitting Torah to a new generation.

The people in that congregation knew that while government policy and officially sponsored anti-Semitism were not killing Jews, they were killing Judaism. Not a single Yiddish school was permitted to function in Russia, not a single course in Yiddish or Hebrew or in Jewish history. In addition, viciously anti-Semitic propaganda was allowed to circulate, such as the notorious tract called "Judaism Without Embellishment," published under the auspices of the Ukrainian Academy of Science. In an effort worthy of Goebbels, it set out to prove that Jewish moral teaching degrades labor and encourages people to exploit others, that the Ten Commandments and other Jewish moral principles from the Bible and Talmud apply only to fellow Jews, that Judaism was a facade for an international imperialist conspiracy. Against this unrelenting attack, it seemed that there could be no hope for the future.[10]

But on our third visit, in the summer of 1969, we felt a new spirit among the Jews. To a large extent, it was the impact of the Six-Day War. Young Jews cared about Israel. They were studying Hebrew. I sensed that the prophecy of Ezekiel was being fulfilled: the dry bones of Soviet Jewry were being clothed with flesh, and the spirit of life was breathed upon them.[11]

---

8. Compare the 1959 sermon above.

9. M. Pe'ah 1,1.

10. On "Judaism Without Embellishment," see Benjamin Pinkus and Jonathan Frankel, *The Soviet Government and the Jews, 1948–1967: A Documented Study* (Cambridge: Cambridge University Press, 1984), 314, 336–39.

11. Alluding to Ezekiel 37:6.

The Soviet officials were aware that their policies had failed. Tens of thousands of applications for emigration were received, despite the social ostracism suffered by anyone who applied to leave. The applications were refused, but they continued to be submitted. Some individuals had the courage to put their names to petitions, protesting government restrictions, demanding the right to emigrate. They were arrested, and others joined them, sending new petitions. Some of these were smuggled out to foreign correspondents, to Israeli leaders, to United Nations officials. These petitioners put their lives on the line. Their intrepid courage was a modern manifestation of the Maccabean spirit.

The Soviet government condemned Israeli policies with ever-greater vehemence. It initiated an anti-Jewish campaign. But it could not stop the swell. Something was bound to happen. On June 15, the eleven arrests of the alleged hijackers were made at the Leningrad airport. The same day, numbers of others in different cities were arrested. Although it is Soviet policy not to publicize crimes until long after the event, the hijacking arrests were announced the same day in Leningrad papers. Apparently, they had been alerted in advance.

Even if these people accused and condemned and now sentenced had been guilty, the severity of their sentences reveals flagrant inhumanity. Remember that they never even entered the planes it is alleged they were planning to hijack. But the record of the Soviet Union is not such as to elicit confidence in the legitimacy of the trials, even when confessions are announced. It is significant that no foreign correspondents were permitted to attend them, and no detailed report of the proceedings has been published.

What was the real crime of those convicted? It is revealed in their statement before the court, remembered by relatives, smuggled out of Russia, and reported in yesterday's *New York Times*. "My only goal," said one, "is to live in the State of Israel, which for a long time I have considered my homeland." The wife of one of those sentenced to death asserted, "I do not doubt for a moment that some time I shall emigrate to Israel. This dream, sanctified by 2,000 years of hope, will never leave me. . . . 'If I forget you, O Jerusalem, let my right hand wither.' 'Next year in Jerusalem!'"[12] A young Leningrad Jew, Viktor Boguslavsky, wrote an impassioned letter to the Soviet Prosecutor, General Rudenko: "Their only crime was that they were born Jews and sought to remain Jews. Love for one's people cannot be considered an offense." Shortly afterward, he too was arrested.[13]

It becomes unmistakably clear. Their "crime" was that they wanted to leave the land of their oppression and to join their people in Israel. The Declaration of Human Rights of the United Nations, to which the Soviet Union is a party, guarantees the right of any human being "freely to leave the country of his domicile." We can understand the reluctance of the Soviet leaders to recognize the vitality of this age-old dream. But they must come to understand that whatever

---

12. *New York Times*, December 28, 1970, A3. The statement was made by Sylvia Zalmanson, Kuznetsov's wife, who was herself sentenced to ten years in a labor camp.

13. Boguslavsky, another "refusenik," was arrested on November 13, 1970, for distributing anti-Soviet material. He went on trial in May 1971.

may be the disadvantages in letting Jews go are as nothing compared to the condemnation that will be theirs if they pursue their current barbaric policy.

This is our message. To the victims who are literally behind prison bars, to all the Jews of the Soviet Union who are figuratively behind prison bars, we pledge, "We shall not forget you. We will not remain silent in your hour of affliction. We shall give your tormentors no rest until justice is done. Your pain is our pain; your fate is our fate. *Chizku v-imtzu,* 'Be strong and of good courage.'"

To the forces of civilized humanity, we appeal, "Remember the bitter prophecy of Obadiah, who condemned those who did nothing in the time of Israel's tragic ordeal.[14] Jews have ever been a testing ground for the conscience of humanity. Let the Soviet leaders know that if they persist in their senseless tyranny, they shall be as pariahs before the world."

To the leaders of the Soviet Union, we say, "Cancel these barbaric sentences. Let those who wish to *live* as Jews do so. Let those who wish to *leave* as Jews do so. Do not forget that the history of the Jewish people is also the story of oppressors who sought to destroy them but went down to their own destruction."

To Almighty God, we pray: Look with mercy upon Thy people. On this closing night of the festival of Dedication, when the entire Menorah is aglow in all its beauty and splendor, grant that the light of freedom and justice and peace may shine forth through all the world, for the Jews of the Soviet Union, for the people and faith and land of Israel, and for all mankind.

---

13. Obadiah's bitter condemnation of the Edomites for having "stood aloof when the aliens carried off [your brother Jacob's] goods, when foreigners entered his gates" (v. 11), was frequently invoked by Saperstein in discussions of bystanders who allow evil to occur by failing to take a stand.

43

Dissent—Jewish Style
February 19, 1971

*The following sermon reflects a certain ambivalence toward the Jewish Defense
League. From Saperstein's very earliest preaching, he had emphasized the need
for Jewish assertiveness in defense of Jewish rights and expressed his impatience with passivity, fearful acquiescence or quiet diplomacy. The pacifism of
the 1930s had long since been abandoned. The experience in the American
Army during the Second World War fostered an awareness of the respect won by
Jews who showed themselves capable of physically fighting, if necessary, for a
worthy cause. The sermons of the late 1940s reveal genuine esteem for the defense forces of the Palestinian Jewish settlement, which became the Army of the
State of Israel, and even a grudging appreciation of the motives and courage, if
not the tactics, of the radical Jewish splinter groups. These feelings were powerfully amplified by the experience of 1967, when the very survival of Israel
seemed to depend upon the Jewish will to fight and skill in the use of force. This
ambivalence is perhaps expressed in the hypothetical "defense" of the JDL at
the beginning of the sermon. In responding to activist, militant American Jews,
there would be no automatic condemnation of as a matter of principle.*

*Nevertheless, by February 1971, the Jewish Defense League had become a
major problem for the organized Jewish community in the United States. Its
in-your-face, confrontational style seemed to many to be an expression not of
appropriate Jewish assertiveness, but of offensive arrogance. More than this, in
the arena of public opinion, its tactics appeared to be dangerously counter-productive, harming the cause of Soviet Jewry, to which Saperstein felt so
deeply committed. As president of the New York Board of Rabbis—the office of
which was invaded and vandalized two months later by twenty-three members of
the JDL—Saperstein was convinced that a stand had to be taken.*

*The first part of the sermon, which outlines a possible defense of the JDL
based on the Torah lesson and the tradition of resistance in Jewish history, may*

be merely a rhetorical technique of communicating the impression of balance and fairness before the attack. Perhaps more than this, it seems to express the genuine anguish and sadness, evoked in the very first sentence, at the need to condemn other Jews in whose sincerity the preacher was still ready to believe.

I GIVE THIS SERMON IN SADNESS, for I must criticize Jews whose purpose I commend but whose tactics I deplore. I refer to the group called the Jewish Defense League. Time after time, people have asked me what my opinion is of the JDL. I do not feel the issue can be dodged any longer. I have therefore decided to address this theme tonight.

If I were to give a defense of the Jewish Defense League, I could have chosen my text from the opening verses of this week's *Sedra* [Torah reading]. You recall that it speaks of the Jew who was sold into slavery. In accordance with Jewish law, after six years he was to be set free. The next verses, however, state that sometimes a person does not wish to receive his freedom—he prefers servitude, with its lack of responsibility. In that case, a ceremony is performed in which his ear was pierced, and he was permitted to live out his life as a slave.[1] The piercing of the ear was a sign of shame and humiliation, indicating that the individual lacked the courage to face life as a free man. Supporters of the Jewish Defense League would say that Jews must no longer go through life and history with pierced ears, that we must stand up and show the courage to be free.

The student of history could find many examples in the story of our people to support this stress on courage, active dissent, and self-determination. There is the story of Moses: when the Egyptian was afflicting the Israelite he did not debate with him, he smote the Egyptian. There is the story of the Exodus itself: when the children of Israel finally rose up against their oppressors and refused to remain slaves. There is the story of the Maccabees, who stood up and fought against odds when the Syrians sought to stamp out their faith. There is the story of Masada: of Jews who fought to the death, and finally took their own lives rather than yield to the enemy. There is the story of Bar Cochba, who carried on a desperate but hopeless rebellion against Roman tyranny in the time of the Emperor Hadrian.

In our own generation, there is the story of the Warsaw Ghetto rebellion (which, incidentally, will be presented and interpreted through film and discussion at our adult education session this Thursday evening). There is of course the story of the Jews in Israel, who three times stood up and threw back the enemy who was determined to drive them into the sea. There is the story of the contemporary Jews in the Soviet Union: once the "Jews of Silence,"[2] they have now found their voice and are ready to place their lives in jeopardy with public proclamations of their Jewish loyalty, such as that expressed in the "Meditations" in

---

1. See Exod. 21: 5–6. The Pentateuchal lesson for the week was *Mishpatim* (Exod. 21–24).

2. A phrase made popular by Elie Wiesel's book of that title (New York: Holt, Rinehart, and Winston, 1966).

today's program.[3] It is this tradition which the JDL claims it represents in the current American-Jewish scene.

A word of background. The JDL was founded in the spring of 1968 under the leadership of a young Orthodox rabbi, Meir Kahane. It was based on the premise that anti-Semitism is exploding all over America; its stated purpose was to defend Jews against bigotry and attack. It came to the forefront during the tragic confrontation that occurred during the teachers' strike in 1968, which unfortunately became a confrontation between Jew and black.[4] There were many expressions of black anti-Semitism against Jewish teachers and others.[5] During this period there were areas in New York that once had been largely Jewish and that now contained large representations of other ethnic groups—black and Puerto Rican. Many of the Jews who remained were Orthodox—unable to move to safer and more comfortable areas, still tied to their religious institutions. Many of them found it dangerous, sometimes impossible, to venture through the streets on their way to synagogues and schools. The JDL set itself up as a self-appointed protection agency.

Rabbi Kahane stepped into this situation with a new philosophy—the philosophy of meeting fire with fire, violence with violence. He gathered together a group of young people and set up classes in karate and rifle practice. "If somebody calls you a Jew bastard," he said, "hit him so hard that he'll never forget it. You know what you'll get," he concluded. "Respect." When he urged Jews to get guns and learn how to use them he answered criticism by stating, "If other groups are going to prepare themselves with guns, why not us?" He established a summer camp in the Catskills, where about 150 youngsters were trained in karate self-defense and in shooting skills.[6]

The statements and program of the JDL shocked a number of Jews, particularly those in the establishment. But it made a positive impression on many others. The response was in part an expression of guilt, particularly for mature peo-

---

3. Referring to the four-page handout distributed to worshippers at the Friday evening service. The proclamations may well be those cited in the previous address, delivered less than two months earlier at the end of the Leningrad Trials.

4. Several strikes were called by the United Federation of Teachers at the beginning of the 1968 school year because of problems with the governing board of the experimental Ocean Hill–Brownsville school district. As many of the teachers were Jewish and the school district was largely black and Hispanic, ethnic tensions, which had simmered during the preceding year, became extremely volatile. See *American Jewish Year Book, 1969* (Philadelphia: JPS, 1970), 79–85, with bibliography on 81, n. 5.

5. The most notorious of these expressions was a poem, purportedly written by a fifteen-year-old girl, read on a New York radio program by the vice president of the African-American Teachers Association, which began, "Hey, Jew boy, with that yarmulka on your head/ You pale-faced Jew boy—I wish you were dead." For the full text of the blatantly antisemitic poem, see *AJYB, 1969*, p. 84. See also *Confrontation at Ocean Hill–Brownsville*, ed. Maurice R. Berube and Marilyn Gittell (New York: Frederick A. Praeger, 1969), 163–76.

6. Compare Kahane's *The Story of the Jewish Defense League* (Radnor, Pa.: Chilton Book Company, 1975), 129–34.

ple. The JDL's motto was "Never Again," referring to the period of genocide under the Nazis when the Jews of the world failed to do all that might have been done to rescue their brothers in lands of persecution.[7] To some young people it was an assertion of dignity and courage, calling on them to stand up and not be pushed around. It was a call for a kind of militancy that is attractive to many in these times. The number of members of the JDL never amounted to very many. Kahane's estimate of 10,000 is certainly exaggerated. But there were undoubtedly many sympathizers.

I was urged at that time to denounce Kahane. I met with him on three occasions. On one of them I arranged for him to meet with representatives of some of the major establishment organizations, who had previously had no contact with him at all. I was hoping to get him to accept a measure of group discipline that would enable us to harness some of his zeal but modify his tactics. We did not succeed. But I was not ready to make a public denunciation.

Then the JDL entered a new arena. It appointed itself the defender of Israel and of Soviet Jewry. They beat up minor Arab official representatives at their offices in the United States.[8] They supported an attempted hijack of a Russian plane. They disclaimed responsibility but endorsed the bombing of the Soviet Cultural Mission in Washington and the Offices of Intourist and Tass Airlines in New York.[9] They have interrupted concerts and other cultural programs presented by Soviet groups.[10] They have picketed and demonstrated outside official Soviet establishments in the United States and harassed Soviet personnel.[11]

As this program developed, it became clear to me that what they were doing was not just another way of achieving the objectives we were seeking, but was definitely harmful to the cause of the Jewish people. I finally found it necessary to issue a statement, which I did about a month ago. Let me read it to you:

---

7. On the motto "Never Again" (the title of Kahane's 1971 book), see Janet Dolgin, *Jewish Identity and the JDL* (Princeton: Princeton University Press, 1977), 69.

8. As Kahane put it, following a May 1970 guerilla attack near the Lebanese border in which eight Israeli schoolchildren were killed, "Two Arab offices in New York, one a front for the terrorists and the other the office of the chief Arab lobbyist M. T. Mehdi, were attacked and the occupants savagely beaten. . . . Jewish militants were active" (*The Story of the Jewish Defense League*, 283). Saperstein returns to this incident later in the sermon.

9. The bomb exploded outside the Soviet Cultural Embassy on January 8, 1971, following the Leningrad trial verdicts (see the preceding sermon). On November 25, 1970, a pipe bomb went off at the Intourist and Aeroflot offices. In both cases, callers informed the press services, concluding their message with the words "Never Again." See Dolgin, 35; Kahane, 18–19, 29.

10. For example, disrupting a performance by the Omsk Siberian Dancers at Carnegie Hall on January 28, 1971.

11. See, for example, the *New York Times*, December 28, 1970, A3, the very page Saperstein had cited in his December 29 address; eleven demonstrators, including Kahane, were arrested in a clash with police when they tried to move through police barricades outside the Soviet Mission to the United Nations.

The New York Board of Rabbis, comprising more than 900 Rabbis, Orthodox, Conservative and Reform, deplores the statements and actions of the JDL. Pretending to defend the Jewish people, this group, through its resorting to harassment and violence, has greatly harmed the cause of Jewry. The Soviet Union is guilty of cruel persecution and unjust denial of rights in respect to its Jewish population. Orderly demonstrations throughout the world have expressed the moral condemnation of humanity. The JDL, however, has enabled the tyrant to assume the pose of the victim. It has given the Soviet leaders additional fuel to stoke the fires of their bigotry and an excuse to besmirch the name of the Jewish people and of Zionism.

We wish to make it unmistakably clear that the JDL has no official connection with the Zionist movement, that it perverts the ideals of our religious heritage and that it represents only a tiny misguided minority of the Jewish community. It is repudiated by the great majority of Jews and Jewish organizations. At the same time we call upon the Jewish community to continue in a disciplined, resolute and non-violent program of demonstration, on behalf of our afflicted Jewish brothers and against the barbaric anti-Semitic policies of the Soviet Union.[12]

Let me explain my reasons for this criticism. I shall do so by answering two of the claims that have most commonly been made to me by those positively impressed by and sympathetic to the JDL. The first is the claim that the JDL activity produced results—that it did get a mitigation of the Leningrad sentences and exit permits for some of the Soviet Jews who had requested them.[13] I can tell you without any measure of doubt that this assumption is altogether false.

It is true that the Soviet Union is very much concerned about world public opinion. Soviet officials were startled and caught off guard by the intense reaction to the Soviet trials. But it is childishly unrealistic to assume that they are frightened by the protest activities of a handful of youngsters in America. The JDL plays into their hands. They couldn't condemn the rest of the world, which was almost unanimous in condemnation of them. The JDL made it possible for them to condemn, in their words, the "Jewish hooligans" who were attacking them.

When the Soviet Union canceled the visit of the Bolshoi Ballet on the basis that their performers were being interrupted in their performance, they blamed it on the JDL.[14] That wasn't really the reason. They canceled those performances because they were afraid of defections, which had already taken some of their best dancers. The JDL gave them a convenient out.

---

12. The statement, in the form of a press release, was dated January 14, 1971, and signed by "Rabbi Harold I. Saperstein, President," following approval by the officers and governing body of the New York Board of Rabbis at its January 1971 meeting.

13. On December 30, 1970, the Russian Republic Supreme Court commuted the death sentence of Dymshits and Kuznetzov and reduced the sentences of three other defendants.

14. The announcement of the cancellation was made on December 11, 1970; the Soviet spokesman attributed it to the American failure to "take necessary measures" against "Zionist extremists" (Kahane, 20).

When the mitigation of the Leningrad sentences were announced, I can tell you it was not the JDL that brought it about. It was the fact that all over the world, protest meetings were held. Here in our congregation we sent hundreds of telegrams and letters and this was replicated all over the country. It was the fact that a great national meeting was convened in Washington.[15] There, as a result of my experience in Belgium during the war years,[16] I was instrumental in getting the Belgian ambassador to intercede with his government to get a message of protest to the Soviet government. Other delegates got similar results from other embassies. Contacts that we had resulted in a statement from the Pope. The JDL was like the fly on the back of the chariot in Aesop's Fables, who proudly asserted, "What a big cloud of dust I am kicking up."[17]

The other claim made for the JDL is that at least it kept the fate of Russian Jewry in the public eye, on the front pages of the newspapers. But in truth, what the JDL did was to take Russian Jewry off the front pages and put the JDL on the front page. If the Soviet Union could have exactly what it wanted, it would have wished for nothing better than the JDL to do exactly what it did. It enabled them to turn the tables. Public sympathy went out to the Soviet wives who were harassed in the supermarkets, to the Soviet officials who were hounded in the streets, to policemen who were injured in the course of demonstrations.

The same was true when they beat up two Arab cultural attachés after a school bus in the Galilee had run over a mine and eight Israeli youngsters were killed.[18] The JDL's attack made it possible for the Arabs to complain as if they were the aggrieved ones, the ones who suffered attack and persecution. And in the discussion of JDL violence, the original tragedy was all but forgotten.

Let me tell you something that I suspect but for which I admit I have no proof. When bombs were exploded at Soviet establishments in Washington and New York, the JDL disclaimed responsibility but asserted its approval. Most people assumed that somehow the JDL had been involved. To me there was something very strange about the whole business. The bombs exploded at a convenient time. There was little damage. There was no personal injury. The police who were anxious to show results could find no evidence to incriminate anyone. I suspect that these bombs may well have been set off by the Russians themselves to divert attention from what was happening in Russia. The JDL played right into their hands.

Even if you recognize the need for active dissent, the mistake of the JDL is that they forget where the action is. The Al Fatah are not in New York, but in the Arab countries. The Kremlin is not in Washington, but in Moscow. When

---

15. This was reported in the *New York Times* of December 31, 1970, noting that Jewish leaders in Washington visited thirteen foreign embassies to ask for diplomatic intervention with the Soviet government.

16. Saperstein was actually in Belgium following the surrender of Germany; see above, the sermon for Rosh Hashanah 1945, delivered in Namur.

17. See *Brewster's Dictionary of Phrase and Fable* (New York: Harper & Brothers, 1953), 370.

18. See above, n. 8.

underground groups fought against the ancient Syrians, against the Romans, against the Nazis, against the British and Arabs in the land of Israel, they were fighting where the action was, and where they had no other recourse but to fight.[19] If the JDL went to Egypt or to the Soviet Union and carried on their demonstrations there, taking the risks entailed, I'd say more power to them. But in America, our government is responsible for the safety and security of foreign property and personnel. The JDL is not fighting the enemy; it is fighting the American government. Their efforts bring them notoriety, but for our cause, they are counter-productive.

What is the alternative? It is not to sit back and do nothing. There are legitimate, disciplined, non-violent demonstrations to which we can give our support. Their effectiveness will depend on the numbers of those who attend them. There is one at Mitchell Field this Sunday. At the same time, it is my honor to be the chief speaker at a demonstration being held in New Jersey.[20] Other demonstrations are being held around the country. The time for silence is no more. We must make ourselves heard. This, and not the way of the JDL, is the way we can truly say, "Never again." Never again shall Jews be victims of genocide. Never again shall we be guilty of indifference to the fate of our brothers!

---

19. Here Saperstein returns to the models mentioned earlier in the sermon and claimed by the JDL to establish its Jewish authenticity, arguing that the JDL does not really follow in this tradition of Jewish heroism at all.

20. According to press reports, this rally, held at the Teaneck Jewish Community Center on Sunday, February 21, drew more than 2,000 Bergen County residents, many of them teenagers.

44

Keepers of the Keys
June 4, 1972
HUC-JIR Ordination Ceremony
Temple Emanu-El, New York

The following sermon was delivered at the ordination exercises of the Hebrew Union College—Jewish Institute of Religion; Saperstein was invited to speak because his older son, Marc, was being ordained as a rabbi. The nature of the occasion required a communication different from the topical sermon delivered at a Friday evening or Rosh Hashanah service. While delivered before a large audience (at Temple Emanu-El of New York), it was addressed especially to those new rabbis and cantors who were launching careers of Jewish service. It is therefore closer to the 1957 sermon given at the convention of the Central Conference of American Rabbis: intended primarily for colleagues, it delineates the challenges and opportunities of the profession. Both the subject matter and the more extensive use of traditional Jewish source material reflect this context.

The occasion was certainly appropriate for reminiscence, and the sermon begins recalling the preacher's own ordination and the charge given to the members of his own entering class by their mentor, Stephen S. Wise. But the main focus of the sermon is the present—"an era fraught with pessimism"—and future. Current trends in Jewish life and projections for the years ahead are evaluated, with reference to the Biblical account of the spies who rejected the pessimism of the majority, drawing frequently from the experiences of a full career—almost forty years at that point—in the congregational rabbinate, as well as special experiences in the larger Jewish world. The peroration, beginning in the sixth paragraph from the end—"there will also be rich and wonderful satisfactions . . ."— was one of those powerful moments of uplift that remain with some listeners throughout the years.

IT IS JUST THIRTY-SEVEN YEARS SINCE I STOOD IN THE SANCTUARY of the Jewish Institute of Religion and received *Semicha* [ordination as a rabbi]. Thirty-seven, in *gematria* [numerical equivalents of the alphabet letters] is "*zayin lamed*," the abbreviation for the words *zichrono livracha*, "of blessed memory." And truly on this day my thoughts go back in reverent reminiscence to the great teachers whose lives illuminated the pages of the history of this school and who have passed to the *Yeshiva shel Ma'ala* [the Academy on High]. Foremost among them are two giants of the human spirit, Stephen S. Wise, who so powerfully exemplified the prophetic ideal and the love of the people of Israel, and Nelson Glueck, who so truly exemplified devotion to Torah and love of the land of Israel. It is their challenging mantle that has passed to the shoulders of our distinguished President, Dr. Alfred Gottschalk.[1]

When I first came to the Jewish Institute of Religion, Dr. Wise said to our entering class, "In choosing the Rabbinate you are linking your lives to the two most difficult and unpopular causes in the world: the cause of religion and the cause of the Jew." Times change. Each generation, each decade, often each year brings its unique tasks and problems. But now again the causes of the Jew and of religion rank high among those that carry the onus of difficulty and unpopularity.

Significantly, the Torah portion to be read this coming Sabbath is *Shalach L'cha*, which describes the incident of the twelve spies, sent on a reconnaissance mission into the land of Israel. You will recall that ten of the twelve returned with a pessimistic report. "The people who inhabit the country are powerful and the cities are fortified. . . . We cannot attack that people, for it is stronger than we" (Num. 13:28, 31). Only two, Joshua and Caleb, spoke in terms of optimism: "The land that we traversed is an exceedingly good land. Let us by all means go up, and we shall gain possession of it, for we are able to overcome it" (Num. 14:7, 13:30).

What caused the difference between these two conflicting reports? All twelve had started out as men of good repute, princes of their tribes, heads of the children of Israel. All of them had surveyed the same land and observed the same people. Yet their reactions were so profoundly contradictory. The medieval commentators posed an answer to this problem. Rashi, drawing upon the Talmud, indicates that of all the spies Caleb alone had gone to Hebron, making a pilgrimage to the graves of the patriarchs.[2] From them he drew inspiration to withstand the enticements of his colleagues. He had in essence renewed his allegiance to his heritage and to his people.

Respecting Joshua, Rashi translates the phrase *Vayikra Moshe l'Hoshea bin Nun Yehoshua*, "And Moses changed the name of Hosea bin Nun to Joshua" as "Moses prayed regarding Hosea bin Nun, May God save you,"[3] which is the literal meaning of *Yehoshua*. Thus Joshua was the beneficiary of the prayer of

---

1. Nelson Glueck, a well-known archaeologist, died in 1971. This was the first year that his successor, Gottschalk, presided at the Ordination ceremonies.

2. Rashi on Num. 13:22, based on B. Sotah 34b.

3. Rashi on Num. 13:16, also based on B. Sotah 34b.

Moses. From it came the spiritual strength he needed in time of crisis. These two then were distinguished from their fellows in that they were guided and strengthened by the bonds that linked them to their people and their faith.

You who become rabbis and cantors today must serve in an era fraught with pessimism. There is much to fill our hearts with foreboding.[4] After a quarter century of heroic existence, Israel still struggles on the precipice, surrounded by enemies committed to its destruction. Despite the miracle of Jews emerging from the valley of dry bones to rediscover their Jewish voices and souls, Soviet Jewry is still threatened with spiritual genocide. Our own nation is still bogged down in a needless and immoral war, which has turned the American dream into a nightmare. In the Jewish community youth has been alienated, the rate of intermarriage is uncontrollably advancing, the measure of Jewish literacy is abysmally low. In the general community, racial confrontation and polarization has become ever more disturbing, and our position in the American spectrum, which had seemed at last so secure, appears again to be threatened. It is not easy to be a spiritual leader in times like these.

From the darkness come the voices of the prophets of doom and despair. Some of them are our own colleagues.[5] We are told that the synagogue is no longer a viable institution, capable of answering the needs of the contemporary Jewish community.[6] We are told that the role of the rabbi is atavistic, no longer serving any meaningful purpose. We are told that worship as we have known it is vacuous and ineffective. If any considerable part of these negative evaluations is warranted, it would seem that all of us are losers, that we have reached the point of no return, that much of what my generation seeks to preserve is doomed, and that you, who as rabbis and cantors are dedicating your lives to the faith and the synagogue, are unrealistic idealists preparing to tilt at windmills or arrant opportunists seeking to milk the last profits from a dying business.

But I am not willing to embrace the dogma of despair so readily. Such thoroughgoing pessimism is essentially un-Jewish. Even on the threshold of the gas chambers in Nazi-dominated Europe, Jews sang *Ani Maamin*, "I believe with perfect faith in the coming of the Messiah." No, I am not prepared to relegate the synagogue into limbo or to negate the role of the Rabbi or to acquiesce in the

---

4. The rest of the paragraph, formulated in uncharacteristically bleak terms, lays the foundation for the plausibility of the negative report by the majority of the modern "spies" in assessing the Jewish future.

5. Leaders of the Reform rabbinate were aware of a sense of "malaise" within their ranks in the late 1960s. In order to assess this, they commissioned a study by the sociologist Theodore Lenn, published in 1972 as *Rabbi and Synagogue in Reform Judaism* (West Hartford: CCAR, 1972). Lenn reported that in his pre-questionnaire interviews with Reform rabbis throughout the country, "many expressed concern that Reform Judaism was in the midst of a crisis" (184).

6. Michael Meyer, historian of Reform Judaism, describes a sense of "severe self-doubt and anxiety about the future" beginning in the late 1960s. "Only a handful of new congregations joined each year; membership lists in existing congregations either remained static or slightly declined; a few temples had no choice but to merge in order to remain viable." *Response to Modernity* (New York: Oxford University Press, 1988), 369.

bankruptcy of religion. There are still sources of affirmation—precisely those factors that sustained Caleb and Joshua in their hour of testing.

The first is that which tradition indicates gave strength to Caleb: identification with his heritage and people. When I was a student we debated the problem of whether Jews were a religion or a nationality. I think we have transcended that discussion now. We recognize that these are concepts which simply do not apply to the Jew. In Biblical study, a word that occurs only once and that can therefore be understood only in its own context is called "*hapax legomenon.*" The Jew has been the *hapax legomenon* of history. The people of Israel must be conceived as a consecrated people—embracing both peoplehood and faith.

Through the years of my rabbinical service it has been my avocation to visit far-flung Jewish communities throughout the world. I have met Jews whose appearances, whose customs, whose languages were different from mine. But I have always been conscious of the fact that their ancestors and mine walked the same path. Their paths diverged, perhaps a hundred years ago, perhaps five hundred, perhaps nineteen hundred, but when we face each other we know that we belong together, that we are one people. I became particularly conscious of this on Shavuot 1967, the first day the civilian population was allowed to visit the Western Wall in Jerusalem.[7] I was among the 200,000 who made the pilgrimage that day. Among us were Sephardim and Ashkenazim, kibbutzniks and yeshiva *bachurim* [students], soldiers and Chassidim, but all were bound together in unity of spirit emerging from the sense of a common historical heritage.

This concept of *k'lal Yisrael*, the totality of the Jewish people, which was the theoretical foundation on which this school [the Jewish Institute of Religion] was founded, must impinge upon our religious orientation. The era when Reform Judaism had to justify itself by the negation of Jewish peoplehood and tradition should be over. The times demand rather that the bonds which link us with other Jews be emphasized. I recently had the opportunity of reading the report of a discussion by some members of this ordination class, expressing their views of their function as rabbis. I was impressed to note that many have instituted a return to traditional forms, which bridge the chasm separating them from more traditional groups. I do not believe that this in any way compromises their dedication to liberal religious principles.

The *k'lal Yisrael* concept is involved also with the moral dilemma implied in the trend toward ethnicity. Our young leaders will find themselves torn by ideological polarization.[8] There are those who insist that Jews must be con-

---

7. On June 14, following the Israeli seizure of East Jerusalem in the Six-Day War. When Jordan controlled this area (1948–1967), it prevented Jews from visiting the Western Wall. A *Jerusalem Post* description of this mass pilgrimage to the Wall is cited by Martin Gilbert, *Jerusalem in the Twentieth Century* (New York: John Wiley & Sons, 1996), 294–95.

8. The tension between Jewish "particularism" and "universalism" was heightened by issues such as the teachers' strike in Ocean Hill–Brownsville and the behavior of the Jewish Defense League (see the previous sermon). In his study, Lenn mapped out positions on what he termed a "Particularism–Universalism Index" (*Rabbi and Synagogue*,

cerned primarily with the problems of the larger society, ready to make whatever sacrifice is necessary to solve these problems. To others, Jewish survival is
central and paramount and all other considerations must be subsidiary to it.
There is a temptation to be doctrinaire, to insist on one or the other. But we must
understand that "*Elu ve-elu divrei Elohim Chayim*," both positions have spiritual validity.[9] We are *both* Jews and human beings. Our faith is *both* particular-
istic and universalistic. It would be tragic if we were to abandon the social idealism of our prophetic heritage. It would be self-defeating if we were to make
ourselves the last generation of Jews, while searching for a broader humanitari-
anism. We must be ready to walk side by side with all men toward our goal of
peace and justice, but there is no moral imperative for us to commit group suicide in the effort to implement our ideals. It will be your task to walk that razor's
edge: to remain firm and unyielding in your dedication to humanitarian principles, yet committed unquestionably to Jewish survival. There will be painful and
difficult decisions to be made. But the negation of either of these goals would be
moral disaster.

The other source of strength is that which, according to tradition, enabled
Joshua to withstand the pressure of the pessimistic majority. It was the efficacy
of prayer and faith. The religious function of our spiritual leaders has been held
up to severe challenge in recent years. The report of God's demise, so widely
circulated some years ago, is conceded to be greatly exaggerated,[10] but most
Jews go on living and acting as though it were true. The fact is that a great numbers of our co-religionists do not storm the doors of the Temple on Sabbath eve
even though the sermon be superb and the music magnificent. The fact is that
among young people there is widespread indifference, and in circles where there
is concern there is often deep dissatisfaction. This is reflected in the diminishing
tendency of rabbinical students to select the congregational rabbinate as their
first career priority.[11]

There are many who are ready to concede the vacuity of our worship services and the failure of the synagogues. Various, sometimes desperate, remedies
have been suggested. Some maintain that a new prayer book couched in relevant
terms is the answer.[12] Unfortunately, nothing is more quickly dated than the

---

240–50). Saperstein denies the polarizing dichotomy and argues for a creative balancing
of both components.

9. Literally, "these and these are the words of the living God" (B. Erubin 13b).

10. A reference to the "Death of God" theology quite fashionable, especially in Christian circles during the 1960s. See Richard Rubenstein's 1966 essay "Death of God Theology and the Jews," in *After Auschwitz* (Indianapolis: Bobbs-Merrill, 1966). By 1973,
Eugene Borowitz could write that the Jewish "death of God" movement, spearheaded by
Rubenstein, "died quickly in the Jewish community" and is "now of only academic interest, in the most invidious sense of that term." *The Masks Jews Wear* (New York: Simon
and Schuster, 1973), 200.

11. Lenn reported that less than half of the students in the HUC-JIR definitely planned
to become pulpit rabbis (*Rabbi and Synagogue*, 329–30).

12. Lenn found seminarians were generally more critical of the *Union Prayer Book*
than were rabbis in the field (*Rabbi and Synagogue*, 331–32), although 49 percent of the

relevant. Prayers that were relevant only last year may now be more incongruous than the traditional prayers of the liturgy.

Others grapple with the inadequacies of the synagogue. They maintain that its weakness lies in its establishment character and in the prevalent cult of bigness. The obvious answer then would be to make the synagogue structure more informal and to limit its size so there could be intimate person-to-person contact. In actual practice, however, small congregations do not necessarily have a greater proportion of committed participants than large ones. The informal religious group may permit more intensive spiritual experience to those already committed. It does not guarantee to attract those who are marginal to begin with.[13]

The flaw in these solutions is that they stress external form rather than inner motivation. The real trouble is not in the prayer book but in the fact that our generation has in large measure lost the sense of the necessity and value of prayer.[14] The real weakness is not in the size or form of the synagogue but in the lack of conviction about the value of religious experience. I would not discourage experimentation and creativity. There is nothing sacrosanct about established forms and structures. We have not been so successful that we can afford to neglect any promising innovation. But I warn you: do not place your hope on some ingenious formula, do not expect to find some magical panacea. What we need is faith in an era of cynicism. To elicit this we have no better means than the example of the religious leader himself. Whether you worship with a robe or without one, whether you use the "Union Prayer Book" or another, whether you serve a large or a small congregation, it will soon be evident whether your life is totally committed to the values you proclaim.

It has become fashionable to decry the changes in the rabbinical role that have developed on the American scene. The rabbi's role as preacher, as leader of the liturgy, as representative of the Jewish community, as pastor to his people, is criticized as a departure from tradition. Such criticism evidences a limited historical outlook. The role of the rabbi has never been fixed; it has been subject to constant flux. The question is not whether his contemporary functions parallel those of former generations. The question is whether they reflect the needs of the contemporary situation without diminishing his moral stature. Out of the years of my experience I would urge you: do not sell these functions and their possibilities short.

---

rabbis (and 68 percent of the seminarians) found a representative passage to be "an example of why so much of the Prayer Book needs to be revised." The "newly revised" version of the *UPB*, almost universally used by Reform congregations at the time, had been published in 1940. The *Gates of Prayer*, which would replace it, was published in 1975.

13. This paragraph refers to the *havurot* movement, which began in the counterculture of committed young Jews as an alternative to the traditional synagogue, but was beginning to be incorporated into certain large synagogues as a way of counteracting the impersonal structure. For perspectives not long afterward, see essays in *CCAR Journal* 22 (Winter 1975), 31–40.

14. Compare the position cited by Lenn in *Rabbi and Synagogue*, 123–34.

But let me be honest with you. There will be many occasions of frustration and disillusionment. There will be overwhelming challenges for which you will feel professionally unprepared and personally inadequate. There will be dark hours of despair. But there will also be rich and wonderful satisfactions. To the young, groping and searching in the darkness of a world they never made; to those of mature years, so engrossed in their problems they have lost sight of their purpose; to the aged, whose eyes are dulled more by loneliness than by the years; to all of them you will have the opportunity of bringing the message that life is meaningful.

In a world thirsting for identity, you will have the exciting task of sounding the summons to your people to be Jews—strong and proud of their Jewishness, custodians of a heritage deep in its understanding of the human heart and lofty in its vision of humanity's goals.

In a time of moral confusion, you will have the privilege of drawing sustenance from the bottomless well of Torah, dealing with problems of the hour but deriving your strength from timeless sources. For yourself there will be the opportunity of integrating life and work in a measure that no other profession can equal. There will be rewards of the spirit and of the ego far beyond what most of us merit.

In Talmud Ta'anit we read that when the first Temple was destroyed, groups of young priests assembled and, holding the keys of the Temple in their hands, ascended the Temple roof and said, "Master of the Universe, since we have not merited the privilege of being Thy faithful treasurers these keys are handed back unto Thee." Thereupon they threw the keys toward heaven. And the figure of a hand appeared and received the keys from them, after which they cast themselves down into the fire beneath.[15]

The young priests in this ancient legend were consumed with tragic pessimism which history has not justified. True, the Temple was in ruins. But somehow Judaism uncovered the secret of eternal renewal. Its institutions assumed new forms. It moved in new directions. And it lived on.

You, rabbis and cantors, will be the keepers of the keys. You take over their custody in a difficult and revolutionary time. Your task thereby becomes all the more significant and all the more crucial. May you prove equal to the challenge of this great and consecrated cause. Like Joshua and Caleb may you summon your people, "Let us go up and possess the land for we are able to overcome it" (Num. 13:30). And may God be with you *bechol y'mechem uv'chol darkechem*, in all your days and in all your ways.

---

15. B. Ta'anit 29a.

- 45 -

The War of the Day of Judgment
October 10, 1973
Sukkot Evening

No Jews who lived through it will readily forget the outbreak of the Yom Kippur War in 1973, the sacrilege of a coordinated full-scale attack launched by Syria and Egypt at 2:00 PM local time on the Day of Atonement, when the Jewish population of Israel is maximally oriented toward spiritual matters. Or the harrowing uncertainty of the following days between Yom Kippur and the beginning of Sukkot, when reports of devastating initial losses mounted, and the very survival of Israel seemed once again uncertain. The life and death events of the Middle East intruded upon and totally disrupted the rhythms of the holy day season.

Jewish communities throughout the world organized emergency fund-raising appeals. Because the holiday calendar already required so many gatherings (Yom Kippur ended on Saturday night, Sukkot began on Wednesday night, leading into Shabbat), many of these appeals were held at worship services. The sermonic message was intended to articulate the feelings of the congregants, dramatize the danger and the need, and culminate in a request for sacrificial financial support. There was little need for elaborate homiletical device. The use of the two passages from modern Hebrew literature established a precedent for an emergency overriding of traditions associated with the holy days and provided a vivid image of sacrifice. Reference to the memories of the Six-Day War and the visit of a group from the Temple the previous spring created a personal link. This was not a matter of convincing a reluctant or hostile audience. It was a time of shared, powerful emotions, reinforced and channeled by the preacher's words.

MY MESSAGE TONIGHT INCORPORATES A HEBREW STORY and a Hebrew poem. The story is by one of the classical writers of modern Hebrew literature, David Frishman. It is called, *Shelosha Sheachlu*, "Three Who Ate," and it is based on an actual incident that occurred in the Pale of Settlement in the latter part of the nineteenth century.[1]

At the end of the summer, an epidemic had broken out in the town. By the time of the High Holy Days, it had taken the lives of many in the Jewish community. On Yom Kippur, which fell that year on Shabbat, the people gathered in the synagogue, many of them with feverish eyes and bodies weakened by the ravages of illness. Most remained in the synagogue throughout the night. The next morning, the Rabbi rose to speak. Beside him were two *dayanim*, Talmudic scholars, who assisted him in matters of Jewish law. As the Rabbi spoke, his face showed strain, his voice was on the edge of breaking.

"This is the holiest day of the Jewish year," he said. "In accordance with the commandments of our Torah, it is a day of fasting. But the law was given to us that we might live by it, not that we might die by it. Therefore, by virtue of the authority of my colleagues and myself as a *Bet Din* [religious court], I give you permission to eat on this day that you may live."

Silence gripped the congregation. No one moved, and no one spoke. The rabbi continued, desperately. "Return to your homes and eat. If there be sin, it will be upon me." No one moved and no one spoke. The rabbi consulted with the two *dayanim*. In a moment they reached agreement. The *shammas* [sexton] was sent out; in a few moments he returned with a loaf of bread. There, in the presence of the congregation, on Yom Kippur that fell on the Sabbath, the three leaders joined in the blessing and ate the bread, that the congregation might learn that life comes before all else: customs, traditions, laws.

I tell this story because tonight is Sukkot, *zeman simchatenu*, "the season of our rejoicing," when in accordance with tradition the heart should be joyful. But I am going to speak in somber terms, from a heart filled with fear and concern for the people and the land of Israel. I do so because *am Yisrael chai*, the people of Israel must live, and their life depends in some measure upon us.

As we gather here, in the Sinai Desert—where once our people made a covenant with God and thereby entered into a rendezvous with eternity, where once our ancestors participated in a great pilgrimage to freedom—Jewish youth stand fighting against tremendous odds in defense of their homes, their land, their loved ones. We are a part of that battle. In the days of Rabbi Akiba, a great revolt was undertaken against the tyranny of Rome under the leadership of Bar Cochba. Bar Cochba was the military general, a man of heroic stature. But Akiba gave him the support of the religious community and galvanized the people with faith and the spirit of sacrifice. That is our task.

---

1. See the translation of the story in Leo Schwarz, *The Jewish Caravan* (New York: Farrar and Rinehart, 1935), 300–4. The quotations in the sermon were not taken from this translation, however; they appear to be Saperstein's own free translations, based on the collection of Frishman's Hebrew stories that he owned.

The poem to which I referred is by Nathan Alterman, one of the outstanding contemporary poets in Israel. It was written during the prelude to the Israeli War for Independence. He called it, "The Silver Platter." The title was derived from a statement by Chaim Weizmann, first president of the newly created State: "A nation is not given on a silver platter." Alterman describes a day of national celebration. A great parade is taking place. Amongst the marchers two young people, a boy and a girl, are passing silently. They are dressed in torn, battle-stained uniforms, their weapons in their hands, immeasurable suffering and weariness reflected in their faces. They are the living or the dead—the poem does not make this clear. But it concludes, "We are the silver platter on which the State of Israel is given."[2] Let me say now, *sacrifice* is the silver platter on which alone the State of Israel can survive in this critical hour.

You all know how critical the situation is. I am sure that like my family, each of you is glued to the radio and the news reports. Last night I awoke in the middle of the night in a cold sweat of apprehension and fear. This morning's paper carried reports that had come to me independently during recent days. Israel knew that the enemy was amassing its forces. It could have reacted with a preemptive strike as it did in 1967. In modern warfare, the nation that attacks first gains forty-eight hours of time, and those forty-eight hours for Israel could have meant tremendous combat advantage. The matter was debated bitterly in the Cabinet. It was decided that, in view of the world's readiness to condemn Israel, they would not strike that first blow.[3] In reaching that decision, they knew that it would mean many additional casualties and the loss of much war materiel. And so the Syrians and the Egyptians struck first on Yom Kippur that fell on a Sabbath—an attack that will go down with Pearl Harbor in the annals of human infamy.

Remember that Israel's standing army is a very small one. Israel is a small country, an island of three million Jews surrounded by a vast ocean of 100 million Arabs. The Arabs are able to have large regular armies. Israel's is predominantly a civilian army of reserves called up in time of emergency. When the fighting began, little groups of armored forces had to face entire battalions, outnumbering them in tanks and men ten to one. Their job was to hold ground, until general mobilization could take place. At the end of twenty-four hours, there had been more casualties than in the entire Six-Day War. The loss of equipment in

---

2. Alterman's poem was first published in the newspaper *Davar* on December 26, 1947. For a translation, see David Roskies, *The Literature of Destruction* (Philadelphia: JPS, 1988), 608.

3. See the *New York Times*, October 10, 1973, A18:1; Howard Sachar, *A History of Israel* (New York: Knopf, 1996), 754–55. The preemptive strike was urged at an emergency meeting on Yom Kippur morning by General David Elazar, the chief of staff, and resisted by Defense Minister Moshe Dayan and Prime Minister Golda Meir. The American Secretary of State Henry Kissinger, when informed by the Israelis of the situation, also appealed not to preempt.

the first twenty-four hours amounted to 300 million dollars. By now the loss in lives and equipment amounts to many times these numbers.[4]

To Marcia and me, the news is particularly personal. For as she told the women of our Sisterhood in a moving taped message yesterday when she was lecturing out of town,[5] six years ago we watched the men leaving as their units were being called up. We heard the pounding of the artillery; we felt our building shake when it was struck. We saw the planes flying to battle, the tracer bullets and flares lighting the darkness of the sky at night. We witnessed our people rise to heights of heroism and greatness. And we knew what it meant to realize that all over the world the Jewish people was behind us and with us, and ready to sacrifice for us.

Exactly five months ago, we were there in Israel with a wonderful group from our Temple and saw the twenty-fifth anniversary parade. We saw the young men sitting proud and tall in their tanks, handling them with such skill; we saw that thrilling, indescribably impressive fly-over by the Air Force, some of the best pilots in the world flying with perfect precision. But in modern warfare against sophisticated electronic weaponry, even skill and courage cannot guarantee safety. Many of those wonderful boys lie blackened by the flames of burned out tanks, mangled in the wreckage of those magnificent planes. They are the silver platter on which Israel survives.

All indications are that this is going to be a long, hard struggle. It is harder for Israel than for its enemies, for all-out mobilization means that everybody is in the army, and the normal economy grinds to a standstill. Let us not forget what is at stake. Despite their statements, the enemy will not be satisfied to return to the pre-1967 boundaries. They had them in 1967 and were prepared to attack. Their goal is exactly what they threatened in 1967: to crush the Jewish State, to destroy its people. We who bear the pain of the Holocaust with its six million victims in our hearts bear the prospect of another Holocaust with three million more victims. *It must not be.*

A war is fought with military equipment. But there are two other elements that make equipment effective and possible. One is human beings, the other is money. Israel is paying with both. But they alone are paying with lives. Your children went home with you after Yom Kippur services last Saturday. In Israel, many young men folded their *talleisim* [prayer shawls] in the synagogue, and quietly kissed their loved ones goodbye. You know where your sons are tonight. Tonight they are praying that their sons are still alive. Should we not pay for that privilege?

That is what we're here for. Everyone has an envelope. Each one contains two forms. One is a purchase form for Israel Bonds. The other is a donation

---

4. By the end of the fighting, Israeli casualties reached 2,552 dead (compared to 759 dead in the Six-Day War) and over 3,000 wounded, with an estimated $4 billion loss in equipment. See Sachar, 786–87.

5. During the 1960s and 1970s, Marcia Saperstein was frequently invited to speak to various women's groups, usually about topics relating to world Jewry, based on their travels together.

form for the UJA Israel Emergency Fund. In either case, the money goes to the State of Israel immediately, and thus supports the war effort. It is for you to choose the medium you wish to use. The difference is that the bond is an investment, the UJA is a gift. With the bond, Israel will eventually have to pay it back to you; with the donation there is no such obligation. But I repeat, in either case, Israel gets the needed finances now, and that is what is so important.

One of the Israeli generals called this war *Milchemet Yom Hadin*, "the War of the Day of Judgment." It is a fitting name. On the Day of Judgment, all must render account for themselves. The nations of the world are being judged as to whether humanity and justice are mere words or realities. The little nation of Israel is being judged as to whether it will endure. And *we* are being judged as to whether we accept the challenge of being our brother's keeper, of being, as Jews, mutually responsible for each other. Please take a few moments to make your pledge, and then they will be collected. This is our *Yom Hadin*. Let us not be found wanting.

Slaughter of the Innocent
May 17, 1974

On May 15, 1974, three armed members of the Popular Front for the Liberation of Palestine, a radical splinter group competing with the PLO for influence, crossed the Israeli border from Lebanon and entered the village of Ma'alot in northern Israel. There they encountered a group of 120 children on a field trip from their home in Safed and took them hostage, threatening to blow up the school building where they were located unless imprisoned Arab guerillas were released. Israeli troops attempted to free the hostages, but in the resulting gunfire, twenty Israeli children were killed and some sixty-three were wounded. Vivid pictures of the wounded children being rushed out to ambulances on stretchers were broadcast all over the world.

This act of terrorism, following by about a month a similar PFLP attack in which eighteen civilians of the border town Kiryat Shemonah were killed in indiscriminate machine-gunning, seemed deliberately intended to undermine and sabotage the delicate negotiations of Henry Kissinger's "Shuttle Diplomacy" following the Yom Kippur War. The idea of targeting civilians, especially children, in order to destroy the possibility of an interim agreement between Israel and Syria, seemed particularly depressing to Saperstein, and he expresses this emotion with absolute candor at the outset.

I PREACH TONIGHT WITH A HEAVY HEART. I had intended to speak about exotic Jews in distant lands, sharing with you some of the knowledge and experiences that have come to me in the course of my travels all over the world. That must remain for some other occasion. The events of recent days have touched us all so deeply that I could not refrain from grappling with them in my sermon this evening. Rarely have I felt so personally involved in events, even though everything that touches the Jewish people anywhere has always touched me. But this has had the character of a personal tragedy.

I have not really slept for three nights. And when I have dozed off, I would awaken after a few moments with a start, as one does when he has just known some great personal sorrow. The memory would come flooding back and I would tell myself, it can't be true, I must have been dreaming. This sense of personal involvement was enhanced not only by the fact that I have been in Tzefat [the Hebrew equivalent of "Safed"] where these children lived so many times, but also by the thought that the ambulance donated by the Men's Club to the hospital in Tzefat—which bears my name—was undoubtedly used to carry the bodies of many of those children, dead and wounded.

Before I speak about events of recent days, I must go back a little to place them in perspective. In a previous sermon, I referred to the troubled spirit of Israel since the Yom Kippur War. That war, all things considered, had been an amazing victory—in military terms greater even than the Six-Day War, But the measure of war must be taken not merely on logistical and numerical terms, but in personal, emotional and human terms. We measure a war not just by the number of planes and tanks and personnel destroyed in comparison with those your own side has lost, but also in terms of the spirit of a people. And that war left Israel a deeply troubled people.

There was understandable sorrow. Immediately after the war, you would sit in a bus and see a woman weeping, and you would pretend not to see. Some Israelis told me that when they saw friends whom they heard had suffered a loss in the war, they would walk on the other side of the street, unable to face each other. Who can forget the scene at the mass memorial service in the National Cemetery on Mt. Herzl,[1] the pregnant wife on her knees at her husband's grave repeating one word: *lamah, lamah*—"Why? Why?" The young soldier carrying the baby daughter of his brother, telling her she must be brave, she must not cry. Sadness in war is part of the pattern. We too have known it in some measure. But in Israel it was so much closer to so great a proportion of the people.

Secondly, there was disillusionment. The Israelis had developed a kind of cockiness, a supreme self-confidence that sometimes bordered on arrogance. It is understandable. In the past generation, they had performed miracles. But it was also necessary psychologically. Jews had been pushed around for too long. They had been the objects and not the subjects of history for many centuries. They were tired of being the eternal victim. So it did them good to feel that they had an army rated, man for man, as perhaps the best in the world. They had total confidence in the superb quality of the Israeli Defense Forces and its leadership.

Those of us who were at the twenty-fifth anniversary celebration[2] will never forget the thrill of seeing those squadrons of planes roaring low across the sky

---

1. On the "Day of Memorial for the Fallen of the Yom Kippur War," held November 7, 1973.

2. This refers to a visit to Israel by a group from the Temple, led by the Sapersteins, in May of 1973 for the twenty-fifth anniversary of the establishment of the State. Saper-

with amazing precision, those seemingly countless tanks driven along the parade route with such quiet confidence. Many of the boys who drove those tanks and piloted those planes are dead now. And Israelis suddenly became aware that all the courage in the world cannot guarantee safety against modern, sophisticated push-button weaponry, and that leadership was human and capable of mistakes in judgment—with tragic results. This disillusionment was increased by the post-war political activities and mutual recriminations of so many of their military leaders. The leaders they had set up as idols too often had feet of clay.[3]

Thirdly, there was terrible frustration. The Israelis had, despite war after war, convinced themselves that peace would ultimately come. They persuaded themselves that each war they won would be the last. They sincerely wanted peace. There were exceptions, but the average Israeli did not hate the Arabs. All he wanted was to live at peace with them. I remember vividly how impressed I was after the Six-Day War by the attitude of the Israelis: there was no venom, no gloating, just a feeling of exhilaration—at last we have the holy places, at last we can forget about fighting.

That hope proved illusory. The Israelis would have been at that moment [after the Six-Day War] ready to give up virtually everything for peace. But the Arabs even in defeat were not concerned with peace. They wanted the end of Israel and they refused to enter into peace negotiations.[4] The Israelis refused to give up their hope; they would show that Israelis and Arabs could live together. And so they maintained a more open policy of military government than has ever existed on the part of a conqueror any place in the world. In West Jordan you could drive for hours and never see an Israeli military installation. The bridges across the Jordan were kept open so that merchandise could be exchanged between Arabs on both sides of the river. Young Arabs from all the Arab countries were encouraged to come to Israel to visit friends and relatives there and see its reality with their own eyes. Surely this was an enlightened policy which would bring peace.[5]

But peace did not come. There were terrorist attacks. There were hijackings. People were killed. Still the Israelis clung to their hope. Then that was crushed in the Yom Kippur War. This time, they were saved by a miracle. I have since driven across the Golan along the path of the Syrian advance. I have seen the

---

stein described the experience in a sermon delivered on May 25, 1973, and referred to it in the sermon given near the beginning of the Yom Kippur War.

3. This undoubtedly refers to the interim report of the "Agranat Commission" submitted on April 2, 1974, which recommended the dismissal of Chief of Staff David Elazar and several other top generals. On April 11, Prime Minister Golda Meir submitted her resignation, resulting in the selection of a new generation of Labor party leaders, who took office on June 3: Yitzhak Rabin as Prime Minister and Shimon Peres as Minister of Defense. See Sachar, *A History of Israel*, (New York: Knopf, 1996), 802–6.

4. Referring to the "Three No's" adopted in the Khartoum summit conference of August 29–September 1, 1967: no peace, no negotiations, no recognition.

5. This refers to the "Open Bridge" policy initiated by Moshe Dayan. See Shlomo Gazit, *The Carrot and the Stick: Israel's Policy in Judaea and Samaria, 1967–68* (Washington D.C.: B'nai B'rith Books, 1995), 176–94.

tanks that had come to the farthest forward point. They were almost within gunshot range of Tiberias. Why did they stop? The Israeli forces were not large enough to stop them. It was because they themselves stopped, fearing they would fall into a trap. But you can't rely on miracles. Israelis asked themselves, where will it all end? How can we keep on fighting over and over?

Months passed. Negotiations began. The mood of the Israelis was chastened. Even the hawks were willing to make concessions. They realized that military power alone cannot guarantee survival. On the other hand, bitter experience had shown that political guarantees could not guarantee peace. They were ready to negotiate. To give up all but that which was essential to their security, in the hope that peace might be forthcoming. As Kissinger carried on his negotiations, despite their skepticism and their weary, troubled spirits, hope again began to bloom.[6] Then came Kiryat Shemonah and the murder of innocent civilians, and now Ma'alot and the slaughter of innocent children. Now that hope is crushed, and the mood of Israel has become not just low but ugly. Now people turn with hatred, and call for revenge.

Incidentally, the phrase "Slaughter of the Innocents" comes from the New Testament. It refers to the events in ancient Palestine when Herod was supposed to have received word of the birth of the Messiah and called upon his soldiers to murder every newborn male child in the land.[7] Even so, the slaughter of these young people, the age of our own youth group—on an innocent *tiyul*, a hike through the land—could serve no purpose except to forestall the Messiah, to prevent the coming of peace.

What lessons are to be learned? First, we know now that the terrorists do not want peace. We know that the Arab nations really do not want peace. I remember Golda Meir telling us wearily, "If only it was a matter of giving up a piece of land here or there it would be simple. The problem is that they want us to give up our existence." Yesterday afternoon, at Staten Island Community College, a celebration was held honoring the Palestinian terrorists. The program included speakers and a belly dancer. It is hard to imagine a group of college students, gloating over the death of innocent teenagers. The Arab nations themselves are responsible for terrorism because they encouraged it, and honored the terrorists, and gave them sanctuary.

Second, we see once again that the Jews are virtually alone in the world. I once heard Gideon Hausner in Israel speak at impressive exercises at Yad Vashem, that unforgettably haunting structure in Jerusalem, a memorial to the six million, commemorating man's inhumanity and at the same time the glory of the human spirit. Hausner asked, "Why must there be such a place?" He answered, "Because of the hatred of men and the indifference of the world."[8]

---

6. On the Kissinger "shuttle diplomacy" leading to the disengagement agreements with Egypt and Syria, see Nadav Safran, *Israel: The Embattled Ally* (Cambridge: Harvard University Press, 1978), 506–60.

7. See Matthew 2:16, speaking of male children age two and under in Bethlehem.

8. Hausner, Israel's chief prosecutor at the Eichmann trial and author of *Justice in Jerusalem*, was appointed chairman of the Yad Vashem Council in 1968.

Even those who have been reluctant to admit it must now realize that there is a double standard of morality in the world. Each time there has been an act of Arab terrorism, the denunciation has been strangely silent, at most an expression of individual feeling. Each time there was retaliation by Israel, all the nations of the world and the United Nations itself jumped to condemnation. They act as though if only Israel would let its people be murdered without striking back, there might be hope for peace. And since Israel won't follow that script, they blame Israel for the continuation of bloodshed. The criticism might be in better taste if even once the world had taken decisive action against the acts of terrorism and violence by the Arabs that instigated the retaliation by Israel.

Today's *New York Times* listed twenty-one acts of terrorism in the last three years.[9] They involved the murder of dozens of innocent civilians. In connection with them, terrorists were arrested and placed into custody in various countries of the world. Today, all but seven of them are at large, free to continue spreading hatred and death.

Let me make myself clear. I am not proud of Israel's response to the attack at Ma'alot.[10] Violence is wrong and the killing of civilians is wrong, even though I cannot equate an attack on areas that unquestionably harbor terrorists with the slaying of athletes at the Olympics,[11] or workers in a village, or children on an outing. At another meeting, Golda Meir said, "I can forgive the Arabs for having killed our sons. I shall never forgive the Arabs because they have forced us to kill their sons."[12] Retaliation is evil and ugly and wrong. But let the responsibility rest where it should. The moral guilt lies with the terrorists and the Arab nations and the civilized world that have forced Israel to compromise its own humanity.

Yet despite everything, I still cling to hope. The ultimate sin in Jewish life is to lose hope. There may be some who say that Israel itself was a great mistake. Think back before there was an Israel. Remember the refugee conferences at Evian and Bermuda, where the nations of the world pondered but could find no place for even a handful of the hundreds of thousands of potential Jewish refugees.[13] Remember the ships bearing their burden of suffering Jews to the shores

9. Apparently referring to *New York Times*, May 16, 1974, A20:1.

10. Referring to massive Israeli air attacks against Palestinian bases in Lebanon on May 16 and 17, following the Ma'alot attack. Lebanese and Palestinian sources claimed 48 deaths, 20 missing, and 174 wounded in the May 16 Israeli air actions.

11. Referring to the killing of eleven Israelis at the Munich Olympics of 1972 by members of the Palestinian "Black September" organization.

12. The authoritative version of this statement, made at a London press conference in 1969, is a bit less absolute: "When peace comes we will perhaps in time be able to forgive the Arabs for killing our sons, but it will be harder for us to forgive them for having forced us to kill their sons." *Golda Meir Speaks Out*, ed. Marie Syrkin (London: Weidenfeld & Nicolson, 1973), 242.

13. The Evian Conference was initiated by the Roosevelt Administration following Germany's annexation of Austria in 1938. See *American Jewish Year Book* 5699, vol. 40 (Philadelphia: JPS, 1938), 345–48; Arthur Morse, *While Six Million Died: A Chronicle of American Apathy* (New York: Random House, 1968), 207–29. The Bermuda Conference

of Palestine and turned back to perish in the waters of the sea because the doors of the Promised Land were closed.[14] Remember the concentration camps themselves, when Samuel Ziegelbaum, former President of the Jewish community of Warsaw, told the world of what was happening and pleaded for action and got nothing but a deaf ear—finally taking his own life in the hope that this might somehow touch the conscience of humanity.[15] That is what we had before the State of Israel. Is that what we want to go back to?

The pain of Ma'alot is the price that must be paid for having our land and our freedom. I will never forget trying to console my friend and colleague Rabbi Moses Cyrus Weiler,[16] who lost one son in the War of Attrition and a second son commanding a tank unit in the Golan on the fourth day of the Yom Kippur War. He said to me, "This is the price we must pay. Only it is such a great and bitter price!" It will not be easy to continue. Our strongest weapon is *ein bereirah*, "we have no choice."

The name Ma'alot, where this last tragedy occurred, is taken from the Psalms. A whole series of Psalms sung in ancient times on the pilgrimage to Jerusalem have the title *Shir Hama'alot*—a song of the ascent. The 129th Psalm is one of those. It begins, "A song of Ma'alot. Much have they afflicted me from my youth up, but they have not prevailed against me. Let them be ashamed and turned backward, all they that hate Zion" (Ps. 129:1,2,5). Our brothers in Israel must pay the price, their children must pay the price. We and our children need not die for our people. It makes it all the more incumbent that we must *live* for them. The time is dark, and events are somber. But behind the clouds the sun still shines. Our hope has not died, and despite everything, we dedicate ourselves to a better tomorrow.

---

was initiated by the British and the Americans in response to public reaction to the published reports of German mass murder of European Jewry. See *American Jewish Year Book 5704*, vol. 45 (Philadelphia: JPS, 1943), 356–62; Morse, 52–66.

14. Most famously, the *Struma*, a ship carrying 769 Jews from Romania who were denied entry to Palestine by the British. The ship sank, with only one survivor, after being towed out of Istanbul harbor by Turkish authorities in February 1942. For the reaction in the United States and Britain, see David Wyman, *The Abandonment of the Jews* (New York: Pantheon, 1984), 158–59.

15. The report of Ziegelbaum's suicide of May 12, 1943, with the full text of his protest letter, was published in the *New York Times* on June 4. For a powerful contemporary response, see Alfred Kazin, "'In Every Voice, in Every Ban,'" *The New Republic*, January 10, 1944, reprinted in *The New Republic Reader*, ed. Dorothy Wickenden (New York: Basic Books, 1994), 55–59.

16. A South African liberal rabbi who immigrated with his family to Israel.

- 47 -

How My Mind Has Changed
January 31, 1975

The following is a sermon not of youth but of maturity. It reflects back upon some four decades of a rabbinical career, work that entailed constant articulation of positions on abstract values and concrete issues. The elements of continuity are noted, but particularly pronounced in this context are the areas of change. As has already been seen, some of the most passionately defended commitments of the 1930s had been abandoned in a process that must have been excruciating. For most in the congregation in 1975, hearing that their rabbi had once been a pacifist and a socialist must have come as something of a shock.

This type of message runs the danger of implying a kind of ethical relativism, an unstable moral compass, a ground always susceptible to radical shifts. Perhaps for this reason, the sermon begins with an evocation of what is permanent: the eternal principles of truth embodied in the Ten Commandments. Furthermore, unlike many colleagues who might have included a shift from anti-Zionism to Zionism in such a retrospective, Saperstein's consistent Zionist commitment is made clear. The sermon thus attempts to communicate the changes as evidence not of an absence of courage or commitment, but rather of openness to new ideas, to changed realities, to deeper insights coming with the years, to new insights that can be achieved without compromising the core principles of religious conviction.

THE STORY HAS SOMEWHERE BEEN TOLD that a group of nations, concerned about impending catastrophe that could wipe out our total civilization, decided to pool their intellectual resources to see how such tragedy could be prevented. They gathered the greatest minds in every field of human endeavor. For many days they shared their wisdom as it referred to man's destiny and human relations. All of it was programmed into the most advanced computer existing in the world. When at last they were done, the computer was asked, "On what basis can the world endure?" The giant machine whirred for a second, and then spelled out the answer, "I am the Lord thy God. . . . Thou shalt have no other gods before Me. . . ." And so on—the Ten Commandments.

I begin with this story tonight because this is the Sabbath when the Torah portion brings us the Decalogue at Sinai [Exodus 20:2-14]. There are certain principles the truth of which is eternal. The Ten Commandments must be placed in that category. But the application of these principles in real circumstances, the ideas by which we guide ourselves and set our goals, may well change with changing times.

I thought of this as I was considering my sermon for this evening, entitled "How My Mind Has Changed." I have been a rabbi, as you know, for more than forty-one years—longer than the lifetime of most of the people in the congregation tonight—all of it, with the exception of World War II, in this congregation. I entered the rabbinate with certain convictions and motivations. I had a deep love for the Jewish heritage and interest in Jewish studies. I wanted to serve the Jewish people; I was committed to the Zionist ideal. I was interested in the social implications of religion, convinced that religion could make an important contribution to the painful problems of society, to the struggle against injustice and war and prejudice. I was eager to give of myself to help others. The narrow sense of religion—faith in God, formal worship, observance of ceremonies—played a lesser part in the forces that moved me. I believed that the liberal interpretation of religion was the wave of the future, and that it alone could satisfy my religious needs.

Many things have happened in my own life and in the world during these more than forty years. They include the Great Depression, the economic revival and the current recession. They include World War II, the Korean War and the Vietnam War. They include the New Deal of the Roosevelt Era, the tragically curtailed charisma of the Kennedy era, the moral decline of the Nixon-Watergate era. For Jews they include the tragedy of the Holocaust, the establishment of the Jewish State and Israel's struggle for survival, the so-called religious revival of the fifties and the flood of intermarriage of the '60s. They include the civil rights revolution, the youth revolution, the moral revolution. There have been few periods in human history so fraught with significant change.

Looking back, my basic thinking has remained fairly constant. I still adhere to the values that impelled me to the rabbinate and sustained me through my career thus far. But in the application of these values, there have been many changes. I would like to deal with some of these changes this evening.

Let me begin by saying that I am less doctrinaire than I used to be, less certain that a particular formula will solve our problems. Sometimes it makes me feel terribly old-fashioned, but so often in Temple life when a young member comes up with a challenging idea for change, I am tempted to throw cold water on the enthusiasm by saying what is true: "It's a good idea but I don't think it will work. You see, we tried that twenty years ago."

The same thing applies in the larger realm of world affairs. I entered the Rabbinate during the years of the Great Depression when radical political thinking was very current in intellectual circles. I was never a communist, but I considered myself a socialist. Many sermons of those days called for a new social order based upon cooperation, not competition, motivated by service and not by profit. Around that time I took some courses at the Union Theological Seminary—a non-denominational Protestant Seminary. One course, with a professor named Harry F. Ward, was on "Religion and Social Change." Ward was an economic radical who had a profound influence on many of his students.[1]

I wrote a paper for him on the Jews in Soviet Russia. In it, I tried to show the effect on Jewish life of living in a communist society. I reached the conclusion that the obvious imperfections were only temporary, that in the long run, anti-Semitism would be eliminated. On my last page, I wrote, "In conclusion, we might say that with the classless society, the mainsprings of anti-Semitism would be destroyed. It would no longer be necessary to find a scapegoat to bear the sins of an exploiting society." And so on. I believed that then. I no longer do. I am convinced that prejudice and injustice are not solely the result of the social structure. They are deeply rooted in the human condition, and the fight against them is a universal and eternal one.

The same pattern manifests itself within our own society. I was and still am an earnest advocate of what we called the New Deal. I thought that if only we could have social security and decent housing for the poor and educational opportunities for all and the elimination of racial and religious restrictions in employment and housing, everything would be well—crime and violence would be largely eliminated, and all people would live decent lives. Well these things, which we once looked upon as so radical, are now in large part taken for granted. But the ideal world is still far removed. Public housing has often been turned into slums, violence and crime are more rampant than ever, social services like Medicare and nursing homes and educational opportunities for minority groups have all too often been exploited for personal profit by those who administer them.

I came into the rabbinate during the pacifist heyday of the 1930s. Our prophets were Gandhi and Einstein. Together with many other students I had taken the Oxford Pledge that never under any circumstances would I participate in any war.[2] As a rabbinical student I remember marching as part of a contingent from

---

1. Ward was Professor of Christian Ethics at Union Theological Seminary from 1918 until his retirement in 1941. His early books had titles such as *The Social Creed of the Churches* (1913) and *Social Evangelism* (1915). Not long before Saperstein's course, he published *In Place of Profit: Social Incentives in the Soviet Union* (New York: Scribners, 1933).

2. The "Oxford Pledge" originated in a decision taken in February 1933 by undergraduate members of the Oxford (University) Union that they "will in no circumstances fight for King and Country." It spread to other English universities and the United States, where it was adopted by increasing numbers of students between 1934 and 1936. See Charles Chatfield, *For Peace and Justice: Pacifism in America, 1914–1941* (Knoxville:

the Jewish Institute of Religion, led by our President Stephen S. Wise, in an antiwar parade through the streets of New York.[3] I preached many sermons on pacifism. I remember telling our people that if war should ever come again and the entire nation be caught up in war hysteria, I would pay whatever price was needed but I would not serve.

Years passed. World War II came and my mind was changed. I volunteered to serve as a chaplain in the American Army. I remember throwing away a thick handful of old sermons from my files. Some of them escaped; I have them here. They were preached in the 1930s. Here are some of the titles: "Education for Peace," "Mental Disarmament," "Why Not?" "Can Jews Afford to Be Pacifists?" "Must There Be War?"[4]

I am no longer a pacifist or a conscientious objector. But I can understand and sympathize with those who are. For myself, there are circumstances under which for actual survival, or for values that are greater than life, war is justified. But with the terrible dangers of total [nuclear] destruction, war is unforgivable except as a last resort.

In my early years in the rabbinate, I had confidence in the basic fairness of humanity. I had great hopes for the good will movement in our country. I felt that prejudice was based on ignorance, and that if we could persuade non-Jews that we were good people and that our religion was a good religion, we would have turned the tide. Similarly, I had great faith and hopes in the United Nations. I was confident that if only nations would be willing to gather together and talk, they could solve their problems.

I am no longer convinced of either. The relative silence of the Christian churches during the Holocaust and on other occasions when the fate of Israel and the Jew were being weighed in the balance, the double standard that is applied wherever Jewish interests are at stake, the prejudice of people who are intellectual and scholarly and impartially objective in all areas outside their prejudices, the readiness of the United Nations members to act not as an instrument of justice but as a weapon of politics—all these have given me second thoughts. I still believe that we need greater understanding and that we must have an international body. But I am not sanguine that they represent the solution to our problems.

What about Jewish life? I was always a Zionist. I was brought up in a Zionist household. My grandfather[5] was one of the first Orthodox rabbis to stand beside the young Stephen S. Wise in support of the movement just initiated by Theodor

---

The University of Tennessee Press, 1971), 260, 272, and Eileen Eagan, *Class, Culture, and the Classroom: The Student Peace Movement of the 1930s* (Philadelphia: Temple University Press, 1981), 57–71, 184–97.

3. For Wise's renewed pacifism in the early 1930s, see Melvin Urofsky, *A Voice that Spoke for Justice* (Albany: SUNY Press, 1982), 308–10.

4. The last two of these are printed above. It should be noted that Saperstein's rejection of pacifism in the context of the struggle against Nazism was fairly typical, but not universal among his colleagues. His friend and classmate at JIR, Rabbi Jerome Malino, maintained his own pacifist commitment during this period and throughout his career.

5. Rabbi Hyman Lasker, ordained by Rabbi Elhanan Spector in Kovno, who served for most of his career in Troy, New York, where Saperstein grew up.

Herzl—at a time when political Zionism was taboo with most of his colleagues.[6] I was confident then of what was classic Zionist doctrine: that when there was a Jewish State and Jewish life would be normalized, anti-Semitism would disappear. We would no longer be an anomaly in the world: a people without a land. I believed that once we had a large Jewish community in the land of Israel, it would serve as a spiritual center to inspire Jewish life all over the world, to reinvigorate the Jewish faith and instill Jewish loyalty. As one of the first rabbis in the area to visit what was then Palestine, I lectured all over the metropolitan area on this subject.

I am still a Zionist, but I am no longer hopeful that a Jewish State in our ancient homeland will automatically resolve all the problems of Jewish communities in the Diaspora. More and more I have come to realize that there must be both Israel and Diaspora, that there must be a bridge between them, that they need each other, and that therefore we cannot assume that survival is automatic.

There are many other subjects about which I could speak. Time permits me to touch upon only one. When I started, I had the feeling that if only we could make our worship service more attractive and exciting, we would get people to come. I was one of the pioneers in what is now called the "creative service." At a time when the Temple had no office and no secretary—only a broken-down mimeograph machine in an old closet—almost every Sabbath had me typing stencils, running them off, and collecting them. I hardly ever conducted a service without hands stained with mimeograph ink.

I no longer have that confidence. Changing the words in services, more or less music, ancient or modern literary selections will not bring people storming the doors of the sanctuary. The failure to attend services is more deep-seated.[7] We are living in a non-religious age. It isn't that people fail to be attracted to a particular style of worship; it is that many people no longer feel the need to worship, or are convinced of the value of worship, however attractive. Yes, make the service as attractive as possible for those who do come. They deserve the best you can give them. But in all honesty, they would probably come anyway. And don't expect that others will be attracted in great numbers. It may very well be, as I have said before, that we will need to reconcile ourselves to the possibility that only a minority of our people will be deeply involved. That does not worry me too much. Minorities of dedicated people have fashioned the direction of world history time and again through the centuries.

Yes, my mind has changed in many ways over the decades. This must sound like a pessimistic report, as time and again I have seemed to lose confidence and hope in something that once seemed to offer promise for a better future. But it is not despair that prompted these changes. It is realism. I am more than ever convinced of the importance of religion, of what we stand for. That there is no sim-

---

6. In 1897, most Orthodox rabbis, like Reform rabbis, were opposed to the new political Zionist movement, though for different reasons.

7. The rest of this paragraph picks up a theme expressed in the 1972 Ordination sermon above. Actually, compared to many other congregations, attendance at Friday evening services, which averaged about 300 during this period, was considered quite respectable. The issue discussed arises when this number is compared with 1,000 family members.

ple panacea to insure the triumph of faith and decency and justice and humanity does not mean that they are any less important. It merely means that they require greater sacrifice.

The Midrash tells us that the Decalogue was offered to other nations first, who refused it because they were unwilling to make the sacrifices that its observance entailed. Only the children of Israel accepted it without argument.[8] As I go forward, I still believe that religion is the most important, most rewarding activity in the world, but in serving it, we must not be guilty of intellectual and spiritual arteriosclerosis. We must keep open minds and open spirits. We must be ready to reformulate our programs and to change our minds. The ideals themselves are eternal. To them we must constantly renew our dedication.

---

8. See sources in Ginzberg, *Legends of the Jews*, 3:81 and 6:30–31.

48

The Dream Shattered
November 14, 1975

Some of the rhetorical elements of this sermon will be familiar to the reader: the explanation of a change from the previously announced topic because of the urgency of the recent event, the assertion of intense personal involvement. This was not a sermon intended to convince an uncertain or wavering audience of the speaker's point of view. No one in the congregation that night would have supported the UN General Assembly's resolution condemning Zionism as a form of racism. Even those who might not have defined themselves as Zionists were offended, infuriated, deeply hurt. The sermon therefore functions as an attempt to articulate the depth of the outrage felt by American Jews along with Jews throughout the world, as well as to formulate a response to the powerful Arab public relations effort buttressed by strong support in the Soviet bloc and "Third World."

This was not, therefore, the occasion for a nuanced analysis of different streams of Zionist thought, or for a balanced discussion of Israel's policy toward its own Arab citizens. Saperstein's visceral support of Zionism, seen in his 1948 sermon following the establishment of the State, had been deepened by the experience of being in Jerusalem during the Six-Day War. At the same time, the struggle against racism—whether the Nazi antisemitic ideology or the prejudice that pervaded the American South as the civil rights movement crystallized— was a core commitment throughout his career. The assertion that Zionism was racism, endorsed by a majority of the world's nations under the auspices of the institution founded to foster international understanding and peace, seemed not just unbelievable but almost surrealistic. The sermonic response drew upon the skills of the debater, beginning with an appeal to the most powerful association at hand: the analogy with Hitler and the "Big Lie."

The final part of the sermon draws upon a motif we have encountered before: the dream, the vision of a brighter future. Saperstein had frequently re-

ferred to the "American dream" (see, e.g., the sermon of September 6, 1963). At President Kennedy's death, he cited Lillian Smith's Killers of the Dream *and concluded, "You can kill men, women, and children. But you cannot kill a dream." Here, however, the dream is "shattered," the hopes are "crushed." It is one of the bleaker moments in Saperstein's preaching. Yet the weekly Scriptural reading leads the sermon to a dénouement at odds with the tone in so much that came before. Jacob, fleeing for his life, lays his head on a hard stone, yet dreams a vision of God's promise. No empirical support from the present reality is brought to justify this hope, and one senses that, at least at that moment, the preacher's heart was not fully in it when he urged that even in this time of disillusion, a "vision of the heights" must remain.*

YOU WILL NOTE THAT THE SUBJECT OF MY SERMON TONIGHT has been changed. I had planned to speak about American Jewish history in light of the centennial celebration of the Hebrew Union College—Jewish Institute of Religion, our Reform rabbinical seminary. But sometimes something breaks over the horizon that captures our attention and stirs our emotions and demands that we address ourselves to it. Such a subject becomes, as the prophet described it, like a burning fire in our bones [compare Jer. 20:9], that will not let us rest. And so tonight I am going to speak about the vote at the General Assembly of the United Nations last Monday, which passed the resolution condemning Zionism as a form of racism and racial discrimination that threatens world peace and security. This resolution was approved by a vote of 72 to 35, with 32 abstentions.

It is significant that it came on the eve of Veterans Day, which in the minds of Americans commemorates our struggle with the forces of tyranny, and only a few days before the first anniversary of the address of Yasir Arafat before the United Nations, which marked the beginning of a process through which the dream that organization embodied has been shattered.[1] For Jews it is painfully ironic that the vote was taken on the anniversary of Kristallnacht—that tragic event in 1938 when the physical attack upon the Jews of Germany was launched with the shattering of windows, the destruction of synagogues, the burning of books, and the humiliation, arrest and mob attacks against defenseless Jews. Kristallnacht was the harbinger of the Holocaust; the passing of this resolution comes with ominous warning to Jews all over the world.

Rarely have I seen such deeply felt gut reactions on the part of Jews. As you know, I was with our Temple delegation at the Union [of American Hebrew Congregations] Biennial Convention in Dallas, Texas. The news of the vote came to us at a session to be addressed by the Israeli Consul General from Chicago. That afternoon, we passed a strong resolution, commending our own Gov-

---

1. Arafat spoke to the General Assembly of the United Nations on November 13, 1974; with a pistol visible in his belt, he indicated that he was demanding a state for all of Palestine that would replace the State of Israel. See Howard Sachar, *A History of Israel* (New York: Alfred A. Knopf, 1996), 811–12.

ernment for its powerful position on this matter. Feelings were tense that evening. One of the highlights of the conference occurred when the young people took over. They had prepared a list of 3,000 signatures written on a wide strip of wrapping paper 300 feet long, and it was unrolled as the entire assembly sang "Am Yisrael Chai."

Then a Yahrzeit [memorial light] was kindled and Kaddish was recited for the dream of the United Nations, while a recording played an address made at the launching of the UN, describing the role it was expected to fulfill and the hopes that were launched with it. When we sang "Hatikvah," the song of the hope of our own people, I could not keep back the tears. Upon returning, I was told by a number of our people who attended the great rally held in New York outside the Brotherhood in Action Center of the tremendous emotional fervor of that meeting.[2] Here at our Temple, we devoted one hour of our Wednesday evening study group to the discussion of this theme, and our people were obviously absorbed and deeply involved in a very personal sense.

Why did this UN Resolution have so powerful an impact on Jewish consciousness? After all, we might have said, "It is just words. The General Assembly of the UN has no authority and little influence. Should we not treat it as the Israeli representative did when he tore the paper containing the resolution into pieces?" But no! Something deep in the Jewish soul told us to beware. There was an immediate gut reaction on the part of Jews everywhere. They felt, without knowing just why, that this resolution was a warning sign.

Let us try to examine what was behind the intensity of our feelings. First, I think, there was the realization that this resolution is not the end but the beginning of a new systematic and calculated effort to destroy Israel. How would this be done? Hitler showed the way. You must first prepare the ground; you must build up an acceptance of inhumanity on the part of those who will proceed to destroy your intended victim. You do that by creating a demonic picture of your victim, as Hitler did about the Jews—as an evil force that undermines nations and seeks world domination. In this way you remove your victim from the category of humanity; you remove the nation you wish to destroy from the legitimate family of nations. To do this, you use the "big lie." That is exactly what is now being done. And so we find the "big lie" directed against Israel, and Zionism.

Zionism is charged with being a racist philosophy, a threat to world peace. The fact is that Israel is one of the meager handful of truly democratic nations in the world. The fact is that none of the countries that voted against Israel is democratic, that most of them are totalitarian tyrannies, practicing racist policies and often bloody barbarism. What a travesty it is that the Soviet Union denounces Israel for denial of human rights—having denied to its Jews both the right to live [as Jews] and the right to leave. What a travesty that Uganda denounces Israel for racist discrimination, after it has driven out its Indian minority and expropriated their wealth.

---

2. A mass rally of tens of thousands gathered in New York's garment district on November 11 to protest the UN resolution; see the *New York Times*, Nov. 12, 1975, A1.

What a travesty that Sudan condemns Israel for racism, after it has massacred its black non-Arab population. What a travesty that Lebanon voted against Israel, even as its Moslem majority waits for the moment when it may seal the fate by bloodbath of its Maronite Christian minority. What a travesty that Saudi Arabia dares to speak of racism, when it will permit no foreign contractor to bring into the country a single Jewish employee. It seems that every dictatorial regime joined the bandwagon, while every democracy—concerned with moral values—gave its support to Israel. Unfortunately, they were all too few.

An example of the "big lie" was apparent in an article on the Op-Ed page of yesterday's *New York Times*. It was written by A. M. El-Messiri, advisor to the UN office of the League of Arab States.[3] I spoke to a group of Protestant ministers on this subject this morning and took the article point by point, showing how sometimes by unmitigated lies, sometimes by quotations completely out of context, the slander of racism is supported.

To give two brief examples. The author states that the phrase "Oriental Barbarism" is frequently found in Zionist literature. I have read this literature and cannot recall a single use of the phrase.[4] He attributes to Ahad Ha'am the term, "the super-nation." I have read virtually everything Ahad Ha'am has written and the phrase is completely contradictory to everything he stands for.[5] He was interested not in politics but in spiritual values, in having Israel become a spiritual center for Jews all over the world. At another point, El-Messiri interprets the conquest of the soil as being exclusivist and discriminatory. The concept was the theme of a Hebrew philosopher, A. D. Gordon. His purpose was to avoid colo-

---

3. *New York Times*, November 13, 1975, A40.

4. El-Messiri wrote that "Zionist literature is rife with such phrases and terms as "oriental barbarism." While certainly not common, see, however, Theodor Herzl's statement: if the Sultan of Turkey were to give us Palestine, "We should there form a part of a wall of defense for Europe in Asia, an outpost of civilization against barbarism." *The Jewish State*, in Arthur Hertzberg, *The Zionist Idea* (Philadelphia: JPS, 1959), 222. A less polemical response might have been to contextualize this statement by noting how widely prevalent such language was in the contemporary discourse of Europeans, and Americans. Note, for example, the far more extreme statement by Theodore Roosevelt, justifying not peaceful settlement but American military conquest: "The warfare that has extended the boundaries of civilization at the expense of barbarism and savagery has been one of the most potent factors in the progress of humanity." *Presidential Addresses and State Papers of Theodore Roosevelt* (New York, 1970), 1:62–63, cited by Norman Finkelstein, in *A Nation on Trial* (New York: Henry Holt and Company, 1998), 85, n. 76.

5. Ahad Ha'am did apparently introduce this term into Hebrew literature, as Saperstein knew from having read him extensively in Hebrew and having marked the following passage in his copy of the English of "The Transvaluation of Values": "If we agree, then, that the Super*man* is the goal of all things, we must needs agree also that an essential condition of the attainment of this goal is the Super*nation*"—*Selected Essays by Ahad Ha-'am*, ed. Leon Simon (Philadelphia: JPS, 1912), 228. The main point is correct, however, that the term is not used in the racial or political sense, as is clear from the continuation: "that is to say, there must be a single nation better adapted than other nations, by virtue of its inherent characteristics, to moral development, and ordering its whole life in accordance with a moral law which stands higher than the common type."

nialism, to prevent Jews from coming in and exploiting Arab natives for the hard labor. He insisted that there was dignity in what he called *avodah shechorah*, "black labor," the labor that gets your hands dirty.[6]

It is significant also that the same day that this resolution was passed, another was passed calling for participation of the Palestinians in any further negotiations in Geneva.[7] The Palestinians have never concealed the fact that they call for the destruction of Israel. The present resolution is a strategic step intended to lead to that ultimate goal.

Secondly, Jews felt instinctively that this was not merely an attack upon Israel but an attack upon Jews. The defenders of the Resolution insist that they are not anti-Semitic, that they are not against Jews or Judaism, but that they are against only Zionism and Zionists. But we Jews know that they mean all of us. Of course there are Jews who are not Zionists. There are also Jews who do not believe in God, or Jewish rituals, or the synagogue. But all these things are part of Jewishness, and Zionism and mainstream Judaism cannot be separated.

What is Zionism? It is not complex or mysterious. Zionism is the oldest movement of national liberation in history, going back for 2,000 years. Zionism is the movement to establish a homeland for the Jewish people in the ancient land of Israel. It has its roots in the Bible. In this Sabbath's Scriptural reading, we find a repetition to Jacob of the promise given originally to Abraham.[8] It was expressed in the words of the Psalmist, *Im eshkachekh Yerushalyim*, "If I forget thee, O Jerusalem, let my right hand forget its cunning" (Ps. 137:5). It was preserved in Jewish life and liturgy, in the Jewish heart and home through all these generations. It was proclaimed at each festival when the Jew recited the formula, *Leshanah Haba'ah berushalayim*, "Next year in Jerusalem."

In essence, even when separated from the land we have preserved a government in exile through thousands of years. And is it really unjust to expect that in an area of the world where there are forty Arab states with 120 million inhabitants and 2 million square miles of territory, there might also be a tiny country of 8,500 square miles where Jews may develop their own culture and heritage and way of life? No, the battle starts out against Israel and Zionism, but it threatens to let loose an avalanche of anti-Semitism against Jews wherever they are.

Thirdly, we are concerned because in this resolution we have seen the shattering of a dream. Probably no people welcomed the establishment of the United Nations more than the Jews. True, it included nations that were anti-Semitic and anti-Israel. But when the majority of the world's nations approved of the establishment of Israel, it was a day of glory not only for Jews but for the United Na-

---

6. Gordon's views on the need for and dignity of Jewish manual labor were available in his *Selected Essays* (New York: League for Labor Palestine, 1938, see esp. 23–28 and 50–91), and Hertzberg, *The Zionist Idea*, 371–86.

7. This resolution passed by a significantly larger majority, 101 to 8, with 25 abstentions.

8. See Genesis 28:13, from the Scriptural lesson *Va-Yetse*. The final paragraph of the sermon returns to the beginning of this passage.

tions as well. Its purpose was justified. It had achieved an act of historic justice. It promised to be the champion and the preserver of peace for the world.

How our hopes have been crushed! The United Nations has developed into another political instrument, whose actions are separated from any consideration of justice or right. Someone has said that if one of the Arab countries should present a resolution to the effect that the world is flat, or that two plus two makes five, that resolution would receive a majority of votes at the General Assembly. Why then did they vote as they did? Some because they wanted to destroy Israel, some out of anti-American feeling, some out of Moslem unity, some out of anti-Semitic prejudice. Many voted because of crass material motives, because of their need for oil, or their desire for investment of some of those petrodollars. Some—we know this without question—were simply paid off for the votes in cold cash.

There is a little island in the Indian Ocean called Mauritius. On our last sabbatical, on the way to Australia, we stopped over there one night. It is a nothing island—its one industry is sugar cane—with a population of about half a million. Its vote, however, counts as much as does the vote of the United States. Its representative was quoted in the *New York Times* as saying, "We don't really know what Zionism is. We only know what the Palestinians told us it is."[9]

The real victim is thus the United Nations, whose moral authority has been destroyed and whose word has now become meaningless. The shame is on those nations who allowed themselves to be bribed or browbeaten. The resolution was an act of blasphemy, obscene in its cynicism.

Should we call for America to get out of the UN? A proposal to that end was presented at our Convention in Dallas. It urged withdrawal of our country and efforts to bring about the dissolution of the organization. But the Convention voted down this proposal, and I think it is to their credit. The United Nations has betrayed and disappointed us. It has shattered the dream. But we are the transmitters of the dream. We must continue to work with the UN despite disappointment and defeat and frustration. For mankind needs that dream, and some day, hopefully, it will be renewed.

Our Bible reading tonight began with Jacob's dream of the ladder rising from earth to heaven. Let me remind you that before he dreamed, he laid his head to rest on a stone (Gen. 28:11). That has been the genius of the Jew: that out of our suffering we have seen a vision of the heights.[10] Despite everything, in this hour of darkness, let us raise our eyes and continue to hope.

---

9. See *New York Times*, Nov. 12, 1975, A17.

10. Compare the use of this motif in the sermons for 1948 and 1950, above. There the statement, cited from Berdichevski, affirms a people's need for territory of its own as a foundation for cultural and spiritual creativity. Here the stone represents not the territorial prerequisite for such creativity, but the hardships that may inspire it.

49

The Harvest of '77
December 30, 1977

As can be seen above, during the 1930s and early 1940s, Saperstein generally used his Rosh Hashanah evening sermon to take stock of events during the previous year and their significance for Jewish life. Later in his career, he often used the Friday night nearest to the secular New Year's eve for this purpose. The following is an example, surveying the ebbing 1977 from a general and a Jewish perspective.

After a kaleidoscopic review, including quick reference to many areas of conflict throughout the world, he narrows the focus to four. The first was a milestone of American cultural history: the enormous influence of Alex Haley's Roots, *especially on television. The enormous audience that viewed this series enabled it to cut across ethnic and socio-economic lines, a shared experience for much of American society—like the assassinations of President Kennedy and the Rev. Martin Luther King in the 1960s, except that this, despite its vivid evocation of suffering, was ultimately uplifting. The searching for roots was of obvious relevance to assimilationist Jews as well as to blacks; as Saperstein notes, it helped launch a significant new interest in genealogical research.*

The other general event was of particular importance to Saperstein on a personal level. During the summer of 1977, he and Marcia had made another visit to South Africa. There he met a young man named Stephen Biko, who had formulated an ideal of "Black Consciousness," described by one scholar as "a liberation movement of the mind, [a] psychological revolution aimed at forging Black thought and feeling into an amalgam of Black pride and ultimately Black unity" (Millard Arnold, see below, n. 8, xiv). Saperstein reported on his visit, including his meeting with Biko, in his sermon of September 23, 1977. Biko's death in custody just one week later, hit him like the death of Jonathan Daniels in Alabama, 1965. As few Americans could fail to be outraged by this, it was another unifying experience.

The Bakke case, argued before the Supreme Court and awaiting a decision, was quite different. A test of the kind of affirmative action involving set-aside goals to guarantee a higher number of blacks in American professional schools, it raised issues that split American society, and the Jewish community as well. Many of those who had been committed to the civil rights movement in the South were concerned about what looked like a new imposition of quotas and a kind of "reverse discrimination," in which fully qualified whites, including Jews, were passed over in favor of what looked like less qualified blacks. Saperstein was somewhat torn on this issue: the legacies of his civil rights work and his representing of New York Jewry as President of the New York Board of Rabbis were pulling in different directions. He tries to define a middle ground, but it is not clear how he would have voted had he been on the Supreme Court.

The final event—the spectacular visit of Egyptian President Anwar Sadat to Jerusalem—was recent and vivid to the listeners and required no extensive treatment. Both the historic significance of the visit and the warning not to be overly optimistic about immediate success in peace negotiations are emphasized. Yet the buoyant mood contrasts dramatically with the discouragement and anger of the sermons from May 1974 (Ma'alot) and November 1975 (UN "Zionism is Racism" Resolution). The prophetic hope at the end of this sermon seems now grounded in something real.

THIS SABBATH WE BEGIN A NEW BOOK OF THE BIBLE: Exodus. Last week's portion ended with the death of Joseph; this week's begins, "And these are the names of the sons of Israel who came into Egypt with Jacob" (Exod. 1:1). *V'ayle shemot*: it seems strange to begin a new book with the word "and." It is intended to indicate that the entire Torah is a continuous narrative, so that each book is connected to what which follows.[1]

The same is true with calendar years. As we finish the year, we throw away the old calendar and put up a new one. We like to speak of starting with a clean sheet. But life and history don't work that way. Life is continuity. The present moment is never isolated; it is unbreakably linked with memories of the past and hopes for the future. That is why tonight, as we stand on the threshold of 1978, I am going to speak about the harvest of '77.[2]

What kind of year was it? I am reminded of Dickens's opening words in *Tale of Two Cities*: "It was the best of times, it was the worst of times. . . . It was the springtime of hope, it was the winter of discontent." We can rejoice that in the

---

1. The continuity between the end of the book of Genesis and the first words in Exodus is emphasized by the rabbinic Midrash and several of the medieval commentators.

2. This kind of sermonic review was not an uncommon among rabbis in all branches of Judaism. Israel Mowshowitz, a leading Orthodox rabbi, introduced a published sermon entitled "The Five Most Important Jewish Events of 1960" as follows: "On the first Friday night service of each new year, I address myself to the five most important Jewish events of the year just ended. This has become an exciting tradition at Hillcrest [Jewish Center], and the members look forward to it with great anticipation." Mowshowitz, *To Serve in Faithfulness* (New York: Ktav, 1975), 51.

world at large, 1977 saw no major wars. But all over the world there was continued conflict between people who need each other: between French and English in Quebec, between white and black in South Africa and Rhodesia, between Protestant and Catholic in Ireland, between North and South in Korea, between East and West in Germany, between Turk and Greek in Cyprus, between India and Pakistan in Asia, between Arab and Israeli in the Middle East.

In our country, all in all it was a relatively quiet year. On our college campuses, the turbulent student rebellion that characterized the '60s and the early '70s is over. Students are concerned about grades and job opportunities. From reports, job prospects for June graduates are the best in years. There was a measure of terrorism and crime in 1977. The "Son of Sam" killings and similar murders in repeated patterns in other cities stirred popular imagination.[3] The seizure of the B'nai B'rith office in Washington, D.C., by the Hanafi Muslims brought the grim specter of terrorism close to home.[4] But statistics indicate that throughout the nation last year, the crime rate was down.

Hatreds generated by controversies over bussing in communities such as South Boston and Chicago have been curbed. There have been no major political scandals. And on the plus side, we can note that Broadway is flourishing more than it has for a long time; reports are that attendance at museums is higher than ever; the divorce rate is increasing with painful rapidity, but marriage and birth rates are also up. On a national level, charities report a record high level of donations. Not too long ago our nation was being torn apart by the nightmare experiences of Vietnam and Watergate. Last year, the tattered social fabric of our country was beginning to be rewoven. There are still unresolved problems—inflation, unemployment, the energy crisis—but basically people are regaining faith in America. And that, of course, is to the good.

So much for the general picture. I turn now to a few special events that I think have special significance for us as Jews. I have picked four; two of them to not affect us directly as Jews, two of them do touch us directly. But all, I think, are of special interest or concern.

The first is the publication of a book, later presented in a series of television programs, which probably reached more people than any other program in me-

---

3. The first in a series of deadly attacks in Manhattan occurred on January 30, 1977; in a total of eight incidents, six were killed and seven wounded by someone who called himself "Son of Sam." On August 10, David Berkowitz was apprehended and charged with the murders.

4. On March 9, 1977, Hanafi Muslims entered and occupied three Washington, D.C., buildings: the B'nai B'rith national headquarters, the Islamic Center and Mosque, and the D.C. City Hall. They held more than 100 hostages, and demanded that the premiere of a movie they considered offensive be cancelled and that men convicted in the 1973 slaying of Malcolm X and several Hanafis be turned over to them. Through the mediation of three Muslim ambassadors, the hostages were released the following day, and a surrender was negotiated on March 11.

dia history. I speak, of course, of the book *Roots*, by Alex Haley.[5] It is the story of an American Negro's tracing of his family history and his seeking for roots, which brought him back through generations of slavery in America and ultimately to a village in Africa. The strict accuracy of the book has been challenged by historians and anthropologists. But that doesn't really matter. If some of these particular names and places were not precise, if some of these events are not literally true, they are historically true. People like these did live in Africa, were forcibly abducted and sold into slavery, did survive through generations, did eventually move forward into freedom with all its problems and its challenges and its promises. The important part of the message of *Roots* was, first, the capacity of people to preserve dignity under the most adverse circumstances, and second, the right of people to take pride in those whose trials and suffering and sacrifice made their lives possible.

I say this is of importance to us because it has awakened a new interest in Jewish genealogy. We Jews can justly take pride in our roots—in a culture that reaches back through the centuries, in a history marked by intellectual creativity and spiritual heroism, despite oppression and persecution and periodic uprooting. Not many Jews have been able to trace their own families back very far beyond their migration to this country. That isn't so important. We're all one family, and the Jew who wants to find his roots need merely to study the heritage and the history of our people and faith. *Roots* stirred many to that quest. As such it was a significant event.

The second event took place near the end of the year in South Africa. Steve Biko met his death in a prison hospital in South Africa under circumstances that strongly indicated official brutality and negligence as causes of his death.[6] I was particularly interested in the case because less than a month before his arrest, I met with Steve Biko. He came to see Marcia and me and two friends at our hotel in King William's Town. At that time he was under the ban, which means that outside of his family he was not permitted to meet with more than one person at a time.[7] There were four of us there that day. I asked him whether there wasn't danger of trouble. He answered, "The street outside is swarming with secret service officers. I guess they are here to protect you," he joked. "But don't worry, I don't think they'd dare do anything to me now." Yet he was arrested shortly afterward. He was brutally beaten. Critically ill from apparent brain

---

5. The television series was shown on eight successive nights beginning January 25. Nielson ratings reported that 80 million Americans watched the final episode, the largest audience in television history at that time.

6. Biko, at age thirty the head of South Africa's Black Consciousness Movement, died on September 12, following interrogation by the Security Police.

7. Biko had been "banned" in 1973. In a description of the ban imposed on Donald Woods, a close friend of Biko's, apparently as punishment for his investigation of the circumstances of Biko's death, a reporter for *Time* Magazine wrote, "For five years, Woods may not meet with more than one other person at a time except for members of his family; he may not write for publication or be quoted—he has become, as a result, a public non-person" (*Time*, November 7, 1977, 38).

damage, he was transported naked more than 600 miles in an automobile to a hospital, where he died shortly afterward.[8]

Steve Biko was a natural leader. He exemplified the hopes of his people for human dignity. He was not an extremist. The black people of South Africa will not continue to tolerate a system that negates basic human values and denies them the opportunities for a life of dignity. Men like Biko could have helped work out a solution that would be positive and constructive. The authorities in South Africa fail to realize that force cannot sustain an evil system. The successors to Steve Biko may not be as reasonable. Nobody has been punished for his death. But I am convinced that the price will be tragically paid.

What gives this case significance is the fact that it became a matter of worldwide concern. The newspapers reported it in detail. The fate of an oppressed people may be taken for granted, but the fate of a single victim of an evil system stirs the hearts of the world. So long as people throughout the world can be stirred by the death of one black man, there is hope for a world in which all will be free and justice will be colorblind.[9]

We come now to America. One of the events that impinge directly on Jewish life was the Bakke Case. I need not spend much time on the details of the case. Simply stated, Allan Bakke had applied for admission to the Medical School of the University of California in 1973 and again in 1974, only to be rejected. At the same time, sixteen black students were admitted to places that had been specifically reserved for them. Bakke claimed that he had been a victim of discrimination. White students with a grade average of less than 2.5 were not even considered. Bakke had a grade average of 3.5. But minority applicants were admitted with averages as low as 2.1. No white student would ever be considered who scored below the 50th percentile in science and verbal ability. Bakke was in the 95th percentile. The average of specially admitted students was well below 40.

The University's defense was that affirmative action required special treatment of minority applicants to balance out the cultural disadvantage and discrimination under which they have been suffering. Bakke's position, endorsed by most Jewish organizations,[10] is that racial preference and quotas, even when intended for a worthy objective, is a form of *reverse* discrimination. In opening opportunities for one group, it deprives people from other groups of opportunities for which they are completely qualified.

---

8. For a report on the Inquest into Biko's death written by the dean of the University of Pennsylvania School of Law, see *Steve Biko: Black Consciousness in South Africa*, ed. Millard Arnold (New York: Random House, 1978), 279–98.

9. The South African government was apparently taken by surprise at the international reaction to Biko's death. One consequence was the decision by American institutions to consider divesting their holdings in companies that did business with South Africa, led by the trustees of the University of Massachusetts on September 15.

10. The Anti-Defamation League, American Jewish Committee, American Jewish Congress, National Jewish Commission on Law and Public Affairs, and Jewish Labor Committee, all submitted *amicus curiae* briefs on behalf of Bakke.

That is where the case stands, still awaiting a decision from the Supreme Court.[11] It leaves us in a position where we must not go to either extreme. We must not reject the policy of affirmative action. Everything must be done to open up opportunities for minority groups that have long been deprived of them. More effort must be made to give special training to worthy minority candidates to help them qualify. New admissions procedures, which do not discriminate one way or another on the basis of race, must be found. Jews must continue to emphasize the importance of equal rights and opportunities. Minority groups must be able to climb to whatever heights their capabilities entitle them. But we must not be expected to lie down so that they can climb over us. There must be better ways of achieving the goals of justice and equality.

The final event of the past year was the historic meeting of Sadat and Begin in Jerusalem initiating negotiations that we hope will lead to peace. Few people will forget the human dimensions of that first meeting in Jerusalem. Marcia and I watched at 5 o'clock in the morning—the plane landing in Israel, Sadat greeting Golda Meir, his visit to Yad Vashem, the wreath he placed beside the memorial to Israel's war dead, the Israeli and Egyptian flags flying together.[12]

We must not build up undue optimism. Careful analysis of official positions shows that neither side is ready yet to make the concessions that would be acceptable to the other.[13] Israel is not yet ready to give total independence to the Palestinians, the Arabs will accept nothing less. More concessions will have to be made on both sides. Otherwise, despite all the fanfare and the friendly gestures, they are on a collision course that will leave an aftermath of disillusion and bitterness and a hopelessness that can lead to tragic conclusions.

But there are two things that give us hope. First, that leaders with sufficient courage and vision can make the breakthrough on the road that leads to peace. Second was the obvious fact that people in the streets of Jerusalem and in the streets of Cairo want peace, yearn for it, rejoice when its prospect is brought near. This is something the whole world could see.[14]

---

11. The Supreme Court heard arguments on October 12. It gave its decision on June 28, 1978, upholding by a five to four majority the constitutionality of college admissions programs that give special advantage to blacks and other minorities, but ruling that Bakke must be admitted to the University of California Medical College.

12. President Anwar Sadat of Egypt arrived in Israel on the evening of Saturday, November 19 (early afternoon New York time). The reference to watching at 5:00 in the morning must be to Sadat's activities the following day, when he visited Yad Vashem, placed a wreath at the monument to Israel's fallen soldiers, and later addressed the Knesset. See Howard Sachar, *A History of Israel* (New York: Knopf, 1996), 847–48.

13. A meeting between Begin and Sadat at Ismailia on December 25 and 26, just a few days before the sermon was delivered, seemed particularly tense and unproductive. See *New York Times*, December 27, 1977, A1:6, December 28, 1977, A1:5,6; Sachar, 849.

14. The sight of large crowds in Cairo welcoming President Sadat on his return from Jerusalem, shown on television throughout much of the world, was particularly impressive at the time.

Our Bible reading this Sabbath tells of the oppression of the Jews under Egyptian bondage. But centuries later, the prophet Isaiah spoke of peoples once enemies united under God. He said, "In that day shall Israel be the third with Egypt and with Assyria, a blessing in the midst of the earth, for the Lord of Hosts hath blessed him, saying, 'Blessed be Egypt, My people, and Assyria, the work of My hands, and Israel, my inheritance'" (Isa. 19:24–25). May the year 1978 on which we shall soon embark bring the fulfillment of this prophetic vision.

50

Jonestown and Masada
December 29, 1978

The "bizarre and tragic events at Jonestown" mentioned in the first sentence of the sermon were familiar to everyone in the congregation that late December Shabbat evening. They were triggered by a visit of a group of Americans led by California Congressman Leo J. Ryan to the commune of the "People's Temple of Disciples of Christ" in Jonestown, Guyana. The purpose of the visit was to investigate reports of abuse within the cult. On Saturday, November 18, 1978, when some cult members decided to leave the commune with the group, the visitors were attacked; Ryan, three newsmen, and one of the cult members defecting were killed, while the others escaped.

Guyanese forces entering the site on November 20 reported 405 corpses. Eventually, the number of bodies discovered reached more than 900. Most of them perished from drinking "Flavour-aide" laced with tranquilizers and cyanide, fed first to the infants and children, then drunk by the adults of the community, all at the instructions of their leader, Jim Jones, following a ritualized procedure that had been previously rehearsed. The photographs of hundreds of corpses spread over the grounds of the commune were staggering. The gruesome events became almost an obsession in American public discourse.

Religious leaders were particularly challenged by the murder and subsequent mass suicide orchestrated in the name of religious faith, and justified by the claim that "the time has come to meet in another place." Parallels made in the media with other apparently similar expressions of fanatically self-destructive religious devotion were troubling to many, who felt the need to define the differences between genuine religious self-sacrifice and the abhorrent behavior of the Jonestown community. (On a personal note, during the week when the Jonestown bloodbath occurred, the present editor was teaching for the first time the Hebrew chronicles that describe the mass communal suicide of Rhineland Jews in the wake of the attacks during the First Crusade. The ques-

*tion why those Jews are considered martyrs who fulfilled one of the highest as-
pirations of the Jewish faith, while they acted in a manner not obviously different from the members of the Jonestown cult, was painfully urgent.)*

*Soon after the reports were publicized, Saperstein and other leaders of Tem-
ple Emanu-El organized a series of Friday night presentations by guest speakers, assessing the significance of Jonestown from the perspective of various disciplines, including psychiatry. The following address, which—shorter than most
sermons—may have been part of a symposium, was the last in this series. The
parallel with Masada, announced in the title, did not detain Saperstein for long;
the distinctions are drawn with clarity and vigor. The thrust of his message is to
identify the seductive pitfalls that ensnare promising leaders, and the failings of
American culture that create a need for cults like the "People's Temple." The
conclusion is that both the proper model of leadership—Moses—and the positive
values being sought in the cults can be found in the classical religious traditions
such as Judaism.*

WHEN THE BIZARRE AND TRAGIC EVENTS AT JONESTOWN took place, there
were some analysts who claimed that this kind of self-destruction was not
unique.[1] The analogy was made to Masada, where some 1,905 years ago a similar number of men, women and children—more than 900—took their own
lives.[2] But to make such a comparison is a desecration of the memory of our
forefathers who died as holy martyrs, *al kiddush Hashem* [for the sanctification
of God's name].

The heroes of Masada took their own lives not because of a cultic fascination
with death, not because of blind subjugation of personal will to that of their
leader, but out of a realistic evaluation of the situation. For two years, they had
resisted the siege of the Romans and had fought valiantly. Many of them had
escaped from Jerusalem. They knew what was in store for them. They knew the
cruelty of their enemies towards those they had conquered. They knew their

---

1. Some of the comparisons were with phenomena in Christian history, especially
with the millenarian Anabaptist community in Muenster, led by the charismatic John
Bockelson of Leiden, who, in 1534 and 1555—proclaiming himself Messiah—maintained a reign of antinomian terror and dictatorial control over his fanatical followers.
This parallel was made by the historian Theodore Rabb in the *New York Times*, December 20; for a fuller account, see Norman Cohn, *The Pursuit of the Millennium* (New
York: Oxford University Press, 1970), 267–80. The anthropologist Marvin Harris, wrote
in a *Times* Op-Ed column on November 26, "Messianic movements involving suicidal
armed struggles have recurred throughout history as a response to rapid cultural change
and harsh political, economic and environmental conditions."

2. See, for example, *Newsweek*, December 4, 1978, 40: "The carnage in Jonestown
conjured up comparisons with the Zealots of Masada, who killed each other rather than
surrender to Rome in A.D. 73."

women would be sold into slavery, their men would be crucified, their children would be ravaged. They chose death rather than accept such a fate.[3]

No such fate threatened the people in Guyana. Their suicide was the result of the paranoia of a charismatic but mentally deranged leader, the grand gesture that was the ultimate expression of his lust for power. There can be no legitimate comparison.

Jonestown, then, must be viewed in its own terms. It poses troubling questions, troubling because they represent the extreme form of social patterns that confront us and our children. What was it that enabled this man, Jim Jones, to exert such power over so many people? What caused his transformation from a prophetic proponent of a better world—a world of love and social benevolence—to a sadistic, tyrannical dictator? And what moved his followers to subjugate themselves to him so completely that they relinquished their role as morally responsible human beings and became mere tools of his will?

When I first read about the events in Guyana, I was reminded of a great short story by Joseph Conrad called, "Heart of Darkness."[4] It is the story of a man named Kurtz, who journeys into the interior of Africa to purchase ivory from the natives. He convinces himself that he is spreading civilization among the savages. He is a powerful orator and preaches altruistic doctrines. At first he believes them, but gradually power becomes an end in itself. He portrays himself to the natives as a divine being, and does not hesitate to use violence and murder to preserve his power. His noble rhetoric is based on a lie, because he becomes addicted to the cult of his own worship to power, to cruelty. The "heart of darkness" is not only the interior of Africa; it is also the interior of his own soul.

This, I fear, is what happened to Jim Jones. He seems to have started out as a sincere idealist. I believe he meant it when he spoke of human dignity, social justice, and racial brotherhood.[5] But when idealism brought him the taste of

---

3. Masada was a favorite site of Saperstein in Israel—he climbed it many times with friends and tours he led from the Temple—and a favorite model of Jewish dignity and heroism in his preaching. The second sermon he delivered after returning from his 1967 sabbatical was entitled "Masada Shall Not Fall Again;" its final paragraph begins, "Masada is a symbol: a symbol of the struggle of the few against the many, of the weak against the strong. It is a symbol of those who in every age have been ready to give their lives for spiritual freedom." The description of the motives of the Masada garrison in taking their own lives in the present sermon is based on the celebrated speech attributed to the commander, Elazar ben Yair, by Josephus in *The Jewish War*, book 7, chapter 8.

4. This rhetorical parallel was made by others as well. The lead article in the *New York Times* "Week in Review" section of November 26 begins "'The horror! The horror!' That is what Mr. Kurtz, the civilized man dying in the jungle, tells the narrator of Joseph Conrad's 'Heart of Darkness.'" Meg Greenfield entitled her *Newsweek* column in the December 4 issue "Heart of Darkness," though without actually referring to the Conrad story.

5. After running into trouble as pastor of a Methodist church in Indianapolis because of his integrationist views, he established his own "People's Temple," which *Newsweek* described as "a model of integration and liberalism," with a soup kitchen, employment service, and nursing home. In 1961, he was appointed director of the Indianapolis Human

power, the idealism became subservient. Power is more than a heady intoxicant. It can also be a deadly poison. Once the cult of his power had been established, it had to be sustained. Brutality, lust, greed, dishonesty, corruption—all were utilized if they preserved his image or gratified his ego. And so the road was paved to the heart of darkness.

Judaism developed a very different concept of leadership. The classic leader of the Jewish heritage was Moses, and he was called not "our leader" but *Rabbenu*, "our teacher." His outstanding quality, according to the Bible, was *anivut*, humility (Num. 12:3). When God threatened to destroy the people at the time of the Golden Calf, he pleaded that his life be taken but the people be spared (cf. Exod. 32:32). When people complained that certain individuals were prophesying in the name of God and should be suppressed, he answered, "Would that all the Lord's people were prophets" (Num. 11:29). And when Moses died, the site of his grave was kept unknown that it might not become an object of veneration and worship (cf. Deut. 34:6).[6] To the true leader in the Jewish spirit, the cause remains dominant, not the individual.

What can we learn from the people who followed Jim Jones to Jonestown and to death? No thorough psychological study has been made. Perhaps it will never be made. But there have been numerous reports about individuals. Only this morning, the *New York Times* had profiles of seven of these people: some young, some old; some white, some black; some poor, some privileged; some educated, some practically illiterate.[7] As we read about them, we realize that many of them were *losers*, individuals who for one reason or another had been unable to make it in modern society. The People's Temple came and told them that they didn't need to "make it," that they were important, OK. Others were *loners*, who despite a measure of success had never been able to establish meaningful relationships. Here came a movement which told them that they were accepted and loved. Still others were *seekers*, idealists who were trying to find the right way and had gotten lost and could not make up their mind where to turn. Along came the cult and told them, "You don't have to worry, we'll make decisions for you, we have the way, all you need is to put your trust in us."

These reflect dangerous symptoms in our contemporary world. Our society has become *materialistic*—where a person is valued primarily by what he has, *impersonal*—where a person can walk in loneliness and nobody cares, and *confused*—where there are more choices than ever before and less guidance. In the past, religion and civilization had a body of accepted values that gave one the framework to know right from wrong, to know the direction in which he should

---

Rights Commission by the Mayor (*Newsweek*, December 4, 1978, 55; see also *New York Times*, November 26, 1978, 20:1).

6. This explanation of the mysterious location of Moses' grave is not explicit in the Bible, but it reflects a medieval exegetical tradition, stated, for example, by Levi ben Gershom (Ralbag): "The Holy One, blessed be He, so devised it that no man knows of his burial place, so that generations to come would not go astray and worship [Moses] as a deity."

7. *New York Times*, December 29, 1978, A12.

move. All too often today we have rejected these guides and find ourselves without any compass. And this makes many people ready victims of someone who comes along and says, "I have the answers, I have what you need."

I shall not spell it out, but here I think is where religion comes in. Not cultic religion, but classical religion, and in particular a religion like Judaism, which says, these are the values on which life can be built: the love of God and the love of humanity, the dignity of the human being and the validity of the moral law. Here are the choices, and you must decide. Before you are good and evil, life and death. "Therefore choose life, that you and your children may live" (Deut. 30:19).

51

Farewell to the "Me Decade"
January 25, 1980

As the December 30, 1977, sermon reviewed events of the previous year, the present sermon, delivered five months before Saperstein's retirement, summarized his reactions to trends during the final decade of his tenure in Lynbrook. Throughout his career, one of the central values he emphasized—along with Jewish strength and dignity—was service to others. This was expressed both in his conception of the Jewish role in human history and in his understanding of what is truly meaningful for an individual. This commitment was validated by his own experience; decisions such as volunteering for the chaplaincy in the American Army, doing voter registration work in Alabama, remaining in Jerusalem as the clouds of war gathered, and devoting countless hours to congregants turned out to be among the most fulfilling experiences in his life. Against this background, the preoccupation with self that was raised to the level of an articulated value system in the 1970s seemed alien and disturbing.

The vision of the previous decade is not unremittingly bleak, nor did it rely on a purely romantic idealization of the past. Positive developments from the '70s are noted in the first part of the sermon. But the negatives are cited, to some extent from sociological evidence, but even more from changes observed in his own experience: as an educator overseeing a religious school of 1,000 children, as a rabbi who met with hundreds of couples before their weddings. To the extent that immediate self-gratification began to trump more traditional values such as commitment, perseverance, responsibility and service, Saperstein felt troubled and uneasy. The thundering, prophetic critique aimed against the humanistic individualism of Western society by Aleksandr Solzhenitsyn at the 1978 Harvard Commencement exercises seemed to him a message that needed to be heard. The end of the sermon presents even traditional Christianity as an expression of individualism (though spiritual, not materialistic). Judaism— paradigmatically the biblical prophet—is portrayed as the antithesis of the

"Me-Decade" ethos, which Saperstein knew could not be easily supplanted, but which he hoped would be transient.

WE ARE NOW FOUR-FIFTHS THROUGH WITH THE TWENTIETH CENTURY. Of these eighty years, the last decade—the decade of the '70s—has had a unique character. The '60s were a decade of social consciousness. It witnessed the struggle on behalf of civil rights, the struggle against war in Vietnam, the struggle for freedom of expression in education, in politics, even in religion. Some of these causes carried over into the '70s. But the main emphasis in the '70s was no longer on social betterment. It was instead of personal fulfillment. In an essay written in 1976, Tom Wolfe called it the "Me Generation," and that phrase has been accepted as an apt description.[1]

What specifically do we mean by the "Me Generation"? First, there is the emphasis on self-centered satisfactions as the measure of life. Hillel said, "If I am not for myself, who will be for me?" But he did not stop there, he went on to say, "But if I am only for myself, what am I?"[2] The spirit of the 70s ignored the second half of the statement.

The '70s were marked by an avalanche of books on self-improvement. They told us how to take care of "number one," how to get rid of your erroneous zones, how to tune in on your biorhythms.[3] There was a multitude of new movements. Some were religious, based on eastern philosophers. Some were renewals of old religions: born-again Christians and evangelical groups. Some were pseudo-religions: EST and Scientology and the Moonies' Unification Church.[4] There was an unprecedented number of fads that promised physical and emotional well being: various diets and health foods, jogging and transcendental meditation. And there was a wider use than ever of artificial mood controllers—tranquilizers and stimulants, Librium and Valium, alcohol and marijuana.

---

1. Tom Wolfe's essay, "The 'Me' Generation and the Third Great Awakening," was featured on the cover of the August 23, 1976, issue of *New York* Magazine. It begins, "The old alchemical dream was changing base metals into gold. The new alchemical dream is: changing one's personality—remaking, remodeling, elevating, and polishing one's very *self*... and observing, studying, and doting on it. (Me!)."

2. M. Avot 1,14.

3. Alluding to books such as Robert J. Ringer, *Looking Out for Number One* (Beverly Hills: Los Angeles Book Corporation, 1977); Wayne W. Dyer, *Your Erroneous Zones* (New York: Funk & Wagnalls, 1976); Bernard Gittelson, *Biorhythm: A Personal Science* (New York: Warner Books, 1978).

4. EST (Erhard Seminars Training), was developed by the psychologist Werner Erhard in the early 1970s; its goal was to transform personality to achieve the satisfaction of being in control of one's inner world, known as "getting it." Scientology, based on the teachings of L. Ron Hubbard, includes a form of counseling ("Dianetics") intended to cure emotional illnesses and enhance spiritual awareness; it was established as a Church in 1954. The Unification Church, also established in 1954, is based on the teachings of the Korean Rev. Sun Myung Moon.

Now not all of these things are bad. Some of them indeed are destructive, but some of them—particularly those that contribute to physical health and emotional tranquillity—have much potential for good. There were movements of liberation: women's lib and gay liberation and gray power. And those that seek to correct injustice and to broaden the horizons of equality and freedom are certainly desirable. The point I am making is that so many of the trends of the 70s are concerned with the self, with the "me." The phrase "doing your own thing" has become a contemporary cliché. It sounds very brave and "with it." Properly practiced, it may be very commendable to have the courage to do your own thing—to rise about the conventional, to follow your own convictions, to be true to your own ideals. But too often, this is not what is meant at all. If you press them, they don't really know what their "own thing" is. Too often it is just a cover-up for a desire to escape responsibility, an unwillingness to carry one's share of the weight within the social structure. "Fulfilling oneself" comes to replace concern for others, or it comes to be a way to justify furthering the interests of one's own group at the expense of others.

The second aspect of the "Me Generation" has been its emphasis on fun, pleasure, and self-gratification as the measure of life. We see it in the breakdown of sexual morality. This was a decade of promiscuity. Now let us admit that there was a lot of hypocrisy and dishonesty and psychic sickness in the rigid moral standards that people spoke about and defended officially, but did not always practice in private. The time had come for lifting the veil of prurient secrecy and letting in some fresh air. Judaism never intended that sex should be looked upon as something dirty or unworthy. In this respect, Judaism is a healthy-minded religion.

The Hebrew Bible is quite explicit and outspoken about matters of sex. One book of the Bible, the Song of Songs, glorifies physical love. "The sparks of love are sparks of fire, a very flame of the Lord" (cf. Song 8:6). The joy of love has a spiritual dimension. But the insistence on immediate gratification of impulses is a mark of childish immaturity. Sexuality should be more than a technique for savoring sensual pleasure. The sex that seeks self-centered satisfactions usually soon finds the satisfaction diminishing. I have not noted that the generation which prides itself on throwing away its inhibitions and living the swinging style is any happier than the generations that preceded them.

We see the expression of the "Me Generation" in the realm of marriage and the family. When I meet for a pre-marital interview with a young couple and talk about their plans and goals, it troubles me to hear them say, as some do, that they are still undecided about whether they want to have children. I can remember people saying that back during the Nazi era, when they questioned whether it was proper to bring children into that kind of evil world. I could understand their doubts—though I tried to get them to feel that because there was so much imperfection in the world, it was doubly important not to succumb to the power of evil, but to live in faith and hope for the future. But that is not the concern of these young people today. First, they don't like the idea of being tied down, of having responsibilities that might interfere with plans for their own immediate gratification. And second, I sense that many of them are reluctant to create a situation that would make it more difficult to cut the bonds if the marriage doesn't work out. They want to keep the gate to their "freedom" unlocked.

The '70s might well be called the decade of the divorce epidemic. When I conduct a marriage ceremony and speak of it as an enduring and sanctified relationship, I sometimes wonder whether these have become just empty words. Someone estimated that every child born this year has a fifty-fifty chance of living in a single-parent home before he is eighteen years old. We can see it in our religious school. Each year we have a greater proportion of single-parent homes than the year before. It used to be the rare exception. Now it is an increasingly common pattern. A particularly unexpected and disturbing expression of this trend is the divorce rate among people who have been married for many years.

What has caused this epidemic? Of course, there is no single or simple explanation for any complex social ill. But I am convinced that part of it is the spirit of the "Me Generation." People have a feeling that life owes them continuous and ecstatic happiness. If you fail to experience this, you've been cheated in life. And so people conclude, "Why go on when the purpose of marriage is not being achieved? Perhaps I can do better elsewhere." They fail to recognize that life is not only ecstasy. It is duty and responsibility—yes, and sometimes agony as well.

We see the same emphasis on immediate gratification in reactions to our educational program. If a child comes home and says, "It's boring," or "The teacher or the subject turns me off," the school is condemned for the unpardonable sin. People have the idea that each class ought to be play like kindergarten, and every teacher ought to be fun like Danny Kaye.[5] Nobody wants to accept the fact that learning, like most worthwhile things in life, can be difficult and frustrating and demanding of time and effort. So the children never learn the fundamental lesson that there are no shortcuts and bargains in life, the lesson that if something is worthwhile and is to bring ultimate satisfaction, you've got to be willing to pay the price for it.

And so we run around seeking fun and happiness, and all too often they elude us. Emerson understood it better when he said, "Happiness is like perfume: you can't sprinkle it on someone else without getting a little on yourself."[6] The joy of life comes not when you consciously seek it, but when you forget it in seeking some greater purpose: the happiness of a loved one, or the betterment of the world.

It took one who came from a different world, who had suffered at the hands of a government representing the antithesis of American ideals, to see and point

---

5. The comic actor, perhaps best known at this time for his title role in the 1952 RKO film "Hans Christian Andersen."

6. Saperstein apparently took this quotation from Lillian Watson's *Light from Many Lamps* (New York: Simon and Schuster, 1951), 15, where it is said to be from Emerson but without any specific source. I have not found this quotation in Emerson; it is, however, attested as an American proverb: *Dictionary of American Proverbs* (New York: Oxford University Press, 1992), 279.

out America's failure to be true to its own best self. In June 1978, at the Harvard University Commencement, I heard an address by the Russian author and chronicler of the gulags, Aleksandr Solzhenitsyn. He charged that America was being spoiled by prosperity and self-satisfaction and materialism, that its spirit had become soft and morally impoverished, that it lacked the moral force and spiritual strength which the world so desperately needed. This has been the legacy of self-indulgence in the guise of self-fulfillment.[7]

In its deepest spirit, Judaism repudiates the assumptions of the "Me generation." The emphasis in Jewish observance is not the individual, but the group. Yes, it is possible to pray in solitude. But Judaism gives special merit to praying in a *minyan*, that is, with the community. The cycle of our festival observances emphasizes not the individual but the family. This is what brings the joy into the Sabbath or the Passover Seder or the kindling of the Chanukah lights.

And theologically, Judaism never put its emphasis on individual salvation. One of the great classics of Christian religious literature is John Bunyan's "Pilgrim's Progress." In it, the hero, Christian, leaves behind family and friends to face challenge and danger in order to reach the City of Salvation. The salvation he sought was not for the world, but for his own individual soul. This was the goal that underlined the monastic ideal of those who left the world behind in order to redeem their souls and improve their chances of getting to heaven.[8]

Judaism took the other approach. The prophet in the Bible was concerned not with saving his own soul, but with the salvation of humanity, with bringing the better world of justice and peace in which all could find fulfillment. (The ideal Jew was expected not to leave the world behind, but to enter the real world and put into practice the teachings and goals of his religious heritage.)

---

7. Solzhenitsyn's Harvard Commencement address evoked an outpouring of response in the media; see *Solzhenitsyn at Harvard*, ed. Ronald Berman (Washington, D.C.: Ethics and Public Policy Center, 1980). Quotations from the address relevant to Saperstein's summary include, "A decline in courage may be the most striking feature that an outside observer notices in the West today" (5); "It is time, in the West, to defend not so much human rights as human obligations" (8); "The West has finally achieved the rights of man, even to excess, but man's sense of responsibility to God and society has grown dimmer and dimmer" (17); "Only by the voluntary nurturing in ourselves of freely accepted and serene self-restraint can mankind rise above the world stream of materialism" (19). Saperstein did not address here (nor would he have agreed with) Solzhenitsyn's fundamentalist religious alternative to the humanistic tradition he attacked.

8. This characterization of Christianity as concerned exclusively with individual salvation and therefore "other-worldly" and self-centered—not uncommon in Jewish discourse of the time—may reflect the work of Leo Baeck. See *The Essence of Judaism* (New York: Schocken, 1961), 222: "In Christianity the determining factor is to experience the miracle of grace and thereby be redeemed; thus the 'I' of the individual man stands alone at the center of religion, apart from the fellow man." Or his essay "Romantic Religion" in *Judaism and Christianity* (Philadelphia: JPS, 1958), 211: "The social conscience finds romantic religion [identified with Christianity] repugnant because it is at bottom a religious egoism; . . . in it the individual knows only himself and what God or life is to bring him, but not the commandment, not the mutual demands of man."

These values can be seen in the following representative quotations from Jewish sources. From the Bible: "Love your neighbor as yourself" (Lev. 19:18). From the Talmud, "The world exists only on account of him who disregards his own existence."[9] Albert Einstein: "Only a life lived for others is a life worthwhile."[10] (And our own prayer book: "Help us to be among those who are willing to sacrifice that others may not hunger, who dare to be bearers of light in the dark loneliness of stricken lives, who struggle and even bleed for the triumph of righteousness among men."[11])

The "Me Decade" is over. The future is in our hands.

9. See B. Hullin 89a (a statement by R. Abbahu).

10. This statement is attributed to Einstein in Joseph Baron, *A Treasury of Jewish Quotations* (New York: Crown, 1956), 7. I have not found the actual source (identified as *Youth*, June 1932).

11. *The Union Prayer Book for Jewish Worship I*, Newly Revised Edition (New York: Central Conference of American Rabbis, 1956), 45. This prayer book, copyright 1940, was the one used by Saperstein during most of his career. It was eventually replaced by *Gates of Prayer*, published in 1975.

Days I Remember
September 26, 1973
Rosh Hashanah Evening

*As can be seen from the selections above, Saperstein's Rosh Hashanah sermons
from the 1930s and early 1940s tended to be topical, preoccupied with the tragic
drama of Jewish life being played out on the historical stage. The Yom Kippur
sermons addressed more personal, existential issues of values and problems of
the individual life. In the final decade of his active career, the nature of the Rosh
Hashanah sermons tended to shift to reflection not so much about the present
and future, but about the past. This was especially true on anniversary occasions: the fortieth and forty-fifth year of his service in Lynbrook and similar
anniversaries of his rabbinic ordination. These occasions reinforced the general
theme of introspection on the New Year, producing sermons that look to forma-
tive experiences of the past and draw lessons from them that transcend a particular moment and begin to characterize an entire career.*

*The following sermon, placed out of chronological order as a conclusion to
this volume, is "topical" not in its response to an issue of the current moment,
but in its vivid evocation of dramatic moments in the past. The reader will have
encountered many of these in the preceding pages; in some cases—e.g. the description of the High Holy Days in Grenoble, 1944, and the description of civil
rights activism from 1965—the sermons published previously are illuminated by
the memories articulated in the present text. The autobiographical, deeply personal nature of this sermon might seem inappropriately self-indulgent if delivered in a strange congregation. For an audience of listeners some of whom remembered the preacher's arrival at that Temple in 1933, most of whom had
heard the original accounts of at least some of these experiences, it seemed
more an expression of intimacy, an evocation of shared memories—inspiring*

*and tragic—that defined not only an individual but also a community, which was
now reaching out to embrace newcomers as well.*

MARTIN BUBER, GREAT CHRONICLER OF THE CHASSIDIC SPIRIT, tells this
story about Rabbi Shneur Zalman, founder of the Lubavitcher movement. Denounced to the authorities by his opponents, he was imprisoned in St. Peters-
burg. One day, the chief of the gendarmes entered his cell. Impressed by the
majestic bearing of the prisoner, he began to converse with him, directing questions about the Scriptures. Finally, he asked,

> "How are we to understand that in the Bible, God, who knows all, has to ask
> Adam, 'Where art thou?' (Gen. 3:9)?"
> "Do you believe," the Rabbi answered," that the Scriptures have a mes-
> sage for every generation and every man?"
> "I believe this," the official responded.
> "Well," the Tzaddik continued, "in every era God calls to man, 'Where
> are you in your world? So many years and days of those allotted to you have
> passed. How far have you reached in your life?'"[1]

As many of you know, these High Holy Days mark for me an important
milestone, the completion of forty years of service to this Temple. It was in
1933, immediately after Yom Kippur, that I first stood in its pulpit, a neophyte
rabbinical student not yet twenty-three years old. In the Bible, the number forty
has special significance. For forty years the Israelites wandered in the wilderness. Eli judged for forty years, David and Solomon each reigned for the same
period. In the Ethics of the Fathers, we read, *Arbaim labina*, "forty years is for
understanding."[2]

This New Year is thus an appropriate occasion for looking back and asking
myself "Where am I?" What have I done with the years granted me until now?
Recently I saw the prizewinning play, "That Championship Season."[3] It is built
around the annual reunion of five men, the coach and four of the players who
twenty years before had comprised the High School basketball team that won
the Pennsylvania State Championship. This had been the crowning event of their
lives, their brief hour of greatness, their championship season.

Now, as they reminisce, we see what they have become: each one corrupt in
his own fashion. One is now the town mayor, but involved in small-time shady
political dealings, another in a successful but unscrupulous strip-mining entre-
preneur, another a school principal ready to sell his soul for security, the fourth

1. Martin Buber, *Tales of the Hasidim*, 2 vols. (New York: Schocken, 1947), 1:268–
69. This passage had been used as the introduction of a High Holy Day sermon in 1957.

2. M. Avot 5, 21.

3. Written by Jason Miller, this play opened at the New York Shakespeare Festival in
May 1972 and on Broadway in September 1972. It was given the New York Drama Critics Award for the best play of the 1971–1972 season.

an alcoholic. The coach still dominates them with his philosophy: exploit the other guy's weakness, fight dirty, the only thing that matters is to win. Bored with life and conscious of their ultimate failure, they try to escape for the night to the world where they once played with such beautiful precision. But even the golden past when we see it was not so beautiful, and the "good old days" were not so very good as they try to persuade themselves they were.

But memory need not be an escape from the present. It can be an inspiration for renewal. And so, in the spirit of the High Holy Days, on this *Yom Hazikaron*, this "Day of Remembrance," I propose to measure my life not over one year but over forty, by sharing with you some of the climactic memories of these years. Since the number seven, like the number forty, has always had deep symbolic significance, I have picked out seven days that live on in my memory. They are experiences that not only gave meaning to the moment but which represent the enduring ideals that give meaning to my life. In essence, they embody what I have learned, and what I have sought to teach to you.

I begin with the day when Rabbi Stephen S. Wise, perhaps the greatest American Jewish leader of the past generation, placed his hands upon my head and ordained me as a rabbi. I already had the title unofficially, for I had been serving here for almost two years. My studies of the Jewish heritage during my rabbinical preparation had been deeply significant to me. It was a process of self-discovery, as though I had known these things before and had forgotten them, and was now relearning them.[4] I found in them the roots of my own being.

I had found great satisfaction in my work here[5] as a rabbi. It was a small and intimate congregation. Young as I was, the people had taken me into their hearts. I was eager to share my knowledge and my enthusiasm with them. Somehow I felt uniquely fortunate. Few people are privileged to earn their livelihood by doing the work they would rather do more than anything else in the world. Few people are able to make their lifework the linking of their lives with a cause that is enduring. My work would allow me to study and enrich my inner being, it would allow me the satisfaction of human service, it would allow me to walk with dignity as a Jew, and to inspire others to do likewise.

Materially, those were hard times. It was the midst of the Depression. I didn't know what the future would bring, though I suspected there would be difficulties and hardships. But I was thrilled to have started, and through all these years I have never lost the conviction that the greatest privilege in life is to be a servant of God and a teacher of men.

The second day took place five and a half years later in the same place: the sanctuary of the Jewish Institute of Religion. Our entire congregation of that time was present. The same rabbi, Stephen S. Wise, joined with Marcia's grand-

---

4. Saperstein is alluding here to a Talmudic passage asserting that during the period of gestation, the fetus is taught the entire Torah, but "as soon as it sees the light, an angel approaches, slaps it on its mouth, and causes it to forget the Torah completely (B. Niddah 30b). In this view, clearly influenced by the Platonic tradition, education facilitates a process of remembering what was once known in a higher realm but later forgotten.

5. That is, in Temple Emanu-El of Lynbrook, during his student years of 1933–1935.

father [Rabbi Nathan Rabinowitz of Brooklyn] in pronouncing the words that united us in marriage. Since then, Marcia has shared my enthusiasms, my adventures, my life. In many respects, she has guided my thinking and my growth.

Admiral Byrd, facing death in a lonely outpost of the Antarctic, the temperature 70 below, not knowing whether he would survive, wrote a book called *Alone* in which he outlined the understanding he had gained through his solitary ordeal. He wrote, "At the end, only one thing really matters to a man regardless of who he is. That is the affection and the understanding of his family. Anything and everything else he creates are insubstantial. [. . .] But the family is an everlasting anchorage. [. . .]"[6] How true that is. The most spectacular success in the world becomes like cotton in the mouth to one who walks alone.

The harvest of that day came for me a generation later, when each of my sons in turn stood in this pulpit to preach his first sermon as an ordained rabbi.[7] Whatever else life has brought me, I have learned and I have taught that the deepest happiness is to be found within the circle of a loving family. And the greatest satisfaction is in knowing that your children carry on your ideals.

Thirdly, my memories go back to the years of World War II, when I had the privilege of serving as a chaplain in the armed forces of the United States. War, under any circumstances, is tragic and evil. But we who fought in that war, unlike our country's most recent war, could feel that there was a deep moral purpose to our struggle.

Many memories come crowding in, but to choose one day from them all, let me turn to the High Holy Days of 1944, twenty-nine years ago, when I was stationed in the mountain town of Grenoble, France.[8] I arranged for services to be held in the University auditorium. Announcements were posted. The time of the service came, and to my amazement, in addition to the American GIs there were hundreds of French Jews. They had survived, hiding in isolated mountain farms, using forged identification papers and, like the Marranos, concealing their Jewishness. Now they had learned of our service through some mysterious underground and had come to join us.

Many of them were reunited with old friends for the first time in years. Some only now discovered what had been the fate of members of their own families. On Yom Kippur, as the *Kol Nidre* was chanted, asking for release from vows made under duress, they proclaimed their faith once again and prayed to God for forgiveness. They wept, and I wept with them. I learned the true meaning of the

---

6. See Richard E. Byrd, *Alone* (New York: Putnam's Sons, 1938), p. 179. Saperstein may have found this passage in Lillian Watson's *Light from Many Lamps* (New York: Simon and Schuster, 1951), 250.

7. Referring to Marc Saperstein (the present editor), in June of 1972, and David Saperstein, in June of 1973.

8. Grenoble had just recently been liberated from German occupation. For the Rosh Hashanah sermon delivered on that occasion, see above, "The Call of the Shofar."

Talmudic phrase that I had been trying to teach through all these years, *Kol Yis-rael arevim zeh bazeh,* "All Jews are mutually responsible each for the other."[9]

Fourth, I think of a day in a little town in New Hampshire. A year before I had been present and deeply moved by the great demonstration in Washington when the Reverend Martin Luther King, Jr., made his unforgettable "I Have a Dream" speech.[10] The following spring came the historic freedom march in Selma, Alabama. Afterward, the marchers returned home, but the problems remained. Marcia and I decided to go down to spend part of the summer in Selma. We lived there in the black community, we worked on voter registration in the surrounding counties, I spoke at mass meetings. We made friends with blacks and fellow civil rights workers. We were threatened with violence by local white citizens.[11]

Our closest associate was a twenty-five-year-old Episcopalian theological student who had taken a year's leave of absence from his studies. His name was Jonathan Daniels. It was hard to leave these friends when we had to return home. A week later, we opened the papers and read of the murder of Jonathan Daniels, shot down in cold blood as he emerged from the jail where he and other workers of our group had been imprisoned for a demonstration just the day after we left them. He was buried in the lovely cemetery of his hometown in Keane, New Hampshire. I raised the money from friends in our congregation to bring up from Selma five young blacks who had been with Jonathan when he was killed. Among them was Stokely Carmichael, who was then committed to the principle of non-violence. They stayed at our home. The next day we drove them up to the funeral. After the service, when everybody else had left, we remained around the grave, held hands, and sang "We Shall Overcome."

Times have changed. Our hopes for a speedy improvement in race relations have proved naive. But I still believe that what we did was right—and that some day men will realize what that experience burned into my heart and what I have been trying to teach all my life: that all men of all faiths and races and nations are the children of God.

I think, also, of so many days when I shared important moments in the lives of people in our congregation. I remember many joys, but somehow, tragedy leaves a more indelible mark. I recall victims of car accidents, and train accidents, and plane crashes; victims of brutal murder and those who took their own lives in despair; the deaths of tiny children who had not yet begun to live and old people who had lived beyond their years and yearned for the end. There were those who died by fire and those who died by water; there was a young boy struck fatally by an automobile as he hurried home on his bicycle from volunteer

---

9. B. Shevu'ot 39a. This passage draws from the account published in Louis Barish, ed., *Rabbis in Uniform* (New York: Jonathan David, 1962), 136–37, which itself was based on letters contemporary with the events.

10. See above, "The American Dream, In Color." The chronology is a bit confused, as the March on Washington and the "I Have a Dream" speech occurred in August 1963, two years before the event now being described.

11. Compare above, "On the Freedom Trail in Alabama."

work at the Temple. I remember countless friends, young and old, stricken in the midst of life, by cruel, devastating disease.

Symbolic of them all was the day of the indescribably painful funeral of the Leonard Levy family. Five members of one family—mother and father, two teen-aged girls, a little boy—all destroyed in a tragic fire that consumed their home.[12] They had been cherished friends and among the most dedicated workers of our Temple. And now, five caskets lay before me. The Temple was filled with mourners, and our hearts were joined in grief. It was my task somehow to express what we all felt, somehow to make sense of what was so horribly senseless. That day I learned, and I have tried to teach, the lesson of Job: that tragedy can come to the good and the evil alike. We cannot determine the number of our years. The measure of our lives is how we use them.

The sixth of these days is associated with Israel, which has played such a central role in my life. On our 1967 sabbatical, Marcia and I were in Jerusalem during the Six-Day War. Those were unforgettable times, when an ordinary people rose to unimagined heights of greatness. They were days of terror and of glory, and we felt caught up in a great spiritual event and a modern miracle.[13]

The day of Shavuot, when Confirmation was being held back home, was the first day the civilian population was allowed to visit the Western Wall. We were part of the great throng of 200,000 Jews, young and old, Chassidim and Kibbutzniks, Sephardim and Ashkenazim, soldiers and yeshiva *bochurs*.[14] We danced and prayed, and there was an indescribable sense of the unity of our people and its unique historical destiny. I learned then, and I have tried to teach since, that you can lay waste buildings, but you cannot destroy the faith and the memories that live in the hearts of a people. That whatever happens, *Am Yisrael Chai*, the people of Israel will live on.

Finally, I remember the day this sanctuary was dedicated, coinciding with my completion of 25 years of service here. We had loved the sanctuary of our little Temple. It was, however, hopelessly inadequate for our rapidly growing congregation. Progress is inexorable. Our old Temple building had to come down and our new edifice went up. We are proud of this Temple. It is not as pretentious as some are. There are others in our area with more ornate decor. But I have never forgotten that a Temple is not just a structure of wood and metal and stone. It is something more.

The ancient Rabbis asked why the great emphasis in our Torah upon the tabernacle, the temporary structure in which the children of Israel worshipped in the wilderness. They answer: it was because the tabernacle enabled our people to bring Sinai with them wherever they went. Our Temple too represents the embodiment of the ideals of our faith. It brings Sinai into our lives.

I like to feel that something of me is in this Temple. I am reminded of the inscription honoring the memory of Sir Christopher Wren in St. Paul's Cathedral

---

12. The fire occurred in the night of January 13–14, 1968. It was reported in the *New York Times*, January 15, 1968, A25, and the *New York Daily News*, January 15, 1968, 1.

13. See above, "A Great Miracle Happened There."

14. This incorporates language from the 1972 Ordination sermon above.

in London. It is placed on the wall among others commemorating some of the greatest of England's sons in every area of human endeavor—on the field of battle and in the arena of statesmanship, in scholarship, literature and the arts. This one reads, "If you would see my monument, look about you."[15] For he was the architect who had designed that magnificent structure. The people who make up this congregation, with whom I have shared so much, this building in which so much that is meaningful to me has taken place, this Temple which embodies the memories of forty years that have passed and the hopes of whatever is yet to come—all this I like to think is the monument that I am building.

These are seven of the days of the past forty years. They illustrate what I have learned, not from books but through heart and guts and life, through laughter and tears, hope and frustration, work and prayer. I have learned, and I have taught, that there is nothing more important than people, and nothing more wonderful than love. I have learned, and I have taught, that there is a power in faith beyond human understanding, and that there is no greater reward than the privilege of linking one's life to a great and enduring cause. I have learned, and I have taught, that Jews have a glorious heritage and a divinely ordained destiny. I have learned, and I have taught, that the greatest of God's gifts are the mind open for knowledge, the heart open for understanding, and the hand open for helpfulness.

At the end of John Hersey's magnificent book, *The Wall*, which comes closer than any other to portraying the spirit of the Warsaw Ghetto under the Nazis, the final few survivors emerge from the sewers. Rachel, who had gone through indescribable suffering, who had seen her loved ones die and led her little group with unparalleled courage and sacrifice, turns to them and says—and these are the very last words of the book, "Nu, what is the plan for tomorrow?"[16]

A New Year begins. Perhaps a new era begins. We look to the past for guidance. And then, as we move forward into the unknown with renewed zeal and hope, we too say, "Nu, what is the plan for tomorrow?"

---

15. The inscription, written by the son of the architect, is in Latin: "Si monumentum requiris, circumspice."

16. John Hersey, *The Wall* (New York: Alfred A. Knopf, 1950), 632.

Index